BOLTS FROM THE BLUE

BOLTS FROM THE BLUE

From Cold War Warrior to Chief of the Air Staff

Sir **RICHARD JOHNS**
GCB KCVO CBE FRAES

GRUB STREET • LONDON

Published by
Grub Street
4 Rainham Close
London
SW11 6SS

A CIP record for this title is available from the British Library

ISBN-13: 978-1-911621-09-6

Cover design: Daniele Roa

Printed and bound by Finidr, Czech Republic

NB: The views and opinions expressed are those of the author alone and should not be taken to represent those of Her Majesty's Government , MoD, HM Armed Forces or any government agency.

CONTENTS

FOREWORD

The history of the UK Armed Forces during the Cold War and the period that follows is short of decent interventions– until now. Richard Johns a twice knighted air chief marshal and former chief of the air staff from 1997 to 2000 has produced a fine memoir full of insights and worthy takes from his life as a Cranwell cadet, fighter (and bomber) pilot, flying instructor, reluctant staff officer, air leader, wise commander in NATO and chief of staff.

For me there is a strong and attractive blend of the practical and the philosophical. Honesty, integrity and resilience shine through his whole career. Invariably fair to his colleagues, this narrative links us back to the real uncertainties that lay beneath the apparent military normalities of the Cold War; our own uncertainties (except for the British pathology to save money on defence) which followed the Cold War in the early 1990s and Dick's genuinely fascinating glimpses into the post-Cold War conflicts and operations.

Inevitably there is a focus on air power and air warfare and so there should be; this is the memoir of a very distinguished airman. But, there is more than that. Inter-service relations, relations between the UK military, politicians and civil servants. Relations between allies both traditional and new. All combined to give the reader plenty to think about. A gap in our knowledge has been filled. We should be grateful to Richard Johns for taking the time and trouble to write this fascinating (and full) memoir. I commend it.

Air Chief Marshal Sir Stuart Peach
GBE, KCB, ADC, DL
Chief of the Defence Staff

INTRODUCTION AND
ACKNOWLEDGEMENTS

I joined the RAF as a Cranwell flight cadet on 9th January 1957 to start a career that ended on 10th August 2000. The journey was characterised by many unexpected twists and turns that reflected a talent for good luck. Few if any of my contemporaries could have enjoyed so much good fortune in being in the right place at the right time.

A wide variety of appointments in the air and on the ground thus gave me the privilege of a rare, if not singular, perspective of the RAF, our sister services and national defence matters. As a pilot I was engaged in the last days of withdrawal from Empire and later was to spend the best part of nine years in Germany as a Cold War warrior. As a NATO commander-in-chief during the mid-1990s I had the responsibility of bringing a brand new regional joint headquarters to full operating capability as the political leadership of the Alliance grappled with a raft of problems emerging from the dissolution of the USSR and war in the Balkans. At home, as a lowly participant in John Nott's 1981 Defence Review and later as a fully involved contributor to the 1997/98 Strategic Defence Review, I witnessed a steady decline in the combat power of our armed forces – a decline accelerated at the end of the Cold War by the search for a peace dividend as financial management took precedence over the identification of strategic priorities.

Although the Strategic Defence Review made a valiant attempt to reverse this process, defence spending was soon to resume its downward trend before I left the service. My RAF career thus ended before the devastating events of 9/11 changed not only the strategic environment but temporarily halted reduction in defence spending. The point needs making because my attitudes and thinking as recorded in this book pre-dated the political and military consequences of 9/11 that were eventually to be the principal subject of the Chilcot Inquiry – a public investigation into the circumstances of British engagement into Gulf War II.

I started writing this book with the intention of leaving one electronic copy with my family, to dip into at their leisure, with a second deposited in the archives of the Air Historical Branch. Others, friends all, then suggested that the mixture of autobiography and history could be of interest to a wider readership, hence the publication of *Bolts from the Blue*.

Diaries, notebooks, flying logbooks, speeches and my own 'black book' of observations and quotable quotes on military affairs have provided the raw material for this book. Old friends and colleagues from all three services have been most generous in adding detail and authenticity to the narrative where my own memory and other sources have been uncertain. In particular, I am most grateful for the Prince of Wales's agreement to the inclusion of a chapter, drawing on official records, that describe his pilot training as a member of No. 1 Graduate Entry at the RAF College, Cranwell. I am similarly grateful to Air Chief Marshal Sir William Wratten for permitting me to include his personal account of his meeting in July 1995 with General Ratko Mladic, chief of staff of the Bosnian Serb Army.

Elsewhere others have provided informed comment on some of the more controversial and technical chapters, albeit I remain accountable and responsible for the finality of the written words. That said, I am indebted to Air Vice-Marshal Tony Mason for his constructive and most helpful comments on the narrative and, by no means least, his encouragement. Mr Sebastian Cox, head of the Air Historical Branch, has been ever ready to provide collateral detail on specific events while Harrier field operations are amply illustrated thanks to Mr Philip Ward's kindness in giving me access to his personal photograph albums.

Air Commodore Graham Pitchfork kindly introduced me to Mr John Davies, the publisher, and publication would have not been completed without the enthusiastic assistance of Wing Commander Martin Hooker who took on the unenviable task of proof reading and spelling out the many abbreviations. All of this hard work would have come to nought had not Mrs Julia Hardy volunteered to type every single word as dictated by me from handwritten scripts. I place on record the sincerity of my thanks to both.

CHAPTER 1
EARLY YEARS

My flying career nearly came to an early and spectacular ending. Shortly after my first solo in a Tiger Moth, aged 17 and a few days, my instructor (a veteran of the Royal Flying Corps) decided to introduce me to aerobatics. After some loops and barrel rolls he inverted the aircraft to demonstrate the effect of negative G in straight and level flight. As my weight was taken up by the seat harness I felt something rip and realised that the buckle had sheared from the lap strap. This left me hanging on to the cockpit coaming with my hands and with my feet wedged under the instrument panel.

The instructor interpreted my yells down the Gosport tube, the means of communication between the front and back cockpit where I was positioned, as cries of sheer delight. When the aircraft was turned the right way up I was able to explain my discomfort which reflected the lack of a parachute and our close proximity to the mud in Langstone Harbour. We returned to Portsmouth Airport, now an industrial estate, landed and the instructor inspected my harness. "Not a word to anyone sonny," he said. Happily, this early scrape did not dim my ambition to join the Royal Air Force.

My mother, sometimes prone to exaggeration, claimed this aspiration stemmed from observation of the Battle of Britain from Dene Park just south of Horsham where I was born. Only one year old at the time of that great battle, such precociousness can be safely denied. However, four years later now living in Walmer just south of Deal in Kent I can vividly remember Doodlebugs (V-1 flying bombs) overflying towards London, some of which were shot down or crashed nearby with a deafening explosion. My mother and I sheltered under the kitchen table as there was no bomb shelter in the garden. I retain a vivid impression of ships burning in the Channel and recall the sky darkened by a vast armada of aircraft, far too many to count. In later years I learnt that these aircraft and gliders were on their way to Arnhem as the first airborne assault of Operation Market Garden. And in Deal I first encountered Americans cruising around in their DUKWs, an amphibious assault vehicle, presumably as part of the D-Day deception plan. A friendly wave was often rewarded with a shower of 'candy'.

When I was born in July 1939 my father was at sea as captain, Royal Marines, on board HMS *Cumberland,* a County-class heavy cruiser. He endured a long and arduous commission which included service in the South Atlantic, the Mediterranean and on Arctic convoys including the disastrous PQ17 which suffered the most grievous losses – 24 out of 35 merchant ships were sunk after the Admiralty ordered the convoy to scatter. The quality of father's service was recognised by the award of the MBE (Military Division). On returning to England in autumn 1943 he was posted to the Royal Marines Barracks at Deal where my sister was to be born and where we lived together as a family for the first time. But not for long, as in late 1944 father was posted as second-in-command of a Royal Marines infantry battalion serving in north-west Europe where he remained until the end of the war.

A short spell at Lympstone, now the RM Commando Training Centre, followed before we moved to Portsmouth in January 1947 where my education continued at Boundary Oak Prep School, an establishment not then noted for pastoral care. Beatings were run of the mill, boxing was mandatory and many of the masters were, with the benefit of hindsight, psychologically disturbed – possibly as a consequence of wartime service and what we now know as post-traumatic stress. I survived and left with a sound grounding in the 'three Rs' and a reputation as a good boxer having won my weight in inter-school competitions. Boxing taught me an early and valuable lesson. Rather fancying myself with my fists, I intervened in a fight when I saw a bigger boy bullying a friend. For my pains I in turn got beaten up. From this I deduced that electing to punch above your weight was not necessarily a good idea when given choice – a lesson of contemporary strategic and military relevance.

My parents planned for me to go on to Christ's Hospital at Horsham. But in 1951 father was posted to Malaya as second-in-command of 40 Commando, Royal Marines. He took command a year later and was away for the best part of three years. Father decided I should stay at home and I was entered for Portsmouth Grammar School through common entrance examination. I joined PGS in the summer term of 1953 and to my surprise entered the A-stream which was full of academically gifted boys. Consequently I took my O levels shortly before my 15th birthday and my A levels two years later.

By contemporary standards my childhood was amazingly free and unrestricted, possibly because my father, a stern disciplinarian and very tough man, was away for much of the time leaving me in the care of my mother. She had trained as a nurse at St George's Hospital then beside Hyde Park Corner and now the Lansdowne Hotel. She was an unconventional woman, entirely self-reliant with no interest in material things. She happily existed on the bare necessities of life which were selected purely on their utility. On the other hand she was a voracious reader who in the 90 years of her life accumulated an amazing fund of general knowledge. Well into her seventies she could still demolish *The Telegraph* and *Times* crossword puzzles before lunch and she was the meanest of Scrabble players. Kind to a fault she nevertheless expected me to look after myself as indeed did my father. Thus from an early age a bicycle gave me the freedom to roam far and wide with my mother rightly assuming I would come home when hungry. As a schoolboy I was a keen supporter of Portsmouth Football Club when crowds of 40,000 were the norm at Fratton Park as Pompey ruled the roost in the First Division. Going to matches alone I cannot remember ever being frightened or experiencing crowd trouble. As I grew older I started to transfer my sporting allegiances to rugby and cricket, interests that survive to this day. But I still follow the fortunes and misfortunes of Portsmouth FC as an ingrained habit, and a fat lot of good that's done them.

I enjoyed my three and a half years at PGS. The quality of teaching was superb and discipline maintained with firmness and fairness by masters who dominated by strength of personality rather than random and underserved beatings which I still associate with my prep school days. PGS was unashamedly meritocratic and educated boys from a wide mix of family backgrounds which generated an early and sympathetic social awareness to the benefit of all. Grammar schools were a great engine of social mobility – a reality of life ignored by the patrician socialists who helped to do away with them. My academic progress was unspectacular with cricket and rugby the principal focus of my energy, while girls from Portsmouth High School became something of a distraction. But I made some memorable friendships, among them Rudyard Penley. He entered the Royal Military Academy Sandhurst about the same time as I joined the RAF and was the first Sandhurst cadet to be commissioned directly into the Parachute Regiment. Sadly he was killed a few years later while participating in a parachute jumping competition.

Also at PGS the teaching of an outstanding master, Ted Washington, developed my passion for history which over the years has concentrated mostly on military aspects with a special interest in the Georgian Navy as a result of many visits to HMS *Victory* and an early taste for the novels of C S Forrester. Years later my interest was reinvigorated by a naval friend who introduced me to the fascinating and exquisite tales fashioned by Patrick O'Brian. However, as a schoolboy I was also addicted to *Biggles* books by W E Johns, sadly no relation, which probably explains my early interest in aviation. But I can also well recall my excitement at seeing for the first time a jet aeroplane flying at high speed and low level. I must have been about 12 at the time. The aircraft was a Supermarine Attacker of the Fleet Air Arm displaying at the RNAS Lee-on-Solent.

After joining the Combined Cadet Force at PGS – scouting offered the only escape – I transferred to the RAF section and eventually won a flying scholarship. This involved 30 hours flying, dual and solo, to achieve a Private Pilot's Licence. I started on 1st August 1956, three days after my 17th birthday, and finished the course by the end of the month. At the same time I received the good news that I had passed my A levels, which together with a clutch of O levels, gained me exemption from the Civil Service Commission Navy, Army and Air Force Entry examination. My ambition to join the RAF, undimmed by early proximity to accident statistics, was now firm and I started the process of application with medical and flying aptitude tests at RAF Hornchurch and selection testing for a cadetship at the Royal Air Force College Cranwell.

My father's friends could not understand why I did not want to follow him into the Royal Marines and fly with the Fleet Air Arm. For my part, badly bitten by the flying bug, it seemed to me that the service whose whole *raison d'être* centred on flying was the best place for a career in military aviation. Apart from condemnation as a black sheep by father's pals, I have to admit that my childhood influence on his career was wholly negative. While at Deal in 1944 my parents took me to tea with his commanding officer and wife who lived in a Georgian house with a long, gently sloping lawn. For amusement, and out of adult sight, I played with a heavy garden roller. Unfortunately, with gravity proving the stronger, I lost control of the roller which accelerated down the lawn to smash into smithereens an ancestral statue much loved by the colonel.

Two years later at Lympstone my parents left me in the car while they enjoyed drinks in the mess after a Sunday church parade. Like the lawn at Deal, the car park had a distinctive slope such that when I released the handbrake – with nothing better to do – gravity again took control propelling the car backwards to achieve sufficient momentum for an effective and square-on collision with another vehicle. Both were prominently and undeniably damaged. The other car was owned by my father's latest CO.

In my last year at home father decided to teach me poker. At first Sunday evenings passed pleasantly enough as we played for matchsticks until eventually I accepted his suggestion that we moved on to real money. Three weeks later I was in debt to the tune of two month's pocket money and called quits.

Father's comment was uncompromising. "You will never be any good at cards and you are a hopeless bluffer. My strongest advice to you is never gamble at cards." I accepted his counsel and recouped my losses in my final Easter holiday with part-time employment as the stoker on Southsea miniature railway. It didn't take long for my hands to blister from shovelling coal and I sought advice from the driver, a retired Welsh coal miner. "Go behind that bush," he said "and pee on your hands. That will toughen them up." And it did.

In early December 1956 a letter arrived from the Air Ministry requiring me to report to the Royal Air Force College Cranwell on 9th January 1957 for enlistment, this subject to my parent or guardian's consent as I was just under the 17½ entry age limit to the college. My father signed with alacrity and took me to Moss Bros on The Hard outside Portsmouth dockyard where he bought me a suit, an overcoat and a pair of black shoes. "That's the last you get out of me," he said "you are now on your own." He meant it as he stayed true to his word.

Some more words on my family background. My mother was the second daughter of a rich New Zealander who came to England for medical reasons just before World War I. He decided to stay and took up farming only to become a casualty of the economic crash in 1929; he was declared bankrupt in 1931. Thereafter he lived in a small terraced house in Horsham where my mother and I spent the first three years of my life. I remember my grandparents with great affection which probably points to the fact that I was a spoiled brat. The circumstances of my mother's childhood also probably explains the fierce streak of independence which remained with her to the end of her life. Shortly before her death in hospital suffering from emphysema, she was asked if she had any allergies. "Yes," replied mother "I am allergic to men with beards." These were her last recorded words.

My father came from a less privileged background and a long line of Royal Navy seamen. He told me that one of his forebears had served on HMS *Victory* at Trafalgar. It is a fact that a 'Johns' was on the nominal roll of the crew in October 1805, but I have never verified the truth of this ancestral boast. His own father joined the Royal Navy as a boy seaman in 1898, retired as a chief yeoman of signals in 1922 and died shortly after of throat cancer. During World War I he was at sea throughout the conflict serving for the most part on the battleship HMS *Hibernia.* He was mentioned in despatches 'in recognition of distinguished services during the war'. His death left my father as the eldest of three children with my grandmother, from memory a rather unpleasant and domineering person, looking to him as the principal breadwinner for the family. Father was academically gifted with a particular bent for mathematics and the sciences as demonstrated by his distinguished examination achievements at the Royal Grammar School High Wycombe where he was considered a strong candidate for a university scholarship. However, grandmother insisted that he left school at 17 to take up employment as a bank clerk. This he tolerated for six months before enlisting in the Royal Marines without telling his mother. Subsequently my father paid her a portion of his income until she died in 1960.

After recruit training father served in HMS *Suffolk* on the Far East Station for two years before he was awarded a King's Commission as a probationary second lieutenant. He passed out top of his training batch and was presented with a ceremonial sword for meritorious examinations by the Lords Commissioners of the Admiralty. Far more than I was to achieve. He excelled at rifle shooting and, after World War II, captained the Royal Marines team and represented England at international events.

Following service with 40 Commando in Malaya and the Canal Zone he returned home as second-in-command of the Royal Marines barracks at Eastney in Portsmouth where we lived together for three years before I joined the RAF. In April 1957 he was told that he would be prematurely retired as a consequence of manpower reductions required by the Sandys Defence Review. Of his contemporaries he alone had not attended Staff College. He left the RM in August that year, two months before the announcement of a 'golden bowler' scheme which would have made a significant difference to his financial wellbeing in the later years of his life. Short-changing service people who have given long and distinguished service to their country in war is by no means a new phenomenon.

Father never spoke about his wartime experiences and the only time he showed emotion was during a TV programme on the war at sea which explained the significance and dangers of Arctic convoys. As the story of PQ17 was told he spat out one word: "Shameful". He died in 1977. His obituary in the *Globe and Laurel,* the journal of the Royal Marines, concluded:

> "At the end of the day the real test of a man's worth is his behaviour in adverse circumstances. When the going got rough it was a wonderful thing to have competent, tough, and utterly reliable Johnno at one's side."

I deeply regret not having learnt more about my father in his lifetime.

CHAPTER 2
CRANWELL

The aim of the RAF College was to train the future permanent officer cadre of the service. Some 300 flight cadets were resident for a course lasting three years with pilots going through basic and advanced flying training so that, on graduation and commissioning, they went straight to operational conversion units. Navigator flight cadet training followed a similar pattern while ground branch cadets (administrative and supply) completed their own specialist courses.

The first two terms at Cranwell were tough. The new intake was accommodated in the South Brick Lines (now demolished) – five new cadets with a mentor from the entry above. The daily routine was focused on drill (foot drill for the first term), kit cleaning and preparation, and academics which provided some welcome relief from other pressures deliberately applied to test resolve and commitment. In the second term, having passed off the square in foot drill, arms drill was introduced. However, before then our .303 Lee Enfield rifles, personally issued and retained for 2½ years, had to be burnished. Woodwork was bulled (spit and polished) with a mixture of ox blood and black shoe polish to the necessary high-gloss mahogany-coloured finish. On parade the first arms drill movement taught was ground arms which removed the bull from one side of the weapon to be replaced that evening with a further application of boot polish. I think my entry (No.76) was the last to endure this absurdity which was stopped on order from the Air Ministry but not before arms drill was mastered and the entry was judged fit to parade with the rest of the college.

Elsewhere a number of other hurdles were encountered. The first visit to the swimming pool, constructed within a World War I edifice, involved climbing into the rafters and jumping into the deep end; no-one asked if you could swim and some couldn't. First term boxing against a flight cadet of approximate weight and height from another squadron was put on as after-dinner entertainment for the rest of the college. Some flying careers were inevitably lost to injuries incurred during the two-round slugging contest. Soon afterwards the junior entry was welcomed by the senior entries at a guest night after which the juniors were obliged to entertain their seniors in the college lecture hall. Failure to provide adequate amusement earned a forfeit of fiendish ingenuity or physical discomfort. Walking 14 miles in the dead of night to recover drill boots from the satellite airfield at RAF Barkston Heath – placed there without the knowledge of the owner – in time for the morning drill parade was no joke.

The final hurdle at the end of the second term was survival camp held in the Hartz Mountains in Germany. Preliminary exercises concentrated on orientation and map reading with ever-increasing long marches in sections of a dozen or so to build up stamina and to test leadership. All of this was the preparation phase for a five-day escape-and-evasion exercise in three-man teams. Enemy forces were the German border guards, German customs police and British soldiers. We moved only at night from rendezvous (RV) to RV for further briefing on our 'escape route'. If captured, the evaders were returned to their starting point to start all over again. Rations (emergency Mk 5 packs) sufficient for three days marching were provided which assumed that some ingredients could be 'brewed up'. But as lighting fires in a densely forested region was forbidden, the entry returned home fit and certainly the leaner for a spot of leave before the start of the third term.

While the parade ground and academic subjects split between science and the humanities filled at least half the working day, sport of all disciplines, ranging from traditional activities – rugby, football, cricket etc – to the not-so-common individual events within athletics and pentathlon, filled any spare time. With some 300 extremely fit young men, the majority medically fit for flying duties, it was not surprising that there was a wealth of sporting talent in the college. Cranwell more than held its own against the vastly superior numbers at Sandhurst. More importantly sport was the great mixer which brought together flight cadets from all levels within the college and from different squadrons, albeit inter-squadron sports competitions were fiercely contested, and on the rugby field, certainly not for the faint-hearted.

Discipline was rigidly enforced. Although expulsion was the ultimate punishment, restrictions or 'strikers' in the jargon of the day, confined miscreants to the bounds of the college with five extra parades a day; all involved a change of uniform and inspection with additional drill on two of the parades. A rather juvenile prank involving the assistant commandant's car landed me and twelve others in hot water such that for some of us a greater part of our second term was spent on restrictions. Once on 'strikers' a spot of misplaced blanco could be punished immediately with two extra days by the inspecting duty under officer. The challenge was to keep kit in a condition to pass inspection on both restrictions and entry drill parades. This forged a bond in adversity with roommates also under punishment. As all of us in my hut were charged and found guilty for our 'impertinence' with the assistant commandant's car, we fashioned a production line of uniform and kit preparation which was a very model of the efficient use of time and space. Most regrettably two of the five of us, Euan Perreaux and Malcolm Maule, were killed in flying accidents after leaving Cranwell.

During our first two terms at Cranwell the flight commander in charge of all three flights within the junior entry was eminently forgettable. He was obsequious to his superiors and in awe of his senior NCO, one Flight Sergeant Jack Holt. Peter Symes, fellow flight cadet and old friend, described FS Holt as "a tall, barrel-chested Yorkshireman with a ruddy face sporting a stubby ginger moustache, hence his nickname 'bog brush'. There was theatre in the man. While criticism was expressed with crystal clarity, its volume could reverberate. When drill was merely excellent he would glare in disdainful silence, amble off for a few paces, pause for effect and look to the heavens beseeching divine assistance. His pace stick was a designator as precise as any laser at marking out errant cadets. His invective was often spiced with brilliant metaphor and he drew some of his ammunition from circumstances of the Cold War, much of it unrepeatable in these days of political correctness. Certainly his dynamism, sheer force of personality and total commitment to his training duties left an indelible impression on the 1,300 or so cadets who passed through Cranwell in his years of service there." Today a memorial is placed in a wall of the college bearing the inscription:

JACK HOLT MBE BEM
CADET WING FLIGHT SERGEANT 1952-1961
REVERED BY
FLIGHT CADETS OF THAT ERA

If Jack Holt was the dominant influence in our day-to-day life within the junior entry, the college ethos with its clear focus on the development of commitment to the service was maintained with flinty resolution by the commandant and the assistant commandant. For most of my time at Cranwell these appointments were filled by Air Commodore D S Spotswood and Group Captain H N G Wheeler. Both were highly decorated for operational service in World War II with a brace of DSOs and several DFCs between them. The inner steel of the Cranwell hierarchy was of the highest quality and had no trouble in dealing with mischief-making by high spirited flight cadets as I found out to my cost.

I did not enjoy my first year at Cranwell. The stern discipline, ruthless punishment of the most trifling misdemeanour, drill and then more drill with the fiercest attention paid to the most trivial details – as I judged them – was far removed from the familiar comforts of my home and school. Moreover, 24 hours basic navigation training, stuck down the back end of a tail-wheeled Valetta, was for me poor compensation for misfortunes of my own making suffered elsewhere within the college. But, and it is a very big but, like it or not I was learning self-discipline and to take strength from adversity while cultivating that certain bloody-mindedness which is the bedrock of determination to succeed. And I was making friendships, ever-strengthening during three years together as flight cadets, that have endured to this day.

The second and third years at Cranwell concentrated on professional development with the satisfactory completion of basic and advanced flying training earning pilots their 'wings' and navigators their brevets. Although my second year got off to a disappointing start, for the most part my memory is of much fun and laughter as we moved towards the goal of our passing-out parade as commissioned officers. In parallel with this process the ground-training syllabus aimed to exercise steady and controlled development of cadets towards the attainment of their commissions. For most of us this was a rather bumpy ride. The suspension rate was high, for example in No. 76 Entry only half of those who entered completed their training at Cranwell. In 1957 RAF manpower was in the order of 200,000 with National Service in full swing. Cadets could be suspended for a wide variety of reasons not to mention self-exclusion by those who found the regime at Cranwell intolerable. But given National Service manpower there was no problem in manning a front line of 11 commands worldwide and the instructional staff could afford to be choosy. Indeed, flight cadet scuttlebutt had it that a trip with the chief flying instructor at Barkston Heath was an automatic 'chop ride'. This probably was the consequence of the wing commander being forced to bail out on his first flight with a cadet.

To correct a probable picture of a spartan existence, the second and third years at Cranwell permitted a gradual relaxation of the rules that governed the life of a 'crow' – a member of the junior entry. Selection for a sports team ensured some time away from the college while the occasional long weekend permitted absence from the compulsory Sunday morning church parades. During term time cadets attended a wide range of single and tri-service demonstrations and hosted incoming visits from foreign military academies, most notably by the first class of cadets from the newly established United States Air Force Academy at Colorado Springs. Comparison of the Cranwell/Colorado Springs training convinced me that Cranwell was the easier and more enjoyable experience, a judgement warmly endorsed by contemporary USAF cadets who I was to meet again in the years ahead. Leave periods, coinciding with school holidays, were not holidays by definition. Cadets had to visit service installations, RN and Army as well as RAF, and participate in some authorised activity. My choice was offshore sailing and I am certain that my education benefited from early exposure to the traditions and attitudes of our sister services.

Off-duty, local pubs were guaranteed steady trade while invitations to dances at teacher's training colleges – Lincoln and Retford come to mind – provided at least some opportunity to enjoy female company. Given the comparative geographical isolation at Cranwell, and with Sleaford out of bounds to flight cadets, the pleasures of off-duty relaxation were critically dependent on the availability of private transport. Cadets from their third term onwards were allowed to keep cars in the Cadet Wing garage, an old hangar in East Camp, long since demolished, which housed a remarkable collection of vehicles. A few contemporary sports cars and saloons financed by generous and rich parents represented the top end of the market. But by far the majority of vehicles were 'bangers' some of pre-war vintage characterised by mechanical under-reliability and questionable roadworthiness. Most bore the scars of misadventures with a few being obvious write-offs having suffered damage beyond economic repair. During their time as flight cadets, most suffered the indignity of a long trudge back to the college after a breakdown or prang. That no-one was killed in the days before 'drink-drive' and seat belts remains to me one of the sweet mysteries of life.

While I, and most of my friends, departed with a sense of pride and achievement, a minority within the entry to this day remain bitterly critical of a regime within which as much time was spent on the drill square (let alone in the preparation of kit) as was devoted to flying and other professional instruction. Although this imbalance of training effort was to continue for a few more years, the eventual replacement of the Piston Provost and Vampire/Meteor by the Jet Provost introduced single-type flying training through to wings standard with a commensurate shortening of the course length. Within a decade the flight cadet entry was phased out to be replaced by the Graduate Entry Scheme in 1971.

A university degree became a prerequisite for a direct route permanent commission in the RAF. Like many other Old Cranwellians I was not convinced by the rationale for such an abrupt change which apparently was based on the belief that the attainment of a degree was an essential precondition for a successful career. Failure to tap into this fashionable trend would leave the RAF at a disadvantage as other professions and our sister services sought to attract high quality candidates with proven intellectual capability for officer training. For my part I felt that the service was distancing itself too far from young men who would have preferred to fly military aircraft on leaving school rather than at the end of three years of abstract study of subjects many of which were of little relevance to a career in the RAF.

An obvious solution was for the service to introduce a programme which would allow officers to study for a degree, useful and valuable to the RAF, as their career progressed and at a time of their own choosing. Forty years later I was in a position to do something about this.

CHAPTER 3
FLYING TRAINING

My pilot training on the Piston Provost at RAF Barkston Heath did not get off to a good start. A year and a half after gaining my Private Pilot's Licence I had lost what little aircraft handling skill I had learned. Moreover, my clumsy and ham-fisted performance did not commend me to my new flying instructor. I did not warm to him and more to the point, he did not warm to me. His instructional technique was, to say the least, forthright and unforgiving. Failure to absorb a lesson instantly provoked harsh remedial action. Unbelievable as it may seem to professional airmen, I recall that I found it difficult to keep the aircraft in trim. To teach me a lesson I was told to trim the aircraft fully nose up and then to fly it straight and level for five minutes – not good for the aeroplane and certainly stressful to my right wrist. Stupid errors, such as misaligning the P-type compass, were punished with a whack on the side of my bone dome (flying helmet) with the crowbar normally stowed in the right side of the left-hand seat to assist, optimistically, escape from the wreckage of a crash. Cockpit hostility came to an early showdown after I made a mess of an approach to land and was forced to overshoot. This was the culmination of another below average trip which had clearly irritated my instructor beyond the short limits of his patience. As we climbed away a couple of whacks from the crowbar kindled within me such a feeling of furious outrage that I let go of the controls and sat with my arms folded. The aircraft, predictably out of trim, started a steep descending turn. The instructor then took control and completed the circuit to land. Not a word was spoken then or after our return to the squadron. That night back at Cranwell I thought I would soon depart for RAF Innsworth to complete my National Service with a broomstick in my hand rather than the joystick of an aeroplane. Next morning, I fully expected a call to my college flight commander's office to be told to pack my bags. But nothing happened and when I returned to Barkston Heath my name was on the flying programme with a new instructor, Flight Lieutenant Benji Hives. I owe him a great debt because after a total of some 17 hours instruction, mostly under his tuition, I achieved my first solo on the Piston Provost. This was a record length of time to first solo which remained so until a year later when it was beaten by Reg Hallam who went on to become a distinguished test pilot.

After this rather awkward start to my service flying career, Benji Hives saw me through my first term of flying training before he moved on to take up a flight commander's appointment. Flight Lieutenant Bill Mackeson became my new flying instructor for an exciting summer term. On our first trip together he took me low flying, or rather literally hedge hopping. This was certainly stimulating but just a foretaste of what was to come. With 140 knots on the airspeed indicator Mac asked me what aerobatic manoeuvre was started at that speed. I replied that it was the speed for looping, and up we went. As the aircraft came over the top of the loop the ground seemed disconcertingly close, and at that point Mac looked at me and said, "we are not going to make it". Before I had time to think that at 18½ I was too young to die, the stick was pushed hard forward and we bunted out getting very close to the field below on the negative G limit – minus 2½ if I remember correctly – before the aircraft was rolled the right way up; the aircraft then accelerated and climbed into the vertical where Mac completed an immaculate stall turn. "That was fun wasn't it?" he asked. I couldn't help but agree and thereafter on nearly every dual sortie that summer Mac threw in a manoeuvre or a stunt that left me spellbound or speechless, sometimes both together. Sadly the fun ended in September after Mac had been court-martialled for a low-flying escapade when flying a CCF cadet on an air experience flight while we flight cadets were away on summer leave and other extra-curricular duties. Flight Lieutenant Dennis Milburn, a brand new qualified flying instructor (QFI) then took me on to see me safely through my last term and the flying tests that had to be passed before moving on to advanced flying training at Cranwell.

The year at Barkston Heath taught me many lessons other than eventually how to fly the Piston Provost. In 1958 the Cranwell/Barkston Heath complex was surrounded with active airfields. Apart from our relief landing grounds at Spittlegate, Folkingham and Fulbeck for circuit training there was a basic flying training school at Syerston (Piston Provosts) and an advanced training school (Vampires) at Swinderby. RAF Manby and RAF Strubby were home bases to a variety of aircraft as well as looking after refresher flying on Meteors. Elsewhere operational airfields were situated at Wittering, Cottesmore, Waddington, Scampton, Binbrook and Coningsby all within 50 miles of Cranwell. Such congested airspace placed a high premium on lookout. But, above all, the death of Flight Cadet Peter Baird in a flying accident, the first to die in my entry, underlined the simple fact that although military aviation might be fun and exciting, progress and survival required hard work and self-discipline as well as a determination to succeed.

In mid-December 1958 towards the end of basic flying training, all student pilots taller than 6 ft had to visit the medical centre for measurement of their thigh lengths, this to ensure that ejection from a Vampire would not remove kneecaps. There must have been 15 or so of us with long legs and I was the last to be measured. As the flying doctor ran out his tape to measure the distance from my backside to kneecap – we sat against a wall – he whispered "would you like to fly Meteors?" Being a good Cranwell cadet now well-versed in replying positively to any question I replied "yes sir". So that was that. Sometime later I heard from an admittedly unreliable source that one inch had been added to my thigh measurement to ensure that one flight cadet from 76 Entry would join the Meteor Flight thus allowing the flight commander (Flight Lieutenant Peter Harding) to retain his full aircraft establishment. It was my good luck to be the last in line because the doctor had forgotten until the final moment his alleged promise to Peter Harding that he would ensure one cadet would meet the parameters for Meteor training.

Recalling my plodding start on the Piston Provost, my excitement at the prospect of flying the Meteor 7 for dual instruction and the single-seat Meteor F8 day fighter for solo flying was tempered with some nervousness. The jump from the Provost, maximum speed 170 knots, to the Meteor, maximum speed 515 knots, represented a test I knew would both stretch and stimulate me. I was also aware that the Meteor's flight safety record was by far the worst of any aircraft type flown by the RAF in the 1950s. Many years later I learnt that in 1952 alone, 94 pilots were killed in 150 Meteor write-off accidents; the majority were the consequence of practising single-engine flying in an aircraft whose asymmetric performance was, to say the least, unattractive. I was also aware of the 'phantom dive' phenomenon. Selection of undercarriage down with the air brakes out could cause the nose to drop and the loss of elevator effectiveness which could be distressing if this error was made in the circuit prior to landing. But my enthusiasm for the challenge ahead was unabated and I was to profit hugely from having the same instructor throughout my final year at Cranwell.

Having taken 17 hours to go solo in the Provost, I achieved my first Meteor solo in nine hours despite lack of continuity caused by winter bad weather. Rather to my surprise I felt immediately at home in the Meteor and had little difficulty with single-engine flying which was an element of almost every dual sortie. While high level flying at 30,000 ft in the unpressurised Meteor 7 was a chilling and gaseous experience, aerobatics, formation flying and tail-chasing remain most memorable pleasures of my advanced flying training. I sustained steady progress throughout the year and passed my final handling test and final instrument rating test towards the end of November 1959. I was thrilled to receive my posting to the Hunter operational conversion unit (OCU) at RAF Chivenor. However, as the commandant was pinning on my 'wings' the evening before the entry's passing out parade he told me that my posting had been changed. I immediately thought that my nightmare of a posting to the expanding V-Bomber force had become reality as this had been the destiny of my predecessors on Meteor Flight. But the commandant went on to say that I was to go to the night-fighter OCU at RAF Leeming to train on Javelins as the experimental first 'first tourist' in that role. Up till then a tour on day fighters was a mandatory requirement before moving on to night fighters. This step into the unknown provoked similar feelings to the news a year earlier of advanced flying training on the Meteor.

In New Year 1960 I was posted to RAF Strubby for continuation flying on the Meteor before moving on to Leeming in March. This was not the end of my association with the Meteor, however. Shortly after joining No. 64(F) Squadron at Duxford I had a checkout ride in the Station Flight Meteor. Thirty minutes into the trip at the end of some medium level aerobatics, the port engine was gently throttled back to idle and I was asked to return to Duxford to land. Everything worked out well and my single-engine approach and landing was satisfactory. Not a word from the back seat until we cleared the runway. "What was all that about?" asked Max Bacon. "That's how I've been taught," I replied rather huffily. "Well, we don't do it like that in Fighter Command," said Max, "bloody dangerous. Take me back to where we were when I simulated the engine failure." This I did. Max then took control, throttled back the port engine, lowered the nose, put full power on the starboard engine and rapidly accelerated as we descended back to the airfield. Overhead the runway he broke downwind – high G hard turn to port, starboard throttle closed – and completed a power-off glide approach without any of the knee trembling associated with single-engine flying in the Meteor. "Now, that was much more comfortable wasn't it?" asked Max. As a newly arrived junior pilot, disagreement with my deputy flight commander was not prudent, but I did think to myself that misjudgement of a glide approach to end up in the undershoot was well within my scope, so probably best if needs be to stick to what I had been taught.

To return to Cranwell, apart from the sheer pleasure of flying solo in the single-seat Meteor F8, Peter Harding's flying and ground instruction ensured that the whole new experience of jet flying was both enjoyable and rewarding.

While he rightly demanded the highest standard of performance, his own example of enthusiasm for flying and good humour could not fail to inspire effort and commitment. The relationship forged between QFI and student is not only necessarily close but it is also enduring and one never knows when it might be resurrected in future careers. Shortly after Air Chief Marshal Sir Peter Harding was appointed chief of the air staff (CAS) in 1988 he visited HQ RAF Germany where I was serving as the senior air staff officer. During staff discussions we got involved in a robust debate on flight safety. I thought I was doing rather well before he cut me off with the words "I should have chopped you when I had the chance". While these words were spoken with a smile, others I have known may feel it a shame that the opportunity was missed.

CHAPTER 4
NIGHT FIGHTING

The Javelin OCU was based at RAF Leeming in North Yorkshire. The course started with two weeks ground school with pilots and navigator/radar operators learning the technical intricacies of the aeroplane. This fortnight also gave pilots and navigators (normally referred to as nav/rads) the chance to sniff around each other before deciding to pair up as constituted crews which would be posted to a front-line squadron at the end of the course. No surprise that none of the nav/rads seemed eager to join up with a 20-year-old guinea pig with only 320 hours in his logbook. But eventually Flying Officer David Holes, with a night-fighter Meteor tour under his belt, decided he would give me a go; my lucky break as he was the best nav/rad on the course. Before our first flight together he shook my hand and wished me the best of luck before he lowered himself into the rear cockpit. That was the start of a very happy association that saw us through the OCU and a full tour on 64 Squadron, first at RAF Duxford with subsequent moves to RAF Waterbeach and RAF Binbrook.

Night fighting was a team effort. The nav/rad would commentate to the pilot once a target had been picked up with sharp instructions to manoeuvre the aircraft into an attack position. The pilot flew the aircraft with the highest achievable degree of accuracy in response to the navigator's commentary which controlled speed, rate of climb and descent and turning performance. Speed increase/decrease instructions required 50 knots plus or minus; the huge, variable airbrakes could produce remarkable deceleration. 'Starboard hard' demanded a forty-five degrees bank level turn; harder and ease required 15 degrees addition or subtraction. Climb and descent instructions meant 2,000 feet rate of climb/descent. Each command required a precise flight configuration either singly or in combination. Within these broad parameters crew team work steadily developed to achieve 'kills' against evading targets on the darkest of nights. Training focused on visual identification of a target before engagement with either guns, or later on, Firestreak air-to-air missiles. The range of identification varied according to the light conditions. Pitch black and the aircraft would be closed to well under 100 yards before the pilot could make an accurate visual identification. On other nights the moon would help out allowing earlier ID and sometimes jet pipe glow could be picked up at much longer ranges. After ID a guns kill with our four 30-mm cannons was standard procedure which required an ideal range of some 400 yards as the wing-mounted guns were spot-harmonised to that distance. The introduction of Firestreak missiles fired from a far greater distance was not allowed to spoil the fun of getting in close with a subsequent gun attack.

At Leeming we flew the Javelin Mk 5 which was not an impressive aircraft principally because it was underpowered. On joining 64 Squadron we upgraded to the Javelin Mk 9 which was a very different kettle of fish. With a 40% power increment over the earlier marks of Javelin, 40,000 feet could be reached in seven minutes and at that altitude the aircraft could out-turn most other contemporary jets. The Mk 9 also had a rudimentary reheat system which boosted performance above 20,000 feet. That said, having enjoyed the pleasure of flying many other aircraft types since those far-off days, I can say without fear of contradiction that none exhibited the totality of idiosyncrasies that came with the Javelin. They have been well described elsewhere, particularly in Peter Caygill's book, *Javelin from the Cockpit – Britain's First Delta Wing Fighter.* So, suffice to say, such incidents as superstalls, centre-line closure, jet-pipe fractures and start-up fires/explosions all added to the excitation generally associated with a tour on Javelins.

Day-flying sorties were flown as pairs out over the North Sea and started with practice interceptions under ground radar control until the pilot called "Judy", the codeword that meant no more help from the ground was required to complete the interception. Sometime would be spent on cine weave, a gunsight tracking exercise closing on an evading target which was filmed from 800 yards down to 250 yards for ground assessment and marking. Most sorties would be completed with one versus one air combat before the pair returned home. The return was sometimes delayed by involvement in furious dogfights, principally against Hunters, which sometimes erupted over East Anglia. For a new boy this could be quite hair raising. Night flying was more sedate and from time to time we operated over land. Looking down on London, brightly lit on a cloudless night from a height of 40,000 feet, never lost its fascination. Thursdays were Kingpin Adex nights when Bomber Command would return from long-range sorties to attack the UK on a broad front to exercise Fighter Command. This exercise was flown lights out but I recall one night when a bomber aircraft switched on his navigation lights. Within seconds the sky was ablaze with flashing green and red colours as everyone followed suit. It was disturbing to note the close proximity of so many aircraft in the pitch black and on the squadron we all agreed that 'lights out' was a far more relaxing environment.

I retain the happiest memories of my time on 64 Squadron. Some very experienced fighter pilots took me under their wings to bring me to combat-ready status in four months. Vin Morgan, my flight commander, Geoff Roberts, Don Headley and Bob Lockhart all come to mind as exemplary fighter pilots who taught me hard lessons about air combat as well as developing my airmanship nous, so important to survival in a rather quirky aeroplane that we were expected to fly at night in the very worst of weather conditions – and quite rightly so given the aircraft's role designation as a night/all-weather fighter. But there were some close calls. I remember a major air defence exercise in late September 1962 just after the squadron had moved to Binbrook in north Lincolnshire. There was no radar talk down and after a mass-scramble at night from Lincolnshire and East Anglian airfields all Javelins were diverted to RAF Leuchars in Scotland because of a rapid weather deterioration. Two of us, taking on the most southerly targets, were behind some 40 other Javelins all heading north and all at minimum fuel states. For us, a stab at Binbrook was the only available alternative where we beat the encroaching fog by less than two minutes. After landing and clearing the runway we had to be towed back to dispersal as thick fog enveloped the airfield. Less than a month later the Cuban Missile Crisis had the world teetering on the brink of general war and for two weeks I wondered if I was going to have to earn my keep for real. It was a sobering experience that was a timely reminder of my ultimate duty.

The Javelin was a comfortable aircraft to fly. A roomy cockpit with excellent and convenient lighting and easy handling characteristics throughout the speed range – as long as you avoided a stall – gave pilots a first-rate instrument flying platform for bad weather operations. To avoid stalling the aircraft low speed warners operated at about 150 knots if the undercarriage was up and performance stall warners sounded during hard manoeuvring if the aircraft was flown into too deep a buffet. The AI 17 radar gave typical target pick-up ranges of 20 nautical miles and once the navigator had locked onto the target (having controlled the aircraft through the difficult geometry of an interception) the pilot could follow the target represented as a green dot on his gun sight via a collimator system. On a night of impenetrable blackness keeping an evading target within a five-degree cone on the gun sight required smooth and aggressive flying and an absolute concentration on the flight instruments to overcome disorientation.

Simply put, the Javelin was a bomber-destroyer and the later marks of the aircraft were capable of attacking targets up to 55,000 feet. Against a mass raid by Soviet bombers each Javelin was credited with a three kills potential per sortie, two with Firestreak missiles and one with guns. For the latter, we sometimes practised an attack which involved a snap-up manoeuvre from 5,000 feet below the target to avoid radar-laid guns which could engage a line-astern attacker at a range of 1,500 yards. A snap-up guns attack boiled down to a race between the bomber's guns achieving radar lock and the Javelin pilot's skill in acquiring and tracking the target with the gun sight before firing. This form of attack was based on a number of assumptions all of which were variable. Any divergence from a single assumption let alone several would upset the geometry of the attack with unquantifiable consequences. Practice of snap-ups during night-training sorties is, perhaps, best described as 'stimulating' for both the attacker and his target. Seeing the dark outline of a Javelin hurtling upwards in a steep climb adjacent to one's wing tip was rather unsettling. Post-sortie debriefs were characterised by much nervous laughter and puffing of cigarettes.

In rotation with other squadrons, night quick reaction alert (QRA) was a regular feature of our life. Operation Halyard required two aircraft and their crews 'on state' from dusk to dawn. Each crew spent 1¾ hours strapped in and 1¾ hours out of the cockpit alternating throughout the long winter nights. The time in between cockpit stints was spent in air traffic control where the WAAFs cooked an excellent fry up and proved themselves to be quality cribbage players. Although my behaviour at the time was hallmarked by a carefree attitude to life – some may say feckless – I was very much aware of my responsibilities as the guardian of UK airspace in a fully-armed aeroplane capable of getting airborne in under a minute to intercept, identify and if necessary shoot down any intruder. I was very proud to have this duty.

I only experienced one serious incident when flying Javelins. During an air gunnery live-firing sortie flown from RAF Nicosia in May 1961 the aircraft's elevators jammed as I completed an attack on the target flag towed by a Meteor. Fortunately my aircraft was going upwards at the time and at a safe altitude of some 20,000 feet. To regain control I started a series of barrel rolls while fiddling around with power and the variable air brakes. Eventually the aircraft was returned to straight and level flight albeit the control restriction was solid with the stick unmoveable fore and aft. Full aileron control was available. My leader and a very experienced pilot, Flight Lieutenant Ken Scott, told me to position the aircraft overhead RAF Akrotiri, point it out to sea and then eject. But after more fiddling around I found that using the Javelin's variable air brakes and with some small amount of available nose-down elevator trim, the aircraft could be put into a steady rate of descent in the landing configuration, albeit at a high indicated air speed of some 180 knots. I decided with youthful optimism that it would be worth having a shot at landing on the long runway at Akrotiri having ejected Dave Holes overhead the airfield. But Dave said he would prefer to stay with me although he would have his hands on the ejector seat blind ready for instant departure to get out of my way should I lose control on approach to land. With radar monitoring I then started a long approach to Akrotiri at a rate of descent of approximately 500 feet per minute maintaining a steady 170 knots and aiming at the runway threshold. Eventually we hit the concrete and the aircraft bounced so high that I thought I had blown it. But the large delta configuration came to my rescue with a ground-cushioning effect so that we landed again hard and with sufficient runway left to stop the aircraft.

A servicing party was sent immediately from RAF Nicosia and discovered that a bolt was jammed in the elevator control lines. This was removed and after full control movements had been checked my CO told me to fly the aircraft back to Nicosia that evening. Before dinner Dave bought me a couple of drinks in the mess – I might have been aircraft captain but a recently pro-moted flight lieutenant buying drinks for a flying officer with only five months seniority merits mention. Soon afterwards a technical instruction arrived from HQ Fighter Command requiring checks to be made on the mark of ejector seats installed in our Javelins. Both of our seats were found to be unservice-able and we probably would not have survived ejection. That evening Dave bought me another drink and a few months later AOC 11 Group awarded me a Green Endorsement to be entered in my logbook.

The three-month detachment to RAF Nicosia from April 1961 was my first overseas deployment. The emphasis on practice interceptions was reduced although the squadron maintained a 24-hour Battle Flight standby at 20 minutes notice in the crew room rather than at two minutes in the cockpit as at Duxford. Air-to-air gunnery against a flag target towed by a Meteor flying at 180 knots introduced me to this new and exciting discipline. The exercise required precise positioning on a 'high perch' position flying a parallel track 1,500 feet above the Meteor displaced by 1,500-2,000 yards. When cleared to attack the Javelin was turned and descended towards the target setting up a curve of pursuit while building considerable overtake speed as the navigator locked his radar onto the metal towing arm of the flag to give accurate range information. With wing-mounted guns all parameters of the attack had to be spot on to have any chance of hitting the flag. The 30-mm ball ammunition was painted in different colours for each aircraft so when the flag was jetti-soned at RAF Nicosia hits could be counted and attributed to individual pilots. It was hugely satisfying to have achieved only a few hits which was the best I managed.

The attachment was one of wonder and pure pleasure. When night flying over the Med the darkness seemed blacker than at home and I was spellbound by my first sight of the night sky split asunder by dazzling bolts of lightning that seemed to stretch from the sea far below into the space high above. Cyprus was now at peace which meant that off duty we could roam the island in a car hired by a syndicate of six of us junior officers. The Country Club at Kyrenia was our favourite watering hole and the 'slab', owned by the club and in the lea of Kyrenia Castle, was the perfect launch pad for snorkelling and water skiing. The weather was perfect for both flying and recreation and I found it difficult to appreciate, until the arrival of my mess bill, that I was being paid for such pure enjoyment. While my memory always recalls the happy things, I am in no doubt that I was very fortunate to revel in such an agreeable life at so young an age.

No. 64 Squadron was the second Fighter Command squadron to take on in-flight refuelling. We trained with Valiant aircraft tankers streaming one hose. Connection of our probe with the basket at the end of the hose line had to be achieved with an overtake speed of three to five knots. Less than three and the contact would be wet, i.e. fuel pouring out of the hose over the Javelin windscreen. More than five, and certainly at seven knots, the whiplash up and down the hose would snap off the probe head leaving it embedded in the basket. Apart from one's personal embarrassment the Valiant was no longer useable as a tanker.

After completion of the training syllabus the first overseas deployment was from the UK to Cyprus. For this we were required to RV with the tankers over north France and then to accompany them to Malta at around 30,000 feet at an indicated air speed of 230 knots. This needed three refuels and a top-up, one of which was above the Rhone Valley – notorious for clear air turbulence – to get us to Malta before the final refuel after which we were free to climb and accelerate. The squadron's preferred plan was to refuel over north France and then to climb and accelerate to best range speed to arrive over Malta – we reckoned we could find it – and refuel there before turning east and cruise climbing to 50,000 feet to annoy Cyprus-based Hunters which would try to intercept us. To descend, with throttles closed and full airbrakes selected, the aircraft was rolled inverted and pulled down into a near vertical descent with an aileron roll to regain heading – no other contemporary fighter could follow a Javelin in a maximum rate descent. The navigation route plan to get to Cyprus which we favoured, much more economical in terms of fuel burn and resources, was rejected by Fighter Command and to this day I still don't know why.

I can recall clearly the details of my first in-flight refuelling trip to Cyprus and the return journey home staging through RAF El Adem in Libya, RAF Luqa in Malta, the Italian airfield at Pisa and the French air force base at Orange in the South of France. For the outward-bound flight, four crews briefed at 05:00 hours then sat around waiting for confirmation that the tankers were airborne. We then manned our aircraft and took off to RV with the Valiants. While waiting for the go Dave asked me if I would like a coffee. When I said, "no, we have a five-hour sortie in front of us", Dave predictably made some rude comments about the strength of pilot's bladders. Once airborne, with the first refuel completed and close to Paris, Dave said, "I want to pee". "Tough," I replied, "by my rough calculations we only have four more hours to go." Adjacent to Italy Dave tuned into a radio beacon that was playing the theme music from 'The Magnificent Seven' which provoked me into gently cycling the stick to and fro in time with the music (we did not have the luxury of an autopilot). This caused Dave considerable discomfort and increased the volume of complaints that endured for the remaining three hours. As we touched down at RAF Akrotiri Dave immediately asked if we were going to stop OK – a sensible question as Javelin brakes were not noted for their 100% reliability. After he received my affirmative I saw in the rear-view mirror straps flying in all directions. As we left the runway to taxi the short distance to the dispersal area I watched in disbelief as a figure emerged from the rear cockpit, stood close to the trailing edge of the port wing, and relieved himself as we passed by the assembled brass from HQ Near East air force and the station who had come to welcome us. I could not pretend that Dave was nothing to do with me.

On the return journey home, in company with Flight Lieutenant Tom Gribble and Flying Officer George Pierce, bad weather in the UK required us to night stop at Orange where we were hosted by the RAF Flight permanently based there to service the multitude of RAF aircraft transiting to the Near East, the Middle East and the Far East. There was a party that evening to celebrate the promotion of a flight sergeant who had served as an airman on 64 Squadron during the Battle of Britain. The arrival of two 64 Squadron aircraft that evening was deemed an entirely appropriate acknowledgement of a career culminating in the achievement of warrant officer rank. For our part we greatly enjoyed the party and got up next morning not feeling in the best of health for the final leg back to Waterbeach.

After starting both engines I had my head down in the cockpit completing checks when I asked Dave how he was doing. There was no reply and I thought 'dozy so and so, he hasn't turned the intercom on'. But then, looking in the rear-view mirror, I was surprised to see that the rear cockpit was empty and I could have sworn I had seen Dave strapping in as I climbed the ladder having completed under-surface checks as was standard practice in the Javelin force. My attention was then quickly focused on the dense cloud of black smoke engulfing the rear of the aircraft. At the same time I became aware of one of the start-up crew jumping up and down making the emergency cut sign. I thus shut down both engines, unstrapped, climbed out on to the starboard engine nacelle and prepared to jump the ten feet or so down to the ground.

At that very moment I remembered that my aircrew holdall was stowed under my feet in the engine nacelle within which were a bottle of gin, 200 cigarettes and a very expensive bottle of scent intended for a new girlfriend in Cambridge. So, keeping a wary eye on the dense smoke at the back of the aeroplane and the activities of the French fire crew who by now had arrived, I got out from my leg pocket a 16-inch screwdriver and attacked the panel screws to retrieve my holdall. I heard a distant voice call "get mine out too" which I did with some reluctance. It later transpired that one of the ground crew, first noticing the smoke emerging from the jet pipes and having failed to attract my attention, had leapt up onto the trailing edge of the wing, tapped Dave on the shoulder and mouthed "you're on fire". Dave believed he had told me, which he may well have done, but unhappily failing to notice that the intercom was not switched on. The story does not have a happy ending. I presented the bottle of very expensive scent to the new girlfriend who, to my delight, was thrilled with the gift. But her happiness did not last long. Having opened the bottle she found that it contained water, not scent, as it had been emptied and refilled by some nimble-fingered Arab working around or for the NAAFI at El Adem where I bought the gift. That as they say was the end of another fine romance.

My first tour was pure pleasure. I enjoyed the job, I enjoyed the aeroplane, I had two COs and a flight commander who I respected and a circle of friends whose company I relished. The officers' messes at all three stations were full of young bachelor officers sharing a love for flying, a disdain for authority beyond the limits of the station and an inclination for the high life constrained only by a salary of limited bounty. The mess by the standards of the day was our comfortable home with a full house guaranteed by service regulations, financial penalties to those few who dared to marry before the age of 25 and the social attitudes and conventions of pre-Beatles UK.

In the air any lapse in airborne performance by a junior pilot would provoke a roasting from a flight commander. Unauthorised air combat, sometimes involving a lot of aeroplanes from different squadrons, was commonplace in East Anglian air space. Our CO, Wing Commander Bill Mills DFC, had a particular penchant for attacking USAF aircraft operating out of Lakenheath. All rather exciting and great fun. On the ground our seniors were remarkably relaxed about our off-duty behaviour as long as we were appropriately dressed. At guest nights after-dinner mess games and inter-squadron free for all, normally involving mess rugby, added to the weekly casualty list more formally associated with Wednesday afternoon sports and particularly inter-station rugby of the conventional kind during the winter months. Guest nights were often further illuminated by the presence of wartime heroes whose after-dinner speeches were both highly entertaining and inspiring. I well recall Douglas Bader telling the story – the first time I heard it – of the Polish fighter pilot visiting a well-known girls' school sometime after the Battle of Britain to give a talk on his experiences. He told how he was attacked by three Fockes. At this stage the headmistress interrupted to explain that a Focke was a German fighter aeroplane. "No," said the Pole, "I was attacked by Messerschmitts, the Fockes were flying them."

Another recollection so clearly etched in my memory was witnessing OC 54 Squadron at Waterbeach flying his privately owned aeroplane – a Turbulent light aircraft – through a hangar. The hangar was not one of the large brick-built structures but one of the temporary wartime constructions that were significantly smaller in height and width. All the junior pilots on the Waterbeach wing in 1962 (1[F] Squadron, 54 [F] Squadron and 64 [F] Squadron) thought this was, in contemporary jargon, really cool. Sadly someone snitched on OC 54 – the betting was on OC Engineering Wing – and our complementary judgement was not shared by the higher command chain. Soon afterwards OC 54 Squadron was sacked and replaced by Squadron Leader David Harcourt-Smith, no mean firecracker himself, who sustained 54's reputation for *joie de vivre*.

Fifty years on all of this may sound rather juvenile but there was much laughter and we lapped up the sense of fun and tradition given to us by station commanders such as Norman Ryder and Archie Winskill who had both fought in the Battle of Britain. I would have followed Wing Commander Bill Mills anywhere and through respect rather than curiosity as to the destination. OC Flying Wing at Duxford, Wing Commander 'Twinkle' Storey, kept us on our toes mainly by the indiscriminate exploitation of thunder flashes, for example, to announce his arrival and departure from briefings. But above all I must acknowledge my debt to the gift of friendships I was so privileged to enjoy. I will never forget names such as Colin Coomber, Sherry Davies, Don Dalton, Geoff Roberts, Andy Dean and a host of others whose company I shared with so much pleasure both in the air and in the mess.

I owe a particular debt of gratitude to Dave Holes. His patience, his good humour and his consummate skill were a constant throughout our three years together. I never cease to wonder how Dave and his fellow navigators so stoically and at times bravely accepted the quirks of their pilots and the peculiarities of such a unique aeroplane as the Javelin.

CHAPTER 5
ADC

My tour on 64 Squadron was marred by several incidents on the ground that did nothing for my career prospects. Amongst the more memorable episodes was a fire in my room at RAF Waterbeach caused by carelessness. As the flames took hold I called "fire, fire, fire" as advised by safety posters. The only response was from a 54 Squadron pilot who shouted "shut up you noisy b....r and go to bed". Eventually others were persuaded of my predicament, a fire engine arrived and the blaze extinguished before it engulfed the entire mess. All of my belongings, including uniforms and civilian clothes, were destroyed. Only the iron frame of my bed survived the inferno. The consequence was a one-sided interview with the station commander and a hefty fine.

Not too long afterwards I managed to skid my car – a battered old Wolsey 6/80 – off the road into a deep ditch. I departed bodily through the front windscreen on impact having rolled out of the way of the steering wheel along the bench seat as impending disaster became obvious. My lifelong friend, Graham Wood, an air traffic control officer driving behind me (we were not racing) picked me up and delivered me to the RAF Hospital at Ely. There my left ear was re-attached to my skull and various other cuts and injuries sorted out. I was not a pretty sight when discharged from hospital a week later, nor for that matter for some time afterwards.

Looking on the bright side I was confident that such mishaps and other misdeeds would have debarred me from appointment as an ADC at a time when most senior air officers in command appointments had pilot ADCs as part of their office furniture and entourage. It thus came as a great shock when I was instructed to report to HQ Bomber Command at RAF High Wycombe for interview by the air officer commanding-in-chief (AOC-in-C) as a potential ADC.

The AOC-in-C was Air Chief Marshal Sir Kenneth Cross, a man of fearsome reputation and huge distinction. As the CO of 46 Squadron flying Hurricanes he led nine of his pilots to their first deck landings on to the aircraft carrier HMS *Glorious* during the evacuation of Allied Forces from north Norway in June 1940. All landed safely and without benefit of tail hooks to engage the carrier's arrestor wires. This courageous effort to save valuable aircraft and their pilots was to no avail as shortly afterwards HMS *Glorious* was intercepted and sunk by German battle cruisers. Sir Kenneth, one of the few survivors out of a ship's complement of 1,400, swam to a raft where he joined 29 others. Three nights and two days later, only Sir Kenneth and one other, a squadron pilot, had survived the arctic cold to be picked up by a passing fishing vessel. Such was the strength of Sir Kenneth's resilience and such was the quality of his courage and leadership in taking his squadron to land their Hurricanes on a carrier; this against the Air Ministry's previous conclusion, after trials, that it was an entirely impracticable undertaking.

As it turned out my interview with Sir Kenneth was not a success. It only lasted for 90 seconds and it was clear from the start that the career brief in front of the AOC-in-C contained a number of inaccuracies. For example, Sir Kenneth understood I was flying Hunters and was stationed at RAF Waterbeach. In reply I had to point out that I was still flying Javelins and had moved to Binbrook. This caused Sir Kenneth some obvious irritation and the interview was drawn to a quick conclusion when he suddenly asked: "What's wrong with you, your face looks a bit of a mess?" I replied that I had a car crash which put me in hospital for a while. "Drunk I suppose," commented the AOC-in-C, "good day to you sir." I returned to my squadron happily convinced that I would be withdrawn from the air secretary's list of potential ADCs. But not so as I was told by my desk officer that like it or not I was going to do a ground tour and there were vacancies in Technical Training Command and on Thor missile sites. This threat softened my attitude to ADC appointments and so I departed 64 Squadron with great reluctance in January 1963 to take on the job of ADC to the commandant of the Royal Air Force College, Cranwell.

The first commandant was Air Commodore Eric Nelson, a charming man and a pre-war Old Cranwellian, who held firmly to the traditions of the college and its training methods. He understood my disappointment at leaving the squadron and promised that, given satisfactory performance, I would be returned to flying duties at the end of his own tour. But, change was in the air and sadly he was moved to another appointment six months later to be followed by Air Commodore Michael Lyne who had graduated from the college in the last pre-war entry. I immediately requested a formal interview with the new commandant who, without hesitation, said he knew precisely what I was going to ask and the answer was no, but do an adequate job and I might earn remission. He would decide the time of my departure and as it turned out this direction, which brooked no argument, would have conse-quences both positive and pleasurable beyond my imagination at that time.

The year and a half working for Michael Lyne, his deputy Group Captain Al Deere, a New Zealander of Battle of Britain fame, and for a short time Group Captain Larry Lamb of Rugby Union distinction was to prove highly educational while curbing the rather distressing element of irresponsibility, now easily admitted, that so far had been evident in my performance as a junior officer. Michael Lyne's primary task as the new commandant was to achieve the smooth merger of Cranwell with the RAF Technical College Henlow which, given the pride of belonging and innate conservatism within any military service, was always going to be a difficult trick to pull off. Add to that a fair measure of concern in the higher ranks of the service regarding the need for a larger measure of academic education in the college's ground-training syllabus, and Michael's task as a reforming commandant was never going to be easy. The spotlight was firmly focused on Cranwell. But Michael accepted his great responsibility, and it was great in the context of the RAF's history, with easy confidence that persuaded even the most traditional elements within the service of the need to accept both the necessity and inevitability of change.

For my part Michael Lyne was to change my whole attitude to the service and my responsibilities within it. As a pilot with three Air Force Crosses to his name he was an inspirational example and leader. In May 1940, flying Spitfires on 19 Squadron, he was grievously wounded in air combat over Dunkirk – in the fight he destroyed a Messerschmitt 110 – and was lucky to escape with his life. With a dead engine he glided back across the Channel and crash-landed on Deal beach. His severe injuries were not helped en route to the hospital when the ambulance driver, looking over his shoulder at Michael, drove slap into a lamppost. A year later, having left hospital, Michael promptly volunteered for the Merchant Ship Fighter Unit and became one of the small and very gallant band of fighter pilots who, in their specially modified Hurricanes, were catapulted off merchant ships to protect convoys from the Luftwaffe. Consider the prospect: the launch, the search, possibly a fight, finding the convoy again, baling out into the sea and then with luck being picked up by a ship before the cold of the ocean claimed a life. And then, once on board, sharing the dangers of convoy life with the mariners of the Royal and Merchant Navies. I once asked Michael why he volunteered. He replied that: "Churchill wanted volunteers for a secret and hazardous duty and that was good enough for me."

Five years later having survived further operational duties in the desert, the Mediterranean and Italy, Michael took command of 54 Squadron which had just converted to its new Vampire jet fighter. There he formed the first jet aerobatic team that he led on its inaugural display at the Brussels Air Show in 1947 thus foreshadowing the success and worldwide renown of today's Red Arrows. Eight years further on Michael was the captain of Aries 4, a Canberra aircraft, which took off from Bardufoss in Norway. After a flight of 6½ hours the Canberra landed at Ladd Air Force Base Alaska, 3,500 miles away, having completed the first jet aircraft flight from Europe to America by the polar route. This pioneering achievement blazed the trail for today's non-stop flights between America, Europe and the Far East. This exploit earned Michael the third of his Air Force Crosses which marked his own distinct and unique contribution to aviation history and the annals of Royal Air Force achievement.

Michael never lost his love of flying and interest in the aerodynamics of aviation. Soon after he arrived there was growing concern about the spinning characteristics of the Jet Provost. It seemed that a small error in the recovery action from a fully developed spin could induce an immediate high rotational spin – most uncomfortable and the more difficult to recover from. At that time my experience of the Jet Provost was just a few sorties cadged as a helpful passenger on air tests and formation leads. So I was surprised when Michael asked me to find out everything about spinning the JP rather than calling in an expert from Standardisation Flight to brief him. I did what I was told and Michael's next instruction was to book an aeroplane to try it out. Off we went, up and down, up and down for an hour as recorded in my logbook. I can't remember how many spins we completed with deliberate mishandling of the controls but by the end of the trip we had covered every possible combination of a bungled recovery. "Good," said Michael, "I can now make some sensible comment on incident reports."

I retain the clearest memory of a man of considerable distinction and great courage, a leader who welcomed responsibility but shunned the limelight and a pioneer blessed with vision and the determination to turn it to reality. During a privileged friendship that was to last for 34 years, I never heard Michael utter a word that could be interpreted either directly or indirectly as boastful. Questions about his achievements were either answered factually and unemotionally or, more often, deflected with a gentle self-deprecating humour that was one of his most memorable and delightful characteristics. While his achievements set an inspirational example, and one to try to emulate, Michael was also a natural teacher who was into everything, questioning, probing, debating, always attentive and invariably courteous. But the impressive ambit of his energy, which could be fiercely focused on those who failed to match his exacting standards of conduct and professionalism, was somehow always relieved by his sense of humour and perhaps more memorably by his occasional eccentricity. One day Michael was to fly himself in a Jet Provost from Cranwell to the Central Flying School at RAF Little Rissington to watch the Flying Training Command aerobatic competition. I went down to the flight line to see him off where I came across an extraordinary apparition about to climb into the aeroplane. Michael, his flying helmet in one hand, was wearing the bright yellow standard Mac West of those days. There reality ended because under the Mae West he was dressed in a Mackintosh worn over his No. 1 uniform. The outfit was set off by leg restraint garters which had already destroyed the sharp creases of his trousers. I hurried up to him, a concerned ADC. "Sir," I said "you can't go flying like that." "Why not?" asked Michael. "Well," I spluttered, "pilots don't fly in Mackintoshes." "They do," said Michael "when it's raining at Rissington."

Michael's energy, his humour, his absolute integrity and eccentricity are abiding memories of that marvellous year I spent with him that taught me so much to my ultimate advantage and benefit. And how lucky I was to be admitted to the Lyne family circle of remarkable cohesion and hallmarked by mutual respect between parents and their four school children, all wondrously polite and intimidatingly intelligent. One evening, when Michael and Joy were out to dinner, I was asked to pop round to The Lodge (the commandant's residence) to check all was well with Roderic, aged 14, who was on holiday and alone in the house. For want of something to do I challenged Roderic to a game of Scrabble and to my discomfort was soundly beaten. It was not a good idea to challenge a youth who was to enjoy a most successful career in the Foreign Office and public service before his appointment as a member of the Chilcot Inquiry where he distinguished himself as the toughest of inquisitors.

Another interesting aspect of my job and of historical note, was sharing the outer office with Michael's personal staff officer, Squadron Leader John MacArthur. John, an Old Cranwellian and a man of mercurial temperament, was grounded for medical reasons, the consequence of a tour of duty which involved flying at extreme altitudes. As I got to know him it gradually emerged he had been one of a small band of RAF pilots – five, one of whom was killed – attached to the CIA in the late 1950s to fly the U-2 aircraft on covert spying missions over the USSR at the height of the Cold War. Their involvement was abruptly ended when the Soviets shot down the American pilot, Gary Powers, in May 1960. During our general chats about flying, which I have never previously referred to, I gradually became aware of the difficulties and challenges associated with flying and navigating the U-2 which left me spellbound with admiration for those who flew these missions then and elsewhere in following years.

I also enjoyed some flying at Cranwell, Chipmunk and Jet Provost, and greater opportunity for sport although a broken ankle in a rugby match against RAF Wittering caused me to cancel my first skiing holiday. The money saved financed a memorable party. Al Deere, who had recently left Cranwell on promotion to air commodore, turned up with his wife, Joan, to collect a debt. Shortly before his departure I had a bet with Al that Wilson Whineray's All Blacks would not win all their matches during their 1963-1964 tour of the British Isles. They were indeed beaten by a Welsh club (Newport if my memory is correct) and I thought the barrel of beer was mine. But Al insisted that the bet only applied to the test matches which the All Blacks had convincingly won. Al had represented the service as both a rugby player and middle weight boxer of distinction, so notwithstanding the discrepancy in our ranks and his fame as a fighter pilot the odds on winning the argument were stacked against me. I lost.

Al Deere was one of the heroes of the Battle of Britain and by the end of the war he had shot down 22 Luftwaffe aircraft with ten more 'probables' plus 18 damaged to his credit. On the debit side Al had been either shot down with a parachute descent or forced-landed with battle damage on no less than seven occasions. Like many others of my generation I hero-worshipped Al Deere. One day I was travelling with him in a car en route to an airfield. It was in August, the sun was shining in an almost cloudless sky, the horizon was clear cut and the visibility was unlimited. For want of something to say I observed, rather vacuously, that it was a lovely day for flying. There was no reply. A minute or so later he turned to look at me, indeed almost a stare without a blink of an eyelid. "You will never imagine," he said "how much I hated days like this in 1940. I used to pray for a clamp" (air force slang for weather so bad it prevented flying). I was taken aback. How could this lion-hearted hero, recognised as one of the bravest of the brave, admit to such fear? How did he disguise it, not just during the Battle of Britain but in the years of war that followed until final victory in 1945?

I think I eventually found the answer in the transcript of a radio broadcast given by one of our greatest soldiers, Field Marshal the Viscount Slim. He said that all of us have some degree of physical courage which is like having money in the bank. We start with a certain capital of courage, some large, some small and we proceed to draw on our balance. As courage is thus an expendable quality some may use it all up. Not so with Al Deere. Indeed his capital of courage was so large that he never came close to overdrawing, albeit he experienced time and time again that nerve-jangling fear that was to leave such an indelible mark on his memory. My friendship with Michael Lyne and Al Deere, which lasted to their deaths in the 1990s, was one of the greatest treasures of my service career.

While passing-out parades and a continuous stream of high level visitors, all eager to give their advice on the future of Cranwell, kept me busy with programming, social functions and transport arrangements, there was time enough to enjoy other more pleasurable activities such as the pursuit of Elizabeth Manning, younger sister of Anwyl who was an officer in the Princess Mary's RAF Nursing Service. Anwyl lived in the mess until her marriage to Flight Lieutenant Michael Allisstone who was serving on the college instructional staff. Two years after our first meeting at Cranwell Elizabeth and I were married and that was the greatest gift of a posting so unwelcome when first notified. In the years ahead I had a companion who provided me with the love and comfort that brought me safely through the occasional darkness of grief and trough of despond. The Royal Air Force was my chosen profession, I sought to do it and was paid to do it. This was not the case for Elizabeth but she was a sublime companion and I can safely record that I knew of no safer refuge or finer friend when the going got tough. Our governments in the future years of our marriage never got a better deal.

In the summer of 1964 Michael presented me with a final challenge. If I could find him an acceptable replacement I could return to flying. Fortunately for me Air Marshal Sir Augustus Walker, Inspector General of the Royal Air Force, was about to retire leaving a redundant ADC. Peter Symes, a secretarial officer and fellow member of No.76 Entry was keen to come to Cranwell to finish a full tour as an ADC and the deal was done. One final and concluding surprise was my posting to Fighter Recce Hunters, an ambition I thought beyond my grasp.

CHAPTER 6
HUNTERS
AND ADEN

In the 1960s the RAF flew a remarkable galaxy of aircraft types. Some like the Belvedere helicopter were troublesome exotica and others such as the Swift and the Lightning made a significant contribution to the commercial success of Martin Baker. The Buccaneer, the Phantom and the Wessex helicopter operated with distinction in the livery of both the RAF and the Fleet Air Arm. And while the Victor was futuristic in shape, the Shackleton was obviously the descendent of the Lancaster. Amongst them and many others there were the real beauties – the Comet, the Vulcan, the Canberra and, most striking of all, the Hawker Hunter.

To fly the Hunter had been an enduring ambition and so it was with delight that I reported to RAF Chivenor, north Devon, in the autumn of 1964 having completed a short flying refresher course on the Meteor at RAF Strubby. At Strubby the officers' mess was a Nissen hut. At Chivenor single accommodation was within wooden huts, warmed by coke-fired stoves, someway apart from central ablutions. All this was a far cry from the luxury of the 1930s messes to which I had become comfortably accustomed. Chivenor was a wooden station of World War II vintage and as such the fighter pilot conversion unit was not a place for the faint of heart. The station buzzed with frenetic activity as staff instructors relentlessly chivvied and chased students in the air and on the ground. Everything was done at the double and criticism of poor performance, particularly any lack of zeal, was forthright and very much to the point. Once airborne, particular emphasis was placed on the development of aggressive flying while acquiring the air combat and weaponeering skills required by the front line. It was all very different from the measured pace of activity at the night fighter OCU.

Conversion onto the Hunter Mk 6 was pure pleasure. Although one could quibble about cockpit ergonomics, aircraft handling and performance met all my expectations. Previous experience saw me safely through the first phase of the course which involved tactical formation flying, air-to-ground weapons and air-to-air firing. But I was well aware that fighter recce was judged to be the most demanding operating regime for single-seat pilots who flew at high speed and ultra-low levels using basic navigation techniques to find and identify targets; these included all forms of military equipment (sea, land and air), others as small as a single radio mast, others huge such as multi-span bridges. Sorties were flown at a cruise speed of 420 knots (483 mph) at 250 feet above ground level with three targets to recce including on occasion a search-of-a-line feature. In-flight reports following a standard NATO format for each target type were radioed to staff chase pilots on selected trips. Full written reports, including sketches, on each target were prepared immediately after landing. No cameras were fitted to the Hunter Mk 6; the challenge of precise low level photography was to come later after posting to a front-line unit.

The theory of high speed, low level navigation was simple. To fly an accurate indicated air speed while maintaining a precise heading for a pre-planned time, monitored with a stopwatch bought at personal expense and mounted on the cockpit coaming, would keep the aircraft close to, if not on, the required track. Map reading should be concentrated on easily distinguishable features well spaced along track allowing time for good look out essential to the survival of a FR pilot operating as a singleton. A route map, 1:500,000 scale, covered the whole sortie and as each target was approached the pilot transferred at an initial point (IP) to a larger scale map, usually 1:50,000. Carrying at least four maps for each sortie required careful preparation in the annotation of heading and time marks with each map folded to a size suited to easy handling and convenient stowage in a relatively small and cramped cockpit. Little FR pilots had an ergonomic advantage over their larger brethren in the context of cockpit management. Today I rather fear that the advent of GPS and inertial navigation systems have destroyed the fun and challenge of high speed, low level navigation, hence for the record this explanation of how we managed.

Simple as the theory was I found it initially difficult to put into practice because I fell foul to the temptation of excessive map reading focused on too small a detail which led to uncertainty and error. But gradually unremitting pressure from the FR instructors, Flight Lieutenant John Morris and Lt Bob Ponter RN invoking a 'bad cop/good cop' routine forced the penny to drop and I left Chivenor in April 1965 as a proficient FR pilot on posting to 1417 (FR) Flight at RAF Khormaksar, Aden. Flight Lieutenant Roger Neal accompanied me to Aden whereas the other student member of the course, Alex Weiss, was posted to 2 (AC) Squadron at RAF Gütersloh.

I arrived at Khormaksar at midday on 20th April 1965 along with 100 or so other passengers in a Britannia aircraft of RAF Transport Command. The flight took 14 hours and my first impression of Aden was not favourable.

Although the temperature reflected from the hardstanding was hotter than I expected, the air was moist and clammy with a rather sweet aromatic smell that I am sure I would still recognise. Met by old friends and designated immediately as a 'moony', the lot of all newcomers, a visit to the officers' mess bar for a cooling glass of beer was most welcome. But this lift to my morale was soon dashed when taken to my room, the closest to the Khormaksar power station which bellowed its cacophony throughout the day and night. Inside the room the temperature was hotter than outside while a ceiling fan revolving at about 20 rpm created no more than a barely identifiable draft. However, within a week and despite my early misgivings I could enjoy the blessing of sweet sleep undisturbed by either heat or noise.

In 1965 the Federation of South Arabia, divided into western and eastern protectorates with a total area of 112,000 square miles including Aden itself, had been promised independence in 1968. The strong running tide of Arab nationalism, hostility to colonialism, weakening political will and economic hard times at home had come together to persuade the British government that sustaining a military presence in Aden was untenable. The announcement of withdrawal increased rather than eased tension within the Federation as political processes and progress were crippled by internal dissent. While the British government tried its best to create a South Arabian organisation capable of self-governance, Arab nationalists were determined to claim the credit for forcing an end to British rule. Egypt was the driving force behind this aggressive nationalism aided and abetted by its allies in the Yemen. The most formidable of many political groups active in Aden were the Front for the Liberation of Occupied South Yemen (FLOSY) and the National Liberation Front (NLF). FLOSY was primarily an urban organisation with its membership largely made up of agitators and misfits. The NLF on the other hand were men of the wadis, tough tribesmen skilled in guerrilla warfare and quick to penetrate the ranks of the Federal Army and Federal Guard such that their reliability in a crisis was uncertain. FLOSY and the NLF were united only by their hatred of the British. By September 1965, their campaigns of intimidation, violence and steadily increasing terrorism had persuaded the British government to suspend the Aden constitution with the High Commissioner, Sir Richard Turnbull, becoming in effect the government of Aden. I never met Sir Richard but have seen him quoted as saying that: "the British Empire left behind only two monuments: the game of association football and secondly the expression 'f**k off'." One of the more memorable maxims I have come across.

In the specific circumstances of Aden, and following the announcement that there would be no defence agreement with the Federation after independence,

Sir Richard said: "in a world of violence and conjecture there is only one certainty: that whatever government might ultimately be in command it would not be a British one. There was no longer any advantage to be secured in supporting us and everybody had to look for a new bandwagon upon which to secure a safe seat." The scene was thus set for a rapid escalation in violent incidents and a similarly quick descent into a "dirty, treacherous, dangerous, disagreeable war – a war of treachery and hate and thuggery and unease". These were the words of the commander-in-chief, Admiral Sir Michael Le Fanu, when he briefed a parliamentary delegation visiting Aden in mid-September 1966.

Such, and in brief, was the political situation during my first year on 1417 Flight, the smallest flying unit on the largest overseas station in the service at that time. While command and control of RAF Khormaksar was exercised through the well-tried and familiar three-pronged station organisation – operations, administration and engineering wings – flying activities were split between three autonomous Wings. Short-Range Transport (SRT) Wing comprised 26 Squadron with Belvedere helicopters, soon to be changed to the Wessex, and 78 Squadron with Twin Pioneers, Whirlwind helicopters and a communications flight operating Andovers and Dakotas. The primary purpose of the Wing was to provide logistic support to the Army throughout the South Arabian Protectorate. Medium-Range Transport (MRT) Wing, 84 Squadron with Beverley C Mk1 aircraft and 105 Squadron with the Argosy C Mk1, also operated in the protectorate but flew far further afield to support RAF detachments at Riyan, Salalah and Masirah along the Arabian Sea coastline and Sharjah in the Persian Gulf as well as RAF Muharraq at Bahrain. Last was Strike Wing consisting of 8 and 43 Squadrons flying the Hunter FGA9, 1417 (FR) Flight equipped with the Hunter FR10 and 37 Squadron flying the Shackleton MR2. Although the SRT and MRT Wings looked after all the vital logistic support functions throughout Middle East Command, Strike Wing was the teeth arm of the Middle East air force, well equipped to deter, to coerce and if necessary to punish.

The establishment of 1417 Flight was six pilots, all flight lieutenants with the most senior and experienced appointed as flight commander, and five Hunter FR10s. Our Hunters were converted from Hunter F6s. Three Vinten F95 strip aperture cameras, installed in port, starboard and nose stations, operated at eight frames per second providing sufficient clarity and overlap up to speeds of 600 knots at ultra-low level, that is 50 feet or so above the ground. Four 30-mm Aden cannons were retained for both offensive and defensive action. Most importantly, the cockpit layout was optimised for low level operations which gave pilots more time to concentrate on look out, map reading and reconnaissance. The cockpit layout of all FR10s was the same with this admirable uniformity contrasting most favourably with 18 possible cockpit permutations in the ground-attack Hunter FGA9. From outside the only obvious visible differences between the FR10 and the FGA9 were the three camera ports and underwing fuel tanks in the normal operating config- uration. The FR10 carried two 230-gallon drop tanks on inboard pylons and 100-gallon tanks on the outboard pylons. The FGA9 was flown without out- board tanks enabling the rapid addition of rockets or bombs for ground-attack missions. In sum, the attributes of the Hunter FR10 in terms of cockpit ergo- nomics, performance (620 knots at sea level was easily achievable) and camera fit made it the perfect platform for recce and attack so justifying the claim that the aircraft was the best of the Hunter breed.

While the Strike Wing operated centralised servicing for all Hunters, the 1417 Flight commander had 14 airmen under command in the photographic section who looked after the cameras and the rapid processing of film. Neg- atives for printing were selected by the pilot and then marked with a north orientation line and a few distinguishable grid references where possible – not easy to achieve in the desert. The wing was commanded by Wing Commander Martin Chandler, a cheerful, breezy and popular leader with his deputy, first Squadron Leader Roy Bowie and then Squadron Leader Fred Trowern, keeping a friendly eye on the activities of six flight lieutenants happily operating as an independent unit. We were well supported and looked after until in late 1966, as the consequence of an aircraft accident, the chain of command decided we needed closer supervision. Derek Whitman, who had been flight commander for little more than a week, took it on the chin with admirable composure. A month later Squadron Leader Dickie Barraclough was posted in and suffice to say that Dickie's leadership and good humour sustained the high morale of the unit through the testing times of our last year in Aden.

The flight's activities embraced a wide range of tasks with some, such as 'flag waves', firepower demos and formation fly pasts, being flown with the ground-attack squadrons. These events demonstrated the weight and reach of the RAF's firepower in South Arabia and beyond. Reconnaissance missions, obviously the bulk of our work, were tasked by HQ Middle East Command through the Air Staff at Steamer Point to station operations and finally to the flight. This lengthy process was adequate for most 'political tasking' which typically required close-up photographs of every building within a defined distance, sometimes as much as ten miles down a specific wadi. The intelligence staffs would then pore over the photos, helped by informants, to identify build- ings used by dissident tribesmen as arms dumps or for other hostile purposes.

Once certain they had the right target, ground-attack Hunters would be tasked to destroy it with air-to-ground rockets. A 1417 pilot would lead off by dropping hundreds of leaflets over the target warning the inhabitants and close neighbours that ten minutes later the building would be destroyed and why this action was being taken. The leaflets were stowed in the flaps of the Hunter so requiring a flapless take-off. I cannot remember anyone committing the faux pas of lowering the flaps and inundating the airfield in a storm of paper. Ten minutes after the leaflet drop the FR pilot took close pre-strike photos of the target and then, if necessary, marked it with 30-mm high explosive cannon fire for the benefit of the circling ground-attack aircraft – this to avoid confusion if the actual target was within a group of buildings. This placed some pressure on the FR pilot as missing was not an option. After the building had been destroyed post-attack photos were taken to complete the mission.

This sedate process so necessary within the political context could extend over several weeks as the intelligence staffs honed in on the target; sometimes further missions were tasked for photos from different angles and directions to achieve a positive identification. But this leisurely pace was far too slow for the purposes of Army units serving 'up country' adjacent to the Yemen border and the Radfan mountains. Soldiers' demands for photographic intelligence were almost invariably at short notice requiring rapid response from the flight. This was frequently achieved by battalion intelligence officers contacting 1417 directly with the task being flown under the guise of a training sortie rather than an operational mission. At the working level everyone was happy with this ad hoc arrangement. However, tactical contentment was not shared by those exercising operational command and with all the benefit of hindsight I can understand why. Nevertheless, this system worked and packages of photographs, suitably annotated, could be bagged up and attached to a drogue parachute which was then lodged in the Hunter's airbrake. Flying low and slow the pilot could drop this cargo to within yards of the intended recipient.

During my two-year tour it was interesting to observe the flight's level of operational activity wax and wane in support of infantry battalions rotating through Aden. Up country some seemed to prefer a comparatively quiet life holding ground well knowing that massive air firepower was available should dissident activity become too aggressive. Other battalions preferred to move out of their bases and dominate the ground with energetic and audacious patrolling making the best use of the photographic coverage the flight could supply to augment poor mapping. I remember the Cameronians (Scottish Rifles), the King's Own Yorkshire Light Infantry, the Royal Anglians and Royal Marines commandos as being particularly hot mustard. Of special interest were the sorties flown in support of SAS patrols. A pilot was briefed on their planned route and would then fly along it through the wadis as low as possible filming with all three cameras to present a detailed line overlap of photographs to assist operational planning. Grid references would be marked up along the planned route so that if a patrol ran into trouble and needed close air support, their position could be quickly identified once radio contact was made. It is perhaps worth adding that once operational, 1417 pilots were all self-authorising down to a minimum height of 50 feet above ground level. This was partly necessary to meet the standby commitment when from dawn to dusk an FR pilot was on two hours standby; there were frequent callouts outside our normal working hours.

Elsewhere the flight was committed to Operation Ranji, the simplest of our operational tasks. This involved flying at high level to a point several hundred miles to the east of Aden and then returning at low level to photograph all shipping, including many dhows, within three miles of the coast. The prints were marked up with a time and position. These missions were intended to gather intelligence, particularly on Soviet and other foreign-flagged shipping, to reduce the incidence of arms smuggling into the protectorate. With what success I don't know as we received no feedback on these missions.

The most demanding operational missions during my tour were involved with Operation Thesiger. In August 1965 two aircraft of the flight were detached to RAF Salalah in the Sultanate of Oman not far from the border with the East Aden Protectorate. The task was to find and identify convoys, allegedly camel trains, bringing arms and supplies across the Empty Quarter to the Dhofar Liberation Front and dissidents in the Sultanate. Flying a pair of Hunters off a rough sand runway required some reordering of standard ground-operating procedures as any movement generated a minor sandstorm. The second aircraft could only start to taxi after the leader was airborne. Thereafter there were two real problems. The only maps available showed a coastline with RAF Salalah accurately positioned. To the north and into the Rub' al Khali (the Empty Quarter) the maps were annotated with a single word: 'unsurveyed'. Secondly, we were briefed not to use the 'Midway' airstrip – now the Royal Air Force of Oman base Thumrait – some 50 miles north of Salalah as a diversion airfield. If an aircraft diverted to Midway because the leader had burst a tyre on landing at Salalah, where there were no crash/recovery vehicles, it would require a brigade-level operation to get jet fuel over the mountains just to the north of Salalah to Midway. So, on recovering to Salalah, the second Hunter dropped into long line astern and only committed to landing once the leader was clear of the strip. If a diversion should be forced, the briefed technique was to jettison immediately the empty underwing fuel tanks, climb to 36,000 feet and set off for Masirah (some 300 miles away) at range speed. At approximately 100 miles from Masirah, the engine would be flamed out and the aircraft put into a glide which, if everything worked out as planned, would place the aircraft at 2,000 ft downwind to land when the engine would be relit. Mercifully this procedure was never put to the test.

Operating deep into the Empty Quarter without adequate mapping at low level concentrated the mind on the crucial need for accurate flying. Bit by bit in August and September 1965 and again in February 1966 we began to build up our own maps of the vast area we were tasked to search by plotting distinctive features such as a bush here and an oil drum there and so on. While I flew most missions in the company of Flight Lieutenant Ken Simpson, I did fly as a singleton when the other aircraft was temporarily unserviceable. I well recall the feeling of total and absolute solitude when alone at low level in the Rub' al Khali among the towering ochre-coloured dunes of the sand sea. It was so different from the topography of the western Aden protectorate where mountains, steep-sided wadis, villages and terraced cultivation within defined tribal areas were commonplace. Further to the east the Hadhramaut, with a landscape reminiscent of Monument Valley in Arizona, told a story of evolution quite absent in the empty wilderness of the real desert. Here and there substantial buildings, three stories high with mud walls several feet thick, dominated lower lying land and the inhabitants of inferior and cruder dwelling places. It was a rare privilege to have flown through the Hadhramaut at low level and to have seen such habitation all bound within a timeless aura of history.

From time to time we were shot at – powder puff stuff compared with the acute dangers endured by our wartime predecessors and indeed successors – and one Hunter Mk 9 was certainly destroyed by dissident action with others suffering minor damage. If forced to abandon an aircraft, protection against hostile tribesman was a 'ghooly chit', a double-sided yellow card containing such useful phrases in Arabic (but without phonetic spelling) as 'whose country is this?' (see opposite). The card also stated in Arabic with English translation: 'I am a British officer and need your assistance to get to the nearest political advisor or government representative. For this good deed the British government will reward you well. This paper is a safe conduct and guarantees that you may return to your people unmolested by the government.' I was never convinced of its value because most tribesmen up country were illiterate and secondly, assuming survival of first contact with dissidents, I was not convinced that a debt-ridden British government would splash out to achieve my safe return in the event of an auction. Happily, my concerns were not put to the test and it says much for the leadership of Strike

FLT. Lt. JOHNS.

RAF Aircrews on Operations

and

RAF Intelligence Officers on

Operations

Assalaam Alaikum	Peace be with you! (initial greetings)
Kaif haalkum?	How are you?
Ana bikhair	I am well.
Eish ismak?	What is your name?
Eish ism hadhal makaan?	What is the name of this place?
Bilad min hadhi?	Whose country is this?
Dhabit sayasi qareeb aw baeed?	Is the Political Officer nearby or far away?
Ana geaan	I am hungry.
Ana dhamaan	I am thirsty.
Ana aayan wa ma aqdar amshi	I am sick and cannot walk.
Min fadhlikum geeby dhabit sayasi aw wahid min riggal al hukoomah	Please fetch a Political Officer or any government official.
Khodhooni ila dhabit sayasi, wal hukoomah ba-taateekum igarah kabeerah	Take me to the Political Officer and the Government will give me a large reward.

انا ضابط بريطاني واحتاج الى مساعدتكم لاصل
الى اقرب مستشار سياسي او مندوب آخر للحكومة ولهذا
العمل الطيب سكافئكم الحكومة البريطانية مكافأة عظيمة
وهذا المكتوب أمان لكم وضمان بأنه يمكنكم أن ترجعوا الى
أهلكم بدون تعرض من الحكومة .

Royal Air Force

I am a British Officer and need your assistance to get to the nearest Political Adviser or Government Representative. For this good deed the British Government will reward you well. This paper is a safe conduct and guarantees that you may return to your people unmolested by the Government.

Wing that during the last two years of our occupation of South Arabia we did not lose a pilot to either hostile action or accident.

I shall never forget my last operational task which I remember with rather a shamed face. The job was to patrol a rough track to the west of Aden leading down from the Yemen border towards the federal capital just to the north of Aden. Any activity was to be reported immediately to an Army patrol which would set up a road block. As I flew northwards at about one hundred feet and a comparatively low speed I spotted a single figure on the track moving towards me. He saw me coming and by the time I was above him he was blazing away at me with a semi-automatic weapon. This irritated me, but rather than return fire immediately with four 30-mm cannons – disproportionate to say the least and well beyond my rules of engagement – I stooged on regardless. A few minutes later and out of sight of my assailant, I turned around, descended to ultra-low level and opened the tap to achieve 500 knots plus. This time he did not hear me coming nor for that matter did he see me. As he disappeared beneath the nose of the aircraft I pulled 6-G up into vertical climb and enjoyed the pleasure of seeing him rolling around in the dust. Deuce I suppose, but somehow I still feel something of a bully.

My two-year tour on 1417 Flight was the most enjoyable of my service flying career. Although challenges to come would prove more testing, the Hunter FR10 remains my favourite aeroplane, while operating in unrestricted airspace and mainly at low level over such variable topography unchanged by time never lost either its excitement or interest.

CHAPTER 7
DOMESTICITY

In October 1965 I returned to England for the week-long Hunter survival and emergency course at RAF Chivenor, a regular feature for all Middle East Command Hunter pilots as there was no simulator in theatre. I tacked on a couple of weeks leave during which Elizabeth and I were married in St John's Church at Stanmore.

My new father-in-law was serving as the air officer administration at HQ Fighter Command and arrangements for our wedding reflected his most impressive organisational talents. The service and reception ran perfectly and my best man, Flight Lieutenant Jerry Saye, not only got me to the church on time but had all the ladies swooning. He was the smoothest officer I knew well and had served as Sir Kenneth Cross's ADC. Having survived that experience I judged he had all the attributes necessary to keep a firm grip on some of my other friends whose behaviour could be unpredictable. Our ushers included three RAF chums, Flight Lieutenants Tim Thorn, John Thomson and Angus Ross and Captain Richard Abbott, Royal Anglians. Two 'civies' supported the military. I had first met Michael Palin through Elizabeth's friendship with Helen forged as students together at the Froebel Educational Institute. Michael and Helen were to marry not long after us and our friendship endures to this day. The second 'civy' was Nigel Talbot-Rice who three years later married Elizabeth's youngest sister, Joanna. Nigel was to be headmaster of Summer Fields for many years and Jo and Nigel's friendship and kindness have been constants in our lives. John Thomson tragically died a year before he was to assume the mantle of CAS. It was a privilege to have counted him amongst my friends. I still see a lot of Jerry Saye, and Tim Thorn from time to time. Richard Abbott, soon to transfer to the Army Air Corps, enjoyed a most successful career in Army Aviation before retiring to work in St Mary's Hospital Paddington where he revealed a well disguised talent for administration. Richard lives nearby so we can still bore the unsuspecting with tales of our time together in Aden.

I was just beginning to really enjoy the reception when father-in-law 'advised' me to bring forward our planned departure time as fog was forecast along our northwards route. So I did as I was told and we set off for our honeymoon in the Scottish Highlands, admittedly my choice and at my selfish insistence because I craved the sight and feel of rain. Scotland did not disappoint.

Elizabeth joined me in Aden on New Year's Day 1966 after we had been allocated a flat in Naagi building, Maalla. Our separation was comparatively short by the standards of the time. The penalty was acceptance of a flat which had been assessed as unfit for civilian occupation, but it was large enough for a childless couple. I was 26 years old and therefore could marry 'legitimately' in the sense that I had passed 25 which allowed me to draw marriage allowance and to live in public accommodation at a rental cost. Before committing to the marriage I had submitted my formal application to the station commander requesting his approval. It was returned annotated with the words 'approved – as long as she is not an Arab'. I do so wish I had kept it.

Elizabeth was soon employed teaching at the service's school at Steamer Point. A month or so after her arrival I was told to hurry home to pack a bag as Ken Simpson and I were off to Masirah for Operation Thesiger 2. I could not tell her our destination or how long our absence, so I wrote a short note saying not to worry and the chaps on the flight would look after her. Two weeks later, coming home from a supper party, Elizabeth found she had misplaced the keys to the flat. Returning to the ground entrance, and keeping a wary eye on the large rats that scuttled around the car parking area beneath the building, she sought help. A passing Royal Marines internal security patrol, ever ready to help a damsel in distress, came to her rescue. A marine shinned up the drain pipe within the inner well and broke a window to enter the flat. The kind boot-neck returned to his duty leaving Elizabeth to ponder the inescapable conclusion that if a marine could climb the pipe and enter through a broken window so could any energetic rat. She barricaded herself into the bedroom and only slept easy when the window was repaired.

In the Maalla Straight all servicemen had to take their turn in off-duty hours guarding the entrance to their block of flats. To present an air of authority and for self defence an ancient revolver and five rounds of ammo was provided and passed one to another at the end of each 'stag'. The duty ended at curfew when the Army internal security patrols took over responsibility. Travel within Aden was strictly controlled with Crater and the back street areas out of bounds to servicemen and their families. Movement was thus largely limited to the road from Khormaksar leading through Maalla to Steamer Point, a very popular destination as a duty-free shopping area, and Tarshyne beach beyond. But I did manage to see the back streets of Aden thanks to Captain David Christie of the Cameronians. Armed with a self-loading rifle and sporting a glengarry I sat in the back of his open-top Land Rover with three other riflemen as he toured the urban sprawl away from the main thoroughfare. I was not a very convincing 'Jock' but David was obviously well known to the locals. Our movement through the cramped streets and squares was something of a royal progress as the locals hailed David by name. It was rather difficult to concentrate on the possibility of someone tossing a hand grenade at us.

Although we were living in the midst of a terrorist campaign this did not diminish an enjoyable social life. On Strike Wing the senior flight lieutenants were much of an age with 1417 known to the more junior pilots as 'Fourteen Canteen' as our crew room offered a level of tranquillity not found in the more robust environment of the ground-attack squadrons. Old bonds with Cranwell contemporaries were sustained as new friendships were made. Local restaurants – I recall with delight the Chin Sing in Maalla – were kept busy while for more formal occasions the Crescent Hotel in Steamer Point provided a level of service unique within Aden. Our own efforts to entertain and repay the generous hospitality of others did not get off to a good start. Elizabeth, having graduated from successfully boiling an egg, decided she would try her hand at a sort of mince mix-up for our first supper party held in the small entrance hall to our flat which doubled as a dining room. The table was illuminated with a spray of candles that gradually raised the temperature of the room to an uncomfortable level. I switched on the ceiling fan – unlike the air conditioning it worked – which rapidly accelerated to a terminal velocity sufficient to spray our guests with molten wax. Over the next 15 months such errors were eliminated and the standard of catering sustained a pleasing upward trend.

In August 1966 I fulfilled a promise to Elizabeth that we would visit Kenya on leave as payback for my insistence on our short honeymoon being spent in rain-sodden Scotland. Middle East Command ran a leave centre at Malindi on the shores of the Indian Ocean for families resident in Aden. We decided that rather than swap Tarshyne beach for another strip of sand in Kenya we would strike off inland from Nairobi where we flew in an Argosy of 70 Squadron – all part of the leave scheme. After a night of unimaginable luxury in the Norfolk Hotel we hired a car and set off for the Highlands Hotel at Molo, some 130 miles distant. Having crossed the Rift Valley we climbed to an altitude of more than 8,000 feet above sea level and arrived in good time to settle in to our bedroom before enjoying a delicious dinner of imperial proportions. The weather transformation from Aden was extraordinary. Aden in August, with temperatures often well in excess of 100°F with accompanying very high humidity, was uncomfortable. In contrast Molo was at least 25°F cooler and the air was dry. The evenings were distinctly cool and the log fire in the bedroom was most welcome. The still silence of the night was occasionally broken by the call of a Colobus monkey, a far cry from the thud of exploding grenades which had become common occurrence in Aden. The view to the east looked down on the Great Rift Valley, presenting an image of distant horizons shrouded in a blue haze that gave no clue as to what lay beyond. My admiration for the explorers who first penetrated the vast and perilous space of East Africa was boundless.

As we looked forward to the next two weeks in this paradise we decided to alternate one day relaxing in the secluded and colourful gardens of the hotel with the next spent exploring. Expeditions to Kericho and Kisumu on the shore of Lake Victoria to the west and to Nakuru and Naivasha to the south passed mainly without incident. Visits to game parks, the Flamingo Lake close to Nakuru and a boat trip on Lake Naivasha accompanied by a new found friend in the hotel, a botanist, introduced us to an unfamiliar and fascinating world that we have been most fortunate to revisit in recent years. But much has changed. The sheer quantity and variety of wild life in the 1960s left an indelible impression which today feeds my anger at the contemporary activities of poachers and murderous thugs throughout East Africa.

One incident threatened the pleasure of our holiday. One afternoon when driving back to the hotel, still some way distant, a young African man on a bicycle suddenly pulled out in front of me. I clipped him with my nearside wing knocking him off the bike and immediately pulled over. He was not badly hurt – some superficial cuts and bruises to his left arm and leg were the only visible damage – but the rear wheel of his bike was buckled. As I helped him to his feet we were surrounded by a crowd which seemed to have appeared from nowhere. I dusted him down, said I was sorry his bike had been damaged and gave him five dinars for repairs although the fault was his – at least in my view. I rejoined Elizabeth in the car and drove off. Later that evening I told the story to the hotel owners who were astonished. They said it was extremely foolish to have stopped and I should have driven on as there was no guarantee of our safety in such circumstances. The crowd could well have taken against me with unpleasant consequences. I rather doubted it but we live and learn.

One day between Christmas 1966 and the new year, along with Roger Neal (1417 Flight) and his wife Anne, we entertained to supper four riflemen from the Cameronians. The commander-in-chief had asked families in residence to invite off-duty soldiers into their homes. The riflemen, one was named

Primrose which I found rather surprising, all came from Captain David Christie's Intelligence Section and had clearly been briefed to be on their best behaviour. As the whisky/lemonades were downed and supper rapidly consumed the evening became happily relaxed as we were entertained with an astonishing array of stories of how they came to enlist and their subsequent exploits. Eventually I drove them back to their encampment in Radfan lines in time to beat the curfew. As we approached the barrier, manned by Coldstream Guardsmen, the windows of my car were wound down and my passengers gave vent to a barrage of obscene expletives the like of which I have not heard since. We were waved through presumably because the profanities were instantly recognisable and could not be mimicked by any other inhabitant of our planet. I returned home contemplating how on earth the Coldstream Guards at one end of the infantry spectrum and the Cameronians at the other could co-exist within the larger institution of the British Army. But such, apparently, is one of the strengths of the regimental system.

In early 1967 I was sent to Mukalla in the eastern Aden protectorate to make contact with the British Resident, and arrange the timing and details of a 'flag wave' over the palace opposite the residence to mark the coronation of the new Sultan of Qu'aiti whose father had recently died of natural causes. I flew from Khormaksar to RAF Riyan in a Dakota which dropped me off before departing to the north. Having met up with the Resident I agreed the arrangements which required me to return a few days later with a radio pack to call in a Hunter formation after the Sultan's fleet of dhows had sailed past the palace. I then drove back to Riyan just in time to see the return of the Dakota which discharged a cargo of manacled tribesmen under a heavily armed escort from the Hadhramaut Bedouin Legion. Apparently the loyalty of the tribesmen, all of senior rank, was questionable and they had been 'persuaded' to come to Mukalla to pay homage to the new sultan and swear their fealty. Democracy was far distant from the hinterland of South Arabia.

That evening I stayed in the mess at Riyan with the two permanent residents, a flight lieutenant air trafficker and a flying officer supplier. They asked me if I would kindly act as barman, and perhaps take a few notes, as they held an extraordinary mess meeting to discuss the arrangements for their Summer Ball. Dismissing a small suspicion of a wind-up I agreed and set to my duty listening with growing amazement as they worked their way through the agenda. Having agreed the date and time they moved on to the guest list which started with the high commissioner and the commander-in-chief with their ladies, moving downwards to the lower but still senior echelons of Middle East Command HQ. That agreed the agenda moved on to catering and it was decided that a buffet would be best because of staff shortages. The supply officer was actioned to procure additional china, glassware and cutlery. While the vital need to replace the mess gramophone with a new-fangled tape recorder was quickly approved there was considerable discussion about what music would be played. To my horror the meeting eventually decided that they should buy a tape recording of 'Swinging Safari'. A year earlier I had been on detachment to RAF Masirah with 43(F) Squadron. Whenever we were in the mess, John Batty played 'Swinging Safari', which after a week drove me to distraction. All efforts to hijack the record were thwarted by John who was something of an artful dodger. Never mind, I was not on the guest list for the ball so the meeting concluded with a final round of gin and tonics and the gratitude of the mess for my assistance was formally recorded. I woke up next morning wondering if it was all a surreal experience. It was not, and I understand that invitations were sent but recipients without exception regretted all pleading a prior engagement. This was hardly surprising given that planning for final withdrawal from South Arabia was proceeding apace.

The coronation itself was educational. Standing on top of the residency I heard an uncommon clamour apparently emanating from a large hen coop-shaped construction on top of the palace roof. I asked the Resident to explain. "That," he replied "is the harem ululating, and if you had just lost a seventy-year-old husband and inherited a twenty-one-year-old replacement you would have something to celebrate." Shortly after a cannon fired, the fleet sailed past and the Hunters overflew on time to reinforce the message of British support to the sultan, not that I imagine it did him much good. For my part, job done and I returned to Aden for the last month of my tour.

From November 1965 until we left at the end of April 1967 the commander-in-chief was Admiral Sir Michael Le Fanu. All of us, sailor, soldier and airman alike, who enjoyed the privilege of serving under his command, will never forget his outstanding leadership in the most adverse conditions. That morale, particularly amongst those living in Aden with their families, remained so high through dangerous times owed much to the example set by the C-in-C. He involved himself in every military activity within his command; he flew with us, he patrolled with the Army and Royal Marines up country, he worked a spell as a stevedore in the docks and all of this while accepting the huge responsibility of planning and activating the complex operation of our withdrawal from South Arabia. Sir Michael and his wife, wheelchair-bound by polio, were the most generous and welcoming of hosts at Command House. To help host a never-ending stream of senior visitors from Westminster, Whitehall and the United Nations, he would invite junior officers from the three services as guests who would be introduced as "the people who really know what is going on out here". He was quick to prick pomposity and there were many stories of his practical jokes as he toured his vast command area. No small wonder he was so respected and admired. After his untimely death in 1970 his ADC wrote: 'The Admiral's real greatness was that among the pressure of internationally important affairs he found time to concern himself with the problems of all the ordinary servicemen with whom he came into contact. I am sure that this was his outstanding achievement and will be remembered long after his policy decisions are committed to the archives.' All so very true.

Before leaving Aden we experienced a truly memorable event. In the early hours of Saturday 1st April 1967 we were woken by an unfamiliar noise which we eventually recognised as rainfall, in fact torrential rain, the first I had experienced in two years. When I got up at 06:00 to prepare to go to work the rain was still pelting down and there were the first signs of flooding down the Maalla Straight. As the rain continued throughout the morning wooden shacks and dead goats from the slopes of Jabal Shamsan started to appear having been propelled downwards by the torrent. Fortunately our block of flats was on the higher ground of the Maalla Straight but not far to the west of us parked cars were soon underwater. Those, living on base at Khormaksar, who did manage to get into work grabbed the opportunity to practise dinghy drill in the Strike Wing car park. The rain stopped at about midday and the waters very gradually subsided leaving behind a deep morass of mud which, as the sun returned, soon generated an unforgettable stench. If nothing else this event cooled for a while the activities of Aden-based terrorists.

Enjoyment of the tour and my admiration for the many fine people I worked for and with cannot disguise one unpalatable historical fact. Our precipitate withdrawal from the Federation of South Arabia left a legacy of disorder, bloodshed and economic collapse. Arab friends who had supported us were left to the cruel mercies of rival nationalist socialist revolutionaries. The departure of our armed forces, which had valiantly held the ring, unleashed a bloody civil war which concluded with the establishment of a Marxist-Leninist tyranny and three decades of repression and impoverishment. While disengagement was primarily driven by military overstretch and national economic weakness, our departure from Iraq in 2009 had similarities which was by no means our concluding engagement with the Arab world, an engagement full of contradictions and wishful thinking. Since then our involvement with the Arab Spring has yet again illustrated a political failure to understand Arab culture and society with a consequent inability to influence events in favour of the western democracies.

CHAPTER 8
CENTRAL FLYING SCHOOL AND CRANWELL

As my tour on 1417 Flight drew to its close I had hoped for a posting to a fighter recce squadron in RAF Germany but there were no vacancies. Instead I was posted to the Central Flying School (CFS) to train as a qualified flying instructor (QFI). CFS was based at RAF Little Rissington perched on top of a Cotswold hill some 730 feet above sea level. The surrounding countryside showed all that was best in England's green and pleasant land, such a sharp contrast to the harsh colours and barren rocks of Aden. We were lucky to find a three-bedroom cottage in Great Rissington at a surprisingly low rent. Not so surprising when we discovered after moving in that our new home was directly under the 400-feet approach point to the easterly runway at Rissy. But, never mind, the cottage was comfortable with sufficient space to house our sparse possessions. It was no more than 10 minutes drive to 'hell on the hill' as CFS was better known to those outside, and perhaps within, the instructional world.

The aim of CFS was to develop and maintain the highest standards of pure flying and flying instruction and to this end the course was divided into three phases. The first, ground school, lasting for several weeks, covered a variety of aviation subjects including principles of flight, airmanship, navigation, meteorology and aviation medicine as well as the aircraft and engine systems of the Jet Provost which all students were to fly in the second phase of the course. Instructional technique was a continuing theme throughout and each student was required to give two 10-minute talks, one on any subject of choice and the second on a service topic, demonstrating their developing teaching skills. I cannot remember my subjects but I do recall Martin Molloy, complete with ironing board and steam iron, giving an outstanding presentation on how to iron a civilian shirt. Full marks were awarded. Several days later, Martin similarly equipped, returned to the lectern to give his service topic titled 'How to iron a service shirt'. 'Nul' point from the staff, much mirth amongst the students.

The course was some 40 strong with by far the majority from a 'heavies' background, most of whom were former V-Force co-pilots. While the toils of ground school gradually shaped the course into an entity with its own distinct and cheerful identity, Rissy to me seemed rather stuffy. Most instructors took themselves very seriously and the knockabout humour and banter of front-line service were rare commodities. This impression was not helped when we started flying. I changed into my flying gear which included the comfortable desert boots I had worn throughout my tour in Aden. This was spotted by the wing commander flying who told me with blunt and brief clarity to take them off and to wear proper flying boots.

My introduction to instructing on the Jet Provost Mk 3 did not generate a morsel of enthusiasm or devotion then or at any time thereafter. Compared to the Hunter it was just plain ugly and so horribly underpowered it seemed to creep around the sky. Although the Mk 4 was an improvement in terms of power, some 2,500 lbs of extra thrust, the instructional sequences we practised starting with effects of controls did not convince me that basic flying instruction was more rewarding than advanced instruction as I had been advised by some friends. So I quickly decided to volunteer for the Folland Gnat which had replaced the Vampire as the RAF's advanced jet trainer. There were four slots for the Gnat course, one already taken by a Royal Navy officer and one by a RAF student who had been re-coursed for medical reasons. For the other two places there were two volunteers, one other and me, so selection was not exactly competitive.

The Gnat Flight of CFS was based at RAF Kemble, 20 miles south of Rissy, and co-located with the Red Arrows under the legendary leadership of Squadron Leader Ray Hanna. The atmosphere at Kemble was noticeably different from the rather cheerless ambiance at Rissy due, principally, to the personality of our flight commander, Dennis Hazell. Instructors and students alike could not fail to respond to his most positive and cheerful leadership. His whole attitude to flying and instruction was conditioned by the view that, while military aviation was a business ultimately of deadly intent, the whole experience of flying should be both enjoyable and rewarding. And perhaps never more so than during the process of pilot training when an instructor's example of enthusiasm and good humour would inspire both effort and commitment from those entrusted to his care.

My instructor, Flight Lieutenant Bob Patchett, a keen disciple of the Hazell school of instruction, was great fun to fly with as we progressed through the instructional sequences. It was definitely a big leap from the undemanding Jet Provost to the technically complex and high performance Gnat with its up-to-date presentation of flight instruments and navigation systems. Understanding the longitudinal control system was a challenge in itself but it had to be understood if students were to cope with the consequences of a hydraulic failure. Looking at a Gnat today I wonder, with due allowance for a coefficient of personal physical expansion over the years, how on earth I fitted in to such a mini aeroplane. But others, most notably Major Bob Jerman, a USAF pilot on exchange, who topped 6' 2" and was some 14 stone of pure muscle, managed to do so thus setting an example to more diminutive folk as they acclimatised to the compact cockpit.

Flying the Gnat was a joy with its impressive performance and delightful handling characteristics coming as a most welcome 'pick-me-up' after the pedestrian Jet Provost. More importantly the Gnat posed a real challenge to student pilots as they experienced a considerable increase in aircraft performance while learning to deal with complex emergencies – mostly and fortunately simulated – and making the most efficient use of the navigation system. Observing students getting to grips with the Gnat was pleasingly rewarding and rather to my surprise I was really enjoying flying instruction. But all this was to come and I must acknowledge my debt to Dennis Hazell and Bob Patchett for seeing me through the CFS course with patience and good humour. Sadly both these fine men were killed in separate flying accidents a few years later.

I graduated from CFS as a QFI in October 1967 and we moved directly to 4 Flying Training School at RAF Valley, Anglesey. I looked forward to a full tour on the Gnat but this was not to be as I was posted on promotion to squadron leader at the end of 1969. The 17 months we spent at Valley had their highs and lows. On the plus side the flying was superb. I averaged 30 hours a month, was made a flight commander, achieved an A2 QFI category and enjoyed the pleasure of instructing some very talented students who in years to come held command appointments in the RAF's front line with some moving on to air rank. At Valley I was back in the fighter world where most of the instructors had a Hunter or Lightning background. My squadron commander, Ernie Powell, who I had first met at Chivenor, was the archetypal fighter pilot while my flight commander, Bob Jerman USAF, had already accumulated a wealth of operational experience in South East Asia. No. 1 Squadron 4 FTS was a very happy outfit and I hope that the students who passed through our hands recall their training, tough and demanding as it was, with some modicum of pleasure and pride in their achievement. The final plus was promotion which I can honestly say was unexpected and all the more pleasurable for that.

But with promotion came a minus. Having completed a fair, albeit rather short-lived, quota of flying instruction I felt well placed to return to the front line as Phantoms, Buccaneers and Harriers were being introduced to service. However, my posting officer told me that all front-line flight commander appointments were filled so pack your bags and go to the RAF College Cranwell to command 2 Squadron flying Jet Provosts. Given my rather snooty misgivings about the Jet Provost and my quite deliberate avoidance of basic instructing this was not good news. At about the same time, Elizabeth became desperately ill suffering from nausea and vomiting while experiencing a sudden and frightening excessive weight loss. She was eventually diagnosed as having contracted Coeliac disease after admission to a NHS hospital in Hertford to be close to her parents. Before then we had packed our belongings for the move from Valley to Cranwell.

Preparations for 'march out' from our married quarter were not helped when the chimney cowling was blown away in a gale which caused a cascade of pitch black soot that smothered all surfaces in the ground floor of our home. At that time junior officers living in married quarters were allotted one morning of 'batting', that is domestic help from a locally employed civilian. My mother-in-law soon arrived to help clear up and her assistance was reinforced from time-to-time by a kind squadron leader's wife. I was thus surprised to be asked by the wing commander president of the mess committee how and with what authority had I arranged extra 'batting' – a neighbour, few doors removed, had complained. When I explained that the extra 'batting' was in fact my mother-in-law, the wife of the air officer administration Fighter Command, no more was heard of this petty vindictiveness.

At Valley the squadron, including the CO and flight commanders, numbered a dozen QFIs and I never had less than three students in my charge. At Cranwell, on Flying Training Wing, I inherited a squadron of 24 flying instructors each looking after a single student, all flight cadets in 1969. Four of the instructors were from fighter backgrounds (I had served with Rod Harrison, Bob Screen and Daz James in Aden and Ian Macfadyen had flown Lightnings), two had been Canberra pilots and several others had qualified as captains on large aircraft. The remainder were former co-pilots from either the V-Force or Air Transport Command. I took over from John Delafield, an exceptional fighter pilot and internationally famed glider pilot, who was well known to me as he had been my first mentor at Cranwell and we had served together at Duxford. He explained that most of my flying would be checking the progress of a cross-section of students through tests at the end of each phase of training culminating in their final handling tests. I would also fly regularly with QFIs to check the standard of their pure flying and to help rectify any identifiable weaknesses, most commonly formation flying. Importantly, I would be responsible for recommending to the chief flying instructor (CFI) suspension of students who failed to make the grade in any phase of their training.

After a brief refresher on the Jet Provost at CFS I was prepared, qualified and keen to take over my first command where I was to discover that there was more to basic instruction than my prejudices had led me to believe. Student pilots posted to Valley were, on arrival, much of a muchness in terms of their flying skills. It was the Gnat which in 70 hours flying sorted out the truly above average from the steady, middle of the road performer. At Cranwell I soon learned that the students had a far wider range of capabilities with progress through the 140 hours flying syllabus varying from the workaday to the impressively quick.

Many years ago, Claude Graham-White, a pioneer of national aviation, wrote a book in 1917 titled *Air Power,* the first so-named in the history of aviation. In it he wrote:

> "Flying instructors must be men of sympathy and understanding capable of an estimate of character and they must have sufficient interest in their work to treat each pupil individually. Flying brings out a man's temperamental peculiarities. One man may be extremely cautious, another foolishly daring. One may be slow and disappointing in getting any sort of feel for his machine; another may pick up the whole business with facility. But the instructor may not feel disheartened by any apparent stupidity nor over-elated when a pupil is unusually quick.
>
> "Often a man who is slow in the early stages will turn out in the end a sound, reliable pilot; while the pupil who is very quick in learning to handle the machine may be found to lack the judgement and discretion which are essential. A large proportion of accidents which have marred the progress of flight have been due to the fact that men have gone ahead faster than their experience has justified."

These great words of wisdom are a timeless message every bit as relevant in 1969 as they are today. They should be drawn to the attention of anyone with an ambition to teach people to fly. The first paragraph is particularly relevant to basic instruction while the second concerns unjustified overconfidence, a failing that in my total experience of military aviation has killed far too many.

I commanded 2 Squadron at Cranwell for 14 months and flew with a number of flight cadets who were to enjoy distinguished careers. Flight Cadet Prince Sultan returned to the Royal Saudi air force before embarking on a diplomatic career and appointment as the Saudi Arabian ambassador in Washington. He was a cheerful and popular member of his entry who certainly enjoyed life to the full and that is perhaps why I remember him as the student who came closest to killing me. With a QFI in the right-hand seat, he was formating on me as I led him down through cloud. Descending and turning inbound to the airfield he drifted away and was about to lose visual contact when he made a desperate lunge back towards my aircraft ending up almost inverted on top of my cockpit. I stuffed the nose down to avoid a mid-air collision by the narrowest of whiskers and disappeared in the cloud; we returned to Cranwell as singletons. His QFI should never have allowed this to happen, but anyone with experience of flying instruction let alone general aviation, will well recognise that a comfortable situation can almost instantly go to pot through a handling error or straightforward misjudgement. Valuable lessons were learned by all three of us.

Other luminaries on my squadron were Flight Cadet Jock Stirrup who was to become chief of the defence staff, a life peer and Knight of the Garter, and Flight Cadet Richie Thomas who flew two tours with the Red Arrows, the second as leader and was one of the very few genuinely exceptional pilots with whom I had the privilege of sharing a cockpit.

One of the pleasures of my job was flying with students towards the end of their course who had been selected to fly in the RAF College's own aerobatic competition. Only the best achieved this and I cannot remember having to take control of an aircraft to avoid the possibility of a disaster. I also flew with QFIs eager to represent the RAF College at the CFS annual competition for the Wright Jubilee Trophy awarded to the best aerobatic display pilot in Flying Training Command. This was considerably more demanding than flying with students as the manoeuvres were more complicated, the sequences much tighter and the base height 500 ft as opposed to 1,500 ft above ground level. I have a clear recollection of one practice sortie flown in the early evening at RAF Barkston Heath.

I was checking out a very talented pilot whose aerobatic sequence included some slow speed rather esoteric manoeuvres requiring very sensitive handling. I was a little edgy but pretty confident he had the skill to cope. My unease was not, however, misplaced because with the aircraft pointing vertically upwards at about 2,500 feet, with an airspeed rapidly reducing to zero and a half application of rudder, the aircraft flipped over onto its back immediately entering a fully developed spin. As aircraft captain I decided in the available split second it was best to leave control with the aerobatic tyro; he had got us into the mess and was probably best placed to get us out of it which he did, albeit at a very low height. We returned to Cranwell and decided that some amendment to that particular part of his sequence was well advised. But, had I failed in my duty in not mentioning my earlier misgivings let alone requiring some editing of his sequence? In retrospect I failed but got away with it. Should I have taken control as the aircraft entered the spin? In principle as aircraft captain, yes, but in practice given the time/altitude imperative it was best to leave things to the highly accomplished handling pilot. As a footnote to the story, during our debrief the QFI said he had admired my silence during the exciting seconds we had shared. I could only reply that this had nothing to do with my powers of self-control as he had left me "******* speechless".

After a year as squadron commander, also memorable for the birth of our first child, Victoria, I was moved on to take over as deputy chief flying instructor. It was disappointing to leave 2 Squadron for a job which involved more administrative work although my flying hours, now spread across the wing, did not suffer. But this was not to be for long as in late April 1970 I was summoned for an interview with Air Vice-Marshal Derek Hodgkinson, then acting AOC-in-C Flying Training Command. No reason was given and I set off from Cranwell haunted by the spectre of several misadventures in recent years while wondering which one had caught up with me. The AOC-in-C's outer office staff at the headquarters steadfastly refused to drop any hint about the purpose of the interview which only added to my unease. Some minutes later, having been ushered into the AOC-in-C's office and invited to sit, Air Vice-Marshal Hodgkinson asked me, "How would you like to be the Prince of Wales's flying instructor?"

CHAPTER 9
GOLDEN EAGLE

Time has not dimmed the memory of that verbal bolt. I cannot remember my exact answer or the subsequent questions and points I was invited to discuss. The interview lasted about 30 minutes and I was dismissed with the instruction not to reveal its purpose. I would be told the outcome in due course. Then, as June approached, word came that the captain of The Queen's Flight wished to speak to me before the visit of The Queen and the Duke of Edinburgh who were to honour the Royal Air Force College with their presence at the parade to mark the 50th anniversary of Cranwell's foundation. The captain, Air Commodore Archie Winskill, my former station commander at RAF Duxford, told me that I was to take over from Squadron Leader Philip Pinney as the Prince of Wales's QFI to instruct him through the full jet training course to wings standard in the summer of 1971. Beforehand I would be detached to The Queen's Flight to convert onto the Basset CC1 – a small twin-piston-engine five-seater communications aircraft – to achieve an instructional category on that aeroplane and an Air Transport Command instrument rating. This was to be completed by the end of the year so I could start flying with Prince Charles after Phil Pinney departed for Staff College in January. This was a lot to take in and marks an appropriate moment to place on record a broad outline of Prince Charles's flying training.

As an outside observer it seemed to me that both Prince William and Prince Harry went through their flying training with the minimum of fuss and, pleasingly, were allowed to progress to full operational status in their respective roles. However, back in 1969, there was considerable concern in the RAF hierarchy when Prince Charles stated his ambition to complete the full jet training syllabus so to earn his 'wings' without fear or favour. In a nutshell, concern centred on the risk to the life of the heir to the throne. Although the horrendous accident rate of the early 1950s had abated in parallel with a considerable reduction in the size of the service and assimilation of hard lessons learned, in 1968 the RAF wrote off 51 aircraft with 43 aircrew killed. Given that the air officers of the 1960s would have survived World War II and lived through the introduction of jet aircraft to front-line service with an eye-watering accident rate, it is perhaps not surprising that their concern for Prince Charles's safety was so evident. This anxiety was apparent in the HQ Flying Training Command Operation Order issued for Exercise Golden Eagle, the rather pretentious nickname for Prince Charles's flying training.

At the RAF College the overall responsibility for all aspects of his training was vested in the commandant, Air Vice-Marshal Desmond Hughes. The routine supervision of flying training and associated ground subjects was exercised through Group Captain Gerald Pendred, the station commander, and the chief flying instructor, Wing Commander Brian Huxley, to me as the authorised QFI with specific responsibility for flying instruction and tutorials in the ground subjects. The more specific definition of my duties was qualified with the concluding order that I was "to treat as absolutely overriding the requirement to ensure HRH's safety throughout all aspects and phases of his flying training".

I was tasked to give a minimum of 80% of the dual instruction and was allowed to authorise my appointed deputy, Squadron Leader John Robinson, to carry out those sorties necessary to provide a check on standardisation and progress. Instrument flying tests were assigned to the senior instrument rating examiner at Cranwell, while the night flying and final handling tests were to be flown with the CFI. An air traffic controller was appointed to be on duty whenever Prince Charles was flying at an AR1 radar position with associated communications for his exclusive use. A Golden Eagle discreet radio frequency was also allocated as, when clear of the circuit, Prince Charles was to be under radar surveillance when flying either dual or solo.

The engineering orders concerning the Golden Eagle aircraft, two Jet Provost Mk 5s, required their servicing to be carried out by tradesmen selected and trained to The Queen's Flight standard. Supporting bay servicing was also undertaken by similarly selected and authorised personnel. Composite servicing was forbidden. Primary servicing and special servicing were required after 50 hours flight time and primary star servicing at 100 hours. Complementary to ground servicing, flight air tests were flown on completion of acceptance checks, within two months of the previous full air test, if the aircraft had not flown for six days and on completion of routine scheduled servicing. Further detailed instructions covered the servicing documentation, servicing procedures, aircraft preparation and appearance and security. Not a single aircraft unserviceability was recorded during Prince Charles's flying training!

There was one aspect of the operation order that caused me considerable concern. HQ Flying Training Command decided that Prince Charles, authorised as aircraft captain, should be accompanied by a navigator for safety reasons during some general handling sorties involving aerobatics, on some navigation sorties at day and night and on solo formation sorties. This decision reflected anxiety about the collision risk in the local training airspace, an obvious area of high air traffic density. The collision risk was real and I agreed that two extra eyes would supplement radar protection. However, my constant worry was the thought of an engine malfunction, caused by bird ingestion or mechanical failure, in the critical period after take-off or shortly before landing, when the decision time concerning possible abandonment of the aircraft was absolutely critical. The decision would have been Prince Charles's alone.

To confront the problem I frequently briefed and discussed the considerations of aircraft handling and captaincy when faced with such situations and during dual sorties often checked Prince Charles's reaction to unexpected situations in the circuit. Even so, it was impossible to cover all permutations of circumstances and as authorising officer I had to put my complete faith in Prince Charles's own judgement. I felt, and still do, that consideration for Flight Lieutenant Malcolm Gaynor, the lookout aircrew, may have added a vital second to any critical decision. The question also arose as to whether or not this imposed an unfair responsibility on Prince Charles who had only limited captaincy experience, principally on the Chipmunk, before the start of the course. The accompanied solo policy was amended before the start of the formation flying phase of training when the AOC-in-C authorised formation sorties to be flown as true solo after Prince Charles had requested this through the commandant. Malcolm Gaynor came with me in the lead aircraft.

In the event, the birds steered clear and the engines performed to specification so it's all history with a happy ending. But I like to think that Prince Charles's pilot training, programmed within rigid guidelines with an emphasis on risk avoidance that arguably went too far and was potentially counter-productive, had some influence on the shaping of flying instruction given to Prince William and Prince Harry.

By the time I started flying with Prince Charles he had passed the Private Pilot's Licence flying test and qualified for the award of the preliminary flying badge on the Chipmunk aircraft. After graduating from Cambridge and still with Phil Pinney as instructor he moved on to the Basset CC1 in which he notched up a further 90 hours flying before I took over. My first two instructional sorties with Prince Charles were flown in the Basset at night in January 1971 from RAF Marham where strong winds and rain showers made circuit conditions difficult. He coped well and I digested one painful lesson; Prince Charles's check of full and free movement of controls was a vigorous and full-blooded examination. My avoiding action was too slow. Two bruised kneecaps so symbolised our first flying association.

Shortly afterwards I returned to Cranwell to prepare for a CFS Examining Wing visit. Squadron Leader Brian Jones examined me and John Robinson in general handling, instrument flying, formation and night flying to ensure we were officially up to scratch for the task ahead. The tests were flown in the new Jet Provost Mk 5, a significant improvement on the earlier marks of that aircraft in terms of performance, cockpit layout and, dare I say, aerodynamic shape. Happily we passed and I returned to Benson to fly some continuation training on the Basset and to make the necessary air traffic arrangements for Prince Charles's arrival at Cranwell, flying the Basset, on 8th March 1971 where he joined No. 1 Graduate Entry (GE) in the rank of flight lieutenant. It had been decided that Prince Charles would not be outranked by any other member of No. 1 GE. Several were flight lieutenants through accumulated time spent in the reserve as members of university air squadrons. Failing finals and staying on for an extra year achieved sufficient length of service for promotion to flight lieutenant. This was news to many of us. As the station commander, Gerald Pendred, commented during his welcome, "fail finals often enough and I suppose you will end up as group captains".

After settling into his accommodation, which Prince Charles shared with three other No. 1 GE students, there followed the inevitable round of arrival briefings, interviews and the fitting of flying clothing. With the necessary preliminaries completed we got down to two weeks of ground school covering technical subjects concerning the Jet Provost Mk 5, combat survival, emergency drills and cockpit procedures. As the course progressed Prince Charles was to spend 1½ days per week at lectures as the ground syllabus expanded to cover airmanship, aerodynamics, meteorology, aviation medicine and navigation. I shared technical instruction with John Robinson and parts of other subjects were farmed out to Flying Wing specialists to save Prince Charles from an undiluted and indigestible diet of one QFI. Although not technically minded, and that made two of us, Prince Charles mastered the essentials of each subject while maintaining a polite interest in even the most dreary aspects of the ground syllabus.

Prince Charles started his jet flying on 19th March 1971 and passed his final handling test, examined by Wing Commander Brian Huxley, on 8th July 1971. In between he achieved his first solo on type after eight hours instruction and then moved on through the well tried and tested system of instruction, solo flying and test sorties. A typical general handling progress/test sortie involved a mix of aerobatics, maximum rate turning, full and incipient spins, practice forced-landings and circuit flying. Navigation, instrument flying and night flying were obviously more narrowly focused. Prince Charles's progress in all phases of his training was marked by a pleasing and steady improvement as his confidence grew. This culminated in a final handling test judged as 'well above the average' which was just reward for his hard work and implacable determination to succeed.

More than 40 years later I can still remember that some observers, particularly in the media, implied that Prince Charles's success as a student pilot was assured from the moment he donned an RAF uniform. This was not the case as there are no foregone conclusions in the training of a military pilot, nor for that matter can there be any relaxation of the required standards if a student is to fly solo. I still consider that Prince Charles's decision to undertake the full wings course was a brave one in view of the inevitable public interest that the exercise would arouse. To put it bluntly he was on a hiding to nothing.

While Prince Charles was fortunate to possess natural ability he inevitably encountered some minor problems in the various phases of his training as have generations of student pilots. That's when QFIs have to earn their keep even if the instructor talks too much. My only concern prior to a test involved navigation. The system QFIs were required to teach at that time needed a fair amount of mathematical gymnastics using true bearings from ground stations to fix the position of the aircraft. This was not Prince Charles's forte, and from my own viewpoint I thought the time allotted to navigation training would have been far more usefully spent learning the skills of airborne map reading on different scales of maps – a belief borne of my own experience as a fighter recce pilot. However, Prince Charles was quick to cotton on to the simple fact that the challenge of aeronautical navigation could be largely solved by meticulous ground planning and accurate flying to compensate for any minor deficiency in mathematical processing, a deficiency which I have to admit I shared. I also have to admit being pleasantly surprised by the result of Prince Charles's navigation test, the first of his 'qualifying exams' which was assessed as above average by the examiner, Flight Lieutenant Peter Norriss.

At the end of the course Prince Charles, who had clearly revelled in the challenges of military flying and was justifiably proud of the standards he had achieved, asked about the possibility of staying on in the RAF to fly on a front-line squadron. Although he didn't know it at the time, he had been included for consideration by the posting board which decided the future for all graduating pilots of No. 1 GE. Prince Charles was judged as suitable for training on the Phantom FG1 (selection to be confirmed after advanced flying training) which had been introduced to service in 1969. However, apart from delaying his planned onward move to the Royal Navy after graduating at Cranwell, I had to explain that front-line service would be a practical impossibility if the aircraft he was to fly, far, far more complex than the Jet Provost Mk 5, required servicing to The Queen's Flight standard by selected tradesmen. And, I was sure, given the service's earlier attitude to risk and indeed concern in the higher echelons of government about the safety of the heir to the throne, a proposal to implement the recommendation of the posting board would have been rejected out of hand.

To round off I retain two clear memories of my time with Prince Charles. The first concerns the formation flying phase, completed in two weeks, which I think from both our viewpoints was the highlight of the course. John Robinson led the dual sorties, I led the solo trips and Brian Huxley flew the final aeroplane to make up the three aircraft formations. Initial instruction covering flying in the echelon positions was easily received and after flying only two sorties Prince Charles was close to solo standard. To my great surprise he found it difficult to master flying in line astern. Slight over-controlling on the ailerons coupled with a barely noticeable lack of anticipation caused some memorable pendulum-like swings. I could see both fault and cause but cure appeared to be beyond my wit. While relaxed in echelon the line-astern position invoked a tenseness which I had not encountered before with students when flying behind the lead aircraft. It was Prince Charles who found the solution of relaxation by suddenly delivering a spirited rendering of 'Rule Britannia' followed by perfect mimicry of Noel Coward's 'Mad Dogs and Englishmen'. The problem was thus solved in an unusual way as thereafter his line-astern flying was immaculate although I did miss the musical accompaniment in subsequent trips.

Having mastered the three basic formation positions, we moved on to tail chasing – that is following a leader, at a range of 50-100 yards, through a series of hard manoeuvres including loops and barrel rolls. Prince Charles immediately appreciated the importance of visual angle interpretation as a means of gauging cut-off to control range, while his handling of the aircraft was appropriately aggressive. Encounters with slipstream did not perturb him and he was quick to regain position. After my first demonstration and rare comments in the subsequent exercises I had nothing to teach, and so was able to sit back and appreciate flying that showed a wealth of fighter pilot potential. In the last six sorties he was given a rigorous examination in close formation flying which included steep wing overs, formation take-offs, formation radar approaches and formation landings. Prince Charles had the skill and determination to stay with it and so earned his highest flying assessment of 'above average bordering on exceptional'.

After completing the flying course, Prince Charles followed a programme of visits to the front line to fly in a Phantom, a Nimrod and a Vulcan before making a parachute descent from an Andover into the sea after a day's preparatory training at RAF Abingdon. The programme was implemented without incident although bad weather required some adjustments to planned sorties. I accompanied him throughout which was an educational experience for me as well albeit not without occasional embarrassment. We arrived at RAF Leuchars for the Phantom trip early one afternoon in mid-July. After taxiing in I did the shutdown checks as Prince Charles was welcomed by the station commander and whisked off to 43(F) Squadron for briefing. I was left unrecognised, unwelcomed and to my own devices. After signing off the aircraft and handing it over to my ground crew who had pre-positioned the day before, I ambled across to the 43 Squadron crew room where I found Prince Charles sitting at a table accompanied by the station commander, OC 43 Squadron, and assorted QFIs and qualified weapons instructors (QWI) all waving their arms around in that rather frenetic manner so typical of air defenders.

Unnoticed, I slipped across to the coffee bar for a cuppa where I had spotted an old chum from Valley days, Flight Lieutenant Jerry Shipley. No sooner had I enjoyed my first sip than the door beside the coffee bar burst open and in entered the squadron warrant officer obviously in high dudgeon. "What are you doing here?" he hissed. "Enjoying my coffee," I replied not unreasonably. "Can't you see who is sitting over there?" asked the WO. "Of course I can," I answered. At this the WO's complexion took on a deeper hue of scarlet. "You can't stay here," he snapped, "you must leave immediately." Feeling rather unwelcome I was about to mount my high horse but by now the kerfuffle had attracted the attention of the briefing group. The station commander turned around to me and enquired, rather rudely I thought, "who the hell are you?" "Oh sir," I simpered, "I am Squadron Leader Johns and I have just flown in with the Prince of Wales". Up piped Prince Charles: "Oh no he didn't, I have never seen him before." Pandemonium.

In the years that followed I have been asked about my feelings concerning the instruction of Prince Charles during his course at Cranwell. It would be patently false to pretend that I was unaware of any responsibility in excess of those accepted by all flying instructors in the performance of their duties. However, my responsibilities were shared with many others at Cranwell. The airmen of Golden Eagle Flight under Flight Lieutenant Chris Masterman carried out their duties with unfailing zeal and good humour. John Robinson and Malcolm Gaynor were ever ready to fly, to assist or to advise and our airborne ways were smoothed by Flight Lieutenant John Osborne's radar vigil. I was fortunate to enjoy the encouragement and confidence of my superiors throughout an exercise that concluded with No. 1 GE's passing out parade on 20th August 1971 when Prince Charles received his wings from the chief of the air staff, Air Chief Marshal Sir Denis Spotswood.

My duty was more than just a privilege. It meant that as a flying instructor I enjoyed the pleasure of teaching a student pilot who achieved an above average standard and proved he had the ability to make a first class operational pilot. This is the real reward of military flying instruction.

CHAPTER 10
STAFF COLLEGE TO CYPRUS

After two weeks leave I returned to Cranwell to resume my duties as deputy chief flying instructor for the last three months of my tour. The time passed pleasantly enough as we prepared for a southwards move for my posting as a student to the RAF Staff College at Bracknell. With insufficient 'points' to qualify for a married quarter at Bracknell we were allocated a hiring in Fleet. As Elizabeth was expecting our second child in January, close proximity to the military hospital at Aldershot was opportune.

The Staff College commandant was Air Vice-Marshal Michael Beetham – my former station commander at RAF Khormaksar – and the deputy commandant Air Commodore Jock Kennedy. They were an ideal pairing in terms of contrasting character and temperament to run the college: one stern and forbidding, the other genial and sympathetic. Their joint exercise of command and control of 180 students, principally RAF but including a large overseas contingent and students from the RN and Army, was resolute and impartial. Sadly, with some notable exceptions (Roy Hollingworth and Gordon Tripp come immediately to mind), the quality of the directing staff (DS) was no more than mediocre. The majority had reached their rank ceiling and were out of touch with developments in the front line and associated technologies that were rapidly expanding the combat power of the service. Elsewhere, during the Joint Services Staff College month held at Camberley, the quality of the Army DS, mostly young lieutenant colonels specially selected and earmarked for command appointments, was in marked contrast to our unexceptional DS. But to be fair, their job was to train competent staff officers with emphasis on written and oral communication skills the watchwords being accuracy, brevity and clarity. I certainly benefited from strict marking and assessment of the many written exercises completed during the year.

Lectures and presentations in the Brooke-Popham Lecture Theatre, some illuminated by candlelight in the winter months because of power cuts, covered a syllabus of defence, political and economic subjects to broaden the knowledge of students beyond their comparatively narrow military special-isations. This process of learning was accelerated by the companionship of fellow students. Since commissioning I had seldom met up with my contem-poraries who had joined Transport and Coastal Commands let alone those whose careers were progressing through the ground branches of the service. Comparison of experiences since leaving Cranwell was certainly enlightening.

The birth of our second child, Douglas, in late January kept me compara-tively active on the home front although I had a room booked in the Bracknell mess for Wednesday evenings to guarantee one night of sleep with the oppor-tunity to catch up on written work that had been overtaken by domestic pressures. I now have to admit, with two daughters pursuing their own careers and each with three children at school, that sounds rather pathetic but I had my wife to thank for her solicitude. I also must admit that living out at Fleet offered some refuge from the frenetic social activity that was a hallmark of 62 Course's passage through Bracknell and elsewhere – particularly, as most will remember, on the course visit to NATO and RAF Germany. Wing Com-mander Ken Hayr, our course leader, ably assisted and supported by Wing Commander Tony Mason – the only two wing commanders on the course – set a cracking pace at both work and play to the student's delight and the DS's discomfort. Sporting activity was significant with cricket and softball in the summer and rugby in the spring and autumn terms. I had thought my rugby playing days were over, but fellow student Squadron Leader Mike Stear, still playing for the RAF and Combined Services, told me not to be so wet and this persuasive argument won me over. I played in the second row alongside Lieutenant Commander Vince Huth, United States Navy, who provided sub-stantial bulk and muscle to our scrum. Converting Vince from the rules of American football to those of rugby union, an impossible task today in the culture of health and safety, took a while but proved the adage that rugby is the thinking man's game.

Towards the end of the second term all students were asked to nominate their preference of posting. Accepting the inevitability of a ground tour I hoped to be posted on exchange to the USAF Academy at Colorado Springs which I had visited in April 1959 as a member of the first party of Cranwell flight cadets to go there. The prospect of seeing how the fledgling academy had developed since then was most appealing as was the expectation of off-duty adventures in the Rockies. But this was not to be as in the summer break I was sent to Cyprus to be interviewed by Air Marshal Sir Derek Hodgkinson as prospective replacement for his personal staff officer (PSO) who was due to leave in January 1973. Sir Derek, largely responsible for my earlier posting with the Prince of Wales, took me on for an appointment in which it was my good fortune to learn much and to share some excitement.

Elizabeth and I with our two very young children arrived in Cyprus at RAF Akrotiri on 31st December 1972. As we disembarked from a Comet aircraft of 216 Squadron – later the gate guardian for many years at RAF Lyneham – we were met by my predecessor, tall, slim and impeccably dressed. I can still recall his look of distaste as he digested the sartorial consequences of my five-hour wrestle with baby food, nappies and other accessories required for the long-distance transportation of two sprogs. But he quickly recovered his customary urbanity to take us to our new home, a married quarter in Paramali North, the wrong side of the social track as Air House and Flag Staff House were located in Paramali South surrounded at a respectable distance by the larger married quarters occupied by senior staff officers.

Work began immediately and after a short handover I was in post as the senior member of an outer office staff of an ADC, sergeant PA and two corporal clerks. The commander-in-chief we served had three appointments: air officer commanding-in-chief Near East air force (NEAF), commander British Forces Near East (BFNE) and administrator of the Sovereign Base Areas (SBAs). As AOC-in-C Sir Derek had under command all RAF stations and units from Gibraltar in the west to Hong Kong in the east. In Cyprus RAF Akrotiri was the largest station in the service with the Vulcan Wing contributing the most potent bomber force to the Central Treaty Organisation (CENTO). Air defence, transport and helicopter squadrons were co-located along with a RAF Regiment short-range air defence squadron. A Bloodhound surface-to-air missile squadron was positioned on a hill top close to the headquarters at Episkopi. Elsewhere RAF Luqa in Malta was troublesome as Prime Minister Dom Mintoff moved towards the declaration of a republic and the withdrawal of all British forces from the island notwithstanding the bilateral defence agreement renegotiated in 1972. At RAF Salalah in Oman the RAF Regiment sustained a tight grip on the security of the airfield as the ten years war against communist guerrillas moved towards its victorious conclusion. Further to the east RAF Gan in the Maldives remained a staging post to Singapore where British forces made a modest contribution to ANZUS, and onwards to Hong Kong which remained home to a small military presence including 28 Squadron of the RAF.

Within Cyprus the general officer commanding Near East Land Forces, a major general, was directly subordinate to Sir Derek. The major units under command were a resident infantry battalion in the Akrotiri SBA (1st Battalion

Royal Anglian Regiment) and a Royal Signals regiment stationed in the Eastern SBA manning the intelligence-gathering facilities that hoovered up signals intelligence (SIGINT) from throughout the near east and far beyond. In the contemporary age of Edward Snowden and other whistle-blowers it's worthwhile noting that after 16 years in the service I first got to know about the Government Communications Headquarters (GCHQ) after my arrival in Cyprus.

As administrator of the SBAs Sir Derek fulfilled the duties of a colonial governor supported by a civilian staff working for a chief officer, a senior civil servant appointed by Whitehall. Since attaining independence in 1960, two serious outbreaks of inter-communal violence in 1963 and 1967 between the Greek Cypriot majority and the Turkish Cypriot minority sustained continuing tensions beyond the borders of the SBAs. Following the last bout of fighting around Turkish Cypriot enclaves in November 1967, friction between the two communities gradually subsided as the main source of tension transferred to factions within the Greek community. While Archbishop Makarios effectively abandoned 'enosis' (union with Greece) as an achievable goal, many others believed that union with Greece remained the only legitimate political aspiration for Greek Cypriots. In 1971 General Grivas, leader of the EOKA armed campaign against British colonial authority before independence, returned to the island to establish a nationalist paramilitary group while stirring up anti-Makarios sentiment through the creation of pro-enosis newspapers. This brief summation provides some feel for the breadth of Sir Derek's duties and the military and political complexities of life in Cyprus where Archbishop Makarios was now an isolated and vulnerable target.

At the start of the working day the chief of staff BFNE, an Army colonel, and I sat in Sir Derek's office as he was briefed on TV, something of a new and novel concept at that time, from the Joint Intelligence Section Near East located inside the headquarters compound. The brief covered all aspects of Sir Derek's responsibilities and at its conclusion the COS and I took questions. The former invariably answered with masterly confidence while my own replies were confined to the words "I don't know Sir, I will find out". The warmth of my previous interviews with Sir Derek was distinctly absent and after three weeks of continued admission of ignorance I concluded that my tour might well end suddenly and prematurely. But then came a day when I could answer a question and as I got up to leave the office I was told to sit tight. Sir Derek said he wondered how long I could continue with my "don't knows" before trying to bluff to cover my ignorance. "You have earned trust," he said and I left his office with new found confidence and a strong feeling of deliverance.

Sir Derek was a man of undemonstrative character. He had been a prisoner of war for three years which I think moulded his personality into one of absolute self-reliance. In six months' close association I never heard him utter an angry word but there was no need as his unblinking and steely gaze could indicate more than adequate and convincing displeasure. He was an attentive listener and incisive interrogator who was not at all disturbed by the contradictions and intricacies of political and military life within Cyprus, CENTO, Malta and the Near East in general. I only once observed some disturbance of his equanimity. Early one morning the Secret Intelligence Service officer serving undercover in the Western SBA asked to see the C-in-C. When Trevor called it was not a case of saying "I'll see if I can fit you in before lunch", rather a case of "please come now". As Trevor entered the office he asked me to join him. We sat down and Trevor asked the C-in-C which would he prefer first, the good news or the bad. Sir Derek asked for the good. "We have confirmed intelligence that there is a Black September group loose in Cyprus," replied Trevor. "Good Lord, what on earth is the bad news?" said Sir Derek. "We assess you are their target," said Trevor with cool conviction.

Immediate steps were taken to enhance the C-in-C's security. Transport to and from Air House was made in different cars at varying times, number plates were changed and car pennants – one for each of Sir Derek's three appointments – were discarded. From time to time a helicopter was used. The ADC, Flight Lieutenant Peter Wilkins, and I requalified on the Stirling sub-machine gun to reinforce Sir Derek's personal bodyguard, an established post filled by Sgt Doran of the RAF Police. Privately I thought that the ADC and I, tottering around with sub-machine guns, were probably as much as a threat to the C-in-C's wellbeing as Black September. But more professionally, soldiers from the Royal Anglian Regiment were dug in to defensive positions around Air House maintaining 24 hours guard. There was one memorable incident during this deployment.

A solitary peach tree with two peaches stood alone in the garden halfway between the helicopter landing pad and the house. Lady Hodgkinson, a keen gardener, was most protective of the tree and her delight in the fruit it bore was boundless. The inevitable happened. The temptation was just too much for a soldier, or soldiers, sweating it out in the midday sun of May and the peaches were eaten. Later in the afternoon Lady Hodgkinson, walking back from the helipad, noticed their absence and immediately phoned me to record her heartfelt annoyance. As there was little doubt concerning the collective identity of the peach poachers, as no civilian gardener would have dared to commit such a monstrous heist, I telephoned the CO of the Royal Anglians, Lieutenant Colonel David Thorne, and suggested that a gesture of apology could provide the necessary atonement to restore the hitherto excellent relations between his battalion and the Hodgkinsons. My brother-in-law to be, a company commander in the battalion, suggested that the presentation of a silver salver bearing two peach stones might fit the bill. Prudently this proposal failed to gain traction such that the next morning the battalion adjutant arrived at Air House bearing a magnificent bouquet of flowers with an appropriately worded letter of apology. The adjutant's career was to continue to blossom thereafter as he now sits in the House of Lords following his tour of duty as chief of the defence staff.

This incident provided some relief to the tension that endured for six weeks before Sir Derek decided that he and Lady Hodgkinson would visit RAF Gan for the weekend. I went with them having surrendered my sub-machine gun on boarding the VC10 at Akrotiri bound for the Far East. The day before our return to Cyprus I was woken in the early hours of the morning to receive a flash signal from the JHQ. The Black September group had attacked the Israeli embassy in Nicosia and after a fierce fire fight with the Cypriot police all the terrorists had been killed or captured. We returned to the island with a sense of relief and life got back to normality as preparation started for the change of command on Sir Derek's departure in June. Trevor told us that the Black September group, having failed to get close to Sir Derek, attacked the Israeli embassy as their secondary target.

Political tensions in Cyprus continued to simmer with varying levels of hostility directed at the SBAs, and large-scale military exercises in Egypt and increased activity of the Soviet Navy in the eastern Mediterranean were matters of concern to the Command Group. My own primary task at the time was planning the departure ceremony for the Hodgkinsons, pretty straightforward, and the arrival ceremonies for his successor, Air Marshal Sir John Aiken, three days later which was far more complicated. After arriving at RAF Akrotiri with a welcoming guard of honour, Sir John and Lady Aiken moved to Air House to prepare for his swearing in as administrator of the Sovereign Base Areas. This solemn, formal and traditional ceremony took place in the drawing room of Air House before Sir John, the judiciary and distinguished guests moved outside to the garden for the concluding salute. A company-sized guard of honour from the Royal Anglians presented arms as nine Vulcans flew overhead. The timing was perfect and I was relieved that arrangements had worked perfectly which allowed me to enjoy the reception that concluded the programme.

Sir John's tenure of office did not get off to a happy start. Soon after arrival he was invited to take the salute at a Beating Retreat ceremony performed by the Royal Anglians in Happy Valley, a natural amphitheatre between Paramali and the Joint Headquarters. The Aikens arrived spot on time, the GOC several minutes late and strolled past in front of Sir John with no more than a casual "evening air marshal". Such disrespect of Sir John personally, or of the appointments he held, in front of many military and civilian witnesses was inexplicable. No word of apology was offered then or later so relations between the two sank into a permafrost from which there was no recovery. As a naïve and relatively young officer this first close experience of such enduring animosity between officers of very senior rank came as an unpleasant surprise. But in the years to come I was to discover it was by no means uncommon within the higher echelons of public life both military and civilian.

Sir John was commissioned in 1940 into the Queen's Own Cameron Highlanders where he served until 1941 when he volunteered to transfer to the RAF for pilot training, a transfer provoked by his keenness to fly and to get into action. Soon afterwards he was flying Spitfires on offensive sweeps over north-west Europe before he was posted to the Far East where his squadron provided close air support to Australian forces fighting the Japanese in New Guinea. After coming home in 1945 Sir John was awarded a permanent commission and started his rapid ascent of the promotion ladder. By the time he came to Cyprus he had accumulated a wealth of successful command experience within a wide variety of appointments while his staff jobs had, without exception, demanded hard work and selflessness. He was blessed with that quality of natural authority expressed in the steadiness of his gaze, an aura of calmness, the directness of his questions and his absolute attentiveness to the answer. My instinct of self preservation told me that I would be working for a very tough man, physically and mentally, whose expectations I would find extremely challenging. But expectations that in the event would always be expressed with crystal clarity and with a courtesy that was an enduring hallmark of his personality. That said, his expression of discontent was invariably both brief and explicit.

During Sir John's tour two events separated by nine months, each with its own dangers and volatility, called for the exercise of command by a man with a cool head and broad shoulders. The first crisis started on 6th October 1973, Yom Kippur, the holiest day of Judaism. A coalition of Arab states, led by Egypt and Syria, launched a surprise attack against Israeli positions in the Sinai Peninsula and on the Golan Heights, both of which had been captured by Israel in the Six Day War of 1967. The Israelis were not alone in being taken by surprise. That Saturday I was watching a rugby game in Happy Valley when my father-in-law, visiting us on holiday, arrived in unhealthy haste for a man of his age to tell me to phone JHQ immediately. I made contact with the duty intelligence officer, Squadron Leader Reg Hallam, holder of the record time to first solo in the Piston Provost, who asked me to come to the Joint Intelligence Section as quickly as possible. His voice was convincingly urgent. The information flowing in from our radar on Mount Olympus was sufficient to tell us that the Arabs had launched a full-scale assault against Israel with pre-emptive air attacks against Israeli air force bases. Signal intelligence from Dhekelia in the Eastern SBA indicated that fighting was fierce on the Golan Heights. But, who to tell?

Sir John was in Malta visiting RAF Luqa. The GOC was in England for an autumn race meeting at Ascot. The chief of staff was on leave and the command intelligence officer was unavailable – we couldn't find him. The most senior officer in contact was the air officer administration, NEAF, a one-star officer whose presence I requested in JISNE as soon as possible. Meanwhile I sent a flash signal to Sir John informing him of the situation and suggesting an immediate return to Cyprus. By 1800hrs that evening the intelligence staff had prepared a briefing for AOA which described a Middle East confrontation of brutal intensity that threatened the very existence of Israel. Considerable worry was expressed about the vulnerability of the SBAs and particularly RAF Akrotiri. Immediate steps were taken to enhance the security of our bases and not before time as Arab propaganda soon claimed that the Americans and ourselves were supporting Israeli forces from Cyprus which was of course meat and drink to those in the republic who sought our permanent withdrawal from the island. All of this was far removed from the day-to-day toil of AOA's legal and financial responsibilities but he bore up manfully until relieved early on Sunday morning by Sir John.

From then on the JHQ had a ringside view as the Israelis gradually turned the tide. While Sir John's coolness kept the lid on internal pressures within Cyprus, the involvement of the Soviet Union and the Americans was plain for all to see. Streams of transport aircraft, Soviet from the north and American from the west criss-crossed above the Mediterranean to resupply their client states. As the Israelis gained the upper hand and sought to secure a strategic advantage it was hardly surprising that the first ceasefire brokered by the UN for 22nd October failed to hold. Two days later the Israelis had encircled an Egyptian Army in the Sinai desert and the city of Suez before agreeing to the imposition of a second ceasefire. The rapid deployment of a UN Peacekeeping Force to secure the fragile ceasefire line was imperative, and Sir John was given operational control of RAF Hercules aircraft tasked to insert the UN force. The operation did not get off to the smoothest start when the assigned Swedish troops decided to negotiate a pay rise before deploying into the Canal Zone. Sir John immediately trumped the threat of an unwelcome and potentially lengthy delay by instantly accepting the substitution of Irish infantry from the United Nations Force in Cyprus (UNFICYP) to be flown in RAF aircraft – a bold move given the gravity at that time of the situation in Northern Ireland. The first Hercules to depart was captained by Squadron Leader John Horsfall, a fellow member of No. 76 Entry at Cranwell, and one of my oldest friends.

As life in Cyprus returned to recognisable normality I heard that I was to be promoted to wing commander in the new year and then hand over to my successor, Squadron Leader David Crwys-Williams after he had finished the advanced staff course at the Army Staff College, Camberley. This happened as planned which meant that I missed the more exciting year of 1974 in Cyprus. When Sir John took command in June 1973 no-one could have foretold that little more than a year later and, following the overthrow of Archbishop Makarios by a Greek-Cypriot faction, Turkish forces would invade the island. Sir John then faced a multitude of practical problems within a complex political situation of the greatest sensitivity. As 25,000 refugees, including many tourists, flooded into the SBAs seeking sanctuary from the fighting, Sir John had to arrange in parallel the withdrawal of 10,000 British service dependents living in dormitory accommodation outside the SBA boundaries. By the end of August more than 20,000 people had been evacuated from Cyprus by RAF aircraft. After considerable debate at the highest political level Sir John was authorised to plan and implement the rescue of Archbishop Makarios from his precarious refuge in Paphos and his onward travel to a safe haven in Malta.

David Crwys-Williams told me that at one stage during the crisis, and just prior to the evacuation of tourists from the north coast of Cyprus by the Royal Navy, it was evident that Turkish warships had sailed south as if to interfere with the operation. Without hesitation, Sir John ordered a message to be sent from him, via the NATO communications network and also via a Vulcan bomber to Adana airbase, for the attention of the chief of the Turkish armed forces. The message was blunt stating that if the Turkish Navy interfered in any way with the Royal Navy evacuation, he would regard it as an act of war by one NATO member against another. The text, not cleared with any department or person in Whitehall, was timely. Some 30 minutes later the Turkish warships were seen to return to port. Sir John's authoritative handling of arguably the most difficult peacetime international crisis faced by the UK since the end of World War II not only saved many lives but allowed the implementation of an enduring ceasefire and the survival of the SBAs which still remain of the highest strategic value to the defence interests of the UK.

Throughout the duration of the Cold War, with the possible exception of Korea and the Falklands at either end, few if any British senior commanders had to confront and overcome such serious and difficult circumstances as those faced by Sir John during his time in Cyprus. He triumphed because his clarity of thought, his perceptiveness, his determination, his integrity and his moral courage were equal to the challenges. No surprise that I thoroughly enjoyed my year working for two dissimilar commanders-in-chief but who were united in their devotion to duty and their pride in the Royal Air Force.

At home our children kept us amused, surprised and occasionally vexed. We could travel throughout the island without hindrance and the beach at Paramali, with sunshades and as clean as any beach could be, was the perfect place for family relaxation. The cost of living was low, overseas allowances were generous and the pace of life, Black September and Yom Kippur apart, was comfortable. Home help provided by a Turkish woman who adored the children helped Elizabeth enjoy the comfort of our home and there was no shortage of babysitters.

The commander-in-chief lived in a style now all but forgotten. Air House, long since destroyed by fire, and its garden provided a perfect setting for investitures and entertaining. To ensure standards were maintained, the RAF provided a house staff of two SNCOs and nine junior ranks. For travelling outside Cyprus the C-in-C had his own aircraft, an Argosy CC1 named Helios maintained by 70 Squadron and modified for his use. The hold was divided into two sections. The forward section and the smaller of the two was a staff office with seats for six and working tables. On our overseas trips I shared this accommodation with the PA, Sgt Barton, who came armed with his typewriter and other bits and pieces required by his trade. On the other side of the partition the C-in-C travelled in enviable style and comfort. His luxurious suite included bunk beds as well as a dining table, comfortable chairs and a shower and lavatory. The aircraft was perfect for leisurely travel and I thoroughly enjoyed the experience as we flew around the Mediterranean to our regular ports of call in Gibraltar, Malta and Naples. To the east the C-in-C was a frequent visitor to Ankara, Tehran, Muscat and Salalah. The Argosy was no speedster so there was plenty of time to draft thank you letters, reports and staff instructions when returning to Cyprus. In those days life as a staff officer had its compensations. If speed was of the essence a Vulcan bomber was tasked for the journey. The C-in-C flew as co-pilot while I stretched out in the seventh crew position below the cockpit. I did this four times and have never been in any hurry to repeat the experience.

Wearing three hats placed a heavy social burden on the C-in-C which kept the ADC fully occupied. I was content to let him get on with his job and only once got personally involved in the arrangements for a drinks party. Its purpose was to welcome to Cyprus a visiting group from the Royal College of Defence Studies (RCDS), the London-based institution which aimed to prepare senior officers and officials of the UK and other countries for high responsibilities in their respective organisations. The nine RCDS members were led by a rear admiral of the Royal Navy and Cyprus was their first stop before they went on to visit other countries in the Middle East not long before the Yom Kippur war. My job was to gather them up in the officers' mess and to get the group on board the command's brand new VIP minibus. Once accomplished I was to speed off in my mini car to warn the C-in-C of the group's impending arrival so he could personally welcome them to Air House. I went to the mess on time and found the rear admiral and his party in the bar. They had obviously been there for a while and the admiral told me he was much enjoying his 'run ashore'. This was readily apparent. Their drinks finished, the visitors climbed aboard the bus and off I sped. The plan worked perfectly up until the arrival of the brand new VIP bus. The C-in-C and the ADC were positioned under the portico at the front entrance of Air House as the bus approached. But regrettably no-one had measured the height of the new VIP bus against the base of the portico roof. Two inches of best Cyprus cement were thus deposited on the C-in-C and the ADC and the admiral as he emerged from the bus only to trip and stumble to the ground. Poor visibility may have had some bearing on his mishap. After a quick brush down in the cloakroom the party got off to a flying start.

It was at about this time that my posting came through. After six years away from the front line I thought that chief flying instructor at RAF Valley – advanced flying training still flown on the Gnat – would be the best job I could expect as a wing commander. But to my surprise and delight I was named as OC designate of 1 (F) Squadron to take up my appointment after completion of refresher flying and the Harrier OCU course at RAF Wittering. This didn't last long. OC 1 (F) Squadron was sacked and Peter Taylor, a flight commander on 4 (AC) Squadron, a current Harrier pilot and an old friend from Cranwell and Aden days, came back from RAF Germany to take command. My own posting was changed to OC designate of 3 (F) Squadron within the RAF Germany Harrier Force based at RAF Wildenrath.

In January 1974 Elizabeth and I returned to the UK to move into a surplus married quarter at RAF Bicester. Our new home was roughly midway between RAF Leeming and RAF Chivenor where I was to attend flying refresher courses on the Jet Provost and the Hunter. The Jet Provost gave me a useful 30 hours shakedown and re-acquaintance with bad weather flying before I returned to Bicester for a month's leave awaiting the start of the Hunter course. Bicester was also fairly close to Elizabeth's parents which was domestically convenient as I would be away for much of the year leaving Elizabeth to cope with Victoria, Douglas and Harriet who was born on 10th April that year in the nearby RAF Hospital at Halton.

I was delighted to return to Chivenor which had not changed since I had left for Aden nearly ten years earlier. The atmosphere was exhilarating with conversation both humorous and caustic as ever. Getting to grips with the Hunter again left me singing the praises of those above who had released me from the rather restrictive conditions of Flying Training Command. It was only later that I discovered I was third choice as a Harrier squadron commander, two others having turned down the posting for reasons that will become apparent.

The refresher course at Chivenor, 40 hours flying, was completed in six weeks and introduced me to skip bombing and SNEB rockets. Whereas these events and the more standard fare of low level attack/recce sorties were hugely enjoyable, my new rank of wing commander was no protection from sharp criticism if my performance fell below par, and quite right too. At Chivenor I met up with several first-tour junior officers who were to accompany me to RAF Wittering for Harrier conversion with an intermediary stop at RAF Shawbury. There we flew seven sorties each in Whirlwind helicopters – with a patient instructor – to give us a feel for hovering and using marker boards to position precisely over a landing spot. We were soon to experience the test of this achievement in far more demanding and exhilarating circumstances.

CHAPTER 11
THE HARRIER

After hearing the news of my posting to a Harrier squadron I read everything I could find about the aeroplane. It was quite clear that the introduction to service of the Harrier in 1969 was the consequence of brilliant and innovative engineering that produced the relative simplicity of vectored thrust. Thereafter the skill and courage of the test pilots flying the P1127 met the Air Staff requirement for a single-seat fixed-wing jet aircraft that could take off and land vertically. The transition from concept to eventual front-line service of a vertical/short take-off and landing (V/STOL) aircraft was not without uncertainty and difficulty.

In the early 1960s NATO identified the need for a supersonic V/STOL ground-attack fighter. Hawker and Bristol Siddeley formally responded with the P1154 which won the design competition but the RAF and RN could not harmonise their conflicting operational requirements. In 1964 the incoming Labour government identified the high cost of the P1154 which the RAF judged as secondary to the TSR2 project; the Royal Navy meanwhile had withdrawn support in favour of the Phantom. Not surprisingly the project was cancelled and quickly followed by cancellation of the HS681 (a short take-off and landing transport aircraft) and TSR2 programmes. Abandonment of these projects dealt a near mortal blow to the British aircraft industry but Hawker had persevered with the P1127 which was developed into the Kestrel aircraft for evaluation by a tripartite squadron of RAF, USAF and Luftwaffe pilots. Hawker's reward was an order for 60 aircraft, named the Harrier, which introduced the exacting and exiting novelty of V/STOL operations to the RAF's front line.

The original Harrier had a Bristol Pegasus engine for lift and propulsion that generated 19,000 lbs of thrust. In normal wing-borne flight four thrust nozzles split either side of the fuselage were fully aft and aircraft handling was conventional. For jet-borne flight, a nozzle lever operated the four nozzles together to rotate between any position from fully aft to about 15 degrees forward of the vertical to achieve an airborne braking position. Control of jet-borne flight was through reaction controls at the extremities of the aircraft fed by air bled from the compressor and controlled by shutters connected to the associated flying control surfaces. This system of control in jet-borne flight was brilliant in its simplicity but handling of the aircraft was tricky and required close attention.

The first trap for pilots was the position of the throttle and nozzle levers adjacent to one another in a single throttle box. The throttle was outboard, the nozzle lever inboard. To decelerate to a hover the nozzle lever was moved backwards in stages until the lever reached the hover stop. To increase the rate of deceleration the nozzle lever could be raised over the hover stop position further aft to the braking stop. Each rearward movement of the nozzle lever required a compensating forward movement of the throttle as the aircraft transitioned from conventional flight to jet-borne flight. All simple enough but in the heat of the moment movement of the wrong lever by mistake could have disastrous consequences. For example, in hovering too rapid forward rotation of the nozzles would move the aircraft forward and downward very quickly – the key word is quickly. The inevitable consequence of mishandling the huge power of the Pegasus engine through a wrong selection of either throttle or nozzle lever while in a jet-borne flight was instantaneous and if a recovery was achieved it owed as much to luck as to skill.

The second handling problem arose during transition from aerodynamic lift to jet-borne lift roughly within the speed range of 30-100 knots. It was essential to keep the aircraft pointing directly into the relative airflow by using the rudder to eliminate yaw caused by crosswind or any other reason. Failure to do so and intake momentum drag (Google for explanation if needed) would accelerate the onset of sideslip with the leading wing generating more lift than the other. The induced rolling moment could, in no time flat, exceed the authority of both the ailerons and reaction controls so the aircraft kept rolling and was out of control. The 'rolling moment due to sideslip' caused a number of accidents. To help pilots keep the aircraft pointing into the airflow a hinged wind vane was positioned on the nose cone immediately in front of the windscreen – certainly not rocket science but brilliantly effective when sufficient attention was paid to this most basic piece of technology. So, while deceleration from wing-borne lift to a hover over a designated spot required the nozzle lever to be moved rearward to slow the aeroplane down and the throttle moved forward to increase power as engine thrust compensated for reducing aerodynamic lift, the pilot kept a careful eye on the wind vane as well as monitoring the engine temperature gauge and the angle of attack indicator as the aircraft was flown down to a hover height no lower than 50 feet above the ground. Sometime during this process pre-landing vital actions had to be completed. In the early days of Harrier flying all take-offs and landings were filmed. Spectacular incidents of mishandling were brought together in the Harrier horror movie which underlined the fundamental truth that the aircraft was easy to fly if you stayed within narrow and defined limits and easy to crash if you strayed outside them.

To bring the Harrier into service a Harrier Conversion Team (HCT) was formed in 1969 and converted onto the single-seat Harrier under the tutelage of Duncan Simpson, the deputy chief test pilot at Dunsfold. The aircraft had no head-up display (HUD), a very poor primary instrument panel, no navigation system and no auto-stabilisation for V/STOL flight. Two years passed before a two-seater trainer entered service and my admiration for the Harrier pathfinders on the HCT – Squadron Leader Dick Le Brocq and Flight Lieutenants Richie Profitt, Peter Dodworth and Bruce Latton – remains undiminished. The team converted six flights of pilots to form 1 (F) Squadron, 4 (AC) Squadron and the OCU staff on the single-seat Harrier before the arrival of the Harrier T2 two-seat trainer in October 1970. No. 233 OCU was then formed at RAF Wittering to start operational conversion of first tourists. The course lasted six months and was split into two phases. Basic Squadron introduced students to V/STOL, instrument and formation flying, night flying and air combat manoeuvring while the Advanced Squadron focused on low level navigation, attack profiles, recce and weapons training with 30-mm cannon, SNEB rockets and practice bombs simulating the BL775 cluster bomb.

During the course I flew the Harrier GR1 to start and then the Harrier GR3 with the Pegasus II engine producing 21,500 lbs of thrust, 1,500 lbs more than its predecessor. New to me were an inertial navigation and attack system (INAS) and a HUD which was another first for an RAF aircraft. The first tourists, the best from Advanced Flying Training, seemed to have not too much difficulty in accepting the new discipline of jet-borne flight, but older and experienced pilots generally found it more testing to accept control techniques that ran counter to deeply ingrained instincts born of previous experience.

After two dual sorties terminating in slow landings using 65° nozzle and then a conventional landing – touchdown speed of 160 knots and generally agreed to be the most hazardous of all Harrier landings – I was sent solo in a Harrier GR1. So far so good. The next dual trip in the Harrier T2 with my instructor, Squadron Leader John Feesey, introduced transitional flying with a demonstrated vertical landing. John then carefully re-briefed me on the technique for a vertical take-off. Having set 55% power, moved the nozzles to 40° to check duct pressure at the shutters, I moved the nozzle lever rearward to the hover position and slammed to full power. My first effort was quickly terminated by John as the aircraft rolled rapidly to the right in ground effect as full power was reached. My second effort ended with similar abruptness as this time the aircraft rolled to the left. The wind sock was flaccid so wind had nothing to do with this contrary behaviour. John then took full control and surprise, surprise the aircraft lifted off perfectly. With the low fuel light flashing we remained in the hover for 30 seconds before descending to land. "You need to be ready for a possible roll with immediate corrective aileron when you have a go," John explained, with heavy emphasis on the word 'immediate'. I must admit to some nervousness as later that day I set off for my first 'go'. All I could recall of the dual attempts was a blur of movement involving throttle, nozzle lever and control column with a most uncomfortable and rapid sideways tip before we crashed back onto an even keel. But as the senior member of the course it was no time for a fit of the vapours. Even so, my confidence was not helped by Wing Commander Roger Austin who commanded the OCU. Walking out to my aircraft I met Roger who asked me what I was going to do. "Press ups (vertical take-offs and landings)," I replied. "Good," said Roger "may I have your egg if you don't come back?" Not exactly encouraging and the significance of his comment will not be lost on anyone with some knowledge of World War II RAF banter.

A runway controller's caravan was parked close by Bravo North, a large expanse of concrete to the north of the main runway specifically used for V/STOL practice. The caravan was occupied by a Harrier QFI in R/T contact with the V/STOL novice. He was there to offer kind words of advice and hopefully to help avert disaster. I thought his time was wasted. I couldn't hear a word he said because of the noise and vibration and if things went sadly awry I was pretty confident that the onset and conclusion of a catastrophic event would be faster than my reaction to any remedial advice – assuming it was audible. But nothing untoward occurred and I managed three vertical take-offs and landings. Any feeling of self-satisfaction was promptly deflated when the junior members of the course appeared from behind the caravan holding score cards aloft; the best I achieved was a three, but out of how many remained their secret.

The conversion phase onto the Harrier, including ground school, lasted for three months. After 30 hours on type, flown on 50 sorties ranging between five minutes and one hour duration, the course had experienced the full gamut of V/STOL manoeuvres including grass-strip operations at RAF Newton and landing in and taking off from a confined area, Vigo Wood, adjacent to RAF Wittering. My first landing at Newton, a rolling vertical landing (RVL) at 50 knots ground speed, was made onto dew-sodden grass so the aircraft skidded some distance when the brakes were applied. Happily the aircraft stopped short of the hangars which had appeared alarmingly close but I had at least dried off the grass which made things a little easier for the rest of the course as they followed in my tracks one by one. At Vigo Wood I spent far too long positioning the aircraft before vertically landing. On take-off I was very short of fuel so rather than hover taxiing to position for a landing on the main runway, I called air traffic and with permission landed with a RVL straight ahead on the southern perimeter track rather to the surprise of someone else taxiing in the opposite direction for take-off. Air traffic controllers at Wittering were well used to unexpected events as new courses settled in on the Harrier and had correctly assessed there was room for both of us. I was thus saved from some embarrassment. These minor alarums apart, I and the others all grew in confidence in our ability to handle V/STOL flying, but lest we became too confident we had our first viewing of the Harrier horror movie before we moved on to the advanced phase of the course. I left Basic Squadron thankful for the high quality instruction and with considerable respect for the QFIs. Instructing pilots new to the Harrier, no matter their previous experience, was not for the timorous.

A further session of ground school introduced the course to Advanced Squadron. We were lectured at length on the weapons-aiming computer and the INAS but all I can now remember is something called the Schuler Loop which seemed to me to be of academic interest rather than any practical value. More important to me was INAS performance. Sitting in a cockpit with a moving map display which gave your present position on a 1:500,000 chart that could be pre-programmed to route via turning points (it was called ackling) represented a most welcome advance. However, the navigation display had an unfortunate tendency to drift such that not long after take-off a pilot could have a present position error of a nautical mile and growing. With map in hand and eyes outside telling one story and the moving map in the cockpit telling another, seeds of confusion could be quickly sown. If the INAS showed early signs of drift, easily distinguished when flying over familiar ground relatively close to base, I decided it was best ignored and to rely on pure map reading as employed during my fighter recce days.

This was important as we flew nine attack/recce sorties, some chased by A Squadron staff, which were assessed before we deployed to RAF Lossiemouth for the concluding operational phase. In Scotland unfamiliar territory and bad December weather put us all through an exacting three-sorties test before we were judged as competent to join a front-line squadron for further operational training to achieve combat readiness. During our time on A Squadron we also flew weapons sorties, guns, rockets and bombs, on Holbeach range in the Harrier GR3. The weapons-aiming pictures on the HUD were also new to me but easy to use. However, if the nav display had drifted off it meant that the sight was giving an incorrect wind allowance that had to be compensated for during the attack pass. All attacks were filmed and my results were generally satisfactory. But I was cross when a couple of high scoring gun attacks were scrubbed by the qualified weapons instructors, with ill-disguised glee, for infringing the break-off distance from the target which was calculated to avoid the possibility of ricochet damage. The break-off range in the Harrier was 100 yards further out than that applied to the Hunter and being a creature of habit it took me longer than average to readjust my range judgement; I was penalised accordingly.

At the end of the course I was delighted to have graduated on the Harrier. I had thoroughly enjoyed the novelty of flying the first V/STOL aircraft to come into service. Low flying around England and Wales, before our final detachment to Scotland, on attack and recce sorties in the service's latest aircraft with a new-fangled weapons system was an obvious and positive step forward from the Hunter, and no matter the Harrier gave a rougher ride. As the OCU staff struck a perfect balance between criticism and encouragement the course came together with its own distinctive humour and wit reflecting the pleasure of growing confidence in the aircraft and one another. Above all we shared pride in being chosen to fly the Harrier and delight in mastering the many modes of take-off and landing while the brute power of the engine added a further dimension of excitement and challenge. But I was aware that success at Wittering represented no more than one step towards a future that would test me to the full.

The omens were not particularly good. Between the aircraft's introduction to service in 1969 and the end of my course in December 1974 the service had lost 19 Harriers. A station commander designate was killed towards the end of his conversion course and one squadron commander had self-suspended. Two other squadron commanders had been sacked and one, by all accounts, avoided sacking by the skin of his teeth. All this was common knowledge in the UK so perhaps, not surprising, enthusiasm for command of a Harrier squadron was not universal. But this was news to me when I returned from Cyprus and "where ignorance is bliss, it's folly to be otherwise".

Not all of the accidents were caused by mishandling during V/STOL flight and deficiencies in cockpit instrumentation were most probably the cause of at least one fatality. The Harrier itself with its unique capabilities clearly demanded careful handling and confident piloting ability. There was also some haste evident in the service's higher command structure to demonstrate that the aeroplane was a serious weapon of war rather than an amusing novelty. The concept of off-base operations to achieve survival through dispersal and concealment added to the pressures on aircrew, engineers and logisticians who struggled to demonstrate a convincing and developing capability without adequate support equipment. Moreover, command appointments had been filled by some officers who quite simply, and through no fault of their own, were not up to the job of flying the aeroplane while accommodating downward pressures through the command chain. It should also be admitted that one or two more adventurous souls introduced new ideas to V/STOL manoeuvring, particularly for display flying, that were bound to end in disaster. By the time I arrived on the Harrier scene much of this was history and I knew that Group Captain George Black had taken a serious grip on the RAF Germany Harrier Force which laid firm foundations for the successful development of the concept of operations in the years ahead.

George Black handed over to Group Captain Paddy Hine who was to continue this progress of positive evolution. George Black and Paddy Hine were two of the most distinguished service pilots of their generation and blessed with personalities and leadership skills that were more than equal to the challenges they faced as commanders of the RAF Germany Harrier Force. When I took command in January 1975 of 3 (F) Squadron morale was high and the whole force was benefitting from justifiable confidence and pride in the Harrier's unique capabilities. Timing and luck were thus to my advantage but this was by no means the end of the story.

Concept of Operations

In January 1972 3 (F) Squadron joined 4 (AC) Squadron and 20 (AC) Squadron equipped to fly close air support (CAS), battlefield air interdiction (BAI) and reconnaissance missions. Harrier Force (HF) survival in war was to be achieved by dispersal to and concealment within pre-selected war sites located in the First British (1 BR) Corps area of responsibility. Reinforced by the OCU at RAF Wittering, 48 aircraft would deploy to six flying sites with six more available as 'step ups' should any one of the first choice sites be compromised. Two logistic parks, separated from the flying sites, and a mobile Forward Wing Operations Centre (FWOC) completed the off-base force structure.

In transition to a war footing support convoys and ground parties would move to the sites after preparation by Royal Engineers and the installation of communications by Royal Signals both under operational control of the Harrier Force commander (HFC). The sites would have been requisitioned by emergency regulations and all used minor roads for take-offs with recovery by vertical landing onto a 70 ft by 70 ft MEXE pad; the pads consisted of rectangular aluminium planks bolted together and were so named to recognise their design by the Military Experimental Establishment at Christchurch. The pads, firmly latched to the ground by 9 ft 'pins' hammered in by the sappers, were laid as close as possible to aircraft hides to achieve speedy concealment after landing.

Although location of the war sites was highly classified, site preparation was quite straightforward. An unobstructed road, at least 500 m long with a minimum width of 10 m was required with immediate access from a designated operational area that housed the aircraft and the site supporting infrastructure. Typically, light industrial estates and supermarkets met the criteria for a Harrier war site although my own favourite was a brewery. Occupation of that site would have tested both leadership and discipline. Most importantly the locations had to allow good communication nodes for the secure Bruin telephone network from the FWOC to the sites and logistic parks for command and control by the HFC. At the FWOC the HFC was supported by a small staff who looked after aircraft tasking, logistic support and force security. The whole deployed force was protected by RAF Regiment light armoured and field squadrons under OC 33 Wing RAF Regiment who reported directly to the HFC. RAF Regiment protection allowed the engineers to concentrate their skills and energy on the generation of a very high sortie rate that was the operational signature of the HF. Should a site come under ground attack every man was armed and trained in basic infantry skills. If a Harrier site was found and attacked, only a small proportion of the force would be affected and aircraft airborne at that time would be diverted to other sites for re-tasking.

Support convoys and all ground parties would deploy forward in more than 400 vehicles to the war sites as ordered by HQ RAF Germany after receipt of the relevant NATO alert measure. The aircraft would be held back in hardened shelters to fly their first war sorties from the main base and then to land vertically at their war site. In transition to war (TTW) pilots would be briefed on the location and characteristics of their allocated war site; all in all their first sortie would have been a formidable task. Once deployed pilots remained in their cockpits during operational turnarounds – refuelling and rearming. New tasks were passed by telebrief with target maps delivered to the cockpit by runners working for the ground liaison officers (GLOs). The preferred weapon was the BL755 anti-armour cluster bomb each containing 147 bomblets. Five BL755 weapons could be carried by each Harrier with SNEB 68-mm rockets (19 within each of four pods) as a second choice of weapon. The two 30-mm cannon were loaded with a total of 240 high explosive rounds.

So much in brief for the concept of operations, but would it have worked in war? Successful off-base deployment of the force was critically dependent on warning time. From RAF Wildenrath the support convoys had to drive some 150 miles to the rear areas of 1 (BR) Corps. Weapons had to be out-loaded from a munitions storage area at Bracht, located some 30 miles north of Wildenrath, and then carried forward by train. In TTW, although the federal government advocated a 'stay put' policy for civilians, in all probability the eastward deployment of HF convoys and weapons would have been swimming against a tide of refugees moving westwards. More significantly, there would have been a massive eastwards movement of NATO land forces to reinforce the Northern Army Group (NORTHAG) in the forward area which would be running alongside and possibly delaying HF deployment. Thus the forward movement of the HF to RAF Gütersloh, situated within the 1 (BR) Corps area of responsibility, in 1976/1977 was operationally essential as it significantly eased the Wildenrath dilemma, albeit the decision to deploy off base from Gütersloh was still conditioned by progress through the NATO formal alert system – from Simple, through Reinforced to General Alert. Given timely decision making the HF would, in all probability, have had sufficient time to deploy to war sites with weapons stocks in place. However, if intelligence of Soviet intentions got it wrong and NATO faced a counter-surprise situation, classified as State Orange or State Scarlet, the HF would have had to fight from on base. Even so the force could sit out a surprise attack by conventional weapons in hardened aircraft shelters – two aircraft to each shelter – and then use stretches of adjacent roads and grass areas on the airfield if the runway and taxiways were blocked.

Happily, the concept of operations was never put to the ultimate test although it was subject each year to rigorous practical examination by Allied Air Forces Central Europe Tactical Evaluation (TACEVAL) both on and off base. Excepting the truth of the military cliché that no plan survives the impact of war, the Harrier offered unique operational flexibility which I am confident would have been fully exploited by the exceptional people – pilots, ground crew and soldiers alike – who manned the HF in Germany from 1971 until the end of the Cold War.

1. Two St George's Hospital nurses circa 1935. My mother is on the right with Godmother Faithful on the left. (Author)

2. April 1959, Mr Harold Macmillan inspects RAF College, Cranwell. In the photograph I am right marker, centre rank. Mr Macmillan is escorted by Senior Under Officer Tim Elworthy who finished his RAF career as captain of The Queen's Flight B. (Air Historical Branch)

3. Welcome Home – June 1945. 31 Battalion Royal Marines return from Germany. Major H E Johns MBE, RM saluting. (Author)

4

5

4. Self and long-standing friend Tony Pearson in No. 1 drill order at Cranwell. (Author)

5. Self and Flying Officer George Pearce outside the crew room at RAF Nicosia. (Author)

6. Air Vice-Marshal Michael Lyne, commandant RAF College, Cranwell 1963-1965. (Sir Roderic Lyne)

7. Six 64 (F) Squadron Javelin Mk 9s in line astern rehearsing to escort President de Gaulle on a visit to the UK. (D Dalton)

6

7

8

9

8. 'My Hunter Mk 10' under Omani guard, RAF Salalah, August 1965. The guard answered to 'Elvis'. (Author)

9. No. 1417 (FR) Flight, April 1967. From front to rear: Squadron Leader Dickie Barraclough, Flight Lieutenants Derek Whitman, Horace Farquar-Smith, Roger Neal, Ken Simpson, myself and Frank Grimshaw. (1417 [FR] Flight)

10. Flying 'my' aeroplane XE614 down the Wadi Bana. (Frank Grimshaw)

11. A typical scene of a 1417 Flight operation mission. Forward looking before descending into the wadi to photo the target at far end. (Author)

12. Wedding day during leave in October 1965. My parents are on the left and Elizabeth's parents on the right. (Author)

13. Family holiday in the Swiss Alps, 1976. (Author)

14

15

16

17

18

14. The Prince of Wales leaving a Jet Provost Mk 5 after another hard hour's work. (Air Historical Branch)

15. My arrival photograph on taking command of 3 (F) Squadron. (3 Squadron)

16. Primary site engineers taking the mickey out of pilots at field site. This was their idea of a formation take-off. (Philip Ward)

17. No. 3 Squadron display team at the Queen's Silver Jubilee review of the RAF in July 1977. Kneeling from left to right: Flight Lieutenants Neil Wharton, Dave Binnie and Squadron Leader Keith Holland. Standing from left to right: Flight Lieutenant Graham Tomlinson, Squadron Leader Peter Squire, self, Lieutenant Commander Byron Duff (USN) and Flight Lieutenant Ian Huzzard.

18. My departure photograph with some 3 Squadron engineers. (3 Squadron)

19. 3 Squadron jet in field action (Philip Ward)

20. Field operation with aircraft bogged in mud. (Philip Ward)

21. Return to Gütersloh as Harrier Force commander. Group Captain Mike Stear hands over command in field. (Air Historical Branch)

CHAPTER 12
3(F) SQUADRON

I arrived at RAF Wildenrath in January 1975 accompanied by Flight Lieutenants Dave Keenan and Harry Karl, fellow OCU course members. Elizabeth and the children came out at the end of the month and we settled into our new quarters, a five-bedroom bungalow, on the officers' married patch within station bounds.

No. 3 (F) Squadron was the first squadron in the Royal Flying Corps to be equipped with fixed-wing aircraft, hence the squadron motto *'Tertius Primus Erit'*. More than a hundred years later it can be said without fear of contradiction that generations of squadron members have remained true to that motto in war and in peace. Certainly I knew that I would be taking command of a first rate operational squadron that had flourished under the dynamic leadership of Wing Commander Graham Williams. Before he took command in August 1972, Graham had hit national headlines as a participant in the *Daily Mail* Air Race commemorating the 50th anniversary of the first crossing of the Atlantic by Alcock and Brown in a Vickers Vimy bomber. Graham flew the second leg of the race which started at the top of the Empire State Building in New York and ended at the summit of the Post Office Tower in London. The Atlantic crossing was flown in a Harrier GR1 with Victor tanker in-flight refuelling support. Graham, a Boscombe Down test pilot at that time, vertically landed in St Pancras station coal yard and then completed the journey by helicopter and motorbike to the Post Office Tower in five hours, 49 minutes and 58 seconds. He was pipped at the post taking second place to a chap who crossed the Atlantic as a passenger in the comparative comfort of a Victor strategic reconnaissance aircraft.

I already knew that Graham possessed a hard-edged competitive streak. In 1965 he was a flight commander on 8 Squadron when I joined 1417 Flight at RAF Khormaksar. In July we returned to the UK to fly out two Hunters from RAF Kemble via the northern route. Stage one was England to Cyprus via Istres in southern France and RAF Luqa in Malta. After an overnight stay in Cyprus stage two was to continue to Bahrain for a second overnight stop via Dyabakir in central Turkey and Tehran. The final leg to Khormaksar was via Masirah Island off the south coast of Oman. Graham flew a Hunter T7 while my aircraft was a Hunter FR10 with greater power and carrying significantly more fuel. My leader made it crystal clear to me that we were to set the record for the fastest ferry from the UK to Khormaksar and this we achieved in 2½ days.

The total 12 hours 30 minutes flying time was not without incident as Graham could not select powered controls after we started up at Dyabakir. Rather than accept a few days' delay waiting for a rectification party, and most Hunter pilots would have accepted this as inevitable, Graham flew the next two legs to Tehran and onwards to RAF Muharraq in Bahrain in manual control which required considerable muscular effort and no small measure of flying skills. I recall some puzzlement at the long time it took for Graham to call me to check in at Dyabakir, but off we eventually set. On take-off as I formated on Graham it seemed, notwithstanding the high altitude of the airfield and relatively high temperature, that we were taking an awful long time to get airborne. I became concerned and a quick glance out to the front showed there wasn't much runway left so I bottled out, applied full power, and took the lead. Looking back I saw the T7 stagger airborne with the jet wash throwing up a cloud of dust and debris. I politely reverted to my No. 2 position as one didn't mess with flight commanders. Not a word was said until Graham explained the nature of his problem after we landed at Tehran. We continued to Muharraq where the problem with Graham's powered controls was fixed by 208 Squadron engineers, the third Middle East air force Hunter squadron. The next day we completed the ferry to Khormaksar in record time, although I have never had the nerve to ask Graham how much fuel he had left after completing the 900 nautical-mile leg from Masirah to Khormaksar – by my calculation little more than fumes. I am proud to share this achievement which rather sadly, but not surprisingly, has not found its place into the *Guinness Book of Records*. But I tell the tale not just as a comment on Graham's competitiveness but to underline the fact that I knew I had a very hard act to follow when he handed over to me command of 3 (F) Squadron ten years later.

The strengths of my situation were clear. I was inheriting a well-trained squadron with a sharp operational edge. My second-in-command and executive officer, Squadron Leader Terry Nash, was a highly experienced pilot, an outstanding airborne leader and a first rate administrator, altogether a rather rare and admirable combination. He was backed up by two experienced flight commanders, Squadron Leader Al Cleaver and Squadron Leader Stu Penny both now well settled in on the Harrier and with considerable ground-attack/recce experience. I was to see much more to my benefit of Al Cleaver in years ahead. Below the flight commanders there was a sound layer of operational experience among the senior flight lieutenants including some old friends from Aden days. Below them there was a bunch of junior officers all blessed with above-average piloting skills. A charismatic and forceful senior engineering officer (SEngO) guaranteed high aircraft availability. Basic military skills, essential for off-base deployment, were taught with patient enthusiasm by the small RAF Regiment contingent. All in all 3 (F) was an impressive outfit.

On the debit side, I was disappointed to hear that within three months of taking command and before my first off-base deployment in April, SEngO was posted along with 87% of the ground crew that had formed the squadron. By the end of the summer Squadron Leader Terry Nash, Squadron Leader Al Cleaver and four other pilots out of a strength of 15 were also to be posted. Thus within the first year of command the training task, not least for myself, would be exacting before the squadron faced an off-base TACEVAL in the autumn. A multi-national team, some 150 strong, would test all aspects of squadron operations over a three-day period. At the end of the exercise HQ Allied Air Forces Central Europe would award ratings to the Harrier Force overall and individual squadrons for operational efficiency, logistic sustainability and survive to operate against both air and ground threats. The parameters of the evaluation were set out in the Supreme Headquarters Allied Powers Europe (SHAPE) Tactical Evaluation Manual (STEM) which allowed no latitude for ad hoc arrangements. The TACEVAL would tell whether or not the squadron was well on the way to regaining the high level of operational effectiveness that I had inherited from Graham Williams.

In progressing towards this goal I was again to enjoy good fortune. Terry Nash proved the most generous guide and mentor and I could not have asked for more powerful support. Terry saw me through my in-theatre operational work-up while organising and leading a demanding tactical training phase that certainly pushed me on an upwards and steep learning curve simultaneously absorbing many facets of the supervision of complex and potentially hazardous manoeuvring of tactical formations at low level. Seven years out of the front line left me with a lot of catching up to do so the accolade of being 'an arbitrator of good taste and judgement' was hard earned. Beyond this Terry organised an on-base mini deployment to give all of us newcomers some taste of what was to come as well as leading the final Exercise Dark Horse sorties.

This exercise was set up under the control of the Central Trials and Tactics Organisation (CTTO) to examine the feasibility of Harrier night ground-attack operations. No. 3 (F) Squadron was detailed to carry out the trial. Prior to my arrival a night-flying work-up demonstrated, not unexpectedly, that the Harrier cockpit lighting was unsuitable for the task. The squadron developed workarounds (botch jobs) with filters on the HUD, masking tape to cover some lights and with more masking tape used to secure two filtered penlight torches. The lack of a radar altimeter and known shortcomings of the INAS were deficiencies beyond correction.

I joined the trial in February 1975 flying with Terry Nash in the back seat of a Harrier T4 flown from the German air force base at Fassberg in north Germany. Six aircraft carrying Lepus flares transited from Wildenrath to Fassberg in the late afternoon; I flew a Harrier GR3 as did Flight Lieutenant Graham Tomlinson who was working up with me to combat readiness. The low level transit training involved the manoeuvring of a four-aircraft tactical formation against a two-aircraft 'bounce' or attacker; all good stuff for me as my previous operational experience as a night-fighter and fighter-recce pilot mostly involved flying alone. After landing at Fassberg, refuelling and briefing, I transferred to the back of the Harrier T4 for two-night sorties before we returned as singletons to Wildenrath.

The sorties were flown at 500 feet above ground level and radar monitored. Navigation to the Bergen/Hohne range was mainly speed/heading/stopwatch stuff due to INAS inaccuracy. After clearance to fire the aircraft entered a 20 degrees climb with a 4 G pull up, flares were released at 2,000 feet immediately followed by a roll to 120 degrees of bank with a 4 G pull down to return under the flares to shoot. After landing back at Fassberg, pilot turnarounds and the movement of flares between aircraft were completed in preparation for the second sortie. Humping flares around in the freezing cold of a February night in north Germany amidst passing snow showers was not much fun. Nor for that matter was flying overland at 500 feet in the pitch black without a radar altimeter. More seriously I now know for a fact that two of the trial pilots came very close to disaster. One missed the ground by only a few feet as he pulled out from an attack. The second was still in cloud flying on instruments when his flares illuminated. The world inside his cockpit turned brilliant white so he could not read his instruments which caused complete disorientation. He ripped the filters off the HUD which gave him enough information to recover from a steep dive as he came out of cloud. These incidents were certainly close calls for both pilots and underlined two obvious lessons from the trial. First, the Harrier GR3 was totally unsuitable for night ground attack. Secondly, the installation of a radar altimeter along with an accurate and reliable navigation system and adequate cockpit lighting was essential for single-seat night ground attack.

For my part I was pleased to have observed the trial from the back seat of Terry Nash's aircraft because next year CTTO proposed to investigate the viability of night operations from deployed sites. On the evidence of Dark Horse I flatly refused to accept the task and said I would not authorise any pilot on my squadron to participate in such a trial until identified deficiencies in the Harrier GR3 were rectified. Some 15 years were to pass before the aeroplane achieved a viable night capability. I have little doubt that in the climate of those days had we lost an aircraft on Dark Horse, or worse a pilot, I would have received a 'yellow card' warning notwithstanding it was early days in the job. The skill and indeed guts of the pilots involved, none of whom received the public recognition that was their due, saw me through the first test of my command and I was the wiser and better for it.

In the months ahead the departure of so many experienced pilots and engineers was more than adequately compensated by the quality of their replacements. The new SEngO, Squadron Leader Ned Billings, was the very opposite of his extrovert and charismatic predecessor. On first acquaintance, reserved, quietly spoken and rather diffident, there was no doubting Ned's technical competence and his determination to do his very best for the squadron. Moreover, his adroit and sensitive leadership of some outstanding SNCOs, certainly the most tenacious and purposeful bunch I came across in my career, boosted my own confidence as the new team settled in. During this process of change I was told the squadron would be the first to receive a full complement of a new trade group called flight-line mechanics. These were young men, recruited and trained to a lower standard than formerly applied to airmen mechanics, whose role was limited to flight-line handling. Despite some misgivings it was soon apparent that their enthusiasm generated most welcome energy that would also stimulate the supervisory capabilities of their NCO superiors to the overall benefit of the squadron.

I was similarly fortunate with my pilot replacements. Terry Nash and Al Cleaver were replaced by Keith Holland and Peter Squire. Both had learned the ground-attack role on Hunters and whereas Keith came directly from instructing on the Harrier OCU, Peter was new to the aeroplane. At about the same time we received the first US Navy exchange pilot, Lieutenant Commander Byron Duff, a test pilot who I understood had been posted to form an objective opinion of the value of the Harrier to balance some rather extravagant claims emanating from the US Marine Corps Harrier fraternity. Byron was accompanied by Flight Lieutenant David Binnie, ex-Red Arrows; they were quickly followed by two first tourists, Malcolm White and Pete Kirton. Two other experienced Harrier pilots, both ex-1 (F) Squadron, Neil Wharton and Paul Hopkins, joined soon afterwards. Within six months more than two thirds of the squadron's personnel establishment changed over with new 'ownership' from top to bottom.

Group Captain Paddy Hine was my first force commander. I knew all about his reputation as an exceptional pilot. Tours on two fighter squadrons and a tour as a Meteor flying instructor at CFS preceded his membership of the 111 (F) Squadron, the Black Arrows formation aerobatic team, still the best flying display I have ever seen. As a squadron leader he commanded 92 Squadron (Lightnings) and as a wing commander 17 Squadron (Phantoms). By any yardstick this was an impressive pedigree. But there was much more to Paddy than the traditional extrovert image of a fighter pilot, and for the time being I shall leave it there apart from recording my good fortune as having Paddy as my first HF boss during the critical settling period at Wildenrath. His encouragement and support still means a lot to me.

The annual programme of HF activity by now was well established. Three off-base field deployments, each of two weeks duration culminating in an off-base TACEVAL during the autumn exercise, was par for in-theatre training. The squadron deployed to the Italian air force base at Decimomannu, Sardinia, for a four-week armament practice camp in the winter months. Sandwiched in were home and away week-long squadron exchanges with a fighter/ground-attack squadron from another NATO air force, more a test of social stamina than airborne training value. Exchanges with Canadian air force squadrons based at Baden-Solingen were particularly hazardous and eventful. Our Canadian chums had an appetite for burning pianos and seized any opportunity to create social mayhem. On one detachment to Solingen our hosts greeted us with lapel badges to wear throughout our stay bearing the logo 'Stamp out Frog Power'. Feelings were running high in the Canadian air force about preferential promotion for French-speaking officers.

Sometime within the annual programme we could expect a no-notice Part 1 TACEVAL which required the generation of 70% of our aircraft declared to NATO, 36 aeroplanes at Wildenrath, all fully armed with practice weapons in a war configuration. This had to be achieved in 12 hours, but typically RAF Germany stations achieved the target within six hours. After generation the aircraft would be live armed and all pilots flew a sortie to Nordhorn air-to-ground weapons range to qualify to the required Allied Command Europe standard in all three events – strafe with guns, retard bombing and rockets.

While a watchful eye was kept on the allocated war sites, off-base training was conducted from field sites that aimed to replicate wartime conditions, but without too much success. Concealment of aircraft was provided by camouflaged aircraft hides alongside wood lines with a take-off run across a field either on the natural surface or a metal strip laid down by the sappers. To judge suitability for take-off, a Land Rover was driven down the proposed strip at 30 mph. If the driver's head did not make contact with the canvas roof the strip was assessed as being adequate for a Harrier short take-off. The MEXE landing pad was sited as close as possible to the hides but at a distance which ensured that the hides and ground equipment would not be disturbed by jet blast as an aircraft vertically landed. Typically there were six aircraft on a site each with its own hide and with its own team of engineers led by a corporal. In charge of each pair of aircrew hides was a chief technician (C/T) usually assisted by a sergeant armourer. The C/T did the paperwork and was the direct link via Storno radio and landline to the ops caravan. On wet and muddy ground more 'tin' was put down for the main wheels and outriggers as taxiways to and from the take-off strip and landing pad. Keeping an aircraft on three narrow tin strips required great care; not many Harrier pilots escaped the embarrassment of slipping off the tin and bogging in to await rescue by ground crew and sappers.

Although the HF sometimes exercised in a low flying area 50 miles to the east of the Rhine and north of the Ruhr conurbation, most deployments took place in and around the Sennelager training area close to Paderborn. A HF training deployment required large numbers of specialist vehicles to carry essential engineering and logistics equipment as well as other facilities for field living such as tentage, generators, water tankers and so on. All these facilities and the operations infrastructure were hidden in woodlands while fuel bunds were dug under thick camouflage netting. Here it should be stressed that setting up a war site would have been much simpler and a lot of the stuff we took for exercises would not have been required in the better-found war locations.

"Train hard, fight easy" may be a military adage but our training field deployments proved the validity of this old chestnut. My own introduction to field operations in April 1975 was a two-week mud bath. A prolonged spell of rain before deployment to sites in Low Flying Area 2 and a rising water table limited flying operations to vertical take-offs and landings as it was impossible to lay a strip. To achieve a vertical take-off required a reduction in aircraft all-up weight achieved by only partial refuelling. Sortie lengths were no longer than 20 minutes. But the high sortie rate, up to eight sorties per aircraft within normal low flying operating hours, was an excellent shake-down for all of us on our first field deployment. Much of this activity was undertaken with ground crew encumbered by nuclear, biological and chemical

(NBC) protective clothing and gas masks. The ground conditions could not have been more testing or further removed from the comforts of main base operating. Shared discomfort and some pride in achievement in adverse conditions laid the foundations for the development of team spirit and individual self-reliance in equal measure from top to bottom of the squadron.

Some truly memorable characters emerged from the ranks of our engineers. Under Warrant Officer Douglas's ever-watchful eye, Flight Sergeants Jeremy and Sharp established their authority while Chief Technician Jim Andrews set an inspirational example of commitment and stamina. Among the junior NCOs Corporals Merv Cook, Ian Hudson, Phil Ward and Clive Handy sustained their good humour along with an element of mischievousness that was to add spice to squadron cabarets which were to become a feature of all future detachments and deployments. And none of us will ever forget Senior Aircraftman Dick Chadwick. His personality radiated much more than the sharpest wit which somehow or the other always stayed (just) within acceptable limits of good order and discipline. No matter the hardship, no matter the pressure, no matter anything with a hint of negativism, Dick Chadwick always found words that made light of difficulties. Such men are worth their weight in gold.

In the summer of 1975 the HF achieved Army agreement to use a section of the tank road encircling the Sennelager training area as a Harrier training site. The site, called Eberhard, situated at the north end of the training area allowed the HF for the first time to operate in conditions far more closely aligned to the wartime locations and without the perpetual worry of excessive rain and marshy ground limiting aircraft operations, particularly during the spring and autumn deployments. Summer 1976 was at the opposite end of the weather spectrum. The HF deployed into Low Flying Area 2 in mid-June when the daytime temperature regularly exceeded 30°C with little or no wind. The consequent reduction in engine thrust caused some excitement and not least for myself when I landed very heavily having run out of thrust, engine temperature and good ideas all at the same time when I approached the MEXE pad. My abrupt and ham-fisted arrival also proved the point that the probability of being watched is directly proportional to personal demonstration of professional incompetence.

Back in the cool of the wood I mulled over the circumstances of my misadventure and quickly concluded that the environmental temperature had been further heated well beyond 30°C by my wing man. I had sent him in to land first and he spent a long time fiddling around in the hover before descending. I should have twigged the consequence. Happily there was no damage to my aeroplane and I knew that I should have gone through the engine limiters and risked burning out the engine to give me proper control over the rate of descent. More importantly, this raised the question of why the HF was not using the water injection system which generated for about a minute an extra 1,300 lbs or so of thrust. Water injection was not used because we didn't think we needed it and taking out the ground equipment was yet another addition to the logistic tail. Summer '76 changed our thinking as well as curbing any personal inclination to overconfidence with two years of experience on the Harrier now under my belt.

The summer exercise also brought home to me an important lesson on the utility of air power. The Harrier Force field deployment was examined on exercise by DS drawn from the HQ and RAF Germany stations. The aim was to warm up for TACEVAL in the autumn. To help us prepare HQ RAFG had kindly arranged for a SAS squadron to provide the exercise enemy. Before we deployed I was tasked to brief the SAS squadron commander on the Harrier Force concept of operations. When we met, the major – later to become Director Special Forces – was accompanied by his sergeant major. After briefing I asked for questions. "I've got one," said the sergeant major "you've talked about aircraft, weapons, fuel, ground equipment and so on, but where do the pilots hang out?"

With an eye for the quick kill, the sergeant major had immediately identified the most critical component within the complex structure of the deployed Harrier Force at that time. He had recognised that air power is the product of many parts, some more important than others, but all vulnerable to ground attack. This critical vulnerability was, and remains, conditioned by the comparative speed of replenishment of losses whether human or material. Suffice now to say that it takes a long time to train aircrew to combat readiness. It is the simple truism of air power's vulnerability on the ground that has underwritten my longstanding and enduring support of the RAF Regiment as an integral part of the Royal Air Force.

A glance at my logbook brings back distinct memories of each of my nine field deployments as CO. I particularly recall the circumstances of my first off-base TACEVAL in October 1975 when the primary site operated from Eberhard with the sub-site located not too far away at a field location called Moosdorf. Before we moved out of Wildenrath on the 150-mile eastward trek I had been told by the new HFC, Group Captain David Leach, that a week after returning to base the primary site would return to Eberhard to prepare for a visit by HRH the Duke of Edinburgh. During the TACEVAL I had hoped that the team, knowing of our royal commitment, would not require us to site move. A forlorn hope as on the second day of TACEVAL the operational situation, fed in by the examining team, gave me no option but to divert airborne aircraft to other sites, to scramble those on site awaiting tasking and to order our ground crew to prepare to move to the step-up site at Mandalay.

With the aircraft safely departed and essential ground equipment added to vehicles partially pre-loaded in preparation for site evacuation, I waited for confirmation that Mandalay was clear of enemy and ready for occupation. I expected to receive this within 30 minutes but it was not forthcoming. Fearing a communications breakdown, and conscious of the TACEVAL staff's growing impatience for action, I decided to set off to see for myself accompanied by Flight Lieutenant Tony McKeon. We covered the 30 km in quick time, but as we approached Mandalay we were worried by the absence of RAF Regiment pickets. We stopped, got out of the Land Rover, and took a close look at our destination which revealed the presence of Belgian paras (exercise enemy) who luckily had not spotted us. As I was considering my options, and I couldn't think of many, to my great relief I saw emerging from an adjacent wood a fighting patrol of 2 Squadron RAF Regiment. As they advanced towards the pre-positioned operations tent they looked most menacing, a judgement shared by the Belgian paras who beat a hasty retreat abandoning in the process a radio with a card detailing all 'enemy' exercise frequencies.

The subsequent move of our convoys from Eberhard to Mandalay under close RAF Regiment escort was completed without further ado and flying operations soon recommenced. Meanwhile, listening to chatter on enemy frequencies gained intelligence that I passed to the FWOC where it was gratefully received. I thus earned a totally undeserved reputation for tactical acumen.

CHAPTER 13
ROYAL EVENTS

At the end of TACEVAL the squadron was awarded top ratings across the board which satisfied my first objective on taking command. Now there was the royal visit. David Leach was rather nervous about it as a visit in the early days of the deployment by a German VVIP had not gone too well in the judgement of the C-in-C. He had escorted the VVIP too close to a field strip to watch a Harrier take-off. Both C-in-C and visitor were then inundated by a deluge of grass that gave their clothing a distinctive green hue. Not exactly David's fault but he was left in no doubt that if the royal visit failed to meet the C-in-C's expectations his head was on the block.

A week after returning to Wildenrath the pilots had washed the mud and cow pats off the aircraft before the engineers got to grips with various unserviceabilities. The deployment kit had been cleaned and sorted out as it was recovered from Eberhard, Moosdorf and Mandalay. A Flight then went back to Eberhard to prepare for a preliminary inspection by the deputy commander, RAF Germany. The programme was simple. Royal arrival, introductions, a briefing on the HF concept of operations, four aircraft to start up and to take off from the road strip before returning to land and taxi to their hides. The intervening time between take-off and landing was to be spent meeting ground crew and viewing weapons displays. All pretty simple stuff until the deputy commander got into the detail.

His first concern was the noise caused by generators which he asked to be switched off for the period of the visit. I pointed out that a briefing in the ops tent illuminated by torch as opposed to an electric light bulb would not create a convincing impression of a force at the cutting edge of contemporary technology. Nor for that matter could I use the slide projector (PowerPoint was still a long way off) with its pretty pictures which hopefully would help illuminate my briefing. Finally, the fridge wouldn't work so the vodka, specially provisioned for the C-in-C's refreshment as ordered, might well sink below optimum serving temperature. This was the clincher and the deputy commander agreed the generators could run, albeit we had to build a wooden bund around them to muffle the noise. The rest of the programme was satisfactorily concluded without the imposition of a 'practice lunch' although I had admitted that we were not bringing out mess silver, table cloths, linen napkins etc; lunch would be served in our standard mess tent at trestle tables sitting on field-issue collapsible chairs. The deputy commander was a little anxious about my unsophisticated attitude which apparently ran counter to the Army's inclination when hosting royal visitors. Whatever, I felt that His Royal Highness would be more appreciative of reality than fantasy.

With all now agreed on the social arrangements, the operational display was completed without incident and we settled down for a quiet weekend. On the Sunday afternoon several of us visited a German flying club at Paderborn Lippstadt airfield which had been used as a Harrier site on previous exercises. We were warmly welcomed and sat down in the October sunshine to enjoy a glass of beer with club members. An hour or so later the local hunt arrived pulling up in front of us after a canter across the airfield. The master, one-armed and possibly well fuelled with schnapps, rode his horse up the steps of the clubhouse but unfortunately forgot to duck as he went through the doorway. He fell backwards off his horse but immediately sprang to his feet. His mount continued into the clubhouse and drank deeply from a sink beside the bar. We were entranced by the spectacle and I introduced my pilots to the new arrival, a most distinguished-looking man – lean, fit, silver haired and with a charming smile. He was delighted to discover we were RAF pilots and proudly told us he had served in the Luftwaffe and lost his arm in combat. All his war service, rather predictably, had been on the Eastern Front. The arrival of the hunt kicked off a party that Peter Squire, with a well earned reputation for social stamina, judged to be a truly memorable affair. We arrived back at Eberhard to our 'green worms' (sleeping bags) later than planned but with a spare day before the royal visit to complete preparations; this included final construction of the noise bund. Rather surprisingly my ground crew considered the bund a test of their technical ingenuity and had gone at it hammer and tongs to construct an edifice of truly impressive dimensions.

The weather on the day of the visit had taken a turn for the worse. Thick, wet fog threatened to put a complete dampener on the day but happily visibility improved sufficiently to get four aircraft airborne although recovery to the site was out of the question. The royal party arrived by road from RAF Gütersloh, 45 minutes drive away. The ground part of the programme went as planned and I survived the ordeal of some penetrating questions from the Duke of Edinburgh without causing too much concern to the C-in-C and the force commander. At lunchtime we sat down at the trestle tables minus four pilots now dining comfortably in the mess at Gütersloh. Conversation started with a lively discussion on the perils of bad weather flying. HRH told us that he had recently been flying an Andover of The Queen's Flight a few hundred feet above a flat layer of stratus cloud. He could see the shadow of his aeroplane and was intrigued by a visible and clearly defined rainbow around the shadow. At this stage the C-in-C spoke up, "was it in daylight sir?" he asked. There was a deathly hush eventually broken by the sound of Flight Lieutenant Harry Karl choking in his soup. Harry survived and the royal party departed on time to a musical accompaniment. Flight Sergeant Jeremy played an appropriate farewell on his bagpipes. There was an amazing array of talents in the ranks of 3 (F) Squadron.

The next day we returned to Wildenrath where, a year later, David Leach told me that HQ RAF Germany required a Harrier display team to participate in the Royal Review of the RAF in July 1977 to mark the Silver Jubilee of The Queen's reign. My tour end date would be extended to accommodate this task. The size and format of the display was for me to decide. The team would be required to attend a full-scale rehearsal at RAF Finningley in Yorkshire (now Robin Hood Airport) in April shortly after the squadron had redeployed to RAF Gütersloh at the beginning of the month. The move to Gütersloh required the disbandment of 20 Squadron – shortly to reform as a Jaguar squadron – as there were only two sites of hardened squadron accommodation on base. In the autumn of 1976 the squadron strength thus grew from 16 to 24 pilots with a commensurate increase in ground crew numbers. No. 4 (AC) Squadron were first to move to Gütersloh in November and 3 (F) Squadron followed four months later.

For the display I decided we would use eight aircraft. Two would be running spares to fill in if I, as leader, or another member of the team suffered an unserviceability on start-up. It was thus essential that the two spares, Squadron Leader Peter Squire and Lieutenant Commander Byron Duff, were not only full members of the team but exercised during work-up training. The display itself aimed to contrast high speed, low level manoeuvring by two aircraft each carrying four SNEB pods co-ordinated with the remaining four aircraft flying a synchronized demonstration of jet-borne manoeuvring. I and Dave Binnie, my number 2, would start the show emerging from aircraft hides for a formation short take-off. Thereafter we whizzed around at low level pulling lots of G while the others lifted off vertically from MEXE pads for a continuity display that required handling skill of the highest order. The show culminated with two aircraft bowing to Her Majesty – a unique Harrier manoeuvre – before vertically landing in unison, two others carrying out rolling vertical landings on the main runway with Dave and me joining in as numbers 5 and 6 behind them as we all landed immediately in front of the royal box.

Four MEXE pads were laid at Wildenrath and we worked up the display bit by bit during the winter months following a four-week-long detachment in November to Decimomannu for our annual armament practice camp, my favourite detachment of the year. I remember that APC with particular pleasure as it was the first and last time I fired four full SNEB pods of rockets in a single attack. The targets, a variety of old vehicles, had recently been scattered by the Italian air force in the tactical range area. I led seven other aircraft on the single-pass attack and we obliterated all targets to the considerable annoyance of our Italian hosts. When I asked for permission to carry out the same attack with eight aircraft there must have been some misunderstanding as the Italians thought we would fire one rocket from each pod. I obviously failed to get over the message that we were filling all the pods with rockets that were approaching their time-expired date. Whatever, it was all most satisfying from our point of view.

On 4th April 1977 I led 14 aircraft off on a farewell to Wildenrath. I was asked to avoid the HQ at Rheindahlen as the noise might disturb staff deliberations and the tranquillity of their environment. Sadly, but to my private pleasure, low cloud and poor visibility to the south allowed no deviation from the northern route and permission to overfly the HQ was reluctantly given. We marked our arrival at Gütersloh with an airfield attack which caused immediate collywobbles because of noise sensitivity in the local area; this was a recurring problem that I had to confront a few years later when station commander.

On 15th April we set off again, this time to RAF Finningley to take part in the two-week work-up for the Royal Review. Along with Peter Squire, Dave Binnie and Byron Duff came my two most experienced Harrier pilots, Keith Holland and Neil Wharton, and two exceptional first tourists, Graham Tomlinson and Ian Huzzard. I could not have had a better balanced team and our ground crew ensured that we did not lose a single sortie through aircraft unserviceability. The whole of the planned RAF display was presented to the Air Force Board on 29th April 1977. Sitting in my hide on the south side of the airfield I felt proud as the flypast of so many different types of aircraft embracing all roles of air power thundered overhead in immaculate formations. The formation flypasts were interspersed with various role demonstrations involving the RAF Regiment and search and rescue forces which included a model air-sea rescue launch which motored past the royal box on wheels. Most spectacular was a scramble by four Vulcan bombers which conveniently covered the noise of eight Harriers starting up on the south side of the airfield. We were the penultimate display with the Red Arrows providing the finale.

The 3 (F) Squadron display went off without a hitch and I was feeling rather cocky and just a little relieved when summoned for a chat with the senior air staff officer RAF Germany, Air Commodore Mike Beavis, who told me that CAS was well satisfied with our contribution. However, he would like some reduction in the noise as he had no wish to deafen The Queen. So, having stumbled at the last fence we returned to Gütersloh and a week later went back to Wildenrath where fortunately our MEXE pads were still in place to readjust some of the jet-borne manoeuvring. Three days later the air member for personnel, Air Chief Marshal Sir John Aiken, came out to watch the amended display and declared his satisfaction. We then returned to Gütersloh in time for the summer off-base deployment in mid-June which passed without memorable incident.

Shortly afterwards Elizabeth and I were privileged to attend The Queen's Silver Jubilee Review of the Army held in the Sennelager training area. It was the most spectacular military occasion I have ever watched. The whole of the 4th Armoured Division, tanks, guns, armoured personnel carriers etc, some 580 vehicles with their soldiers were paraded in review order fronted by the massed bands of the Cavalry, Infantry and Scottish Regiments numbering some 750 musicians. After HM The Queen had reviewed the parade from a Land Rover escorted by Major General Nigel Bagnall, General Officer Commanding 4 Division, in his armoured personnel carrier (APC), all the vehicles started together in a spectacular concoction of noise and smoke. Thereafter they rumbled past the saluting dais with the main battle tanks, four abreast, turning their turrets and dipping their guns in salute. The drive past took some 30 minutes to complete and the salute concluded with a flypast by Army Air Corps helicopters.

A week later we flew back to Finningley to take part in final preparations for the Royal Review of the RAF on 29th July. We quickly got back into the swing of our display and to ensure combat skills remained well-honed we flew four aircraft versus two low level evasion sorties before returning to Finningley for display rehearsals. Everything went smoothly until the day before the review. I was telephoned by a MoD official to tell me that there had been a low flying noise complaint from a Derbyshire MP. The timing and place of the complaint left me in no doubt that it was us and I said so straight away while adding that I was 99 per cent certain that none of my team would have infringed the 250 ft above-ground level limit. If there was to be any further action I asked if it could be delayed until after the review as my mind was on other things. Happily that was the last I heard of it.

The Queen arrived on the morning of 29th July to present a new Queen's Colour to the Royal Air Force at the conclusion of a spectacular parade with every squadron in the service represented by colour parties escorting their own squadron standards. We were allowed to watch the dress rehearsal in our flying suits, we travelled light, before being banished back to the south side of the airfield to our 'gypsy camp' as described by one supercilious Strike Command staff officer. The hapless fellow was clearly content with his own comfortable but pitiable life within the corridors of HQ Strike Command. On the day the flying display started after lunch. The weather conditions were ideal and to my relief the temperature was 19°C which meant that I had no worries about engine performance. The whole display was completed without incident but the secretary of state for defence, Mr Fred Mulley, stole the headlines as he was photographed asleep next to The Queen in the royal box. This was probably the consequence of a good lunch washed down with vintage wines specially chosen for the occasion. Nevertheless, I was confident that the secretary of state would have been awake during our display notwithstanding the token noise adjustments. On Saturday the whole flying display was repeated for the general public and on Sunday we returned to Gütersloh as the station was vulnerable for a no-notice Part 1 TACEVAL.

Five weeks later we deployed for the ninth and final off-base exercise of my tour. I flew a minimum of three sorties each day in the mistaken belief that Exercise Hack Fist would be the last time I would enjoy the excitement and stimulation of Harrier field operations. Back on base I started to clear the decks for handover and flew my final sortie on 3 (F) Squadron which was 1v1 combat against Dave Binnie. I think the emotion of the occasion overcame Dave as I won. So ended a tour that fulfilled an ambition and most happily concluded without a single fatality. The squadron lost one aircraft due to a mechanical failure in the engine and the pilot, Flight Lieutenant Peter Kirton, ejected safely. The town of Borken, a few miles east of the Rhine, awarded Pete a medal at a civic reception for his supposed skill and bravery in steering his aircraft clear of habitation before ejecting. I had to accompany Pete to the presentation to ensure he stuck to a script not of our composition. At the end of October I handed over command to Wing Commander Richie Profitt, a founder member of the Harrier Force. There could not have been a better replacement to bring new enthusiasm and fresh ideas to the duties of squadron command.

CHAPTER 14
MINISTRY
OF DEFENCE

Command of a squadron is the proper ambition of a military pilot. I had two bites of the cherry but there was more than a wealth of difference between command of a training squadron and a front-line operational squadron. The measure of success in the former was essentially sorting the wheat from the chaff – those who had the determination and mental and physical attributes to progress to front-line combat readiness from those who conclusively lacked an essential element of a military pilot's make up. During my extended tour as OC 3 (F) Squadron I was fortunate to enjoy the company of some outstanding fighter pilots; apart from those I have already mentioned, Bob Iveson, Arthur Gatland, Roger Gault, Gavin McKay all come immediately to mind. The Harrier Force in the 1970s certainly had the cream of the crop of young pilots produced by Flying Training Command. Not altogether surprising that Harrier pilots gained a reputation of arrogance provoked perhaps by an element of envy. Twenty years later I had forgotten this when I offered my flying boots, well-worn in and sumptuously comfortable, to son Douglas when he was flying Hercules at RAF Lyneham. A Harrier pilot's flying boots were uniquely distinctive in having the laces covered with a flap – this to protect the laces from being cut or burnt as a pilot ejected so to prevent the possible loss of boots which would have made for a more painful landing. Douglas refused my offer. "If I wore those at Lyneham I would be lynched," he explained. Reputations within the armed forces die hard.

It is worth reiterating that the squadron's performance in gaining the highest assessments on two off-base TACEVALs owed much to the contributions of the Royal Engineers and the Royal Signals. The relentless and fiercely focused energy of the sappers kept us flying in gruesome weather that waterlogged sites. On one occasion they lifted and re-laid an entire take-off strip overnight after a wayward junior pilot had lifted the edge and rippled the surface. The signallers ensured our communications within the deployed force and outside to tasking HQs at corps or ATAF level were sustained with only the occasional interruption. Both sappers and signallers were ever ready to help our ground crew if it was all hands to the rescue of a bogged-in aircraft or when another minor crisis threatened flying operations.

Any tribute to the Army's contribution would be incomplete without mention of our ground liaison officers (GLO). After the move to RAF Gütersloh each squadron had three GLOs, all majors, whose on-field deployments provided the critical link between the tasking agency and pilots in their cockpits. Essentially GLOs translated requests for air support into 'pilot speak' while including land battle information relevant to the task. After landing pilots were debriefed by a GLO who passed pertinent information back through the Army chain of command with mission reports being transmitted to the tasking HQ. Their role went beyond the processes of operational tasking and debriefing. Back on base the GLOs were responsible for regular briefings to aircrew on all military equipments, tactics, strengths etc. of both friendly and enemy forces while maintaining the most accurate information available on the disposition and strengths of Warsaw Pact formations, land and air. GLOs liaised with the air/ground elements of NORTHAG divisions and were on hand to advise squadron commanders on Army matters.

During my tour four GLOs served under my command with good humour and commendable patience as they readjusted to an unfamiliar environment and lifestyle. There can be no doubt that a good GLO could, through personality and loyalty to the squadron, exercise a powerful and most welcome influence on morale. One such was Major John Hickie RA who came to us directly from 2½ years in Londonderry where he served with the Special Branch of the RUC as a military intelligence officer; he described the job as 'hairy'. John had been specially selected for the appointment by the General Officer Commanding (GOC), General Sir Frank King, to re-establish trust and confidence between the Army and the police as relations had broken down. John was successful and he brought to 3 (F) Squadron the same mindset which had underwritten his success in Londonderry. He, and his attractive and most energetic wife Mary, enjoyed their time with 3 (F) such that John was to complete two further tours with Harrier squadrons before he retired in 1989.

John had no difficulty in keeping junior pilots under control as he was a master of banter and the appropriate put down if his patience was tried. As CO, much as I liked John as a person and appreciated his hard work, I kept a wary eye on him during high profile visits to the Harrier Force of which there were many. On one occasion we welcomed the US ambassador to the Court of St. James who was visiting British Forces Germany. Mrs Anne Armstrong, a most attractive woman with a personality that mixed warmth with an aura of authority, stumbled on a step as she entered the crew room. There I was to introduce squadron officers. First in line was Major John Hickie. "Did you have a good trip?" he asked politely. "Yes," replied Mrs Armstrong favouring John with an old-fashioned look. I moved quickly on to the junior officers who in such circumstances were by and large more predictable and reliable.

Towards the end of the tour the air secretary sent me a form asking whether I wanted to sign on for further service after my 38th birthday in July 1977. 'Delete yes/no' as applicable and return to sender which was not exactly a resounding call to commit to a further 17 years of service. But the very bluntness of the question made me take stock of my situation. So far my time in the RAF revealed that I had a talent for good luck. Circumstances of timing and opportunity had played into my hands. Many strong friendships within and outside the RAF had made life agreeable. I could withstand pressure and was willing to press my luck knowing that the consequence of failure or discovery would have been career termination. In balancing reward against risk I was determined, first, to accept responsibility for possible failure and secondly, not to whinge if called to account. On 3 (F) Squadron I recall two specific occasions when the reward in terms of benefit to squadron morale was worth the risk. One example will suffice. HQ RAF Germany promulgated an order that two-seat combat aircraft were not to be used to ferry servicemen to and from the UK – hitherto seen as a 'perk of the job'. A couple of weeks later Warrant Officer Douglas told me that the mother of one of our young airman had been admitted to hospital and was not expected to live long. There were no transport aircraft returning home for two days. Later that morning after kitting out and briefing, the airman was in the back of a Harrier T4 en route to RAF Wittering where onward transport to Birmingham had been fixed. I authorised the trip and happily no-one outside the squadron questioned its purpose. Had the HQ or indeed my station commander got to know about it I would have expected at the least a severe wigging if not greater punishment, and quite right too. I will go no further lest others should be encouraged to disobey command routine orders to their possible and ultimate distress.

Our life in Germany, enjoying generous overseas allowances, shielded us from the financial stress suffered by those at home as armed forces pay lagged further and further behind civilian comparators. Family life in RAF Germany, with few job opportunities for wives, was a strong element of squadron spirit. Victoria and Douglas were but two of a horde of squadron youngsters all starting their education at a service primary school while Harriet, now three years old, kept Elizabeth busy. The high value of such family bonds stretching throughout the structure of a squadron would gradually evaporate in the years ahead with changing social attitudes and family circumstances. For my part, from 1975 to 1977, I was so lucky to enjoy Elizabeth's full-blooded support and her consistent contribution to the wellbeing of the squadron while simultaneously accommodating the needs of three young children. And that is not to mention the demands of a clamorous husband who at times inclined to burn candles at both ends. Elsewhere our holidays in Switzerland and Austria provided happy and energetic R & R while starting a love affair with the Alps that endures to this day.

The issue of commitment to a full career posed a question about my ambition. Promotion to wing commander at the comparatively young age of 35 owed much to the Prince of Wales's survival of my flying instruction as well as generous annual reports by Michael Lyne, Sir Derek Hodgkinson and Sir John Aiken. I was not a workaholic by any stretch of the imagination but was prepared to knuckle down and work hard when necessary. Aged 38, I had no far-reaching ambition; air rank was elevated above my sights and I recognised that while revelling in success a principal motivational force was fear of failure. What would I do if I left the RAF? I had absolutely no idea because I was totally engrossed in service life and civilian aviation did not appeal. I was addicted to flying military aeroplanes and revelled in the company of like-minded people. I was proud to belong to the Royal Air Force and gratified to have served men who had contributed so much courage to its short and valiant history. The icing on the cake was flying the Harrier and commanding so many talented individuals who came together to forge the distinctive identity of 3 (F) Squadron. No wonder I deleted 'no' on the air secretary's form with scarcely a moment's hesitation.

We packed up our home at Gütersloh in November 1977 and returned to England to occupy a quarter on the married patch at Northwood, home of C-in-C Fleet and AOC 18 (Maritime) Group. From there I was to commute to MoD Main Building to start work in the Directorate of Forward Policy (RAF). A staff appointment was inevitable and I would have preferred an operational job; but MoD, an institution of dubious merit as seen from the front line, roused my curiosity.

My first close-up view of MoD Main Building was a disappointment. Its monstrous structure did not blend easily with the older and more elegant premises home to other departments of state. Inside, miles upon miles of corridors – replicated through nine levels above ground – were adorned with cable ducting housing goodness knows what. Whereas the most senior members of the ministry, service and civilian, occupied offices with space to spare for meetings, the majority toiled in poky little rooms often shared by two. It was all rather lacklustre with green and brown décor adding to a gloominess which was much in tune with the mood of the nation in the late 1970s. In November 1977 the firemen went on national strike when their demand for a pay increase of 30% was refused. Some 20,000 service personnel then manned 'green goddesses' (emergency fire tenders) for nine weeks dealing with more than 40,000 incidents. The pay disparity between the striking firemen and service personnel – the latter earning just 50% of the hourly gross rate for firemen – went a long way to explain widespread discontent in the armed forces which had contributed to an accelerating outflow of trained personnel from all three services. Soon after I arrived, Wing Commander Neil Hayward, an old friend from Cranwell and Aden days, popped into my office. Neil, acknowledged as the most talented man of my generation, told me that he would leave the RAF at the end of his tour in command of a Jaguar squadron at RAF Coltishall. "I can no longer afford to stay in the service," he said with typical bluntness. So Neil departed and sought his fortune elsewhere in the aerospace industry.

The Directorate of Forward Policy (RAF) was concerned with the long-term future of the service rather than contemporary problems. This required the drafting of appropriate concept papers that looked ten to 20 years forward which in the troublesome political and economic circumstances of the time meant that the directorate was not in the mainstream of policy definition. For a short while I worked for Air Commodore Mike Armitage before he handed over to Air Commodore Peter Collins. Although dissimilar in service background and personality, both enjoyed debate with their three wing commander subordinates and were constructive critics of our written work and associated staff activities. The latter involved considerable research and tramping of the dismal corridors seeking the tutelage of appropriate experts from all three services. Their specialist knowledge was needed if we were to achieve accuracy and balance in papers addressing the RAF's longer-term contribution to maritime and land/air warfare.

I shared an office with Wing Commander John Willis which was a delight. John, three entries in front of me at Cranwell, had with the exception of one tour as a QFI at RAF Acklington spent his entire career in Lincolnshire before his posting to MoD. A Vulcan bomber man, he was one of the wisest and kindest men it has been my pleasure to meet and bore me no grudge for my own good fortune. That said, his intellect and sharp wit had the measure of any upstart Harrier pilot with ideas above his station. We agreed that few if any ever read our papers through from start to finish. Aim, assumptions, conclusion and recommendations gave enough ammunition to potential critics and destruction of a well argued case in the meat of a paper could usually be achieved by attacking the assumptions. Some were carved in tablets of stone. The Cold War would continue indefinitely, the Warsaw Pact would confront the West for the foreseeable future and the Central Region would remain the decisive area of potential conflict. No argument on these assumptions was permitted but you could have fun with warning-time assumptions and assessment of the impact of new Soviet weapons systems, the timing of their introduction to service and their subsequent deployment. Debate could rumble on for months with each service seeking an interpretation and format of words that best suited their own interest. Argument eventually ceased when the lead department had to submit their paper for consideration. Contentious issues were smoothed out and sometimes deleted before another anodyne paper was presented to the chiefs of staff to take note with no blood spilt.

Under Peter Collins's leadership his triumvirate of wing commander desk officers – Viv Warrington, also a Vulcan man, was the third – were directly involved in two topics of consequence during my 14 months in the directorate. The first concerned General Sir John Hackett's book *The Third World War* which addressed the questions of how, why, when and where would World War III be fought. Sir John asked Air Chief Marshal Sir John Barraclough, recently retired, to produce the chapters covering war in the air and the task descended down from Sir John to Peter Collins via CAS. We were each given the draft of the book as it then stood to read ourselves before writing the air contributions to be delivered sooner rather than later. Peter Collins provided a chapter on the air defence of the UK which was entirely appropriate for a dyed-in-the-wool air defender who had been a member of the team that introduced the Lightning (the RAF's first genuine supersonic fighter) into service. John Willis, who had commanded a Vulcan maritime recce squadron, delivered the air contribution to the chapter on the Battle of the Atlantic while I drafted the chapter dealing with the air war over the Central Region. Viv Warrington was the continuity man who ensured our drafts fitted into the narrative as he checked the accuracy of all references to air throughout the book. Our drafts largely survived the editorial process. Although authorship of the book was attributed to General Sir John Hackett and others, the contribution of the Directorate of Forward Policy (RAF) was not specifically mentioned, nor could it be as officially there was no MoD involvement in its production. So sadly we were not invited to the launch of the book which was to become an international bestseller. However, a year later we each received a £100 voucher to spend at the wine merchants Berry Brothers & Rudd, a most welcome addition to family finances and one that could not be frittered away on far less appealing domestic necessities.

The second task given to

Collins was to identify the long-term operational requirements of the service against the assumed continuation of the Cold War. Peter gave each of us an area of study within which we looked in depth at every role and set out proposals for development. Once a week we met together to ensure each of us was on track and contradictions avoided. The work took several months and concluded with some far-reaching recommendations. The provision of an air-to-surface missile for the Nimrod maritime patrol aircraft, the intro-duction of an in-flight refuelling capability to our transport aircraft and the procurement of a defensive aids suite for our offensive aircraft are three that I remember. There were many more and at the end of our work priorities for implementation were proposed; this was a tactical error that was soon evident as the Air Force Board Standing Committee considered prioritisation to be their territory and that trespass by an air commodore and his three wing commanders was out of order. The directorate's work became known as the 'Blue Book' and its production from my viewpoint was a most valuable pro-cess of education. The book was supposed to be updated regularly as a blueprint for future capability developments, but after Peter left it fell into disuse, although it was a useful document for plagiarism by speech writers gazing into the future with counterfeit perspicacity. I was sad that Peter Collins never received his due credit for masterminding the production of such a constructive volume so relevant to the future operational health of our service.

Not long afterwards, towards the end of 1978, I heard that I was to be promoted to acting group captain to take over from Group Captain David Parry-Evans as the director of Air Staff Briefing (DASB). The welcome news of promotion came as an absolute surprise as I fully expected to complete a full staff tour before even being considered for advancement. If this was a bolt from the blue, appointment as DASB was a bombshell. In short, DASB was the highest profile group captain appointment in the Air Force Department. Supported by two wing commanders, his primary job was the composition of briefs for CAS before he attended meetings of the Defence Council, the Air Force Board (AFB), the AFB Standing Committee (AFBSC), the chief of staffs' committee and chiefs of staffs informal get-togethers. All CAS's visits outside the MoD required an appropriate written pre-brief. DASB was also responsible for the coordination of Air Force Department (AFD) inputs to final drafts of Defence Staff papers and the preparation of CAS's bi-annual report to HM The Queen. Finally he drafted for approval a brief for quarterly circulation to those holding command appointments. The document updated recipients on all aspects of RAF activity and progress on subjects under consideration within the MoD, particularly those concerned with conditions of service. My superiors paid much attention to the 'tone' of the draft – not too upbeat, not too downbeat but judgement of the middle path was very much in the eye of the beholder.

The compliment of selection as CAS's briefing officer was flattering, but I did wonder if my elevation would prove a jump too high. Fourteen months' experience in the MoD, most of it spent considering the long-term future of the service, was not the best introduction to the complexities of day-to-day work within the department, particularly management of the defence budget. Although obviously aware that 15 years of defence retrenchment reflected the national economic malaise, I had only a cursory understanding of its impact within the MoD. And I had yet to understand the baleful influence of Treasury officials all committed to a perpetual struggle with departments of state equally dedicated to spending taxpayers' money. Moreover, within the Policy Division of the AFD – Forward Policy was a subordinate directorate – there were others far more experienced in Whitehall blessed with quick wits and ready primed for promotion. But, in for a penny in for a pound, and after a short handover from David Parry-Evans I took up my new appointment at the beginning of January 1979.

Air Chief Marshal Sir Michael Beetham was CAS and he was a bomber man. By the age of 21 he had flown a full tour as a Lancaster bomber captain against the most heavily defended German targets. He was decorated with the DFC. Thereafter, and having been awarded a permanent commission at the end of the war, his career followed the normal pattern of alternating flying and staff appointments. Both were primarily within Bomber Command when the V-Force was the custodian of the national nuclear deterrent. He also commanded 214 Squadron flying modified Valiant bombers that would soon become the RAF's first dedicated air-to-air refuelling aircraft. Under Sir Michael's command this squadron provided convincing demonstrations over long distances, more than 6,000 nms, of the potential of air-to-air refuelling to extend the reach of air power, a capability that today we take very much for granted.

I had served under Sir Michael's command three times before his appointment as CAS in 1977. He was station commander for most of my tour at RAF Khormaksar, commandant of the RAF Staff College for two-thirds of my year at Bracknell and C-in-C RAF Germany for the second half of my tour as OC 3 (F) Squadron. So Sir Michael was no stranger to me and I had no illusions about his expectations of the new DASB. I knew he would be a demanding and unforgiving taskmaster totally and properly dedicated to the wellbeing and operational health of the RAF. Working directly for him meant you either cut the mustard or were sacked. If CAS asked for a brief, sometimes with the shortest notice, it was provided on time, normally first thing in the morning and no matter how much midnight oil was spent in its preparation. I had a camp bed in my office, quite often used, to anticipate these tasks. More formal written briefs, prepared to a set format for high level meetings, required a precis of the paper for discussion, AFD staff comment signed off normally at two-star level and the likely lines to be taken in discussion by CDS and the other chiefs of staff (COS). The brief concluded with DASB comment that aimed to draw together the key issues with complete and compelling accuracy before recommending 'the line to take'.

The brief was then circulated to all who attended CAS's pre-meeting briefing session held in his office. Those normally involved were the vice-chief of air staff (three stars), controller aircraft (four stars), air member for supply and organisation (three or four stars), air member for personnel (three or four stars), deputy under secretary of state air (a three-star civil servant) and the appropriate assistant chiefs of Air Staff (policy, operations and operational requirements, all two-star officers) and sometimes all three together. I sat at the end of the long table opposite CAS flanked by CAS's private secretary (a civil servant) and his personal staff officer, a wing commander. After CAS opened the discussion my job was to take down the major points of debate and decision from which I fashioned CAS's speaking note for the meeting with the line to take. More often than not for a COS meeting there would be several agenda items each requiring its own separate brief and speaking note. Now and again at a pre-meeting brief one of the air officers would challenge the accuracy or relevance of a point in my written brief. Sir Michael's eyes would glitter as he said to me, "defend yourself DASB".

During my 2¼ years as DASB the major issues of COS discussion were the problems associated with service pay and the military quality of life, the replacement of the Polaris nuclear deterrent, activity levels for training and future equipment plans. Overlaying discussion of these subjects were the consequences of the sterling crisis of 1976 which resulted in cuts to the Defence Vote of £3bn over three years. It could have been much worse had not the CDS at that time, Marshal of the Royal Air Force Sir Andrew Humphrey, led the chiefs of staff to a meeting with the prime minister at which he warned that any further financial surgery to the defence budget would provoke the resignation of CDS and his three single service colleagues. Any hopes that financial pressures on the defence budget would be eased by the election of a Conservative government in May 1979 were soon dashed. Although the phased pay award of 32% previously agreed by the Labour government was immediately implemented and agreement reached on the procurement of a new nuclear weapons system, the Conservative government's monetary policy soon caused severe difficulties, particularly when equipment cost inflation was running some 5% higher than national inflation. Growing tension between the prime minister and secretary of state for defence, Mr Francis Pym, culminated in the latter's replacement by Mr John Nott in January 1980. Mr Nott arrived full of reforming zeal and determined to use his undoubted intellect to eliminate what he interpreted as waste and extravagance in the armed forces. At the same time he would set strategic priorities that could be accommodated within the defence budget. The consequence of his ambition was the publication of the Defence White Paper titled 'The Way Forward' in June 1981.

As DASB I had a privileged 'worm's eye' view of progress of the review from start to finish. By and large the Army sat on the fence safe in the knowledge that their commitments to operations in Northern Ireland and the Central Region of NATO were unassailable. It thus boiled down to a bitter argument between the RN and the RAF as to whose contribution to NATO was of the greater strategic importance. I had no informed insight to CAS's relationships with CDS and his COS colleagues, but there was no disguising bitter feelings within MoD uniformed staffs. Walking the corridors seeking to establish RN and Army views on papers for COS discussion gave an insight to the now almost traditional acrid relations between the Navy and the Air Force borne of the aircraft carrier debate, some would say battle, which had run since the end of World War II. Some staff officers in the Navy Department, knowing I was CAS's briefing officer, would not speak to me. Within the Army Department I was sometimes patronised but the price was worth paying. Helpful information was inevitably spilled to bear out an assumed superiority that owed more to unquestioned and assertive confidence in the Army's future than intelligent thought. That said, friendships with officers in both the RN and the Army were made that have withstood the test of time.

I think most of us shared a common view that the vital interests of national defence would be best served by the chiefs of staff standing shoulder to shoulder against Whitehall opponents whose initiatives were almost inevitably driven by short-term political and financial considerations. Any split opened between individual chiefs would be exploited, possibly to the disadvantage of both and certainly with a clearly defined loser which would upset the balance of national defence capabilities. On the other hand, and at that time, our single service superiors felt it necessary to take a parochial view of their responsibilities to achieve critical examination of risks in a defence budget within which defence policy owed more to the opinions of Treasury officials than military judgement. As the Nott Review progressed to its conclusion I had some sympathy as an amateur student of maritime history with the RN's position. The Army and the RAF had clearly defined commitments to NATO to substantiate their force levels declared to the Alliance. The RN's role, following withdrawal from east of Suez, concentrated on the protection of transatlantic reinforcements during the conventional phase of warfare as set out in NATO's strategy of flexible response. This narrow definition took no account of the RN's need for balanced forces in sufficient strength to satisfy our national commitment to support the Central and Northern Regions in Allied Command Europe while maintaining readiness to react to unexpected calamities elsewhere in the world. But 'unexpected' does not lend itself to objective judgement of risks when defence priorities had to be adjusted within a reduced defence budget. So I was not surprised by the secretary of state's conclusions.

The first two pillars of national defence strategy, the nuclear deterrent and home defence (which needed strengthening) remained unchanged. However, while the British contribution to NATO had hitherto been split equally between the Central Region and the East Atlantic, precedence was now to be given to the former. The practical consequence left the RN far worse off: a rundown of frigate numbers from 65 to 52, the disposal of two aircraft carriers, a reduction in nuclear-powered submarines from 20 to 17 and the closure of the dockyards at Portsmouth and Chatham. The Army were to lose 7,000 men but no units, but the RAF was to benefit from extra Phantom and Hawk squadrons for UK air defence, a one-third increase in the tanker fleet and confirmed commitment to the Tornado aircraft programme with European partners. In reaching these conclusions the secretary of state was supported by his permanent under secretary, Sir Frank Cooper, and the chief scientific advisor, Sir Ronald Mason.

Decades later the circumstances of the Cold War at that time are a fading memory. The Soviet invasion of Afghanistan in December 1979 and their deployment of SS20 missiles, highly mobile with intermediate range and targeted on Western Europe, caused growing concern. Not surprising that neither the chief of the general staff (CGS) nor CAS would give ground to the Navy's case particularly given the vulnerability of surface warships to new Soviet weapons systems. Moreover, and less subjective, their reluctance to help out the RN acknowledged the simple fact that the Army and the RAF would have to foot the bill from within their own underfunded budgets. The failure to establish a unified defence view was to lead directly to the strengthening of the chief of defence staff's (CDS) authority with a commensurate increase in the size of the Central Staffs at the expense of the single service departments. CDS would become the principal military advisor to the government and not just chairman of the chiefs of staffs committee. The committee would remain in being to provide single service advice to CDS but would lose its collective responsibility for the advice CDS gave to the government. In effect the chiefs of staff were no longer a body of strategic advice and the practice of placing financial management above professional military thought was underway.

I left the MoD on posting in April 1981 soon after John Nott had decided the future for the armed forces, a future vision that two years later was to be upset in the South Atlantic. Meanwhile, to my absolute delight I was posted to RAF Gütersloh as station commander and Harrier Force commander to take over from Mike Stear in March 1981. Mike had been PSO to CAS when I took over as DASB and we had played rugby together both before and during our time at Staff College.

I was not sorry to leave the MoD. It wasn't that I couldn't stand the heat in the kitchen, it was the aroma I found distasteful. Although some of my contemporaries flourished in Whitehall and enjoyed being at the centre of policy making, it just wasn't my cup of tea; this probably says more about my shortcomings than personal sensitivity as the thickness of my skin has never been in doubt. For 2¼ years I felt I had been walking a tightrope. No matter the strength of endeavour it seemed that my best efforts were seldom satisfactory. Sometimes I missed the kernel of a debate, sometimes my briefs were too long and sometimes too short as were the speaking notes prepared for CAS's meetings. But above all in the rarefied atmosphere of the highest levels of defence debate other shortcomings were exposed. My professional judgement and objectivity were suspect as my thinking owed more to intuition than rigorous analysis and quick-witted deliberation. While some of my weaknesses may have been self-evident from the start, others became apparent with the passage of time. I can only assume that undisputed hard work was recognised as a saving grace.

It came as no surprise that my farewell interview with CAS did not leave me with a warm feeling of a job well done. Indeed I received a stern talk on the extravagance of pre-appointment training given to station commanders designate – in my case three courses of refresher flying (Jet Provost, Hunter and Harrier), a six-week colloquial German language course (an exam pass was worth £80) and courses concerned with the handling of public and non-public accounts. CAS believed that this could easily be achieved within six months rather than the 11 I was to take. In reply I pointed out that I was doing no more than follow the air secretary's instructions. But I did not mention that I knew I was being moved earlier than necessary to make way for another group captain who the air member for personnel judged needed a high profile appointment to cement a special recommendation for promotion to air rank. In October 1982 CAS visited Gütersloh to meet and talk to Harrier pilots recently returned from the Falkland Islands. In the car going to the 3 (F) Squadron crew room CAS said that he had not forgotten the extravagant inefficiency of the time given to my preparation for station command. The worm turned and I said: "Sir, I think you think that I fixed it." "Quite right," replied CAS. Some you just can't win.

Despite leaving the MoD on a downbeat note the time ahead offered a most attractive prospect. Bags of flying to include my last delightful experience of the Hunter at RAF Brawdy, re-acquaintance with the Harrier at RAF Wittering and a full conversion onto the Puma helicopter at RAF Odiham were to be relished. And in my travels, freed from incarceration in the MoD, I would meet up with many old chums and have more time to spend with my family. All of this was most welcome and like it or not I had absorbed many lessons in Whitehall that were to prove invaluable in the years ahead, not least when I faced as CAS the next formal Strategic Defence Review launched by New Labour in 1997. Moreover, my duties had brought me into contact with a number of two-star officers who gave me cheerful confidence in the future of the service. All were well acquainted with the conduct of contemporary air operations and the pitfalls associated with the operation of the new generation of high performance aircraft. They had not only flown the aeroplanes operationally and passed the tests of TACEVAL and high level in-service scrutiny, but they recognised both the strengths and vulnerabilities of the RAF's air power. Above all they understood the men and women of the service who had inherited its future wellbeing from the World War II generation of commanders. It was indeed my good fortune that I served my time as DASB enjoying the support and understanding of such fine men as John Sutton, Paddy Hine, Ken Hayr and David Harcourt-Smith. These men and others of their generation should not be forgotten when future historians study the RAF's contribution to Cold War victory.

That said, at a time when political and economic pressures came together to threaten a reduction in the combat power of the service, Sir Michael Beetham was at the helm to steer the RAF safely through some very choppy waters. Sir Michael was never a man to court popularity but his single-minded and ruthless determination to do what was best for the RAF earned him the respect of all of us who witnessed him fight the RAF's corner. In his five years as CAS service manpower increased from 94,000 to 98,000, a vital expansion to meet growing commitments; this tells but one story of Sir Michael's effectiveness as the professional head of the service.

Living at Northwood for 4½ years gave the family stability and allowed Victoria and Douglas to start at boarding school before we returned to Germany. This was a wrench. But before they finished their secondary education we had moved a further six times and each move would have required a change of school. The older two, and eventually Harriet, all benefited hugely from continuity of education which we could not have afforded without boarding school allowance. For my part, travelling by tube for two hours for most working days fed my keen appetite for reading drawing on the resources of the MoD library in the Old War Office, a much-neglected facility. My interest in military history was generously nourished as was my appetite for commentary by such distinguished historians as Professor Sir Michael Howard – described by A.J.P. Taylor as "that rare figure, an honest historian". A collection of Sir Michael's lectures and writings published under the title *The Causes of War* remains an erudite and elegantly written examination of the complexities of war and strategic thinking, the latter being a concept that needs continual definition, and perhaps never more so than today. So I remain most grateful for the rapid response of the librarians to any request for new books. And if I acknowledge my gratitude to them, my thanks would be incomplete without reference to my secretary, Janet, whose support throughout my tour as DASB was invaluable. The job just could not have been done without her patience, skill and understanding.

So, I left Northwood for RAF Gütersloh better informed, wiser in the ways of Whitehall and having enjoyed the best part of a year which in all honesty was pure hedonism. My morale was high and I was keen to get to grips with the new job that I was determined to enjoy to the full and to be seen to enjoy it. I had now been a group captain for three years and the novelty of the rank had long worn off. I felt no compulsion for unnecessary demonstration of new-found authority and have always felt that group captains appointed to station command are the better for first completing a testing ground tour in the rank.

CHAPTER 15
RAF GÜTERSLOH

Nothing in my service career fills me with more memories, mostly happy and occasionally sad, than my 2¾ years in command of RAF Gütersloh. The airfield was a pre-war Luftwaffe base and allegedly a favourite haunt of Hermann Göring. A turret at the north-east corner of the officers' mess contained a small drinking den that housed memorabilia from the Luftwaffe's wartime occupancy. A handle, hidden under a long table, activated a hinged beam which split downwards. Legend had it that when Göring was drinking with young fighter pilots he regaled them with stories of his World War I exploits. He ended his tales with a declaration that if he was lying "let the roof fall in on my head". Hence the collapsible beam cleverly engineered by pre-war German pilots. The mechanism was still in working order and regularly exercised for the entertainment of visitors.

The airfield endured a fearful hammering in the last two years of World War II but adjacent administrative and domestic accommodation was soon repaired which allowed the RAF to occupy the base from November 1945. Thirty-seven years later when I took command Gütersloh was the only RAF operational airfield remaining east of the Rhine; at the end of World War II there had been 12. The airfield's proximity to the inner German border (IGB), only an airman's stone throw away to the east (100 kms), rendered the base vulnerable to both air attack and Soviet special forces (Spetsnaz) operations. These were significant threats given the importance of RAF Gütersloh as the main reception airfield for 1 (BR) Corps reinforcements in TTW. In essence the three in-place armoured divisions would be augmented by the arrival from the UK of 2 (Infantry) Division which would assume responsibility for the security of 1 (BR) Corps rear area. The operational importance of the airfield was given a sharper edge with the arrival of the Harrier Force and the augmentation of the Support Helicopter Force when 18 Squadron arrived, post Falklands War, in April 1983. The normal establishment of on-base aircraft was then 36 Harriers, 16 Pumas and 12 Chinooks; the four resident flying squadrons were all reinforced from the UK in TTW. No. 63 Squadron RAF Regiment with Rapier missiles provided short-range air defence

(SHORAD) against the air threat while HQ 33 Wing RAF Regiment looked after on-base ground defence training for RAF personnel. In TTW (and on exercises) the Wing HQ deployed with the Harrier Force with three field squadrons under command to provide force protection. In sum these forces presented a powerful contribution to an air/land battle in the NORTHAG area of operations.

The simultaneous off-base deployment and operation of the Harriers and helicopters was a formidable logistics challenge. The helicopters, unprotected on base, first flew out to dispersal areas as their operating sites were set up with the necessary engineering support and communications. As previously explained the Harriers remained in their hardened aircraft shelters until their war sites were ready to receive them and the supporting logistics parks had been adequately prepared and stocked. The smooth transition from routine peacetime operations to a war footing could only be achieved through regular exercising which gave additional and most welcome zest to life.

On base the simultaneous operation of Harriers, Pumas and Chinooks with such a wide variety of landing options, each requiring regular practice, was a testing task for the air traffic controllers. But there was much more to it. A miscellany of diverted aircraft from other NATO air forces were regular visitors who often arrived short of fuel demanding landing priority. RAF transport aircraft maintained a regular flow of arrivals and departures as they met Army roulement requirements for internal security duties in Northern Ireland and battle group training in Canada. Air movements squadron handled the arrival and departure of a multitude of boarding school children at holiday times. For one week each year the station hosted three air defence fighter squadrons from the RAF, the USAF and the French air force. They practised escorting air transport aircraft down three air corridors simulating access to Berlin as a political signal of Allied resolve to maintain right of entry to the city. Bold Gauntlet exercises took place in Federal Republic air space as fighter aircraft would only be sent down the corridors to Berlin for real. The station was no more than a mounting base for the exercise but the intensity of air traffic reached new highs as did the bar profits in the officers' and sergeants' messes. Finally, and by no means least, the station amenities fund (SAF) ran its own charter airline, SAFAIR, under contract with Air UK providing direct flights to and from the UK for service and civilian personnel and their families. Seat utilisation was more than 80% and the profit provided a steady revenue stream for a multitude of station activities that could not be paid for from official funding. In an average year 150,000 passengers passed through the air terminal, more people than were handled at either of the RAF's primary air transport airfields in the UK at Brize Norton and Lyneham.

Mike Stear signed over command to me at the Eberhard field site of blessed memory from my previous Harrier tour. I was immensely proud to be the first former Harrier squadron CO selected for command of the RAF Germany Harrier Force with the concept of operations by now well established and field proven. Both Harrier squadron commanders, Bob Holliday and Keith Holland, were old friends and I knew 3 and 4 Squadrons were in good hands. I had not met OC 230 Squadron, Wing Commander David Hamilton-Rump, before but I had heard that his squadron numbered amongst its aircrew some well-known 'characters' of intimidating size and physicality when it came to mess games and less legitimate activities. 'Windowing' on a Friday evening was a favourite sport not forgotten by mess members of those days. Engineering Wing, and its subordinate supply squadrons for on and off-base operations, was fully manned and well led by Wing Commander Jack McQuillan. To my delight, OC Administrative Wing was Wing Commander Duncan Herd, a fellow member of No. 76 Entry at Cranwell who was to remain with me throughout my tour.

Back on base I met OC Operations Wing, Wing Commander Paul Constable (another old chum from Hunter days), OC 33 Wing, the senior medical officer, the senior dental officer and the three padres. Even before the arrival of 18 Squadron the span of control was wide which required the ten wing commanders to share with me mutual trust and an absolute determination to give of our best. My job was to set the standard and keep everyone up to the mark recognising that we were positioned within the geographical focus of the Cold War confrontation in Central Europe – a confrontation overlaid by the threat of intercontinental nuclear exchange. Although the focus of our operational attention at Gütersloh was on the IGB, I knew full well that this focus would be kept sharply defined by re-acquaintance with vigorous and regular examination by Allied Air Forces Central Europe TACEVAL both on and off base.

Less than a month after I took command Argentine forces invaded the Falkland Islands which was to exercise an immediate and enduring influence on station activities. The first inkling of what was to come was the arrival of a signal from HQ RAF Germany asking how many of my Harrier pilots had previous air defence experience. Four admitted to having flown Lightnings and were immediately detached to RNAS Yeovilton to convert onto the Sea Harrier and then to join embarked Fleet Air Arm squadrons. Other pilots were sent back to the UK to reinforce 1 (F) Squadron and for trials flying aimed particularly at giving the Harrier GR3 a laser-guided bomb capability. Towards the end of April I was required to train up four combat teams of eight pilots each as reinforcements for the Task Force, in effect two teams from each Harrier squadron. 3 (F) Squadron was immediately recalled from Canada where the squadron was undertaking advanced operational training on Exercise Maple Flag. Led by Bob Holliday the squadron returned without in-flight refuelling support which was probably the longest staging trip ever undertaken by the Harrier Force.

During the afternoon of 7th May 63 Squadron RAF Regiment was returning to base from a field training exercise. I met the squadron commander, Squadron Leader Ian Loughborough, with the news that his squadron was to redeploy on 9th May to Southampton to join the 5 Brigade move to the Falklands. At 10:30hrs on Sunday morning I saluted the squadron as it departed in Land Rovers smack on time in immaculate order. Their Rapier fire units were left at Gütersloh and were replaced with systems drawn from UK-based squadrons before they embarked on RMS *Queen Elizabeth II* at Southampton.

Meanwhile training of Harrier combat teams proceeded apace with detachments to RNAS Yeovilton for ski-jump and deck-landing familiarisation. The Belgian air force generously flew their Mirages against our Harriers for dissimilar air combat training in our local airspace – the Mirage being the primary air-to-air threat of the Argentine air force. Operational low flying practice at 100 feet above ground level involved a lot of going and coming from Scotland as did familiarisation with new weapons-delivery profiles involving SNEB rockets and Sidewinder air-to-air missiles. The consequence of all this was that flying activity and accompanying noise went off the clock which started to provoke difficulties with the local German civic authorities. They thought we were absurd to go to war over the ownership of some sparsely populated and wind-blasted islands many thousand miles away in the South Atlantic. As far as I was concerned they could think what they liked, but as station commander I had a duty to sustain good relations with our German neighbours.

To this end I invited all the political and local government bigwigs to a briefing ostensibly to put over the British government's point of view and to tell them what I could about our activities within the constraints of operational security. The real purpose, however, was to make the point that continuing bellyaching about our station functions was unbecoming of a NATO ally in whose country, and within Stadt Gütersloh in particular, the station annually spent something in the order of DM 50 million. This figure was calculated by a civil servant accountant from Joint Headquarters (JHQ) Rheindahlen who I had invited to go through all our books to estimate the station's contribution to the local economy. The DM 50 million was the approximate sum of personal expenditure of 3,500 service personnel and their families plus a multitude of local contracts covering everything from rat-catching to laundry. I suggested mischievously that should flying operations become untenable our departure would leave a considerable hole in local pockets. The message was received loud and clear and next year when the station was twice besieged by thousands of anti-nuclear protestors (more about this later) we enjoyed considerable help and support from local authorities.

The summer of 1982 brought with it an unwelcome difficulty. The Harrier Force was declared to NATO as 36 aircraft with 52 pilots. As conflict started and preparations to reinforce the Task Force accelerated I asked HQ RAF Germany to seek MoD approval for a down-declaration to reflect the reality of Harrier Force availability. This was refused at some level in the MoD but without acknowledgement let alone explanation. No-one has since accepted responsibility for the decision. The inevitable happened one early morning in June. The TACEVAL team arrived and I authorised the sirens to sound and the recall of personnel living off base. The process of securing the station and generating aircraft in an anti-armour weapons fit started. In the hardened combat operations centre (COC) a quick count confirmed that of my 52 Harrier pilots only 24 were available. Nine were junior pilots not yet combat ready while another three were US exchange officers from the Navy, Marine Corps and Air Force. Several aircraft were away on the 'navalisation modification programme' and both squadrons were also missing significant numbers of engineers. But most fortuitously the TACEVAL team chief was a Canadian air force colonel I knew well. In a quiet room in the COC we struck a deal that if the station generated 24 aircraft in the stipulated 12 hours and if I could put a pilot in each one of them for start-up and taxi he would call it quits and ask no questions. The target was achieved and the RAF is indebted to Colonel Morrison. Others I knew at HQ AAFCE would have enjoyed roasting us to our national and service embarrassment.

The end of June was marked by tragedy. I had decided it was necessary to deploy the remnants of the Harrier Force on a field exercise principally for the training benefit of the non-combat-ready pilots. On 28th June I flew a Harrier into a newly-established site in the Bergen-Hohne ranges in north Germany. From there I drove across to the Forward Wing Operations Centre (FWOC) which had been perfectly set up by Squadron Leader Peter Day – the first man to achieve 3,000 hours on the Harrier – who was the FWOC executive, in essence my chief of staff. The next day Keith Holland flew out to the site to say farewell to 4 (AC) Squadron pilots and ground crew who would remain at Gütersloh when he led his team back to the UK for pre-deployment essential training. Keith phoned me at the FWOC to tell me all was well on the site and said goodbye. The next call I received, ten minutes later, reported that Keith had hit some trees on take-off and crashed. No parachute was seen. A few minutes later came confirmation that Keith had been killed. This was a heart-rending tragedy for his family and an appalling loss to his squadron which had flourished under Keith's command. Keith was big in build, big in brainpower and with a larger-than-life personality. Quick wits, infectious good humour and scrupulous decency hallmarked his leadership which was of the highest quality. Many others far away from Gütersloh mourned his death as I did.

The next day all deployed units returned to base as the site had to be secured for Board of Inquiry examination. The circumstances of the most sudden and unexpected death of such a respected and popular CO cast a pall over the squadron. A steadying influence was needed and forthcoming in the person of Major Charlie Davis, the US Marine Corps exchange officer. His training and operational experience had fashioned a hard nut but one whose disciplined behaviour, sympathetic but unsentimental, set a steadfast example of the primacy of duty over personal emotion. Keith's funeral was held at Gütersloh and his body repatriated for burial in the Wittering village church graveyard. Angela, Keith's wife, and their five young children returned home soon afterwards borne there by a wave of sympathy and solace shared amongst their many friends in Germany and the UK. Angela and her children remain close friends to this day.

Wing Commander Tony McKeon was refreshing on the Harrier prior to taking command of 3 (F) Squadron from Bob Holliday. The latter's tour was extended and Tony came to Gütersloh much earlier than planned to take over 4 (AC) Squadron. In the circumstances of the time there could not have been a better man for the job and I was delighted to welcome him back to Gütersloh.

The summer of 1982 exerted sustained pressure on the station and I must acknowledge my debt to HQ RAF Germany. Air Marshal Sir Jock Kennedy and his deputy, Air Vice-Marshal John Sutton, were similarly supportive and encouraging, while my primary staff contacts, Group Captain Nigel Walpole and Wing Commander Jock Heron, both old friends, did their utmost to protect their station from those who would not recognise that while Gütersloh was facing a substantive threat from the east, it was participating in and supporting a war thousands of miles to the south-west. Victory in the Falklands, achieved against the odds and at considerable strategic risk, did not relieve the load on the Harrier Force. Soon after the Argentine surrender, 1 (F) Squadron set up a Harrier operating site at Port Stanley airfield before being relieved by the first 3 (F) Squadron combat team. Tented accommodation close to the centre of the airfield adjacent to a minefield in the middle of the South Atlantic winter did not make for comfortable living. Work started immediately to prepare the airfield for the arrival of Phantoms to provide air defence against the lingering threat posed by the Argentine air force. Meanwhile, Harrier GR3s, armed with Sidewinder missiles and cannon, sustained QRA in the air defence role. Any hope that this commitment would end with the arrival of Phantoms was dashed when Mrs Thatcher paid her first visit to the islands. She noticed the Phantoms were not flying because of a howling crosswind. She asked how air defence was being maintained. The Harriers with their V/STOL capability can still operate was the reply which condemned the Harrier Force to three more years of Falklands detachments until the new airfield at Mount Pleasant became operational in 1985.

This new task plus the Harrier Force's continuing commitment to manning 1417 Flight in Belize, started in 1975, required the most careful management to ensure Harrier Force declarations to the Central Region and the north and south flanks of NATO could be met. Some very good rugby players at Gütersloh gave up the game to avoid the possibility of injury. The substitution at short notice of a replacement pilot would have an immediate knock-on effect on the detachment programme for a year ahead causing disruption to training and the supervision of flying let alone family life. Maintaining the roulement of pilots and ground crew while sustaining declaration levels in Germany was a permanent problem throughout my next 2½ years as Harrier Force commander.

In July 1982 I asked to visit our detachments – 3 (F) Squadron and 63 Squadron RAF Regiment – but permission was refused because too many COs from all three services were demanding their right to visit detached personnel. In early December, having planned my Christmas programme which involved a number of engagements with the local German community, I was sent to the Falklands with 24 hours' notice. My task was to examine the size and capabilities of the Harrier detachment and to make recommendations for a sustained presence. It took longer than planned to get from Ascension Island to Port Stanley. On the first attempt the Hercules in-flight refuelling probe snapped off whilst in contact with a Hercules tanker. Five hours later we were back at Ascension. The next day 14 hours in the Hercules with three in-flight refuels brought passengers and cargo safely to Port Stanley airfield. The Hercules transport air bridge supported by Victor and Hercules tankers continued for another three years, and those involved have never received the public acclaim they deserved for an outstanding achievement reflecting the very highest standards of professionalism and flying skills.

I stayed at Port Stanley airfield for five days sharing a tent with Tony McKeon who had taken command of 4 (AC) Squadron in August. While there I flew as Tony's wing man on combat air patrol the Phantoms were grounded, crosswind! – which gave me a better informed view of the current operational task and what had been achieved by the task force, particularly those who fought the land battle and the seamen, RN and Merchant Navy, who took such a battering in Falkland Sound from the Argentine air force. Despite the weather, four seasons in a day ranging from bright sunshine to blizzards, the detachment was in very good heart. When I spoke to all ranks I had to tell them that Tony McKeon was required back at Gütersloh for operational reasons. Knowing full well his reluctance to return only halfway through his detachment, it was a good thing that I was able to explain more fully the reasons both to him personally and his men.

With the information to complete my task carefully noted I started the homebound leg as the only passenger aboard a Hercules. I made myself comfortable on the lower bunk at the back of the flight deck as the aircraft was settled at cruising altitude for the long flog back to Ascension Island. Just before midnight some movement woke me from a shallow slumber. The air loadmaster appeared with a cake topped by an array of burning candles to wish the flight engineer a very happy 21st birthday. Congratulations were offered by the two pilots, the navigator and the air loadmaster, the candles blown out and the cake cut as the crew, accompanied by a tone-deaf group captain, sang 'Happy Birthday'. That birthday party under a canopy of the brightest stars I had ever seen and alone in the sky high above the South Atlantic Ocean remains a surreal and most happy memory of aircrew kinship. With the cake consumed the captain told the flight engineer to take a nap on the top bunk. He was soon fast asleep. From there on the crew's aim was to complete the trip without waking him. This was achieved until the wheels touched the runway at Ascension Island. I have never seen anyone wake with such alacrity. He was off the bunk and strapped into his seat within a couple of seconds and before he was properly awake.

That afternoon I continued my journey to Brize Norton by VC10 and arrived in time for a quick nap before being called at 0345 next morning for the onwards flight to RAF Wildenrath, again on a VC10. I was looking forward to getting my head down for another snooze before attending a conference for station commanders chaired by a new deputy commander that kicked off at 1100hrs. The aircraft landed at 0700hrs and I was met by the Wildenrath station commander, Group Captain John Allison. "I am looking forward to your presentation on aircrew fatigue," he said. This was the first I had heard of the task as the agenda had not been set before my departure, but at least I could talk about it from the passenger viewpoint. More seriously, I was concerned about the continuing high pressure on the force, aircrew and engineers alike, as there had been no trimming of our in-theatre commitments for 1983. None was forthcoming.

Lessons learned from the Falklands War were to shape future Harrier Force training. Pilots returning to Gütersloh from the conflict and others posted to the RAF Germany Harrier Force from 1 (F) Squadron had experienced a unique intensity of operational flying and the disagreeable consequences of a convoluted chain of command. For the first time the RAF had used smart weapons to good effect in the form of laser-guided bombs, with ground forces designation of targets, which may have influenced the Argentinian decision to surrender unexpectedly soon. The deployment of reinforcement Harriers direct from Ascension Island to the task force was bold in concept and brave in execution. Four Harrier GR3s, flying separately in pairs on consecutive days, took their final refuel 1,000 nms from the Falklands and pressed on south. The first pair, Squadron Leaders Mike Beach and Murdo Mcleod, were met by a Sea Harrier flown by John Leeming, also a 3 (F) Squadron pilot, then flying with 809 Naval Air Squadron. Beach and Mcleod were led to HMS *Hermes* for their first deck landings at the end of their ten-hour transit. Many other experiences were given a full airing at a Harrier symposium held at Gütersloh in November 1983. Sir Paddy Hine chaired the meeting which was attended by RN and RAF pilots as well as representatives from other arms who had contributed to victory. A happy and memorable professional occasion lasting two days also provided a spirited test of social stamina. All this was more than 30 years ago but I have never forgotten Mike Beach's answer to my question "What was the most important operational lesson you learned?" "Never fly over the Scots Guards," came the immediate reply.

On 20th April that year I flew a Puma to RV with the first three 18 (B) Squadron Chinooks, led by Wing Commander Tony Stables, en route to their new home at Gütersloh. We arrived as a composite formation which marked the start of much-needed augmentation of RAF Germany's support helicopter force. 18 Squadron's new hangar was huge by any standard. It could house all 12 Chinooks and was painted pink. I was told that a Mr Gay, who worked for the ministry of public buildings and works, claimed this was the best camouflage colour for such a sizeable building. HQ took some time to accept that in reasonable weather the hangar was clearly visible from ten miles or more. It cost £18,000 (at 1983 prices) to have it repainted in conventional toned-down green.

18 Squadron's Chinooks included Bravo November of Falklands fame. The helicopter was airborne when *Atlantic Conveyor* was sunk by an Exocet missile; three other Chinooks went down with the ship. In the following three weeks BN flew 110 hours without servicing and with a growing number of unserviceabilities. More than 2,000 troops were carried along with 550 tons of freight not to mention a similar number of prisoners of war. Squadron Leader Dick Langworthy, aircraft captain throughout, was awarded a most well-deserved DFC. Sadly, and having settled into his new home at Gütersloh, Dick returned to the Falklands for a second time where he died. It was a privilege to have known Dick Langworthy, an exceptional pilot, a very brave man and a true gentleman.

That summer I slipped a disc and spent a week in the RAF Wegberg hospital close to Rheindahlen undergoing hydro-physiotherapy. In the evenings I was entertained by a stream of friends visiting from HQ each bearing a bottle of booze, strictly against hospital regulations. Luckily I had my own room but had to plead with my chums, particularly Nigel Walpole and brother-in-law Dan Baily, not to bring refills as my bedside locker was crammed to over-flowing. Kindly sisters and nurses turned a blind eye to this ill-discipline. I was discharged with some good and bad news. After my back was X-rayed I asked the orthopaedic consultant to have a look at my right ankle as 20 years previously, following its third break, I had been warned off skiing. The out-come was clearance to learn to ski – sensibly – as the quality of boots and bindings now gave far greater protection against serious injury. On the other hand I was banned from flying on ejector seats for five months. However, this was turned to some advantage as it gave me time to learn far more about support helicopter operations and to achieve captaincy on the Chinook while simultaneously keeping a friendly eye on Harrier Force activities.

Flying the Chinook and Puma also allowed me to participate in the 6th Airmobile Brigade trial. After satisfactory conclusion of the trial the airmobile role was transferred to 24 Brigade within the UK-based 2 Division. Although 230 Squadron met their airmobile trial commitments with a full complement of aircraft, 18 Squadron, like the Harriers, sustained a Chinook detachment in the Falklands which inevitably reduced home-base availability of aircraft; sometimes this was increased by short-notice deployments such as support for operations in the Lebanon in 1983/84. In very quick time the Chinook, which entered front-line service with 18 Squadron in February 1982, demon-strated capabilities that would remain a vital component of most national military operations long into the future.

Early in my tour I went to Air Movements to introduce myself, as the new station commander, to Lieutenant General Sir Nigel Bagnall, commander 1 (BR) Corps. The general thanked me and said I was not to bother to meet him again as he was such a frequent passenger in and out of the station – advice I happily ignored – but would I please arrange with his military assistant an office call in his HQ at Bielefeld, a relatively short distance away the other side of the Teutoburger Wald. A date and time was agreed with the MA, Lieutenant Colonel Seymour Munro, the son of Air Commodore Sir Hector Munro, the then Honorary Inspector General of the Royal Auxiliary Air Force.

A week later I walked into the general's outer office and was immediately aware of raised voices next door. Seymour said he was afraid that I had not come at a particularly good time. After a while the door to the general's office opened and out scuttled a brigadier in a state of some distress. Sir Nigel stood in the doorway following the brigadier's departure with a baleful stare. He then noticed me huddled in a corner. "Come in," he said and pointing to a chair added "sit down". It was an order not an invitation. Sitting nervously on the edge of the chair I waited for a welcoming pleasantry and waited in vain. What seemed a long silence was abruptly broken when the general fixed me with his penetrating blue eyes and asked without preamble: "How should the Harrier Force be used in war?" If nothing else I was now on familiar ground and replied that the Harrier Force was a cudgel not a rapier. "Explain," said Sir Nigel.

For the next three minutes or so I outlined my view that flying a pair of Harriers under a forward air controller's control against at best a comparatively small grouping of Soviet armour was a waste of effort and capability; this was standard fare on most NATO exercises. Once deployed off base I would far prefer the force to lie doggo in its war locations, if necessary for several days, waiting for the enemy's armour to be canalized by NORTHAG operations or geographic features into large concentrations unable to deploy tactically. That would be the time to launch 24 Harriers each armed with five anti-armour cluster bombs to achieve the maximum concentration of force in time and space. The atmosphere in the office was transformed and I was introduced to Sir Nigel's thinking on manoeuvre warfare. A captivating conversation followed with the general patiently answering my rather elementary questions; this concluded with Sir Nigel asking about my operational concerns and if he could help. I replied that warning time apart I was worried about the level of Royal Engineers' support so critical to the timely preparation of our war sites. There was only one field squadron – No. 10 based in Mansergh Barracks, Gütersloh. The arrival of 38 Engineer Regiment from Yorkshire was a critical component in the deployment plan and the possibility of delay concerned me. A second independent Royal Engineers field squadron based nearby was immediately assigned to Harrier Force support until the arrival of 38 Engineer Regiment.

Following on from this most helpful outcome I was invited to all 1 (BR) Corps study periods. I was given a privileged insight to how Sir Nigel was breaking the paralysis of NATO's operational thinking about how best to absorb the shock of a massed Soviet tank assault. My own thinking was elevated from the tactical to the operational level of war as I listened to the arguments supporting the abandonment of linear defence and attritional warfare. While this would necessarily require Federal Republic territory to be yielded to the invader, the manoeuvre of ground forces at divisional and brigade level could exploit tactical opportunities as the Corps withdrew to fall-back positions. These would be killing zones with the enemy prey to synchronised attack from ground and air forces.

When Sir Nigel moved onwards and upwards to take command of NORTHAG he succeeded in persuading the Germans to adopt his concept of operations which initiated a re-write of the general deployment plan. Such was his professionalism, his strength of character and his leadership which inspired respect and admiration from all quarters, national and allied, in Germany during some of the darkest days of the Cold War.

During my tour the Harrier Force deployed on five full field exercises where I benefited from the support of two exceptional FWOC executives. Peter Day was replaced halfway through my tour by Squadron Leader Keith Grumbley, another very experienced Harrier operator who had led the first 3 Squadron detachment to the Falklands. On deployment we shared a Marshall cabin, a box-bodied vehicle protected against biological and chemical threats and theoretically nuclear attack. The cabin also housed an operations officer who supervised four operations clerks in direct communication with the flying sites; the transmission and recording of accurate information on aircraft tasking and availability was a critical component of force command. The force engineer and OC 33 Wing were accommodated in their own cabins and we regularly exercised in closed-down conditions wearing not just our NBC suits but respirators as well which didn't help telephonic communications. The spring exercise of 1983 had a conspicuous first. On base I had noticed that the female ops clerks in the COC were far better at their job than their male counterparts. I sought permission for them to deploy with the Harrier Force and HQ RAF Germany, ducking the issue, asked me to submit my request directly to the head of the Women's Royal Air Force. Subject to certain conditions concerning their tented accommodation and personal security, Air Commodore Helen Renton agreed my proposal. Given the status of women today in the armed forces and their contribution to operations in the three services all this may sound rather quaint, but it was a first step in the right direction, certainly for the RAF.

Once deployed and ready to go Harrier Force tasking was decided by the commander 2nd Allied Tactical Air Force (2ATAF) who was co-located with commander NORTHAG in the war HQ at Maastricht. The force could be tasked to give offensive air support to one or all of the four national Corps which constituted NORTHAG. But there was a problem. Once the Harrier Force had broken cover from its war sites located relatively close to the forward edge of the battle area, the Harrier's 60-minute airborne/turnaround cycle and cockpit tasking set a pace that was beyond the capacity of the HQ operations staff. In their defence the counter air battle, both offensive and defensive, against Warsaw Pact air forces to gain at least local air superiority required their closest attention and energy. The immediate answer to the Harrier conundrum was simple: direct tasking from a Corps Air Support Operations Centre (ASOC) and preferably 1 (BR) Corps within which there was an RAF team well experienced in both Harrier and support helicopter operations. Direct tasking with one-to-one communications to the Corps ASOC was very much my preferred modus operandi. But the problem of how to form up a large attack package – 24 aircraft – flying from six dispersed locations had so far eluded solution.

The answer, worked out with Peter Day and Keith Grumbley, was simple although success was critically dependent on the precision of timing and the flying accuracy of section leaders. The transmission of an execute order from the FWOC gave each site an exact time to launch its aircraft to fly in an agreed order to a RV so that each aircraft section arrived in a pre-determined sequence. Minimum risk transit routes to the target through the Corps air defences would have been agreed beforehand with the Corps air defence commander co-located with the ASOC. The system worked on peacetime exercises and I very much hoped that if it had to be used for real against slow moving and bunched up enemy armour, the ferocity of the attack concentrated in time and space would have overwhelmed Soviet air defence weaponry. Although the intention satisfied four of our national principles of war – offensive action, surprise, concentration of force and economy of effort – I doubt we would have got away with it scot free.

The pinnacle of training activity was Exercise Lionheart held in September 1984. The simultaneous generation and deployment of the Harrier and Support Helicopter Forces to off-base sites was closely followed by round-the-clock air transport operations in and out of Gütersloh as the full-scale reinforcement of 1 (BR) Corps was exercised. The troops arrived in RAF transport aircraft supported by British Airways jumbo jets and immediately boarded trains operating from the station down to the Corps assembly point in the Sennelager training area. I saw none of this prodigious activity as I had moved out to the FWOC leaving the station in the very capable hands of OC Operations Wing, Wing Commander Al Cleaver, an old friend from my 3 Squadron days. HQ Allied Air Forces Central Europe (AAFCE) had predictably seized the opportunity to TACEVAL the Harrier Force in the field as part of Lionheart. This was to be my Harrier Force swansong and I wanted to make the most of it.

We had operated under full field exercise conditions for the first week when I returned to Gütersloh to give the 'in brief' to the 170 members of the TACE-VAL team. The purpose of the brief was for me to give a few words of welcome and to set out any exercise constraints that applied; the fewer the better and normally there was little else to say except to remind the team that the RAF Police were exercise-exempt. On this occasion I looked a mess as I had been in my NBC suit for a week without the pleasure of a bath. The weather had been typically wet and cold and I was splattered with mud. Casting an eye over the spruce throng in front of me I gently warned them that site conditions at all Harrier Force locations were far removed from the conventional airfield environment. They would be well advised to visit the local Markauf to buy gum boots and wet-weather gear. The evaluation went well and the Force had considerable success in defending itself against French paras enlisted as our ground enemy. Each morning the prisoner-of-war cage at the FWOC was full. Eventually the penny dropped. Our enemy had discovered that night time capture guaranteed a full English fry-up for breakfast before their release back into action. Soviet special forces would not have been so obliging.

The TACEVAL also marked the first time that the FWOC had been required to site-move after an exercise inject that Soviet recce aircraft had fixed its position. With key personnel from the operations, intelligence and logistics staffs I shot off to 4 Squadron's primary site leaving Keith Grumbley to execute the move to the FWOC step-up site some 20 km distant. Transfer of command was well practised with Tony McKeon taking command of the force until I arrived with the FWOC team. At about midnight I heard the FWOC was up and running and ready to assume command; there had been some delay because of communications problems. My team immediately set off in Land Rovers escorted by armoured fighting vehicles (AFV) of the RAF Regiment. In the pitch black I am afraid that the corporal leading the small convoy made a navigational error which brought our cavalcade to a grinding halt in a cul-de-sac in the small German town of Hovelhof. The corporal dismounted from his AFV, came to my Land Rover window and asked rather rudely I thought, "who's in charge of this ******* shambles?" "I thought you were," I replied politely. The corporal recognised my voice if not my face that was striped with camouflage cream. "Good morning Sir," he said making a rapid attitudinal adjustment. After this brief exchange – the tale was subsequently subject to some exaggeration by witnesses – we got on famously as with position fixed we set off again leaving behind a bewildered audience gaping from bedroom windows. Fortunately, the TACEVAL team were all safely tucked up in their hotel beds at the time.

Four days later with the TACEVAL completed the Harrier Force returned to Gütersloh. After a quick bath and brush up I sallied forth into the field again to visit the SH squadrons that were to remain deployed for another week to assist the recovery of Army units to their home bases. Both squadrons had enjoyed a busy and successful exercise under the leadership of Wing Commanders Tony Stables (18 Squadron) and Rob Turner (230 Squadron). I was particularly pleased when the Harrier and SH forces were safely back on base without any casualties or loss of equipment. The station itself, under Al Cleaver's command during my absence with the Harrier Force, had successfully resisted all 'enemy' efforts to disrupt the flow of reinforcements while incidental damage to the airfield facilities caused by jumbo jets was soon repaired. In sum the station made a major contribution to the success of the largest exercise British forces held in Germany during the Cold War years.

Lionheart '84 was my last full exercise as Harrier Force commander and my ninth TACEVAL when on-base exercises were included. Once again the force was awarded top ratings across the board and I was very proud of this achievement.

During my two tours with the RAF Germany Harrier Force I hosted many visitors. Once senior Army officers got over their surprise at seeing the RAF sloshing around in the mud all carrying personal weapons, interest in our capabilities, especially weapons and sortie generation rates, sparked searching questions and professional debate. Visitors from Allied air forces were simply fascinated by the Harrier and how we had adapted to a unique concept of operations. Sadly, but with one notable exception, most politicians seemed only really happy when posing for photos. Very few asked intelligent questions and those that did were not minded to probe our vulnerabilities. The majority struck me as rather arrogant and disinterested. The exception was, predictably, Mrs Thatcher who after the Falklands War wanted to see the force in action. In September 1983 the prime minister arrived by helicopter at Eberhard to follow a programme similar to that arranged for the Duke of Edinburgh's visit in 1975. The programme had been agreed by Air Marshal Sir Paddy Hine who had succeeded Sir Jock Kennedy as our C-in-C.

From the start of my introductory briefing it was clear that Mrs Thatcher had done her homework. Her questions revealed an understanding of our concept of operations and she honed in on our vulnerability to chemical attack and the resilience of our logistics support. It was a stimulating session before we watched four Harriers emerge from their hides and take off in rapid succession. I told Mrs Thatcher that she would meet the pilots in 20 minutes time. After chatting to our engineers and soldiers she watched the four aircraft vertically land on the MEXE pad and quickly taxi back to their hides. As we moved forward to meet the pilots I mentioned that all four had only recently returned from a Falklands detachment. As I introduced the pilots there was a sudden and remarkable transformation in her disposition. Previously serious, focused and impatiently energetic, Mrs Thatcher had given me no feeling of warmth let alone empathy. But then, quite suddenly, an attractive woman glowed with flattering admiration and became quite flirtatious. The pilots, all flight lieutenants, rapidly overcame any jitters at the prospect of meeting their formidable prime minister and it was with some difficulty that I eventually persuaded her that she had to move on if she was to be on time at her next destination. Two later meetings with the prime minister were to give me further insights into the magnetism of her extraordinary personality.

My station commander predecessors had put considerable effort into the important duty of establishing good relations with the local German community. Strong links had been forged with civil authorities, representative bodies – both cultural and sporting – and local industries which included Miele (electrical white goods), Bertlesmans (publishing) and Claas (agricultural machinery). The Anglo-German club was a flourishing society despite the constant drip of noise complaints. The station's contribution to the German economy and national security was generally welcomed. There was, however, a strong anti-nuclear movement which vigorously opposed the deployment into the Central Region of Pershing and Cruise missiles. In March 1984 the C-in-C, Sir Paddy Hine, hosted at Gütersloh a visit by the defence committee of the Bundestag. Group Captain Nigel Walpole and I gave the briefings which covered 2ATAF operations and RAF Germany's contribution. The C-in-C insisted we spoke in German. A few days afterwards in the late afternoon the main entrance to the station was blocked by a large crowd of anti-nuclear demonstrators. Wags had it that the Walpole/Johns briefing in German was the last straw of provocation. Whatever, it was a miserable afternoon for a demo so I got catering squadron to serve the protestors with afternoon tea. This caused some amusement in the local media and crash gates were used for entry to and departure from the station. But when the demonstration dispersed I was left in no doubt that the protestors would return to block all entries to the station.

A few months later several thousand came back on a Sunday with the aim to stop flying on Monday morning. The German police, accommodated beforehand on station, were very quick to snuff out aggressive attempts to penetrate perimeter fencing and those who would not move to make way for a service vehicle leaving the station were treated roughly. Overnight there was stalemate, but I had arranged for the display pilots to fly their sequences starting with the Harrier at 0800 hrs on Monday morning to be followed by the Puma and the Chinook. As station commander I was personally responsible for regular checks on the quality and safety of display flying. As the Harrier did its stuff the morale of the protestors suffered a heavy blow and within an hour the crowds had started to melt away leaving the station to get on with its business.

Although the protests were demonstrations from the Left I witnessed an unusual example of counter-feeling from the Right. In June 1984 the town of Harsewinkel held its annual Shutzenfest – a tradition going back to the 17th century when the people of Nord Rhine Westphalia endured the savagery of the Thirty Years War. Each village and larger conurbation selected a military leader to command their defences against onslaught from either side. Candidates for command had to demonstrate compelling skill at arms. Three hundred and fifty years later Shutzenfest was a carnival occasion with competition confined to a shooting match. A small bore rifle was fired by each competitor in turn at a wooden bird suspended in a tree. The competitor who finally knocked it down was Koenig (king) for the year. As an invited competitor this was a destiny I was keen to avoid as it entailed considerable private expenditure let alone time. With the Koenig selected, a parade followed where I shared the saluting dais with the Burgermeister. When our RAF Regiment Squadron marched smartly past exercising the station's Freedom of Harsewinkel there followed a shambolic multitude of young people waving flowers with some carrying anti-nuclear placards. Towards the end of the procession came a group, some 20 strong, of much older men. Thirty yards or so from the dais an order was snapped and they passed by in a clearly recognisable goosestep with a smart eyes left. Thirty yards further on there was another order and they went back to a casual stroll with much waving to the crowd. At the end of the parade I entered the beer tent and immediately saw the group sitting at a nearby table. Some I recognised as locally employed civilians on the station. Their leader invited me to join them for a glass of beer. Sitting down I asked them what that was all about. "We wanted to show you that some of us have not forgotten how to be soldiers," replied the leader. I asked no further questions lest I would be embarrassed by the answers.

Sometime earlier I had sat next to the Burgermeister at dinner. He told me about the destruction inflicted on the locality by Allied bombs missing the airfield. In turn I asked him if he had served during the war. "Yes," he replied, "in late 1944 aged 17 I was given a choice of enlisting in either the Waffen-SS or the Navy. I chose the Navy which was a good thing because we didn't have any ships left." Much laughter but I had previously heard that the north-west of Westphalia had been a prime recruiting area for the Waffen-SS.

Many other dealings with town and state officials were generally good humoured, albeit my attempts to converse in German were kindly brushed aside as the majority spoke excellent English. If the subject of discussion was sufficiently serious with no room for misunderstanding both sides used Frau Gerda Lohmeyer, the station interpreter. Gerda was indefatigable in furthering Anglo-German relations to the benefit of both communities. She had an encyclopaedic knowledge of the station that was sometimes evident in her translation of my answers to questions. Fortunately I understood sufficient German to recognise Gerda's embellishments which required me to rein in gently her enthusiasm. But enthusiasm is forgivable, indifference inexcusable.

With all the benefit of hindsight I can now recognise that at Gütersloh my talent for good luck had re-emerged. Sir Paddy Hine was C-in-C for the greater part of the tour with Air Commodore David Brook the senior air staff officer. David, a friend for many years, was the CO of 20 Squadron at Wildenrath when I took command of 3 Squadron. We had served together under Sir Paddy when he was force commander so I knew that when problems arose I could speak to superiors who understood the hazards that were part and parcel of Harrier deployed operations.

Make no mistake, flying a single-engine high performance jet aircraft out of a small field and then returning to land on a metallic square some 70 ft by 70 ft contained an element of risk much higher than that found in conventional flying throughout the spectrum of military aviation – save perhaps for night landings on an aircraft carrier. The Harrier Force flourished because the majority of young pilots were the best in the service and they soon warmed to the exhilaration and unique challenge of off-base flying. Pride in achievement and membership of a unique group operating a remarkable aeroplane bred self-confidence and team spirit throughout all elements of the force. Junior officers and junior NCOs were presented with testing conditions to prove their leadership potential and many grasped the opportunity.

As station commander I soon recognised that support helicopter operations required skills not too dissimilar from those taken for granted in the Harrier Force. Flying and navigating a large helicopter at 50 feet above ground level for a concealed approach and departure to and from a six-figure grid reference was an exacting task. When soldiers ask to be landed at a precise location that was exactly where they wanted to arrive. The standard hand signal on landing to the section commander indicating 'north' to assist map orientation was pretty useless if he wasn't where he expected to be. Beyond the practicalities of the flying job, which required close crew co-operation and trust between pilots and crewmen, off-base operations presented similar tests of leadership to those I was familiar with in the Harrier Force. Perhaps not altogether surprising that during my tour as station commander I had serving under command a future CAS and two other future air chief marshals. Two other officers went on to achieve the rank of air marshal, six became air vice-marshals and five more reached one-star rank. As the OC 3 (F) Squadron I can add to this tally of junior officers under command another future CAS, two air vice-marshals and two air commodores. The majority were pilots but the total included an engineering officer, a supply officer and two officers from the administrative branch.

The natural inclination of station commanders is to focus their attention on flying activities and there can be no doubt that regular flying with the squadrons is an essential and enjoyable element of station command. To this end I retained currency as aircraft captain on the Harrier, Puma and Chinook to the end of my tour. But a balance needs to be struck between benevolent oversight and unnecessary intrusion – on the one hand demonstrating interest and confidence in subordinates, on the other unwelcome disturbance of matters that should be left to squadron commanders. There is also the danger, no matter the temptation, that too much time spent with the squadrons leaves insufficient to devote to the vital work of administration.

As a flight cadet at Cranwell I had learned that administration was a principle of war. In recent years administration had given away to sustainability which placed more emphasis on the importance of sound logistics as a pre-requisite for the success of any operation. But the new definition did not overlook the significance of "sustenance of personnel in moral as well as physical terms". Although my Administrative Wing was often the butt of aircrew teasing and occasionally misinformed provocation, the contribution of Wing Commander Duncan Herd and his team to the welfare of all ranks and their families was quite simply outstanding. To solve a problem of chronic overcrowding of junior ranks on base barrack block accommodation, 400 extra married quarters/hirings were taken on charge which meant that married airmen could move directly into their new home on arrival rather than having to wait several months in barrack blocks. This was the consequence of Duncan Herd's unremitting pressure which ultimately convinced a visiting minister of the need. The standard of single-airman accommodation was vastly improved while the station amenities fund (SAF) under Duncan's chairman-ship generated an annual income of DM 200,000 from SAFAIR, the ski shop, the bowling alley and the video library. Caravans bought by SAF and located in the Black Forest, Austria and close to Venice also contributed to the income stream through holiday lettings to service families. Administration of these activities, all constituting secondary duties, was undertaken by officers not liable for short-notice detachment, principally those involved in administrative duties. SAF provided the wherewithal for a huge span of off-duty activities ranging from tae kwon do to gliding. Apart from agreeing and endorsing planned SAF expenditure all I had to do was to take an interest and show my appreciation of the unsung heroes of SAF as well as giving them total support for their commitment to the overall wellbeing of the station and its people.

A RAF station is a microcosm of the service with its three-wing structure bringing together the functional elements that generate air power. While the job of a station commander is to provide leadership to meet the operational tasks, the harmonisation of operations, engineering and administration requires a steady hand, an open mind and clarity of purpose. Disciplinary lines have to be drawn in the sand and the consequences of straying over them clearly understood without the deployment of 'fun detectors' to stifle robust behaviour and the humour which are part and parcel of service life.

Gütersloh provided me with opportunities to exercise independence of thought and action. For example, I banned the sale of alcohol in all messes and clubs over lunchtime; this reflected my concern about young airman technicians coming on duty and having a quick pint or two before dispersing to hardened aircraft shelters. HQ RAF Germany thought I was losing my marbles as those going off duty would be denied a drink until the evening, but I had discovered that my worry was also a major concern among the warrant officers who had the most dealings with manpower on the station. They backed me to the hilt. There were no exceptions to the rule and I took some small pleasure from observing the reaction of senior visitors to the station when offered a tomato juice before lunch. Independence of thought is all well and good when backed by sound judgement which requires a capacity to think outside the confines of previous experience, a willingness to evaluate other points of view and the aptitude and patience to analyse all possible solutions before making a final decision. This process must avoid both dogmatism and self-interest if the decision, no matter how unpopular it may be, is to be recognised as honest and not the offspring of personal ambition. I cannot claim by any stroke of imagination infallible judgement, but I will claim that some of my errors of judgement, particularly concerning individuals, were at least sincere in their assessment.

At the start of the tour my ambition was to enjoy the experience and responsibility. For most of the time it was fun and I had no difficulty in sustaining my cheerfulness and sense of humour. This was important because I had long since decided through hard-earned experience that no-one enjoyed working for a miserable bugger no matter the personal satisfaction he derived from a job well done. I was in no hurry to leave but recognised that after more than 2½ years I was becoming too set in my ways. At a standard morning briefing I was discussing with the wing commanders a long-standing problem to do with road traffic control both on and off station. A newcomer proposed a solution but I cut him off saying that we had tried that two years earlier; it hadn't worked then and it wouldn't work now. After the briefing I recognised that this must have been a deflating and discouraging experience for the new man so I called him to my office and apologised for my irascibility. The next morning at briefing I gave him the floor and at the end of his explanation directed that we try his solution again. This time, with minor amendment, it worked. But it did serve to remind me that military institutions require regular injections of new thought and enthusiasm if they are not to stagnate.

This rather self-indulgent ramble through many memories at least serves to illustrate the simple fact that the appointment of station commander offers many opportunities for the incumbent to confirm his readiness for promotion – or indeed to put a full stop on further advancement. Success or failure thus marked a pivotal point in personal and career development. At the time I did not appreciate quite how far the span and variety of my duties were stretching me beyond the boundaries of previous experience. There was much more to it than the obvious expansion of command responsibility and accountability.

The process of education through closer contact with the Army raised my professional awareness from the tactical to the operational level which was to stand me in good stead. Direct dealings with Command HQ developed a practical awareness of how the staff could be both help and hindrance. Such insight positively defined my own perspective of staff responsibilities within the chain of command. Above all I came to understand that independence of thought, imagination and initiative are not substitutes for discipline, tenacity of purpose and loyalty but are military virtues complementary to them.

I handed over to my successor, Group Captain Frank Mitchell – another old friend from Cranwell days – to drive home with Elizabeth to occupy a married quarter at Bushey Heath in north London. I was to attend the 1985 course at the Royal College of Defence Studies with the added bonus of two promotions – the first to air commodore and the second from OBE to CBE. Such public recognition was most pleasing but I recalled some very wise words attributed to Group Captain Leonard Cheshire VC, one of the greatest men of RAF history and achievement. He wrote:

> "Leaders there have to be, and these may appear to rise above their fellow men, but in their hearts they know only too well that what has been attributed to them is in fact the achievement of the team to which they belong."

So very true, and not just for station commanders.

CHAPTER 16
INTERLUDE

The daily journey to RCDS started from Stanmore tube station at the north end of the Jubilee line. Neither an inspiring nor romantic setting by any possible stretch of the imagination but the station still resonated with nostalgia in my memory. It was there, little more than 20 years before, that I said goodbye to Elizabeth as I started the return journey to Aden after our wedding. Not knowing when we would meet again was an experience shared with many armed forces families before and since and not least with our own parents. Such episodes remain part and parcel of service life but my first experience of an indeterminate time of separation remains a most poignant memory.

The tube from Stanmore to Green Park provided comfortable travel in the morning as start time at RCDS was after rush hour. Syndicate work was normally finished by mid-afternoon so 'tube crush' was avoided in both directions with a guaranteed seat. Two hours travel each day gifted even more time for reading drawing on the excellent RCDS library; Philip Ziegler's biography of Lord Mountbatten, a sympathetic but candid portrayal, whetted my appetite for the memoirs of great men of recent history, most memorably Field Marshal the Viscount Slim and Marshals of the Royal Air Force Lord Tedder and Sir John Slessor. The walk from Green Park to Belgrave Square contributed short but welcome exercise before entry to Seaford House, a white stucco building with four main storeys above ground and a large basement containing the college dining room and kitchen. Seaford House, built in the mid-19th century, remains one of the grandest surviving aristocratic mansions in London and there can be few if any more imposing premises dedicated to education. The aim of the college was to prepare senior people from the UK and other countries for high responsibility in their organisations by "developing analytical powers, knowledge of defence and international security and strategic issues".

The 1985 course, numbering some 76, was equally split between UK and overseas members. The home team was drawn from the armed forces, the civil and diplomatic services, with additional representation from the police and industry. While the majority of overseas members were from

Commonwealth countries, the USA, West Europe, the Middle East and the Far East were well represented. For the first time RCDS was attended by members from Yugoslavia and Algeria. Within the membership of the course there was recent and knowledgeable experience of conflict in Northern Ireland, the Falklands, the Middle East, the Indian subcontinent and South East Asia. Discussion of defence and security matters within the context of the Cold War was thus well informed by personal experience. More importantly, the opportunity to listen to world-renowned experts lecturing on global strategic issues covering all aspects of governance, diplomacy, commerce and science broadened professional horizons as well as generating spirited discussion and debate. To benefit from such education in the handsome and comfortable domain of Seaford House was indeed a privilege.

During the course members visited exhibitions and demonstrations by the RN, Army and RAF while the Royal Marines, not to be left out, hosted their own voluntary visit to the Commando Training Centre at Lympstone which brought back to me a vivid memory of a whacking from my father after the unfortunate mishap involving his car. Early on in the course we split up into small parties to pay week-long visits to UK regions under the supervision of a senior member of the DS. I was fortunate to pay my first visit to Northern Ireland led by General Sir Michael Gow, commandant of the RCDS, for an action-packed week. Each of the five working days followed a different programme investigating various elements of life in the province of which I retain three very clear memories.

During our day with the security forces I was the front-seat passenger in a Land Rover as we drove out of White Rock Army base in Belfast. We had gone no further than a hundred yards when a brick hit the armoured windscreen. I nearly jumped out of my skin; the driver didn't bat an eyelid. On our agricultural day the general left me in charge as he had some regimental commitments – I think he knew what was coming. The last item on the programme was Unipork in Cookstown. On arrival it became clear that Unipork was a pig abattoir. I explained this to the two Muslims in our group and said we would all understand if they wished to remain in the coach. The senior Arab officer asked if we would be invited to eat anything and I replied that it would be most unlikely. So they joined us for the mandatory briefing followed by a tour of the premises as we observed the transformation of a pig on the hoof into recognisable joints within 40 minutes. Not an experience for squeamish souls. My third memory concerns the visit to a factory on the outskirts of Belfast that refurbished refrigerated lorries for the meat trade. When we arrived it was clear that we were either unexpected or very early.

We were in fact spot on time so our escort, a senior civil servant from the Northern Ireland Office, hurried off to find the manager. The escort was a woman of formidable stature and a few minutes later she reappeared with her prey, a little fellow who she dumped in front of General Gow who was already impatient at the delay. Without preamble the general introduced himself and each of our group of nine in turn. Sir Michael concluded with the observation that we were visiting the factory as we had been informed that it was at the forefront of the regeneration of industry in the province. The wee manager opened his mouth for the first time. "Who the f**k told you that?" he asked.

The tour of the province, including a most enjoyable visit to the Bushmills Distillery, was without exciting incident for me excepting the high velocity brick. But discussions with senior military commanders, politicians and officers of the Royal Ulster Constabulary left us in no doubt about the intransigence of the opposing factions and the almost casual brutality of sectarian violence. The threat of anarchy and chaos was very real and the prospect of achieving a political settlement seemed far distant.

At the start of the third term members were once more split into groups for their global tours with each party visiting a different area. I had hoped to be selected for the Far East tour which included a week in China so was disappointed to hear that I was a member of the West European party. Apparently members on the tour in the year before us, with no British representation, had been rather disinterested to the chagrin of IIM ambassadors who had reported their annoyance to the commandant. It was thus decided that the 1985 course would field British members with up-to-date knowledge of Europe and NATO. As the only RAF member recently returned from Germany I self-selected along with Brigadier Tony Makepiece-Warne who had come home from Berlin. Another RAF officer and a RN captain completed the British contingent. We were joined by an Australian (Navy), a New Zealander (air force), a Canadian (Mounted Police), a Brazilian (Navy, with Christian name Nelson) and an Army colonel from Trinidad and Tobago. The leader was Vice-Admiral Sir David Hallifax who had been appointed to succeed Sir Michael as commandant of RCDS at the end of the year. My misgivings were ill-conceived. We spent up to a week each in Czechoslovakia, Hungary, France, Germany and Finland which brought home to me how much my judgement of each country had hitherto been shaped by reading purely military history with insufficient attention given to political and constitutional matters. Thirty years on some anecdotal recollections of that most happy month illuminate the informative value of the tour.

I recall the atmosphere of suppressed and joyless calm in Czechoslovakia. Much of the architectural magnificence within Prague was shrouded in scaffolding that supported planks to protect pedestrians from falling masonry. But risk to life and limb was low as there were no crowds and the scarcity of traffic in both town and countryside presented an impression of a nation asleep. Driving from Czechoslovakia to Hungary we spent an age at the border for documentation checks which demonstrated that the Iron Curtain was more than a north/south-orientated barrier; it also enclosed Czechoslovakia.

In the sharpest contrast Hungary presented an image of energetic industry and we were astounded to find that the country's economy was dynamically capitalist. Our interpreter explained the paradox with a story. He told us that Mikhail Gorbachov, Margaret Thatcher and Janos Kadar – long-time president of Hungary – were driving together through Budapest. They came to a T-junction and the driver asked "which way do I go"? Mikhail Gorbachov replied, "indicate left driver, go left". Mrs Thatcher piped up, "no, indicate and go right, that's the only way to go". Janos Kadar tapped the driver on the shoulder and said: "this is my country, indicate left and go right".

An early visit to a collective farm had got us off to an unimpressive start. The farm cultivated sunflowers, not the most exciting of enterprises, and we spent an hour gazing at the stubble of a recently cropped field while an interpreter droned on with a story of unconvincing propaganda. The next stop was a lamp museum where another hour studying lamps of all varieties failed to raise morale. But things looked up when we arrived at the collective's social centre where we were invited to a wine tasting with white and red served alike in quantity from enamel jugs. Once suitably fuelled, dinner was served – huge chunks of liver on a bed of glutinous rice. Thereafter our hosts asked for our judgement on the comparative merits of Hungarian, Polish and Russian vodka with samples served in rapid sequence. This unsocialist extravaganza precipitated an impromptu singalong. Rather than sea shanties, Captain Bob Hill RN and Captain Jim Dixon Royal Australian Navy led us in a raucous rendering of Abdul Abulbul Amir which apparently was much enjoyed by the audience. Eventually we said farewell to our agricultural hosts, who had shared the banquet, with oaths of eternal and fraternal friendship. As we departed for Budapest the admiral commented that "it had been his best run ashore since '39". That was the second time I had heard an admiral make such an observation and was left wondering if 'runs ashore' had some influence on career success in the RN.

Next stop was France. We arrived at the Quai d'Orsay at the appointed time for our arrival briefing but were kept waiting for an unconscionably long time before being admitted. It transpired that the French foreign service did not want our New Zealander, Group Captain Peter Adamson, to be included. The French were still deeply troubled by the diplomatic and public relations disaster that followed the sinking of the Greenpeace flagship, *Rainbow Warrior,* in Auckland harbour two months earlier. The ship was sunk by limpet mines, placed by frogmen, to prevent it leading a flotilla of smaller vessels to the Pacific island of Moruroa in protest against French nuclear testing. The impasse at the Quai was eventually resolved when Sir David spelt out with crystal clarity to the French authorities that either the whole RCDS party attended the briefing or nobody did. Sir David's will prevailed.

Following on to this rather vexatious start we later visited the Ministry of Defence. In the circumstances it almost beggars belief that we were shown an introductory film on the French armed forces that started with a clip of frogmen attaching limpet mines to a ship! Later on we met with officials to discuss nuclear policy. The French team was led by a glamorous and most attractive young woman with long red fingernails and earrings to match. Although admittedly beguiled, as indeed were the other members of our party, I still recall her patronising dismissal of the British nuclear deterrent as not genuinely independent – true perhaps but at least we didn't sabotage Greenpeace protestors to help guarantee nuclear independence. After Paris we moved south to Toulon where we were most generously hosted and entertained by the French Navy before spending a soporific afternoon in a vineyard with a more cultured and disciplined wine tasting than that experienced in Hungary. Peter Adamson, Kiwi to the core, had the last word. "I still prefer the hop to the grape," he observed as we departed for Germany.

Visiting the Federal Republic as a guest of the government gave me an insight to West German attitudes and foreign policy that came as something of a disappointment. Hitherto I had considered that Anglo-German relations were next in importance to our 'special relationship' with the United States. Within Europe, however, the visit to Germany confirmed the significance of the Paris/Bonn relationship and the relative decline of the UK's influence in Europe. Although victory in the Falklands had boosted our military reputation, British attitudes to Europe were an irritant to German officials who wished the UK to be far more involved in continental affairs beyond our national contribution to NATO. I also noted that while Germans in Stadt Gütersloh would talk about the war, in Bonn our hosts showed no inclination to revisit the past. They had not inherited, nor wished to accept, any responsibility for the crimes of their elders. I did not know at the time that I would be posted back to Germany at the end of the course, but exposure to German attitudes in Bonn, particularly those concerning Anglo-German relations, was to prove most beneficial.

The last lap of the tour took us to Finland. I knew the country was the eighth largest in Europe, was sparsely populated and that the Finnish language challenged the best of linguists. I also knew that Finland had been a Grand Duchy in the Russian empire and since 1919 had fought two wars against the Soviet Union to retain independence before participating in the Red Army's onslaught on Nazi Germany in 1944/45. Since joining the United Nations in 1955, Finland's history and geography had formulated a policy of neutrality in international affairs which was evident in our discussions with officials. The short and violent narrative of Finland's existence as a nation state had quite clearly constructed, or perhaps improved, an already cohesive society of admirable strength. The Finnish defence forces consisted of cadres of professional sailors, soldiers and airmen with rapid mobilisation of substantial reserves numbering some 400,000 judged as sufficient for robust homeland defence. A firepower demonstration – the only one we observed during our tour – left us in no doubt of Finland's determination to safeguard its neutrality. By 1985, 'Finlandisation', a term describing foreign policies adapted to give no offence to large contiguous powers and popularised in the West during the 1960s, seemed outdated and patronising.

The visit ended with a trip to a timber yard north of Helsinki which included a mandatory sauna in a social centre. Having boiled to baby pink in the hot room, Peter Adamson and I accepted the invitation to take the cold dip in the adjoining lake rather than in the sauna house pool. This was our first mistake. We ran to a short jetty and jumped into the water, some 7 ft deep. Such was the shock of immersion we re-emerged in a vertical ascent not unlike the launch of a Polaris missile. We immediately returned to the sauna house and after restoration of body heat decided to take a dip in the sauna pool. This was the second mistake. The pool was colder than the lake water. Any good accruing from this experience, which I have no wish to repeat, was probably undone when we were entertained to a supper of beer and sausages.

I returned to England well aware of the many privileges we had enjoyed on the tour. An insight into the harsh realities of life behind the Iron Curtain, the addition of authenticity to superficial impressions of France and Germany and an introduction to strategic pragmatism in Finland provided us all with a broader understanding of the utility of democracy and the soulless functionality of socialism in action. Once reassembled in Seaford House each group gave a presentation on their tour. Suffice to say that I was left in no doubt that our group had enjoyed the most entertaining and comfortable of tours made even the more pleasant by the congeniality of Sir David Hallifax and the benevolent – for most of the time – supervision of senior member, Tony Makepiece-Warne.

The end of the year at Seaford House was marked by a prime ministerial visit. Mrs Thatcher exceeded already high expectations. Without notes she talked about putting the 'Great' back into Great Britain with fluency and total conviction; she spoke from the heart. Afterwards she answered questions with almost brutal directness with no ambiguity in her replies. It was a bravura performance and a high note on which to end our time at RCDS.

During the year at Seaford House Elizabeth and I had taken great pleasure in the company of old RAF chums, the Chrys-Williams, the Govers and the Hardings in particular, and we all enjoyed the avuncular oversight of the senior RAF DS, Air Vice-Marshal Barry Newton. But RCDS was also the perfect place to establish friendships with overseas members which were to prove productive in the future. For example, after returning to Germany one telephone conversation with Colonel Lee Downer, posted to the USAFE HQ at Ramstein, solved a problem of airspace utilisation which had become something of a trial of strength between the 2nd and 4th ATAFs. Further afield we have maintained to this day our friendships with our antipodean friends which have survived the ebb and flow of success and misfortune on the rugby and cricket fields. In recent years Mike and Marlena Jeffery and Jim and Anthea Dixon from Australia (Mike in his capacity as governor general) and Peter and Pat Adamson from NZ have been frequent and most welcome visitors to the UK. I must add that my 'sauna' pal, Peter, an Old Cranwellian and several entries senior to me but in the same squadron, went on to become the CAS of the RNZAF. At home I was to see a lot more of my RN friends, in particular Peter Abbott when vice chief of the defence staff, Bob Hill as the RN's chief engineer and David Bawtree who recruited me as a governor of The Portsmouth Grammar School. Army colleagues rather sadly faded from view with the notable exception of Richard Swinburn, the archetypal cavalry officer, who retired in the rank of lieutenant general.

While friendships were a delight of the year, it is worth re-emphasising that course members contributed a stimulating variety of experience, opinion and outlook which broadened minds through spirited discussion and tolerant listening. Debate was enriched by the words of successful and often brilliant lecturers that provided ample provender for rumination. All of this encouraged much more than independence of thought. I learned not only to recognise apparent incompatibilities within the military life but to accept them as anomalies of my chosen profession. All this armed me to face a future in which discussion, argument and sometimes confrontation, particularly with ambitious bureaucrats, became ever more challenging.

Meanwhile, two matters of consequence, beyond the confines of Seaford House, became evident and which were to influence future careers in the armed forces. General Sir Nigel Bagnall, now CGS, had been quick to carry forward his thinking on the operational level of war with stress placed on manoeuvre and quick and flexible thought. He instituted the Higher Command and Staff Course (HCSC) to spread the gospel of the manoeuvrist approach to operations amongst Army rising stars in the ranks of colonel and brigadier. The HCSC, with its emphasis on thinking as fundamental to an understanding of the operational art, lasted for four months which created difficulties of selection as the HCSC could not in the early days be harmonised with the RCDS year. Moreover, it took some time for the RN and RAF to appreciate the importance of the HCSC in formulating the need for joint doctrine and training. HCSC became a make or break career course and within less than a decade all key operational-level appointments were filled with HCSC graduates.

The second matter of far-reaching importance was the appointment in 1983 of Mr Michael Heseltine as the secretary of state for defence, a man described as "being of unlimited ambition in a hurry". The MoD presented the perfect platform for enhancing his reputation as a "mover of mountains". By 1985 the Heseltine blueprint for the future management of defence had been implemented. The authority of the single service chiefs and their supporting service departments had been weakened while the secretary of state's control over the defence programme had been strengthened by the creation of an office of management and budget (OMB), largely civilian-manned and reporting directly to Heseltine through a newly appointed second permanent under secretary. The OMB, working alongside central military staff, was responsible for recommending the size and shape of our armed forces. While the chiefs of staff could understand the merit of centralising the control of operations and the allocation of resources, members of the 1985 RCDS course were left in no doubt of the chiefs' concerns about their ability to discharge their duties when even further distanced from the central staff. At the time I noted the words of Air Chief Marshal Sir Keith Williamson, CAS, who was forthright in stating his concern that the OMB would add further complications to the already convoluted processes of defence programming and weapons procurement. Sir Keith was quite right and as we, the RCDS members, were to learn, the Heseltine blueprint not only debilitated the influence of the chiefs of staff as a strategic advisory body but "elevated financial management over professional military thought".

A decade later I became aware that within Whitehall there were some in positions of authority, both service and civilian, who were concerned that the RCDS course made an inadequate demand for hard work. A year spent in reflection and study within a pleasing ambience and an atmosphere of academic enlightenment was an anathema to Whitehall killjoys. Reflection, in my book, is the pre-requisite for innovation and change, and more of it in Whitehall might have saved the taxpayer from the consequences of many failed projects – information technology (IT) comes immediately to mind – due to insufficient understanding of the technology and the real difficulties of implementation. Vast sums paid to consultants could also have been saved if politicians had trusted senior military and civilian officials to do their own thinking –assuming they had the confidence and determination to do so. It might come as a surprise to some, but the MoD has never been short of brain power.

I must, however, admit that in 1985 the high level management of defence did not concern me. At the end of the course my primary objective was to avoid any chance of a return to the MoD. As an air commodore I would have very much liked a posting as commandant of the Central Flying School but my old friend Kip Kemball was in situ and it would have been treachery to wish him misfortune. But I was more than happy when told I was to return to RAF Germany as the senior air staff officer (SASO) in the headquarters at Rheindahlen. Lucky me.

Recalling the aims of RCDS I departed much the better informed on the strategic issues of the day; they were not to last for long. Within a few years the certainties of the Cold War were to give way to the emergence of new threats and vulnerabilities. Instability in one part of an interdependent world could quickly affect security in another. The complications that were to arise boosted my interest in strategic thought which was to be most helpful in distinguishing the difference between theory and practice. And never more so than when successive governments sought international acclaim for punching above their weight when in reality the armed forces were consistently asked to punch above their budget.

CHAPTER 17
BACK TO GERMANY

The RCDS course ended with an interdenominational service in the Guards Chapel, Wellington Barracks, on 13th December 1985. After a final and emotional gathering back in Seaford House, I returned home to put my skates on as I was due at HQ RAF Germany, Rheindahlen, three days later. David Brook was keen to return to the UK before Christmas so having packed the car and made a minimal contribution to preparing our quarter for march out and another overseas move, I was off with batteries fully recharged. And it must be admitted that Elizabeth preferred me out of the way when it came to moving house; apart from sorting out the paperwork and packing uniforms my presence was generally more hindrance than help.

After a short handover I was in the chair as SASO one day before Elizabeth and the children arrived to occupy our new home in Dundee Way, a more spacious and comfortable married quarter than we had lived in during previous tours. There was a large garden which sloped down to a thick wood. After Christmas lunch I led three stroppy teenagers down to the wood for some much-needed exercise. No further than ten yards into the trees and the ground suddenly gave way and I was waist deep in a well-camouflaged bog. Gleeful hilarity immediately succeeded recalcitrant teenage insubordination and it took all my powers of persuasion to convince them that I needed assistance.

This mishap apart the Christmas and New Year breaks gave me time to take stock. Whereas I knew all about Gütersloh from my last tour I had had only a few dealings with RAF Wildenrath (two squadrons of air defence Phantoms and a Pembroke communications squadron), RAF Brüggen (four squadrons of nuclear-armed Tornados) and RAF Laarbruch (three nuclear-armed Tornado squadrons and a Jaguar tactical-reconnaissance squadron). RAF Regiment Rapier squadrons provided SHORAD on each of these airfields. RAF Gatow in Berlin supported British forces based in the city plus providing an important element of our air intelligence-gathering capability. A number of minor units directly supporting RAF Germany or 2ATAF were either under direct or administrative control of the HQ.

My new duties involved direct responsibility to the deputy commander RAF Germany on all matters concerning air staff policy, operational training and intelligence. The deputy commander, an air vice-marshal wearing a national hat, was essentially the equivalent of a group commander in Strike Command. The commander-in-chief was dual-hatted as a national commander and as the NATO commander of 2ATAF. During my three-year tour I was to serve two C-in-Cs and two deputy commanders of widely differing personalities. The first C-in-C was Sir David Parry-Evans: quiet, reflective and undemonstrative. The second was Sir Tony Skingsley, a fluent German speaker, with an ebullient, genial and cheerful personality. The first deputy commander was Derek Bryant, who had a reputation, earned and deserved, as a hard man. His flying pedigree was most impressive and included project leadership for the introduction to service of the Folland Gnat advanced trainer. Derek was a fighter man to the core and a most demanding task master. Growing familiarity with my duties led me into the trap of overconfidence which earned me a hefty kick in the pants for submission of some sloppy staff work. The severity of his disapproval was well deserved and I did not repeat the mistake again of forwarding papers to clear my in-tray when called back to MoD at short notice for some conference or the other. Given his love of flying and his absolute devotion to the operational efficiency of the service, Derek would not thank me for stating, without hesitation, that in our year together I learned more from him about the orchestration of staff work than from any other person before or since.

His successor, Bob Honey, with one important exception, could not have been more different. Bob also came with a fighter pedigree and a well-established reputation as a formidable mountaineer. He was invariably relaxed, almost laid back, and he spent a lot of time sustaining the highest level of physical fitness. He let me get on with my job but I soon discovered he had cultivated a memory of computer-like capacity. He forgot absolutely nothing, could memorise a long speech in a trice and, like his predecessor, was unforgiving of inaccuracy or error. I was fortunate to serve four such contrasting superiors united only in their determination to do their very best for the service without fear or favour.

In 1986 RAF Germany, at the sharp end of 2ATAF's offensive capabilities, was deeply entrenched in Cold War operational thinking that was shaped by the NATO strategy of flexible response. The Alliance adopted the strategy in 1967 to allow a greater range of response to all levels of aggression or threats of aggression than very rapid recourse to nuclear weapons. It was argued that certainty of response but uncertainty over the level of response constituted a powerful deterrent. Our national contribution to the strategy was quick reaction alert (nuclear). When I took over as SASO seven nuclear-armed Tornados, four at Brüggen and three at Laarbruch with one crew from each squadron, were held at 15 minutes readiness throughout the year. Should a crisis develop the number of aircraft committed to nuclear missions would be increased until all available strike (nuclear) aircraft were at cockpit readiness to fulfil SACEUR's composite launch sequence plan (CLSP); this coordinated the release of NATO's tactical nuclear arsenal in northern Europe. Tornado crews could also be tasked for selective use to demonstrate political resolve! An increasing commitment to readiness for strike operations reduced the availability of Tornados for attack (non-nuclear) tasking against Warsaw Pact airfields and other target systems relevant to the battle for air superiority. The transition from attack operations to the CLSP was regularly practised and examined by national and TACEVAL teams.

As a pure 'mud mover' (ground attack pilot) with no practical experience of the nuclear business, I had wondered about the attitude of our aircrews to a nuclear bombing mission knowing full well that if launched it was with a one-way ticket. Having talked to friends who had held QRA(N) readiness it is quite clear that they shared a common conviction that the professionalism of air and ground crews alike contributed to the strength and credibility of NATO deterrence. As long as this was sustained and not weakened by anti-nuclear protest or political back sliding, the likelihood of war in Europe was minimal. That said, the consequence of a nuclear weapons exchange in Europe (if on the receiving end how does one judge the difference between a tactical and strategic weapon?) would be so catastrophic that the fulfilment of a duty as ordered would be the inevitable conclusion of a failed strategy. Determination to guarantee the credibility of the strategy bound together the various air arms of RAF Germany with each contributing its own specialisation to the operational cohesiveness of the command.

The RAF had sustained high readiness states since tactical nuclear weapons were first deployed to RAF Germany in 1958. Twenty-seven years later, President Reagan and Mikhail Gorbachev (general secretary of the Communist Party of the Soviet Union) met for the first of five summit meetings which culminated in the signing of the Intermediate Range Nuclear Forces (INF) Treaty of 8th December 1987. The treaty eliminated all nuclear-armed ground-based ballistic and cruise missiles with ranges between 300 and 3,400 miles along with their supporting infrastructure. In addition, the planned progressive reduction in other unmanned nuclear delivery systems devolved responsibility for maintaining a tactical nuclear capability to dual-capable aircraft such as the Tornado. However, the INF Treaty and emerging political change in the Soviet Union and East Europe reduced assessments of the Warsaw Pact threat which allowed NATO to relax its nuclear force posture in the European theatre. Relaxation of the QRA(N) readiness times was implemented in autumn 1987 and response times changed from measurement in minutes to quantification in hours. Little more than a decade later the UK had retired and dismantled all its WE-177 nuclear bombs leaving the RAF without a nuclear role – a significant milestone in the history of the service.

The reduction in the command's nuclear readiness and response times soon immersed me in the fine detail of amending orders issued to the station commanders at Brüggen and Laarbruch concerning the processes of authorisation and execution of their nuclear responsibilities. Not surprisingly these orders were meticulous in both detail and clarity. While the responsible air staff, led by Wing Commander Dick Howard, completed the hard graft, the orders received my painstaking scrutiny before submission to the deputy commander and C-in-C. The task also underlined the rapidity of change in global geopolitics which was to lift the spectre of nuclear annihilation. But here it is worth remembering that most inter-state conflicts of the past started when one side believed it could win; the aim of deterrence was to avoid that situation. During the Cold War the threat of mutually assured destruction (MAD) was essentially a strategic balance of terror. But credible deterrence required capabilities to respond at an appropriate level to any scale of attack within the spectrum of conflict. And paradoxically the more credible the use of nuclear weapons, both strategic and tactical, the less the probability of their use. In Germany the RAF's nuclear forces, within a complex system of controls to guard against accident or misunderstanding, provided a substantial element of the deterrence which was to sustain peace in Europe for more than four decades.

Memories of 24 hours' confinement in the secure QRA(N) site are mixed. Study and commitment to memory of every detail of the mission was essential but could not fill all hours of the day and night. Some recall the tedium relieved by board games and videos. Others, perhaps the more sociable, considered QRA(N) the ideal opportunity to get to know people from different squadrons to foster a force or wing identity. All remember the welcome presence of a cook who ensured that everyone was well fed. Now, some 30 years later, one thing is for sure. Time spent on QRA(N) was not wasted time and those who carried out this repetitive and onerous duty did so with commendable commitment.

The greater part of RAF Germany's order of battle conformed to the maxims that offence is the best defence and that the most effective defence against air attack is to stop it at source. Offensive counter-air operations against Warsaw Pact airfields required our Tornados to penetrate a dense thicket of ground-based air defence (GBAD) weaponry – mobile anti-aircraft artillery (AAA), man-portable (MANPAD) missiles and surface-to-air missiles (SAM) – to reach their targets. Terrain-following radar allowed the aircraft to attack at night and in bad weather which gave some protection against enemy fighter aircraft and optically-laid weapons. In less favourable conditions the support of escort fighters, electronic jamming and defence-suppression aircraft – principally USAF assets – was unlikely. Nationally the procurement of these capabilities had been judged as unaffordable. Thus the wartime survival of the RAF's offensive forces had for many years been based on accurate navigation to avoid heavily defended areas with aircraft flown at high speed and low level to impede detection and interception. Low flying was thus a core capability of the RAF's operational training flown at 250 feet above ground level. But the Falklands War proved this to be too high so operational low flying at 100 feet above ground level was introduced as a formal training requirement for Tornados, Harriers and Jaguars.

The amendment of training directives and syllabi was simple enough. But by the mid-1980s growing German public opposition to low flying limited Tornado night training to 1,800 feet above ground level with 250 feet day flying the lowest permissible and constrained to a few comparatively small areas. Operational low flying training thus had to be exported back to the UK with the considerable expense of non-productive transit flying. Much further afield month-long squadron detachments to RAF Goose Bay in Labrador gave access to an unfettered environment. This excellent training was ideal preparation for Red Flag exercises hosted by the USAF at Nellis Air Force Base in the Nevada Desert. The Red Flag training concept was born of lessons learnt in the Vietnam War where pilot losses fell significantly after completion of their first ten combat sorties. The aim of Red Flag was thus to provide a contemporary training experience as intense and as close as possible to those first ten missions through the provision of the most realistic operational training environment with measurable results. To achieve this the USAF had mapped out a range area, half the size of Switzerland, to the north-west of Las Vegas. Within it there were a variety of targets ranging from concentrations of AFVs to full-scale airfields configured to represent typical Warsaw Pact bases. The target area was defended by an aggressor squadron of USAF F-5 Freedom Fighters simulating MiG-21 and MiG-23 fighters. Ground threats included genuine ZSU 23/4 radar-laid anti-aircraft guns along with Soviet SAM-3 and SAM-6 missile systems. Radar simulators completed an integrated air defence system which was real in every sense except no guns or missiles were actually fired. However, the Red Flag Measurement and Debriefing System, a computer and software network, provided real-time monitoring and post-mission reconstruction of manoeuvres and tactics with precise assessment of success or failure. Crews participating in Red Flag knew for certain whether they would have survived or died on their mission. In the aftermath of Gulf War I a Tornado pilot told me that operations over Iraq were at the same level of intensity as a Red Flag mission. "This is just like Red Flag" was a regular observation of RAF aircrew and there could be no higher accolade for a training system.

The RAF's commitment to high speed, ultra-low level flight was reflected in the principal weapons procured for attacks on airfields and armoured fighting vehicles. A Tornado tasked against a Soviet airfield would be armed with two JP233 airfield-denial weapons each containing 30 cratering bombs and 215 small anti-personnel mines. The cratering bombs penetrated concrete surfaces and created 'heave' by pushing up cracked and broken concrete. The mines scattered amongst the rubble and craters would threaten and discourage repair teams. A typical airfield attack force would comprise eight Tornados with the potential to deliver on target 480 cratering bombs and 3,440 mines. The BL755 anti-armour weapon, previously described in the Harrier chapter, was an area weapon covering the size of a football field which in the context of a Soviet massed-armour attack was certainly fit for purpose.

Policy changes in response to developing political circumstances generated a heavy workload for the staff. As the certainties of the Cold War permafrost started to melt away, I took it as a staff imperative that we did our very best to ensure that the cutting edge of RAF Germany's operational effectiveness remained well honed. The programming of squadron detachments for armament practice camps in Decimomannu, for flag training in the Unites States and Canada, the sustainment of Harrier detachments in the Falklands and Belize and a Chinook detachment also in the Falklands kept us in touch with the realities of station life. On the other hand, never-ending statistical arguments with the MoD and German air force Tactical Air Command about the sum of our low flying activities was at times some distance removed from reality. I strongly suspected that the low flying returns submitted each month by the squadrons were economical with the actualité while the responsible staff under Wing Commander Bill Rimmer's control added their own fiddle factor to ensure that the stats remained within the bounds of respectability. I accepted them as such.

All of this was of little consequence when the cost of our operational training was counted. Low flying at high speed close to the ground allows little margin for error. Add in hard manoeuvring under high G loads and the risk increases proportionally. But the risk factor was a significant feature of the challenge which forged bonds of exclusivity that tied together the select club of RAF fast-jet aircrew. Fatal accidents were an explicitly accepted part of an exacting occupation. During my three-year tour the command lost 14 aircraft and 13 aircrew were killed. To the best of my memory at least half of these major accidents involved some degree of aircrew error. The common denominator appeared to be overconfidence particularly in aircrew with around 1,500 flying hours under their belt. They may have had the skill and experience to stay out of trouble but a single misjudgement of what constituted the edge of risk acceptability all too often had fatal consequences. The RAF quite properly nurtured aggressive self-confidence in its fast-jet aircrew but the definition of acceptable risk appeared to vary not just between aircraft types but also within squadrons on the same station. And like it or not, luck was a significant factor that protected some and abandoned others. Reviewing Boards of Inquiry into aircraft accidents before drafting conclusions and recommendations for the C-in-C's consideration was never less than a serious and sombre duty which often reminded me of the luck I had enjoyed in my own flying career.

In the Harrier Force Friday afternoons were reserved for ground training before the wing retired to the bar for refreshment. Recce quizzes of Soviet military equipment were a regular feature of ground-training sessions using up-to-date photographs of crystal clarity. The majority of shots were taken from the air and I often wondered about their origin. The introductory brief to my air intelligence responsibilities solved the puzzle when I discovered that I was the authorising officer for Pembroke intelligence-gathering missions flown up and down the three air corridors which linked West Germany to Berlin. Three venerable piston-engined Pembrokes of 60 Squadron at RAF Wildenrath were modified to carry oblique and vertical cameras. Flying along the edge of the ten-mile-wide corridors between 3,500 and 10,000 ft allowed the cameras to be trained on specific targets well into Soviet-occupied East Germany. The morning after landing at RAF Gatow, and under guise of an air test, the aircraft prowled around the Berlin Control Zone collecting further imagery before returning to Wildenrath the next day via a different corridor to recce more targets. I heard that one mission returned with some quality imagery of a nudist camp showing mixed groups playing volleyball. The photos were annotated as SSNBs – soft-skinned naked bodies. But corridor missions flown under Operation Hallmark were not without danger. Aircrew were well aware that if they strayed outside corridor boundaries because of a minor navigation error they faced the real possibility of being shot down.

No. 60 Squadron lived a dual existence. Most of the squadron's aircraft were fitted out for communication flights transporting senior officers and other military personnel to and from the UK and around Europe. While these legitimate activities provided some cover, I still find it extraordinary that the squadron's more clandestine activities remained such a close-guarded secret for so long. No. 60 Squadron aircrew must have enjoyed the odd chuckle as young Harrier pilots, not noted for either their reticence or modesty, strutted their stuff around the station before the Harrier Force moved east from Wildenrath to Gütersloh.

The squadron's collection of photographic imagery was supplemented by our 'listening posts', the most important being No.54 Signals Unit at Celle in north Germany and No. 26 Signals Unit and Radar Squadron in Berlin. Their work reinforced the substantial activities of BRIXMIS, the British commanders-in-chief mission to the commander of the Soviet Forces in Germany, which was set up in September 1946. Initially a British/Soviet agreement, the Russians went on to make similar bi-lateral agreements with the Americans and the French although the British Mission remained the largest. Reciprocal Soviet military liaison missions (SOXMIS) were located in each of the three western zones of the Federal Republic of Germany. The original purpose of BRIXMIS was to provide confidence-building liaison between respective commanders-in-chief to prevent escalation of relatively minor incidents.

By the mid-1950s BRIXMIS had evolved into a purely intelligence-gathering organisation using a variety of vehicles to tour permitted areas within the German Democratic Republic. On average BRIXMIS had three tours, each constituting a three-man team, in action throughout the year. Although some 40% of the GDR was covered by permanent restricted areas, the vast quantity of military equipment and troops serving in the Group of Soviet Forces Germany and 11 Tactical Air Army provided a rich source of intelligence success. Two RAF Gatow-based Chipmunks – single-engine basic trainers of truly venerable age – were ostensibly there to maintain an air presence in Berlin. However, the two-man crew from the RAF element of BRIXMIS, known as Biggles and Algie, flew around the Berlin Control Zone designated as a 20-mile radius from the centre of the city. It was estimated that around 95% of all Soviet ground equipment passed through the limits of the BCZ so aerial observation providing visual reports backed up with photographic evidence from hand-held cameras generated a consistent stream of high quality intelligence.

BRIXMIS tours contained their own element of danger particularly during the mid-1980s when East-West relations were particularly fractious. There was always the risk of crews being beaten up or detained by Soviet or East German forces if touring teams were caught too close to sensitive targets. More seriously in 1984 a French officer was deliberately killed in an engineered traffic accident and the next year Major Nicholson from the US Mission was shot by a Soviet guard when close to a military installation. The Soviets refused to apologise which had an immediate bearing on my own existence. The British, American and French commanders-in-chief refused to meet with their Soviet counterparts with representation at social functions delegated down to one-star level – me for the RAF.

In my three years as SASO I represented C-in-C RAF Germany at SOXMIS receptions held at Bunde near Hanover and at The Queen's birthday receptions in the BRIXMIS Mission House in Potsdam. The drive to Potsdam in a specially modified Opel Senator crossing the Glienicke Bridge – of spy-swap fame – routed through the dilapidated back streets of Berlin. Soviet barracks were similarly neglected while the soldiers were slovenly in dress and lethargic in bearing. The receptions I attended in the Mission House were all blessed with good weather with a band from one of the Berlin brigade regiments adding musical accompaniment to a pleasant evening of champagne and canapés. At my final reception I was surprised when Brigadier John Foley, chief of BRIXMIS, told me that a Soviet air force general had turned up unexpectedly and asked me to look after him. Grabbing an interpreter I hurried over to greet the general and for the next five minutes we conducted a conversation of diplomatic inanities. Becoming rather bored with this vapidity I asked my interpreter to seek the general's agreement to move onto a subject of mutual interest, for example aeroplanes. The general, a short man with a large girth and a galaxy of medal ribbons, listened carefully. His face remained expressionless and I was concerned about the possibility of having provoked a diplomatic incident. He then replied sharply and concisely. The interpreter translated "the general agrees that the conversation should be moved on, but rather than talk about aeroplanes he would prefer to talk about women". I had not expected to meet a Soviet general with a sense of humour.

Back at Rheindahlen the Joint Intelligence Committee (Germany) met regularly to consider the highlights of intelligence garnered from such a wide variety of sources. These meetings also allowed me to keep an eye on brother-in-law Dan Baily's activities as he was a regular BRIXMIS tourer. Some of the intelligence such as details of the new Soviet gun/missile air-defence system known originally as ZSU-X and new explosive reactive armour had immediate operational implications. BRIXMIS ground tours and observation of Warsaw Pact exercises gave an accurate and unique insight to their strengths and weaknesses at the tactical level. This was not true of air intelligence which consisted of modules of accurate but unrelated details of aircraft, weapons systems and range firing, flying rates and so on.

It was Air Marshal Sir Paddy Hine who as C-in-C RAF Germany set up the Berlin Tactical Analysis Cell (BTAC) to fuse all air intelligence so to provide a single comprehensive picture of Warsaw Pact air forces' concepts of operation, capabilities and tactics. The team was led by a wing commander who had recently completed a tour in Germany as a squadron commander. Sadly I have forgotten his name, sadly because he deserves publicly-recorded recognition for the work his team produced which for the first time gave NATO squadrons a precise assessment of how Warsaw Pact air power would be used in war and the tactics employed. This knowledge and successive updating bulletins, warmly welcomed throughout RAF Germany and much further afield, was certainly better late than never – not that we knew that at the time. BTAC was lasting testimony to Sir Paddy's operational vision and tactical acuity.

In July 1988 I received the good news of promotion in the new year and a posting as commandant of the RAF Staff College, Bracknell. I was thrilled to bits and shortly afterwards Derek Bryant, the incumbent commandant, invited me to visit for a chat and a tour around the college with lunch to follow in the commandant's residence. The prospect of a job hallmarked with a high quality of life with the benefit of meeting a new generation of RAF officers buoyed me up for the final five months of an arduous tour. But hard work had its elements of fulfilment and pleasure. The variety of my work and frequent dealings with the Army and NATO colleagues – mostly harmonious and only occasionally testy – guaranteed no dull days in the office. The JHQ also gifted the occasional treat which I shared with my Army opposite number, Brigadier Nick Ansell. Together we presented the British Forces Germany briefing. One such occasion was the briefing we gave to Chancellor Kohl and Mrs Thatcher at the German air force base Fassberg. The two leaders were accompanied by a multitude of ministers, diplomats and very senior military officers. Nick and I gave up trying to calculate the total of 'stars' present but it was a true constellation.

Halfway through the brief, Nick speaking, I glanced at Mrs Thatcher. She had the faraway look of someone who had heard it all before with more pressing matters on their mind. Not so. Nick came to our shared concern about the chemical warfare capabilities of the Warsaw Pact and our vulnerability to chemical attack. Instantly Mrs Thatcher turned on the chancellor with some sharp words of irritation at NATO's reluctance to confront this threat. After a less-than-friendly exchange we were allowed to continue and end the briefing with the normal invitation for questions. Neither of us got a word in edgeways. In such rarefied atmosphere top dogs are always concerned that puppies may make a mess of things so Nick and I smiled amiably and happy that our work was done. But it was fascinating to observe the debate on momentous issues between our political masters with their military advisors hanging on every word as they sought the opportunity to add an opinion of relevance and substance. No-one suggested that the Cold War was nearing its end.

In late August 1988, with Elizabeth and the children, I enjoyed two weeks invigorating holiday in the Bavarian Alps. Walking, cycling and swimming certainly sharpened me up physically but conversations with our offspring, now well-established in their teenage years and not subject to military protocol, often left me floundering for convincing replies to challenging questions and attitudes. I consoled myself with the thought that this was good preparation for Staff College. On the first day back at work I received a telephone call from the air secretary. Air Vice-Marshal Tony Mason didn't beat about the bush. "Has the C-in-C spoken to you yet?" he asked. "No," I replied. "He will soon," said Tony and hung up. Five minutes later I was summoned to the C-in-C's office. Air Marshal Sir Tony Skingsley greeted me with typical bonhomie and the question "do you want the good news or the bad news?" Being an inveterate optimist I asked for the good. "Well," he said, "you are still being promoted but ….. you are no longer going to Bracknell. You are off to Strike Command as the senior air staff officer". Five to six years as a SASO seemed rather excessive but from time to time one has to take the rough with the smooth.

The remaining four months of my tour passed without major incident although a few days before completing my handover to Air Commodore Dickie Duckett, a mid-air collision in bad weather between two USAF A-10 aircraft south of Cologne caused consternation. A colonel from German air force Tactical Air Command telephoned to tell me that all of our low flying in Germany was to be stopped immediately. I commented that the mid-air collision occurred at 1,500 feet above the ground and had nothing to do with low flying. The colonel replied that the German public would not see it as such. The terse conversation ended with me pointing out that as a staff officer I did not have the appropriate authority and his superiors would be best advised to contact commander 2ATAF (COMTWOATAF) as this was a matter for NATO rather than a bilateral national issue. I left the sorting out of this potential hospital pass in Dickie's hands as I completed the round of farewell calls.

I was genuinely sorry to leave a job that I had thoroughly enjoyed. But, as ever, it was the people who made it a congenial experience. I knew some of my staff from the past. Paul Ryan from the RAF Regiment, Bill Whyte, Mike Beach and Malcolm White from Harrier days and Cliff Spink, our air defender, all come immediately to mind. They were right on top of their jobs and brought with them squadron humour and banter to vitalise the rather gloomy corridors of JHQ and their offices in the basement below known to all as the sheep dip. Dick Howard, a Cranwell contemporary, was replaced by Bill Rimmer, a large and robust Scot not given to mincing his words – then or years later when we spent many happy days together off-shore sailing. Mike Heath, a navigator and the only man I have met who cooked a three-course dinner with the aid of a computer, was to play a pivotal role in the Kosovo campaign a decade later. Group Captain Steve Nicholl, a man of formidable intelligence and breadth of interests, filled the crucially important planning post. All of these good men had established their aircrew credentials before arrival in the JHQ and were a pleasure to work with. I did not know at the time that most of them were to play significant parts in navigating the service through choppy waters in years ahead. No words of the debt I owed them and others would be complete without mention of my PA, Sergeant Francis Plowman, who firmly ensured that the multiplicity of our tasks were completed in good time. Finally, and by no means least, I met SAC Dave Smith who through fair and foul was to be my driver for the greater part of the next ten years.

The death in late November of Elizabeth's father, a man I held in the highest regard, cast a dark shadow over our departure. Elizabeth returned home immediately and I joined her for John Manning's funeral before returning to Rheindahlen to complete the march out of our quarter. I lived in the mess for my last week before driving back to join Elizabeth in our new house on the married patch at Bradenham Beeches close to Strike Command HQ. The children were all at home and preparations for Christmas were in full swing. But the joy of the festival was tragically diminished by the destruction of Pan Am Flight 103 overhead Lockerbie on 21st December 1988. The Lockerbie bombing and recent IRA attacks within the perimeter of the Rheindahlen garrison were indicative of a growing terrorist threat which was only to increase in future years notwithstanding the Good Friday peace agreement with the IRA made in Belfast some nine years later.

CHAPTER 18
TO WAR WITH THE ARMY

As SASO RAFG I held the war appointment of commander Air 1 (BR) Corps which required me to go to war with the British Army on exercises in Germany. No need to misinterpret the chapter title. I shall address the Army's hostility to the formation of the RAF later on.

My war appointment was agreed by General Sir Martin Farndale and Air Marshal Sir Paddy Hine when they were the respective commanders of the British Army of the Rhine and RAF Germany in the early 1980s. The Cs-in-C decided that when deployed for war the Air Support Operations Centre (ASOC) within the Corps HQ would benefit from some beefing up. The two separate elements of the ASOC – offensive air support and support helicopters – were commanded respectively by a wing commander and a squadron leader that led the Cs-in-C to conclude that the presence of a one-star officer would provide a single channel of air advice to the Corps commander and carry more weight in representing his air concerns to HQ 2ATAF. My predecessor, David Brook, was the first to take on the new job and I followed in 1986.

As recorded earlier on I had some previous experience of the Army. In Aden, observing and working principally with infantry battalions, I had noted the imbued tribal instincts and loyalties that so clearly differentiated one regiment from another. And I recall an invitation from a senior RAF officer to a lunchtime drinks party; dress was beach wear. Five Hunter pilots turned up in flip flops, shorts and short-sleeved shirts. A similar number of junior Army officers from a Guards regiment arrived in shoes, trousers and long-sleeved shirts with ties. Nothing could more clearly demonstrate the social divide between the RAF's purely functional interpretation of the invitation and the subaltern's understanding of what was more properly fitting. In Cyprus a haughty and rather snooty major general was disinclined to treat his RAF C-in-C with the respect owed to his appointment. But any misgivings I had about working with soldiers, that had more to do with attitudes than operating practicalities, were dispelled during my two tours with the Harrier Force in

Germany. I repeat my admiration and respect for the disciplined energy of the Royal Engineers and the technical skills of the Royal Signals. Without their wholehearted support the deployed Harrier Force would have been non-effective.

My war appointment, held for three years, presented a further fascinating insight to land warfare. Twice a year I joined the Corps HQ on field command post exercises (CPXs) – 'Summer Sales' and 'Winter Sales'. These outings each lasted for two weeks and I took my accommodation with me. A basic Land Rover, driven by SAC Dave Smith, towed a two-wheeled box body which resembled an overgrown rabbit hutch. I much envied the majority of my Army one-star equivalents who were accommodated in purpose-built extensions mounted on the rear base of long-wheeled Land Rovers. The Corps HQ moved every night to a new location most of which were hidden within the bowels of a disused factory that in winter was freezing cold and in summer dank and clammy. All staff elements necessary to support the Corps commander worked in tents within 'the diamond' that was secured by coils of barbed wire with a single point of entry manned by soldiers from a battalion dedicated to the security of the entire HQ complex. The two elements of the RAF's ASOC shared a tent with commander Aviation, an Army Air Corps brigadier, and commander Corps Air Defences, a Royal Artillery brigadier. The offensive side of ASOC was commanded by my old friend Wing Commander Al Cleaver. The support helicopters were looked after by Squadron Leader Mike Leeming. Both Al and Mike filled permanent posts in the Corps HQ's peacetime location in Bielefeld where I also attended Corps study periods and briefings.

Our shared tent was an agreeable place to work. The inevitable banter between the four elements was good humoured and we were united in representing the contribution that air could make to land operations. For my part it was easy, indeed too easy, to persuade HQ 2ATAF to allocate the Harrier Force to 1 (BR) Corps for direct tasking from our ASOC. Both Corps commanders I worked under were attentive to my advice on Harrier Force tasking, that is to say, when to use Harriers, in what numbers and against what target sets. Safe routing through the NORTHAG Corps boundaries was pre-planned for 2ATAF aircraft to avoid engagement by anti-aircraft weapons systems. All well and good if the land battle was static – highly unlikely – so safe routing tended to follow the battle rather than keep up with it. However, within HQ 1 (BR) Corps Al Cleaver and I could speak to Brigadier Mike Shellard to set up minimum-risk corridors through the Corps AOR which could then be passed to the Harrier FWOC along with the mission task.

Each of the three armoured divisions of the Corps included an Army Air Corps (AAC) regiment operating Lynx and Gazelle helicopters. The Lynx were armed with eight TOW (tube-launched, optically-tracked, wire-guided) anti-tank missiles; the Gazelles were tasked for observation and recce. I noticed during exercises that as attrition took its inevitable toll there came a point when command and control of surviving helicopters passed upwards from divisions to the Corps HQ. Like the Corps heavy artillery they became a Corps asset to be tasked directly by the Corps commander. When I asked commander Aviation (Brigadier Simon Lytle at that time) why AAC Regiments were not a Corps asset from the kick-off he told me that the divisions wouldn't stand for it. I was puzzled by this immutable declaration but the chief of staff (Brigadier Peter Sheppard) explained that the allocation of AAC regiments to divisions was more a matter of structural organisation with no implication of operational inflexibility.

The Corps commander, known as Corky when out of hearing range, was briefed twice a day and I was much impressed by the quality of briefing that covered all complex aspects of Corps functions ranging from operations through intelligence to logistics and communications. Within the pattern of HQ redeployment every 24 hours each staff cell, operating in two shifts with one in play as the other relocated, worked under sustained pressure from the Corps commander. More often than not and having set out various options for future operations, briefings would conclude with a succinct recommendation that was spot on. In the first instance this was rarely accepted by the Corps commander who would then task the staff to flesh out in detail other discarded options. The briefing officers, mainly lieutenant colonels, sustained confident delivery based on expertise within their own specialisation that could withstand intensive interrogation. All in all it was a class act. On the debit side I was surprised that we were never required to work in closed-down mode within the Marshall cabins in anticipation of a chemical/biological attack. The cabins were the same vehicles as used full time by the deployed Harrier Force. Working in closed-down mode in full NBC kit, including wearing a respirator, was distinctly uncomfortable but the capability to do so required constant practice before observation by TACEVAL assessors some of whom took too obvious pleasure in our discomfort. I have since been told by former brigade commanders that, unlike Corps HQ, they and their staff endured the same unpleasantness when deployed on exercises.

Two aspects of the briefings resonated in my airman's mind. The first was the weather forecast. Airmen need to know about visibility, cloud base, cloud structure, wind velocity and for Harrier operations in particular, environmental temperature. To soldiers the most important features of a met brief were those that affected 'trafficability' – a new word to me. This boiled down to how much weight would the ground support and how would the weather affect its LCN – load classification number in airman's speak as applied to runways. Heavy rain swelled rivers and canals that added a further dimension of difficulty of manoeuvre that was already conditioned by permanent features such as mountains and forests within the Corps AOR. In three years exercising with the Corps I watched the staff wrestling with problems arising from weather conditions that ranged from freezing rain, deep snow, swamped landscapes to rock-hard ground baked in temperatures of 30°C plus.

The second point of note was the importance of technical skills in all branches of the Corps to enable functional combat efficiency. The exercise of command and control required the setting up and sustainment of a complex communications network. Supplying and servicing fighting units placed huge demands on logisticians and engineers such that they absorbed a greater proportion of the Corps' manpower than the teeth arms. The logistic tail was highly vulnerable to air attack and I noted that the Corps staff paid little more than polite attention to the air situation above their battlefields. Local air superiority seemed to be taken almost as a given. The provision of offensive air support was a different matter. In the second half of my tour the Corps commander at that time, Lieutenant General Sir Peter Inge, required the Royal Artillery's staff to plan with the ASOC (OS) fire plans that combined Harrier air support with Corps heavy artillery when battlefield circumstances required the greatest available concentration of firepower in time and space. This was not a new concept. In the latter days of World War II the operations of tactical air forces were closely orchestrated with Army operations, albeit when the Allies enjoyed air superiority, a luxury as I reminded my Army colleagues not at all guaranteed in the Central Region some 40 years later. Discussion with the gunners before a joint recommendation was made to the Corps commander again so clearly demonstrated how topography in all its elements contributed to the 'friction' of land warfare.

During my three years working with 1 (BR) Corps I served two commanders, Lieutenant General Sir Brian Kenny followed by Sir Peter Inge. Some 30 years later if I was to characterise the two generals in the context of the English Civil Wars, Sir Brian, the archetypal man of action, would transmute to Prince Rupert of the Rhine, a dashing, charming and most professional cavalry officer. To Sir Peter I would attribute the military competence and political acumen of General George Monk, the Roundhead C-in-C and pivotal figure in the restoration of the monarchy in 1660. Sir Peter was also to enjoy the confidence of politicians and the approbation of the monarch as he ascended to the appointment of chief of defence staff and installation as a Knight of the Garter. Although differing in personality and approach to their command responsibilities, both were similarly rigorous in examining the capabilities of their subordinates and in particular during CPXs. Also on staff rides the Corps hierarchy, two stars upwards, would grill brigade commanders on their concept of operations within their boundaries.

For me they were pleasant outings, particularly in the summer months, when I could sit on a hillside overlooking some tactically important feature while listening to brigadiers as they attempted to demonstrate more than mastery of their subject with the introduction of new insights; rather difficult when the Corps' frontage and boundaries had not changed for some four decades. Divisional commanders and brigade commanders were both under the spotlight during CPXs which were quite clearly make-or-break career appointments for the incumbents. As a privileged insider I witnessed some careers accelerate upwards whereas others were soon to languish in obscurity. Most if not all of these men had already passed in Northern Ireland close examination of their professionalism and leadership.

The fierce competition for success and promotion was most evident and came as no surprise. RAF friends who attended the Army Staff College at Camberley all commented on the obvious rivalry within the ranks of their Army peers, not exactly 'dog eat dog' but pretty cut throat nevertheless as a high grading at the end of the year was essential for further advancement. This competitive instinct seemed to me to be one of the consequences of the Army's tribal system. A young officer, growing up in his regiment with the laudatory ambition of taking command sometime in the future, would always be in fierce competition with his contemporaries. Up to the rank of lieutenant colonel operational service for most Army officers was spent in one regiment which forged unbroken bonds of long-standing attachment. In direct contrast a junior RAF officer would serve on a squadron within a force of several squadrons and move between them at the end of the normal posting period of three years. Some others, and here I was particularly lucky, would move between roles albeit one became something of a jack of all trades rather than a specialist in one.

There was another significant difference between Army and RAF life in the front line. As a station commander I would fly with the squadrons more often than not under the leadership of a junior officer. While it gave me an informed judgement of their abilities, if I made an error during the sortie the leader would be polite but unsparing in his criticism during the adrenalin-fuelled debrief. There was no hiding place from even minor transgressions. But out of flying kit and back in light blue I was a force commander with all the powers of command and responsibilities vested in me by the Air Force Act. My Army peers were not expected or required to mix it with their front-line people in the same way for quite understandable reasons. A commander of an all-arms battle group had to adopt a wider perspective that took in all his front-line troops, indirect fire units (artillery), his sappers, his communicators and the whole fabric of logistic units required to support fighting echelons on the move. This fundamental difference between the Army and the RAF may go some way to explaining recent criticisms of the RAF, made by a retired air chief marshal, that middle-ranking Air Force officers "had to work hard to lift their eyes above the tactical". On the other hand one could observe that their contemporaries in the Army sometimes find it difficult to raise their eyes above the visible horizon. There is some truth in the military cliché that soldiers only believe in what they can see, hear and smell.

Of greater concern to me at the time was that assessment of command ability within the RAF stopped at group captain rank. Each year most station commanders faced detailed and critical examination of their leadership, the war fighting proficiency of their squadrons and the full gamut of their on-base support activities. Bad marks on TACEVAL and the station commander's career was dead in the water. But upwards from group captain, air rank officers were not subject to evaluation as were divisional and brigade commanders in the Army. In my third year at Rheindahlen I suggested that 2ATAF War HQ should be subject to TACEVAL. Suffice to say that my floated proposal quickly sank without trace.

Since the far-off days of the Cold War, RAF commanders have experienced continuous commitment to operations with the reality of war fighting requiring command and leadership far in excess of TACEVAL demands. For my part, the time I spent with HQ 1 (BR) Corps was an invaluable experience that benefited me greatly when two and a half years later I was director of operations in the Joint HQ for Gulf War I. I was familiar with the Army, I was aware of their concerns and I had enjoyed the company of some quite admirable soldiers some of whom remain good friends to this day and not least from the Corps of Royal Engineers. In 1994 the engineer-in-chief, Major General Geoff Field, invited me to take on the appointment of honorary colonel of 73 Engineer Regiment (Air Support) Volunteers. I was delighted to accept and in the following eight years thoroughly enjoyed the company of some exceptional sappers from the Regular and Territorial Armies.

CHAPTER 19
HIGH WYCOMBE

After my bruising encounter with Air Chief Marshal Sir Kenneth Cross 26 years previously I had only occasionally visited RAF High Wycombe. So working there as an air vice-marshal was I suppose as good a way as any of getting to know the RAF's primary operational headquarters.

My tour did not get off to a good start. Two days in the chair, after a short handover from my predecessor Air Vice-Marshal Sandy Wilson, I slipped a disc – the consequence of lifting an overweight Labrador temporarily housed with us after the death of my father-in-law. My new AOC-in-C, Sir Paddy Hine, who had been C-in-C in RAF Germany the first time I slipped a disc, sternly advised me not to waste time with doctors but to find a good osteopath. So I turned up the Yellow Pages, found the fellow with the most initials after his name, and booked an appointment. Next day my driver, a young senior aircraftman, delivered me to the address and watched as I laboured up a pathway welded in a near-sitting position. The SAC then saw me arrive at the door and reach up for the knocker. Shortly afterwards the door was opened by a most attractive blond woman who caringly took my hand and led me to the back of the house where I was passed on to a middle-aged chap for the treatment. It worked as by the end of the session I was standing up straight. The receptionist then took me back to the front door and waved me on my way. I got into the car and my driver could scarce contain his excitement. "These osteo....osteo Sir?" he asked. "Osteopath," I volunteered helpfully. "Yes Sir, these osteopaths, is that what I would call a massage parlour?" Rather ashamedly I just smiled my reply. In years ahead we met a few times and he always gave me a look which was a strange amalgam of envy and nudge, nudge, wink, wink, 'your secret is safe with me, sir'.

Back to the office and still in some discomfort I found working from a lectern the most comfortable posture as I got to grips with the responsibilities of an appointment much wider in scope than SASO RAF Germany. Strike Command had been formed in the late 1960s and early 1970s by the merger first of Fighter and Bomber Commands followed by the absorption of Coastal, Air Support and Signals Commands. By 1989 HQ Strike had three groups under command: 1 Group at RAF Upavon contained all UK-based strike/ attack/recce squadrons, all support helicopter squadrons and the complete force of air transport and air-to-air refuelling aircraft; 11 Group at RAF Bentley Priory comprised all air and ground air defence forces while 18 Group at RAF Northwood (co-located with the Royal Navy Headquarters Fleet) encompassed all of the RAF's maritime assets including search and rescue. Each group was commanded by an air vice-marshal with supporting operations, engineering and administrative staffs. The uniform strength of the service was 91,433 of whom 43,655 were serving in Strike Command.

I knew all the group commanders and senior staff at High Wycombe so settling in was not difficult, and it was particularly pleasing to work directly to Sir Ken Hayr who was deputy C-in-C and the chief of staff. Sir Ken was a leading member of the so-called 'Harrier Mafia' (its influence much exaggerated) and readers may recall he was the senior student on the famous/ infamous 62 Course at the RAF Staff College in 1972. Ken was by any yardstick a great aviator but I think he found the transfer of the vital attributes of outstanding airborne leadership to a 'mahogany bomber' something of a trial. But his good humour and lively sense of fun never faltered which made a visit to his office a cheerful event no matter what gloom shrouded the subject for discussion. Ken's passion for flying was unquenchable and it was a desperately sad day when, aged 66, he was killed flying a Vampire at the Biggin Hill Air Show in 2001.

Two pressing issues required my immediate attention as directed by Sir Paddy. The first was to accelerate the progress of the Improved United Kingdom Air Defence Ground Environment (IUKADGE) to full operating capability; it was already well behind schedule and over budget. In essence the project involved the linking together of all ground-based and airborne radar-detection systems to provide a fully recognised air picture of the UK Air Defence Region (UKADR) into the bunker at RAF High Wycombe. The UKADR covered an area of some 400,000 square miles. Sources included nine radar sites and Shackleton airborne early warning (AEW) aircraft operating from RAF Lossiemouth in the north of Scotland and awaiting replacement with Boeing E-3Ds. The project was in disarray. Whilst individual elements were up and running plugging the whole lot together caused the system to crash. That much I could understand but the management and implementation of a software intensive project, let alone understanding the associated technology, was way beyond my experience and comprehension. Most fortunately help was at hand.

Air Commodore Joan Hopkins was the first female RAF officer to command an operational station, RAF Neatishead in Norfolk, one of the three sector operations centres (SOCs) in the UKADR. She had joined the operations staff at High Wycombe on much-deserved promotion from that tour. A fighter controller by background, Joan's professional competence and straightforward force of personality had earned her the accolade of respect and affection in equal measure. It didn't take her long to suss out that her new boss's understanding of radar technology and electronics was superficial at best. So with commendable patience and in response to my invitation she led me through the troubled history of IUKADGE. Her presentations were not contaminated with an overdose of wiggly amps which are normally so attractive to those blessed with a deep knowledge and understanding of things electric. After several sessions she concluded that the future of IUKADGE was in the balance. So what was to be done?

Joan understood the problem of connectivity which she attributed to the contractor's concept of bringing the project to a single and co-ordinated conclusion – in essence the big bang solution. In Joan's opinion a staged introduction of each element sequentially after proof of performance offered a far better chance of success. Moreover she knew that this concept was the preferred solution of one Nancy Price, a technical troubleshooter embedded in the contractor's consortium. I immediately agreed Joan's suggestion that she should work in cooperation with Nancy to implement in stages a programme of increasing complexity with the RAF taking over the running of the software after the completion of each element. Thanks to these two women the programme was put back on track and achieved full operating capability in 1991 presenting in the bunker a recognised air picture that encompassed the whole of the vast area of the UKADR – six years late and about the same time as the last brick was removed from the Berlin Wall. Giving Joan Hopkins a free hand was my sole contribution to the eventual success of IUKADGE. She kept me in touch with regular progress reports and tried to teach me the principles of early computer technology and I was now free to focus on the new bunker built to replace Air Chief Marshal Sir Arthur Harris's wartime headquarters in which he masterminded the World War II bomber offensive against the Axis powers.

Construction of the huge, largely NATO-funded, subterranean structure some four storeys deep had been completed. It was designed to survive nuclear attack in closed-down mode with sufficient utilities to permit continuing operations after a nuclear strike. The bunker, with its own generators and air filtration units, could house 850 people for up to seven days with full sleeping, medical and feeding facilities. My war appointment as director of operations within the UKADR required me to take the lead in achieving full operating capability for the bunker and with the technical capabilities and capacity to operate as a fully functional national joint headquarters. To bring the bunker and Strike Command staffs up to speed a series of CPXs were completed with each increasing in size and complexity; initially these exercises focused on air operations both defensive and offensive.

The culmination of this process was achieved in June/July 1990 with a large-scale joint out-of-area exercise based in Cyprus with operational command of deployed forces exercised by Sir Paddy. The bunker housed staffs from all three services with other participating players in the MoD, HQ Fleet and HQ Land. At the end of the three-week exercise the High Wycombe bunker, now known as the Primary War Headquarters (PWHQ), was judged to have achieved full operating capability. I well recall leaving the bunker at the end of the exercise thinking that this had been my final underground stint before I departed in May 1991 to take command of 1 Group. I relished the prospect but on 2nd August 1990 Iraq invaded Kuwait and my life took another unexpected turn as I was to spend the next seven months working exclusively underground in our brand new and shining bunker. More about this later.

Although IUKADGE and the bunker took up a lot of my time there were three aspects of my appointment which introduced stimulating thought. Two concerned operations. Sir Paddy's patience was stretched by the Soviet air force continuing to probe our air defences. Soviet aircraft regularly transited west of the UK en route to Cuba and Lusaka. Others launched from the Kola Peninsula and tracked by Norwegian radar stations would suddenly descend to low level below radar coverage to reappear at altitude somewhere on the borders of the UKADR. The air staff was tasked to draft an operational plan to intercept these flights at low level using a composite force of air defence fighters and AEW aircraft with air tanker support to give the Russians a nasty surprise. The plan, activated by early warning from the Norwegians, was the comparatively easy one.

The second, a far more adventurous war-contingency operation, was to plan a simultaneous attack on Soviet airfields in the Kola Peninsula with 24 Tornado GR1s armed with the JP233 airfield-denial weapons. The journey to and from RAF Lossiemouth to the Kola Peninsula and back was more than 2,000 nautical miles with the attack sector flown at ultra-low level to make the best use of terrain screening so to achieve both surprise and concentration of force on selected targets. The bomber aircraft on these airfields posed serious threats to both the UK base and transatlantic reinforcements. The operational contingency plan, necessarily very assumption-dependent, went through so many iterations that the staff nicknamed it 'Hirohito', inspired by the longevity of the emperor of Japan. Eventually we received the AOC-in-C's approval and I was tasked to present the operation order for formal approval as a NATO op plan. I went to SHAPE at Mons in Belgium to go through the details with Major General Mike Nelson USAF who listened with intense concentration and no interjections. As I finished he leaned back in his chair and with a nice smile coolly observed, "Gee, you guys are really something" – as polite a way as any of expressing doubt about the probability of success given the complexities of coordination and the attendant risks. I took it as a compliment but I am not convinced it was meant as such. Never mind, planning the operation exercised far more than mathematical conjuring with fuel burn figures and the many other relevant factors that required consideration. And the employment of Tornados on high-low-high sorties let alone exclusively at medium level was to become reality far sooner than any of us expected at that time.

In the summer of 1989 at a routine senior staff meeting Ken Hayr had unexpectedly asked me what we could do to mark the 50th anniversary of the Battle of Britain in September the following year. My first reply off the top of my head was to fly 200 Tornados – a mixture of strike/attack and air defence variants – over London. The idea soon fell on stony ground as some of the squadrons that would be involved did not have the honour 'Battle of Britain' emblazoned on their squadron standards. More importantly, the Battle of Britain Fighter Association, under the chairmanship of Air Chief Marshal Sir Christopher Foxley-Norris, asked that all squadrons currently in service that had fought in the battle should be represented in the flypast. This introduced some complexity because it meant co-ordinating a flypast of fighter jets (Tornado, Phantom, Harrier, Jaguar, Hawk) at one extreme with heavies (VC10, Nimrod, Hercules and the much lighter HS125) at the other with the all-important inclusion of the Battle of Britain Memorial Flight with their Spitfires, Hurricanes and single Lancaster bomber. After I had dismissed some rather wacky ideas from the staff as to how this should be achieved, Air Vice-Marshal Bill Wratten, AOC 11 Group, accepted the invitation to lead the flypast in a Spitfire and to produce the operation order within broad parameters set by HQ Strike Command. The planning brain which solved the problem of co-ordination belonged to Wing Commander David Broome. With Bill at the front of the flypast, 168 aircraft achieved compression in time and space so that the seven main formations flew over Buckingham Palace all within five minutes. It was a proper and fitting tribute to 'The Few' and survivors of the battle had the privilege of marching past Her Majesty.

Although operational planning of aerial activities in war and peace were part and parcel of a SASO's job, the end of the Cold War introduced defence policy matters which were to provoke uncertainty and unease throughout the service. First and foremost was the government's search for the 'peace dividend' under the Options for Change review initiated in late 1989 after the Berlin Wall came down and it became clear that the Cold War was de facto over. The review was intended to recognise the changing strategic environment with the Warsaw Pact by then defunct as a military alliance. Soon after, the reunification of Germany and the collapse of the Soviet Union itself added a further dimension of strategic uncertainty. While it seemed to me that we had already enjoyed the peace dividend with 40 years of relative tranquillity in Europe, the opportunity to reduce the share of GDP taken by defence was irresistible to politicians throughout West Europe. Decisions on the capabilities of our armed forces were taken without structured and wide-ranging debate but with the stated intention of creating "smaller forces, better equipped, properly trained and housed and well-motivated. They will need to be flexible and mobile…" Within the next two decades these words with only the smallest variation were to become a familiar refrain as the size and capabilities of our armed forces were subject to unremitting pressures from continuing reductions in defence spending.

As far as the RAF was concerned the main and immediate consequences from Options for Change were a reduction in air defence capability, the closure of two bases in RAF Germany and a reduction in service manpower from 89,000 to 75,000; this 16% cutback brought the manpower strength of the service to its lowest state since 1938. A week after the Options for Change announcement in Parliament Saddam Hussein invaded Kuwait and our operational capabilities were to be tested against reality rather than hypothesis. However, this imposed no more than a temporary halt on the implementation of cuts which within 18 months were to see the closure of five RAF stations and one RAF hospital and the disbandment of four Phantom squadrons, three Tornado GR1 squadrons, two Buccaneer squadrons, one Nimrod maritime patrol squadron, one Victor tanker squadron and four squadrons of the RAF Regiment. The inevitable consequence of such deep cuts was that matching resources to tasks for all three services would become increasingly fraught. I felt at the time that execution of such cuts on this scale was premature as there had been no evident attempt to identify and assess the exact nature of the post-Cold War security environment.

I cannot recall having any input to the calculations which resulted in such a significant drawdown in the combat power of the service but I was to be deeply involved in the implementation of the disagreeable consequences. Meanwhile, the Iraqi invasion of Kuwait was effectively to end my tour as

SASO as I took up my war appointment in the bunker as director of operations in a Joint HQ where I headed up the Battle Management Group (BMG). Both were rather grandiose titles as I didn't direct any operations and had no hand in the management of battles. But there was more than enough to do which was to keep me very busy for the following seven months.

CHAPTER 20
GULF WAR I

At 0200 hours on 2nd August 1990 Saddam Hussein's troops crossed into Kuwait. The Iraqi Army, more than a million strong, was the fourth largest professional army in the world and included armoured brigades equipped with modern Russian-built T72 tanks which led the main attack across the desert to Kuwait City. Soon afterwards Saddam massed 100,000 troops on the Kuwait/Saudi Arabia border. Despite the prime minister's caution – Mrs Thatcher was reported as having said that she did not wish to "get our arm caught in this mangle" – she decided that the RAF would support the immediate American military response to deter a follow-up incursion by the Iraqi Army into the north-east of Saudi Arabia. All this was made clear to me when summoned to the MoD on 5th August where I was instructed to activate the High Wycombe bunker in preparation for the deployment of RAF aircraft to the Middle East. I briefed the acting C-in-C, Air Marshal Sir John Kemball, while messages went out to recall Sir Paddy from Germany where he was enjoying his summer leave. He returned home in quick time to take command of what was to become Operation Granby.

Within the next week, and in response to the United Nations Security Council Resolution 662, the British government announced the deployment of a squadron of Tornado F-3 air defence aircraft from RAF Akrotiri to Dahran on the eastern seaboard of Saudi Arabia and a squadron of ground-attack Jaguars to Thumrait in Oman supported by two VC10 tankers. Shortly afterwards three maritime patrol Nimrods were also deployed to Oman to support the RN Armilla Patrol which had been operating continuously in the Gulf for the past ten years. All of this is recorded in the first of the six shorthand notebooks I filled during my contribution to Op Granby as the so-called director of operations. I see no purpose in recording the full history of the operation as much has already been written about it by those involved at the sharp end. But I can offer a number of personal observations for the record and in doing so they will reflect my own honest opinions on events and personalities. It is, however, important to understand the structure of command and control for Granby.

The structure for the operation was simple. Op Granby was directed by Her Majesty's government, acting through the MoD in Whitehall, with the operational centre in the UK established in the PWHQ at High Wycombe. The bunker became a fully Joint HQ from 1st October 1990 when RN ships on the Armilla Patrol were placed under the operational command of Sir Paddy. RN staff from Northwood under the positive and good humoured leadership of Captain Paul Canter quickly settled into their new domain. Also on 1st October Lieutenant General Sir Peter de la Billière was appointed commander in theatre with operational control of British Forces Middle East. Shortly beforehand the deployment of 7 Armoured Brigade had commenced which led to Sir Peter's appointment and Air Vice-Marshal Sandy Wilson, hitherto commander British Forces Arabian Peninsula, now appointed as deputy commander/air commander. The upgrading of the in-theatre command appointment from two stars to three stars reflected the War Cabinet's increasing commitment to Op Granby which was to reach some 45,000 men and women deployed – the UK's heaviest involvement in conflict since the end of the World War II as the initial aim of defending Saudi Arabia transitioned to the recapture of Kuwait should Saddam not bend to the will of the United Nations.

Sir Paddy's directive as joint commander from CDS was specific in its statement of military objectives. They were to contribute to the unconditional withdrawal of Iraq from Kuwait and the restoration of the legitimate government of that country at the same time upholding the authority of the United Nations. Having stated the objectives the directive then ran on to 28 pages of close signal type including annexes. Apart from spelling out in fine detail exact limits on the achievement of military objectives, the document covered everything imaginable from logistics through prisoner-of-war handling to the employment of padres. The final directive was the tenth issue and did not include 12 different sets of rules of engagement (ROE).

The words 'command' and 'control' in the purely military context need brief explanation. Operational Command (OPCOM) as exercised by Sir Paddy gave him the authority to assign missions to his subordinate commanders, to deploy units, to re-assign units and to retain or delegate operational or tactical control as deemed necessary. Operational Control (OPCON) was the authority delegated by Sir Paddy to his subordinate commanders to accomplish missions usually limited by function, time or location. Operating within an American-led coalition required the War Cabinet's agreement to Sir Paddy's recommendation that General Schwarzkopf, US Army and C-in-C Central Command, should be given tactical control (TACON) of our in-theatre forces, that is the detailed direction of our forces to contribute to the coalition's achievement of operational objectives. His recommendation was subject to three conditions. First, that tasks allocated to British forces were consistent with Sir Paddy's directive from CDS; secondly, Sir Peter de la Billière would be a member of General Schwarzkopf's command group and, thirdly, British officers would be included in his operational planning teams. These conditions were readily accepted by the general and Sir Paddy's recommendation was approved by the War Cabinet. Eventually some 100 British military personnel were directly involved with the Americans on either planning or liaison duties.

Within the bunker the staff were organised into three tiers. At the bottom of the pyramid were the functional cells, some 32 of them, who reported to ten one-star assistant chiefs-of-staff looking after personnel, intelligence, operations (sea, land and air), logistics, plans, communications and finance. There was a separate special forces cell. The one stars comprised the Battle Management Group (BMG) which I chaired. The BMG routinely met twice daily before I and selected members of the BMG briefed the command group comprising Sir Paddy, Sir John Kemball as chief of staff, the Naval deputy (Rear Admiral Roy Newman at first followed by Rear Admiral Peter Woodhead) and the Land deputy Lieutenant General Sir Michael Wilkes. Mr Andrew Palmer of the FCO joined the group shortly before hostilities as the political advisor. At the end of the briefing and discussion the joint commander made his decisions and gave his orders which I then transmitted to the staffs through the BMG.

Three weeks before the start of hostilities the bunker went onto full 24 hours manning with me taking the night shift from midnight until midday, effectively a sixteen-hour stint given the need for detailed handover/takeover briefs with my two deputies, Air Commodore Trevor Nattrass and Brigadier Philip Sanders. Briefings were held in a specially devised situation room with large-scale maps and charts recording the most up-to-date information we had on the disposition of all friendly and enemy forces. The day of PowerPoint had still to come. Within the bunker this structure proved resilient and effective as were our lateral dealings with HQ Land and HQ Fleet. Upwards from the BMG our dealings with the commitments staff in the MoD were less comfortable and I shall return to this matter shortly.

The principal tasks of the BMG under my direction were to plan the deployment and recovery of British forces, the provision of the necessary combat capability for designated air, sea and land operations and the sustainment of British forces deployed to theatre. To implement government decisions and direction the joint staffs planned and accomplished the deployment of 45,000 service personnel, 157 RAF aircraft, 100 helicopters, 221 main battle tanks, 92 artillery pieces and 29 RN and Royal Fleet Auxiliary (RFA) ships. Some

15,000 vehicles and 85,000 tons of ammunition were transported with 139 ships involved in a sea train over lines of communication some 6,500 miles long. By the new year the daily airlift exceeded 500 tons which equated to the monthly peacetime rate for the whole of the RAF Air Transport Force.

In 1990 we still possessed sizeable, well trained and immediately available forces albeit logistic sustainability was configured primarily for NATO's Central Region and the Atlantic. Moving the focus of military action several thousand miles to the south-east into a desert environment tested to the full the expertise of service logisticians. All RAF aircraft in the order of battle required modifications; to name but a few, engines needed rescheduling for a hot climate, IFF systems required modification and secure radios had to be fitted. To allow for attrition nearly 300 aircraft were prepared for Granby and we were fortunate to have had the time to adapt aircraft to accommodate the demands of a harsh operating environment. In the event actual wartime availability for all types far exceeded peacetime training rates much to the credit of our technicians with round the clock shift work on main bases and maintenance units. The planning and harmonisation in the bunker of the RAF's engineering and support effort, under the leadership of Air Vice-Marshal Mike Alcock, was crucial to the success of the service's contribution to Granby before, during and after hostilities.

The deployment of a second armoured brigade and the decision to bring our combat ground forces up to light division strength also challenged Army logisticians. I was told that the Army was suffering from a chronic shortage of spares, manpower, ammunition and the wherewithal to fight in the desert. To support the deployment of a division every engine was taken out of tanks not deployed, infantry battalions were 'cannibalised' to bring deployed units up to their war establishments and to provide battle-casualty replacements. The build-up in the Gulf of fuel, power-pack (engine and transmission) replacements, ammunition and all other vital paraphernalia was brilliantly handled by Brigadier Simon Firth in the bunker and Brigadier Martin White who set up his force maintenance area next to the docks at Al Jubayl. As deputy chief of staff (support) for all logistics Mike Alcock was a very busy man. And my broad description of logistic aspects makes no mention of such important topics as the provision of NBC kit, desert clothing, tentage, water, fresh rations, explosive ordinance disposal (EOD), battle-damage repair, medical support and so on.

The provision of the necessary communications to allow the exercise of command and control placed special demands on our communicators who, to my mind, were foremost amongst the unsung heroes of Gulf War I. They worked wonders, procuring and pressing into service new and often untrialled equipment, adjusting locations and moving people and kit to meet changing operational circumstances and the needs of commanders and staffs alike. In this domain JHQ's working relations with MoD were first class as communications and information systems (CIS) activities were masterminded by the MoD CIS Committee under the chairmanship of Rear Admiral Rob Walmsley with Air Commodore John Main as his deputy. But there was a rub. The vast array of communications no longer channelled the flow of information through a single conduit to the JHQ. MoD had similar and parallel access to information which increased rather than diminished the political thirst for information. At one stage during the build-up to the war we in the JHQ were under considerable pressure (not from the CIS Committee) to install one-to-one communications from the secretary of state to brigade commanders so that he could be kept fully informed on the progress of land operations. Eventually the joint commander's argument, that brigade commanders in action had more pressing calls on their time, won the day and no more was heard of this nonsense.

Coming so soon after the end of the Cold War with politicians keenly seeking the so-called peace dividend, I should not have been surprised that political interest in Op Granby was so intense and pervasive. In particular, the political spotlight, most enthusiastically focused by MoD officials, was trained on resource implications and particularly manpower. The Civil Service was determined that the armed forces would not be allowed to run amok with their demands as had been, allegedly, the case during the Falklands War. Because of the high political profile the defence secretariat, prompted by the Treasury, went through every submission – particularly those concerning manpower resources – with a fine-tooth comb. The secretariat thus exercised a disproportionately large input to decision making which at times paid scant attention to military judgement and delayed the whole process of implementing the deployment and sustainment of UK forces. Simply put, the time imperative to prepare for war was not appreciated and officials were slow to grasp the military realities of what we were about and the difficulties of deploying such large numbers of men and equipment over considerable distances.

In retrospect I don't think it was until we forced London to consider the disposal of the dead, in particular the possibility of many chemical casualties, that the potential awfulness of what we were facing finally struck home. From our campaign modelling in the bunker, under the direction of Brigadier Sanders, we estimated that in the very worst circumstances involving the widespread use of Iraqi chemical weapons our casualties could top out at some 4,000 per day. Seeking MoD guidance on the disposal of the dead, some if not many chemically contaminated, in a Muslim country caused officials considerable discomfort. That said, we now know that the Iraqis had been warned that if Saddam Hussein used chemical and/or biological weapons the US response, unspecified, would be overwhelming. Saddam most probably interpreted this warning as a threat of nuclear attack and assumed the Americans had nuclear weapons in theatre. So weapons of mass destruction (WMD) were not used against coalition forces; in 1990 their existence was a reality.

The focus on resource implications involved the JHQ in an absolutely unending stream of ministerial submissions proposing the deployment of various units and sections. I remember drafting one that involved just ten men. On occasion, and at some risk of consequent embarrassment, ministerial endorsement of a mission was anticipated because we could not afford to wait a day longer. I got caught with my pants down when I instructed the ship carrying support helicopter engineering equipment to sail without London's permission. Unfortunately the ship ran into bad weather in the Bay of Biscay and had to put into Gibraltar to check the security of its loads below deck. It didn't take long for MoD to question the arrival of a ship in Gibraltar within a timescale that could only have been achieved by a powerboat at full throttle. I confessed my sin to Sir Paddy who administered a sharp rap to my knuckles and then protected me from the wrath of Whitehall. On another occasion we were involved in a month-long argument with Whitehall as to whether the Royal Fleet Auxiliary ship *Argus* should be prepared as a hospital or a primary casualty-reception ship. There are important differences and I did not believe the Iraqi air force would acknowledge the significance of a white ship adorned with and protected by red crosses, hence my preference for the latter in standard RN colours to minimise its distinctiveness. Eventually MoD agreed that *Argus* would remain unadorned.

Throughout Operation Granby obtaining timely MoD agreement to ROE and their subsequent revision to accommodate changing operational circumstances was a running sore that caused great concern and frustration to all in the command chain, but especially those serving in our operational units. The staffing process in London lacked any sense of urgency. Following the move of Iraqi fighter aircraft from their bases in Iraq to airfields in Iran, Commodore Chris Craig, the senior naval officer Middle East, requested a change in his ROE to permit engagement of aircraft judged hostile emerging from Iranian airspace. This was particularly important as two of his Type 42 destroyers formed a vital element of the forward air defence barrier protecting the three US Navy carrier battle groups in the central Gulf. I submitted the request to

MoD and pressed for a quick decision. None was forthcoming and when I spoke to an official I was told the submission was in the minister's weekend bag. I protested that delay was hazarding our ships and their crews only to be informed that the minister needed more time for consideration of the request and that protection of his reputation in Parliament was the official's principal concern. I was very angry and here I must acknowledge my debt to Sir John Kemball who, recognising the breakdown in communication between me and the particular official, took on his own head responsibility for the submission of all future ROE requests. Two weeks later the minister concerned visited the JHQ and asked me if I had any specific worries. I mentioned my concern about slow response to ROE requests only to be told that he left this to officials. I could hardly believe my ears.

Taken in the round, there remains no doubt in my mind and with all the benefit of hindsight that the efficiency of national command and control arrangements during Granby was threatened by an excessively bureaucratic approach that constrained our efforts to prepare for war and caused a great deal of unnecessary frustration and extra work. Moreover, operating within a multinational coalition of 32 nations added to the challenge of sustaining a degree of national political control over our forces under the command of a foreign national. Sir Paddy visited General Schwarzkopf every three weeks and achieved a sound working relationship with him that was mirrored down the chain of command between American and British commanders at all levels. The example set from the top was absolutely instrumental in achieving mutual confidence between ourselves and the US forces in all three elements of warfare.

To minimise the risk of heavy land-force casualties, General Schwarzkopf required coalition air forces to reduce the combat effectiveness of the Iraqi Army in the Kuwait theatre of operations by at least 50%; AFVs and artillery were to be the primary targets. The general set this as a precondition for the launching of a ground offensive correctly judged as necessary to evict all of Saddam's forces from Kuwait. The air campaign to establish air superiority began on the night of 16/17 January. With an enormous array of air power – some 2,000 armed aircraft within the coalition – air supremacy was declared on 28th January. Thereafter the air campaign continued remorselessly until General Schwarzkopf assessed that the level of damage inflicted on the Iraqis was such that it was time to launch the land offensive. The attack began on 24th February and 100 hours later the Iraqi Army called it a day.

In the years that followed two topics about the campaign were regularly raised in discussion. The first concerned the RAF's use of the JP233 airfield-denial weapon and the post-war claim by commentators that our Tornado GR1s were forced up from low level to medium level operations because of an unacceptable loss rate. The decision to discontinue JP233 attacks against Iraqi main operating bases (MOBs) was taken after five to six days of the air campaign when it became clear that the Iraqi air force was making no more than a token effort to counter coalition air attacks. They appeared to be content to sit inside their hardened aircraft shelters (HAS) to await the impending ground assault when presumably their air effort would focus on support for the Iraqi Army. There was thus no point in continuing to attack runways until such time as the Iraqis decided to make use of their ground-attack aircraft. However, counter air operations were continued against enemy HAS on their MOBs with the task allotted to aircraft with precision weapon-guidance capability such as the USAF F-15E, the F-111 and the F-117. As we had no 'smart' weapon delivery in theatre at that time to join in these operations with Tornado GR1s they were switched from low to medium level against a variety of targets including radar sites and weapons-storage areas. We thought we were doing quite well but when the results of American satellite intelligence became available it was painfully clear that we and other freefall bombers were achieving very little.

It was then that Sir Paddy decided that Buccaneers with Pave Spike laser systems had to be deployed if the Tornados, in the absence of previously promised designator support from the USAF, were to make a meaningful contribution to the continuing coalition air effort. Twelve Buccaneers soon arrived at Muharraq (Bahrain) followed quickly by the addition of two pre-production thermal imaging airborne laser designation (TIALD) pods immediately nicknamed by the crews as Sharon and Tracey. The Buccaneer and TIALD-equipped Tornado combination produced such a dramatic improvement that Tornado GR1 operations achieved the most consistent and accurate bombing in the RAF's history to date.

Within 18 days around the clock TIALD sorties alone had hit 229 pinpoint targets. Meanwhile, HAS-bashing had convinced Saddam Hussein that the survival of his more capable ground-attack aircraft could only be achieved by their withdrawal to Iran. That was the moment when the coalition moved from outright air superiority, which we had really enjoyed from the outset, to air supremacy. The further use of the Tornado/JP233 combination against Iraqi MOBs thus became redundant. By the end of the war our Tornado GR1s had flown more than 1,500 operational sorties for the loss of six aircraft. Only one of these was downed while attacking an airfield with JP233 and this flew into the ground after leaving the target. Here, and wearing my airman's hat,

I must record my admiration for the Tornado crews. Their JP233 operations made a unique contribution to the rapid achievement of air supremacy. Flying with a five-ton weapon load for the first time for night attacks, which included in-flight refuelling to reach and return from their airfield targets, required flying skills of a very high order. Pressing home attacks in the face of fierce opposition from extensive enemy anti-aircraft gunfire called for a similar measure of physical courage. They were not found wanting.

The second matter concerned the American administration's decision to implement a ceasefire after 100 hours of the land campaign. The UK was not consulted; Prime Minister John Major was simply informed of the decision. It was Sir Paddy's opinion, and one fully supported by all of us in the JHQ, that we had stopped too soon. Coalition land forces were within 36 hours of completing encirclement of the Iraqi Army inside Kuwait. When achieved this would have allowed all remaining Iraqi armour and artillery pieces to be neutralised before soldiers were returned to Iraq. So what caused the Americans to call a halt to operations? First, Iraqi forces seeking to avoid encirclement would have passed through the Mutla Pass as they retreated from Kuwait City towards Basrah. Their inevitable destruction by air attack would probably have been reported as unnecessary carnage by the international media particularly as withdrawal allowed the restoration of the legitimate government of Kuwait as mandated by the UN. Secondly, General Schwarzkopf had won a spectacular victory on the ground in just four days with very light casualties, 250 killed within the whole coalition. There was a concern that if the Iraqis had been trapped inside Kuwait, remnants of the Republican Guards might have fought much harder so adding to coalition casualties. And thirdly, both these matters concerned General Colin Powell, chairman of the Joint Chiefs of Staff, who it is believed persuaded President Bush to suspend operations.

In the aftermath of the war I was often asked whether or not, given the scale of victory, the coalition should have pressed on to Baghdad. My answer was always in the negative. The UN mandate had been met and it had nothing to do with regime change. Furthermore, Arab members of the alliance would have withdrawn their forces so breaking the legitimacy of the coalition. Apart from these political considerations land forces would have had to regroup and wait for their logistics to catch up before launching northwards. The daily needs of 1 (BR) Armoured Division – some 28,000 men – were of the same order as those for the whole of the 21st Army Group during the early part of Operation Overlord, the D-Day landings in 1944. At the end of hostilities on 28th February, the line of communication from Al Jubayl, the port of entry in the Gulf, to brigade positions was of a similar distance to that between the Normandy beaches and Berlin.

In the round the British forces committed to Operation Granby performed with courage and professionalism that won the respect of both our Allies and the public at home. Within the coalition only the RN joined the US Navy in offensive maritime operations, and although our ships represented no more than 10% of the total strength, they played a proportionally much greater part than implied by numerical comparison. Eleven destroyers/frigates were deployed for Granby supported by an underway replenishment group of 11 fleet auxiliaries. Nine vessels in the mine countermeasures task group made a particularly important contribution in clearing the extensive minefields laid by the Iraqis in the northern Gulf. Two weeks of non-stop minesweeping operations were completed before the port of Kuwait City was declared safe and allowed to reopen.

1 (BR) Armoured Division advanced with remarkable speed across some 200 miles of desert from its start position with logistic resupply and communications maintained throughout. The Royal Engineers overcame many physical objectives met during the advance and the Royal Electrical and Mechanical Engineers ensured that virtually the whole of the armoured vehicle fleet was operational when hostilities were suspended. Within the advance the division destroyed 200 tanks, 100 armoured vehicles and 100 artillery pieces. Eight thousand Iraqi soldiers were captured which left the designated guard force awash with prisoners. All of this was achieved at a cost of 15 soldiers killed and 43 wounded although tragically nine more were subsequently killed by friendly forces air attack. Special Forces operations principally aimed at countering the threat of Iraqi Scud missiles made a contribution to coalition success which again was out of proportion to their numbers. No details of their operations were included in the joint commander's despatch at the request of HQ Special Forces. To my considerable surprise this commitment to operational security was soon broken with the publication of books written by recently retired SAS soldiers, both commissioned and non-commissioned.

Although I was filling a joint appointment, as SASO Strike Command I took more than a polite interest in the activities of the RAF from the start to the end of Granby. The performance of our 'heavies', all Strike Command aircraft, was more than satisfactory. For the record the Air Transport Force of Hercules, VC10s and Tristars logged 12,500 sorties in accumulating 50,000 flying hours – more than twice the peacetime rate. During the air war Victor, VC10K and Tristar tankers flew 730 sorties off-loading 13,000 tonnes of fuel

22. Field action shot of Harrier on lift-off. (Philip Ward)

23. Field action shot of 4 Squadron aircraft in hide, parked on tin. (Philip Ward)

22

23

24. Helping the Army. No. 18 Squadron retrieves the second of two AFVs from a local river to save further embarrassment for the Army cavalry. (Author)

25. Visiting 4 (AC) Squadron at Port Stanley airfield, Falkland Islands, December 1982. Wing Commander Tony McKeon on my right. Flight Lieutenants Loader and Moran (third and fourth to my left) both achieved four-star rank. (4 [AC] Squadron)

26. A farewell photo for the scrapbook. (3 Squadron)

27. Former QFI greets former student at RAF Gütersloh in 1983. (Air Historical Branch)

28. Mrs Thatcher and me during her visit to the Harrier Force in Germany, September 1983. Behind us are Air Marshal Sir Paddy Hine (then C-in-C RAF Germany) and Wing Commander John Thompson (OC 3 [F] Squadron). (Author)

29. Change of command at No.1 Group in 1993 as I hand over to Air Vice-Marshal Peter Squire. PSO Ian Jenkins and ADC Nick Newman on the right, back row. (Air Historical Branch)

30. Office and house staff when I was C-in-C Allied Forces North-West Europe. MA Lieutenant Colonel Clive Knightley on my right and ADC Flight Lieutenant Fraser Miles to Elizabeth's left. Back row, top right, Sergeant Dave Smith – my driver for the best part of ten years. (HQ AFNW)

31. Son Douglas shows me around the Jet Stream. (Douglas Johns)

32. Arriving at RAF Leuchars to attend NATO Air Meet in company with ACM Bill Wratten. Eight stars in a two-seater jet attracted some comment. General view, if we crashed promotion prospects would be significantly enhanced. (HQ AFNW)

33. With the Red Arrows prior to display sortie on 17th July 1998.
(Author)

34. Air Marshal Sir John Kemball hands over to me the staff of office
for CAS and DC-in-C Strike Command in February 1993.
(Air Historical Branch)

35. My one and only sortie in a Eurofighter/Typhoon. (BAE SYSTEMS)

36. Under Iguazú Falls Argentina with ADC Peter Brown and PSO Andy Pulford. I refused to share my umbrella. (Author)

37. Sarajevo, 1995. From left to right: Admiral Leighton Smith (USN) NATO C-in-C South, self as C-in-C North-West and Lieutenant General Mike Walker, Commander IFOR. Behind us is General Helge Hansen, C-in-C Central Region. (SHAPE)

38. Allied Command Europe, Command Group 1995. From left to right: Admiral Leighton Smith (USN), General Sir Jeremy McKenzie (UK), General George Joulwan (US Army), General Helge Hansen (German Army), self and General Peter Carstens (German Army). (Author)

39. Me on board Ivanhoe at Windsor, 2000. (Author)

40. Riding a main battle tank during a visit with Sir Paddy Hine to British Forces deployed to Saudi Arabia for Operation Granby, December 1990. (Author)

to RAF and other coalition aircraft mainly from the US Navy. The four Nimrod maritime patrol aircraft flew 112 sorties over the waters of the northern Gulf during hostilities. Almost one quarter of the RAF Regiment total strength were deployed on airfield defence and in direct support of the 43 helicopters (31 RAF and 12 RN) operating with 1 (BR) Armoured Division. These impressive achievements reflected the quite outstanding efforts of deployed ground crews and logisticians supporting 16 different types of aircraft and the RAF Regiment at the end of a lengthy supply chain. At home many of our aircraft types, optimised for operations in the Central Region, had to be modified and enhanced for desert operations. A total of 242 different modifications were embodied in 300 aircraft at a cost of more than 300,000 service man hours.

In addition to Tornado GR1 operations, 12 Jaguars now based forward at Muharraq in Bahrain, flew some 600 offensive sorties against a variety of targets in Kuwait and Iraq. All Jaguar sorties were flown in daylight, often in the face of fierce opposition from Iraqi ground air defence, without loss. Jaguars were also employed in the tactical-reconnaissance role to supplement the night low level operations of the six Tornado GR1As, the recce variant of the aircraft. Equipped with infra-red linescan, the GR1As provided the coalition with vital intelligence on the dispositions of Iraqi forces as well as participating in the hunt for mobile Scud missile launchers. In targeting Scuds on Israeli cities the Iraqis hoped to provoke retaliation which could turn the conflict into a holy war, so splitting the coalition. This strategic risk diverted considerable air effort into searching for and attacking launch sites.

At the end of the war all of us in light blue in the JHQ shared satisfaction in our contribution to the coalition air campaign. But our pride in a job well done was not complacent. We were aware that our thinking about the employment of offensive air power was stuck in a Cold War rut. For reasons previously explained we trained to penetrate enemy air defences, both air and ground based, by flying low and fast and the RAF was very good at it – probably the best in the world and that is no idle boast. But our front-line lacked specialist defence suppression and electronic countermeasures aircraft. Moreover, our Tornados, Jaguars and Harriers all lacked an integral precision-guided munitions delivery system. While these limitations may have been partly the consequence of budgetary constraints, our doctrine, tactics and training had all been shaped by the service's long-standing commitment to a limited number of tasks in NATO's Central Region. The inevitable consequence was a loss of tactical flexibility. The Granby experience acknowledged the vital role that precision-guided weapons would play in future conflicts with a pressing need for anti-armour munitions not tied to low level delivery and stand-off missiles to reduce the threat of ground-based air defences. The essential need for greater tactical flexibility required aircrews to be better trained and equipped for medium level operations but without loss of low flying skills. All of these matters would become important concerns for me in the decade ahead.

Running the BMG was an exhilarating experience. I was blessed with the company of some outstanding officers from the three services all absolutely determined to contribute their best efforts to the success of a truly joint enterprise. Our sessions were often brightened with good humour and inter-service banter that was witty rather than barbed, so my responsibility of maintaining an acceptable level of inter-service tolerance was not difficult as the team settled to its duties. It was an invaluable experience for me that continued the process of military education which further expanded my understanding of the difficulties associated with maritime and land operations.

Two personal episodes remain permanently etched in my memory. Shortly before the end of hostilities I took a telephone call from the Secret Intelligence Service. An American TV crew, imprisoned by Saddam, had recently been released. During their debrief they mentioned the first names of a number of Brits who they had heard calling to one another in the jail. This was the first positive indication we received that soldiers and airmen, who we knew had been captured, and others who had been posted missing including SAS soldiers, were still alive. Identities were confirmed when we matched first names – there was no duplication – to surnames. This information could not be released; although highly improbable, there was no absolute certainty they would survive Saddam's attentions before release. A few days later watching our prisoners of war leaving a bus under the auspices of the Red Cross was for me the most joyful moment of Operation Granby.

Also towards the end of Granby, the joint commander was informed that The Queen would visit the bunker one afternoon soon. On the day Sir Paddy told me that after I had handed over to Phillip Sanders I was to go home for a wash and brush up and then return to the bunker. When I returned, some 15 minutes or so before her arrival, Sir Paddy casually mentioned that I was to brief Her Majesty on the current situation – the disposition of coalition forces and their achievements with emphasis on our national contribution. There was no opportunity to prepare scripts and notes which Sir Paddy knew full well I would have done given extra warning. So there was no time for stage fright and I had to cuff it which in the event was not difficult and certainly less stilted than reading from a prepared script.

Granby was an American-led campaign in which the British chiefs of staff exercised little if any influence on planning or the conduct of operations.

Although the chiefs may have been side-lined this did not stop other senior officers in the MoD offering the joint commander free advice on how the war could be won in double-quick time. One such proposal was to use JP233 weapons against Iraqi oil refineries and nodal points in the electric power grid system. The author of this proposal entirely missed the point that attrition of the Iraqi armed forces, in particular the Army, was a strategic objective of greater consequence than the rapidity of victory. Although not specifically stated I felt at the time that there was more intent to the lengthy air offensive than preparation for the land offensive. Iraq and its bloodthirsty leader needed to be taught a lesson and this could be best administered by significantly reducing Iraqi war-fighting capability.

It was thus my privilege, as a staff functionary in the JHQ, to witness the exercise of operational command at the highest level that involved not only the application of leadership and management skills but also, and most importantly, political nous. Officers are expected to develop their powers of leadership and management so we work hard at cultivating the necessary attributes. But during Granby I observed at first hand that at the very highest level of operational command there is a step change in pressure which places greater emphasis on certain personal characteristics. While total commitment to the cause and the determination to see it through are self-evident, as is military professionalism of the very highest order, the unremitting pressure of Granby over eight months stressed the importance of stamina and resilience. A considerable reserve of mental stamina was essential in order to master both concept and detail and to maintain concentration over long periods no matter how many diversions occurred. And a similar degree of resilience was needed to cope with these diversions which modern communications guaranteed came thick and fast and mostly from unwelcome quarters.

As an amateur student of military history I have often read about the aura of calmness associated with successful military commanders of the past. When the heat is intense it is essential that those placed in positions of high command can sustain calm deliberation which differentiates precisely between the essential and the not so essential. Without this capacity, the vital sense of balance and proportion can be lost as it is so easy for molehills to grow into mountains under the pressure of vested interests whether they be political, military or economic. Singularly they may be containable but sometimes they can come together to form a tidal wave of pressure that may overwhelm all but the very strongest of character and personality.

Operation Granby involved our armed forces venturing into new and unfamiliar territory, within a disparate coalition of nations, against an unpredictable and heavily armed foe. The stakes were high and the exercise of operational command within the JHQ required leadership by example of all the qualities I listed above, including good humour. We got this in far more than fair measure from Sir Paddy Hine who, without any doubt, was our 'Man of the Match'. There was widespread regret within the service that Sir Paddy, who had previously served as vice chief of the defence staff, was not appointed chief of the air staff, recognition that he so richly deserved.

CHAPTER 21
ON THE MOVE

I handed over my duties at High Wycombe to Peter Squire on 22nd March 1991 and after two weeks' leave moved to RAF Upavon on Salisbury Plain to take command of 1 Group. There I would be responsible to the AOC-in-C for the training and fighting effectiveness of units under command as well as the discipline, welfare and morale of all ranks. I was to succeed Sandy Wilson who was departing on promotion to take command of RAF Germany. Elizabeth came with me to see our belongings into Littlecott House in nearby Enford village before she returned to Bradenham Beeches to prepare our married quarter for march out. Three days later, with my feet hardly under the table and before Elizabeth returned, I took a call from Sir Paddy. He asked me, rather bizarrely I thought, if I was doing anything important to which I replied with a cheek born of distant separation that I was taking command of 1 Group which I considered an important duty. Sir Paddy told me sharply not to bandy words and to get to RAF Brize Norton by 9am the following morning where I was to meet Kip (Sir John Kemball) who would brief me. I asked for any clues as to my destination. Sir Paddy replied, "take KD (khaki drill uniform)" and rang off. Next morning I got to Brize Norton in good time where I met up with Sir John and a large company of staff officers; half drawn from the JHQ were immediately recognisable, the other half, nearly all Royal Marines, were new acquaintances.

After the end of coalition operations Iraqi opponents of Saddam Hussein had been encouraged to rise up and overthrow him and his regime. Saddam was quick to launch attacks on the Marsh Arabs in the south using both land forces and helicopters which General Schwarzkopf had not included in the ceasefire terms. With the revolt of the Shia Marsh Arabs cruelly crushed, Saddam was next to turn his murderous intentions on the Kurds in the north. Having failed to protect the southern uprising the Americans and ourselves were determined there should be no repeat performance in the north and that we would deploy forces to protect the Kurds from his wrath. The Kurds, with horrific memories of Saddam's use of chemical weapons against them in the mid 1980s, were already fleeing their homes to escape a repetition. The mounting of a further operation with the Americans – the Safe Haven initiative as proposed by Prime Minister John Major – required close liaison concerning command and control arrangements and force structures. Thus my job was to lead the liaison team to determine specifically a concept of operations, the force structure and its composition, to identify headquarters siting and structure and to recommend multinational command and control arrangements. In addition we were to consider ROE, recommend deployment plans and the composition of combat and advance parties. The JHQ party was led by Brigadier Mike Willcocks who had been my ACOS Land Operations throughout the Gulf War, and the Royal Marines by Brigadier Andy Keeling, commander 3 Commando Brigade. We were accompanied by Dr Nabarro, the UK civil aid co-ordinator.

Following the briefing we all boarded a VC10 and flew directly to the Turkish air force base at Incirlik where we met up with Lieutenant General Shalikashvili (known colloquially as General Shalli) of the US Army and his deputy Major General Jamerson of the United States Air Force. We settled in quickly and noted the significant distances between Incirlik, Diyarbakir airfield in central Turkey, Salopi on the Turkey/Iraq border and Zakhu in northern Iraq all of which were key locations within a developing concept of operations. Preliminary air efforts to drop supplies to the Kurds from Diyarbakir had already run into problems as the Turks restricted relief flights to the western side of the airfield alongside a live weapons firing range. RAF slots at the airfield were restricted to three VC10 and six Hercules sorties per day which were insufficient to overcome a potential human tragedy involving half a million Kurdish refugees in northern Iraq. I thus thought a visit to Diyarbakir to assess the difficulties would be useful and Andy Keeling suggested that if possible we should continue the recce down to Salopi so he could see the lie of the land.

There were two problems. The first, transport, was quickly solved when I hijacked a RAF Chinook helicopter which was refuelling at Incirlik en route Diyarbakir. The Chinook had been offloaded at RAF Akrotiri from a merchant ship returning to the UK from the Gulf. The second problem was the lack of any formal credentials explaining my presence in Turkey. I knew only too well from previous visits to Ankara during my tour in Cyprus the sensitivity of Turkish officialdom to unauthorised intrusions. My concern appeared justified when after landing at Diyarbakir the base commander said he had been instructed to take me immediately to the office of the regional governor. There I was ushered in to an extravagantly furnished and palatial room where I was greeted with the words "Hello Dick, how nice to see you again". It took me a few seconds to recognise Sadi Erguveng, a fellow student at the RAF Staff College, and now a lieutenant general, governor of the eastern province and commander of the 2nd Turkish tactical air force.

After a genuine exchange of pleasantries I explained my mission and that I was well aware of Turkey's concern about the activities of the Kurdistan Worker's Party (PKK), a left-wing militant organisation, which sought the foundation of a Marxist-Leninist state in the region which would be known as Kurdistan. Given reassurance and explanation about the purpose of Safe Haven, Sadi Erguveng kindly provided me with travel permits and promised to look into our operating problems at Diyarbakir airfield to include the closure of the adjacent weapons range. I returned to the airfield thanking providence for my good fortune and we continued the journey to Salopi where more surprises awaited us. The Americans had beaten us there. We landed alongside a couple of Black Hawk helicopters and some Humvee vehicles where we met up with Major General Jay Garner, US Army, who was on a similar recce mission and much better equipped than us to do so. After a flight around the local area in a Black Hawk, Jay Garner asked if we would like to go with him to have a look around Zahku. I had no authorisation to enter Iraq and no comms to seek permission, but it would have been churlish to refuse the invitation. So I set off with him in the lead Humvee, driven by a US Marine with a passing resemblance to Mike Tyson, closely followed by Andy Keeling in the second vehicle.

The road to Zahku passed through a barren and rather featureless landscape scarred here and there with burned-out vehicles, mostly military. It was ominously quiet as we entered the outskirts of the town without a living soul in sight. But all this changed as we turned sharply left into the main street. A hundred yards or so in front of us the road was blocked by a phalanx of Iraqi soldiers. The driver slammed on his brakes. "Gee, general, what do I do now?" he sensibly enquired. "Drive up to them real slow," replied Jay Garner. Here I have to admit my own instructions, if invited, would have been precisely the opposite. As we approached the phalanx, all armed while we were without weapons, it split allowing us to pass through a central passage with heavy eyeballing from both sides. There was a palpable feeling of tension which gradually eased as we drove out of Zahku. The question then arose as how best to return to Salopi and discussion was not helped by the lack of local area maps. Shortly after we stopped to review the situation there was a banging on my door window which I lowered to be confronted by Brigadier Keeling. "Air marshal," he said "you missed a trick back there. Those buggers didn't salute. You should have got out and gripped them." I could only rather feebly reply that there was a time and place for everything and the situation in Zahku met neither consideration.

We eventually retraced our route to Salopi once more passing through the Iraqi soldiers without incident. Leaving the Chinook at Diyarbakir we boarded a Hercules from the Special Forces Flight of 47 Squadron for the return to Incirlik. Talking to Chinook and Hercules aircrew already involved in dropping food and water to the Kurds fleeing from the mountains presented a vivid impression of chaos which could only be stabilised by the presence of strong ground forces to provide security and control of relief operations. By the time the deployment of coalition 'boots on the ground' was actioned, RAF Hercules and Chinooks had already delivered 650 tonnes of supplies and airlifted more than 800 refugees – including 250 medical cases – to safety.

Back at Incirlik Mike Willcocks had confirmed that immediate humanitarian tasks were located in the mountains, an ideal role for the Royal Marines, and the sooner the first commando battalion was deployed the better. Staff talks with the Americans had progressed rapidly but there was still an urgent need for UK rules of engagement. Meanwhile, recommendations to the JHQ on the UK force structure and the integration of staff within the US HQ were nearing completion. That evening, 21st April 1991, I asked JHQ for an aircraft to bring the recce team home next morning. A VC10 arrived and as we flew back we worked on the presentation that we would give to the joint commander and his staff supplemented by a host of officers and officials from the MoD and other military HQs. We landed at Brize Norton in the early afternoon and a flight of Puma helicopters flew the whole party to High Wycombe where we started our briefing at 1630 hours.

During the return flight I warned Andy Keeling that MoD's interest would inevitably focus on the size and cost of the deployment. I was not wrong. The total manpower bill was close to 4,500 men and included the guns of the Commando Regiment Royal Artillery. This recommendation provoked robust debate and a memorable eruption from the major general Royal Marines that threatened to upset the applecart. Sir Paddy, predictably, restored calm to proceedings before departing to brief the secretary of state by a TV link on our recommendations and the outstanding actions that required further work. Soon afterwards the commando brigade deployed to north Iraq as the second largest contribution to a coalition force that saved and preserved the lives of Kurdish refugees while creating the conditions for them to return home in safety. The commando brigade's order of battle (including their artillery!) deterred the possibility of interference from the Iraqi Army while ensuring that aid, airdropped and trucked in from Turkey, was quickly and effectively distributed.

At the end of the debrief I was relieved of my duty as recce team leader and returned to Upavon to start my real job. This was not to be the end of my association with military operations in and over Iraq.

During my absence Air Commodore Henry Hall, the SASO, had looked after the shop. He was the first of 'my' three SASOs at Upavon as he was followed in succession by Air Commodores David Hurrell and Tony Stables. Having SASO'd for nearly six years it felt rather strange to refer to 'my' SASOs particularly with such a rapid changeover, and one not of my making. My outer office, a more stable environment, was manned by two officers – a personal staff officer (PSO) and ADC – both from the RAF Regiment. Air staff pilots and navigators, including several who had fought in Gulf War I, were a little miffed by this arrangement but consoled themselves with the thought I had one who could write and one who could read.

RAF Upavon, situated on the north-eastern edge of Salisbury Plain, was the birthplace of the Central Flying School, formed there in 1912, and directly administered by the War Office with costs equally borne by the Royal Navy and the Army. After the formation of the RAF in 1918, RAF Upavon's association with military aviation was mostly concerned with flying training until, in the aftermath of World War II, it was occupied by a succession of command and then group headquarters as the size of the service reduced. When I arrived the grass airfield was still active and used mostly for gliding but with frequent visits from Hercules aircraft practising grass-strip take-offs and landings.

Upavon was a popular posting and an early morning hike in agreeable weather from Littlecott House across two miles of the plain to the HQ was a bracing start to the day. Sometimes Elizabeth came with me and on 23rd October 1992, our wedding anniversary, we got hopelessly lost when suddenly engulfed in thick fog. I thought I knew the route like the back of my hand but without a compass and in visibility of no more than a few yards we stumbled around for two hours before hitting a recognisable road and thumbing a lift. As a stickler for punctuality, my absence had not gone unnoticed and caused some worry to the staff. Their concern, somewhat exaggerated in my judgement, was nevertheless encouraging as I grappled with the consequences of Options for Change. Unexpected new operational tasks, the closure of three stations, the redeployment of major units and the disbandment of squadrons all came together to generate unease about the future that lurked behind the pride of achievement borne of Op Granby.

This feeling was not confined to any single group within the 17 stations under command which ranged in size from 4,000 at RAF Brize Norton to

100 or so at RAF Goose Bay in Labrador. My visits to these stations gave me the clear impression that most of our servicemen and women understood that the disintegration of the most immediate threat to our security, as posed by the Soviet Union and Warsaw Pact, required the government to reassess both the threat to national security and what in consequence we could afford to spend on defence. Nor for that matter were our people blind to the difficulties faced by the service board who had to confront a most complex raft of problems in an uncertain political climate prior to the general election in 1992. That said, as a group commander, I was very much alive to the concerns of many who had their legitimate career aspirations put on hold let alone widespread anxiety about redundancy as the service set about reducing its strength from 89,000 to 79,000. In talking to all ranks I was determined to do my best to explain the context of the difficulties we faced and not to promise any false dawns. Although this was my natural inclination, events yet to unfold proved this to be no more than common sense.

In 1991 one could not fail to notice that the greater part of public and media noise and palaver following Options for Change announcements centred on the future structure of the infantry within the Army. The loss of seven Tornado squadrons from our front line and much else besides provoked scarcely a squeak of public protest. In the wake of the Gulf War where the conditions for a quick and successful land campaign were shaped by air power I felt rather let down. In fact I was astonished that implementation of Options for Change decisions was not put on hold until MoD analysis of Gulf War I was completed. It was as if it had never occurred.

Three structural issues kept the staff busy. The first concerned the future of the air transport (AT) and air-to-air refuelling (AAR) squadrons. As SASO at Strike Command I had made no secret of my judgement that 1 Group was disproportionately large. Moreover, in December 1989 the AT and AAR policy and tasking staff had moved from 1 Group to Strike Command leaving the AOC responsible for training and personnel matters. Despite the loss of tasking authority the AOC was still held accountable for the group's fuel budget of which 65% was consumed by the AT and AAR squadrons. This was a nonsense and although I would be sad to see them go I could not argue against the move of RAF Brize Norton, RAF Lyneham, RAF Northolt and The Queen's Flight based at RAF Benson to form a new group, No. 38, which would be embedded within the headquarters at High Wycombe. This was accomplished in November 1992 leaving 1 Group as essentially a tactical formation that was better balanced, more manageable and with proper alignment of authority and accountability.

The second structural matter concerned the Tornado Force which was to live through a period of considerable upheaval. The two Tornado GR1 squadrons at RAF Marham were to move to RAF Lossiemouth to take over the anti-surface unit warfare (ASUW) role from the Buccaneers as they were phased out of service. No. 13 Squadron was to move from RAF Honington to join 2 (AC) Squadron, recently returned from RAF Germany, to form a Tornado recce wing at RAF Marham. The Tornado Weapons Conversion Unit (TWCU) was also to move from Honington to Lossiemouth. Only the Tri-National Tornado Conversion Unit at RAF Cottesmore was to remain in place. There I noticed the planned arrival of pilots from the former German Democratic Republic who had presumably completed a crash course in democracy. Elsewhere the Jaguar OCU at Lossiemouth was to move to RAF Coltishall to join the main force. As the flying units departed Honington the RAF Regiment depot at Catterick was to move lock, stock and barrel to Honington with the airfield placed on care and maintenance with RAF Catterick handed over to the Army. The implementation of these moves required the most careful planning and I have to admit that travelling around the group to brief station commanders was not the most pleasant or easy of my responsibilities; and nor for that matter was informing the staff at Upavon that the HQ was to move to RAF Benson in 1993 with the station then to be occupied by an Army headquarters. While the Army, recognising the significance of Upavon, kindly agreed that their headquarters would be named 'Trenchard Lines', departure from such a historic location was a bitter pill to swallow; but others, similarly distasteful, were soon to follow.

On the plus side, and selfishly, there was still much to be enjoyed. Since leaving Gütersloh I had done very little flying, in effect no more than type familiarisation on aeroplanes new to me and a few 'joy rides' in the Harrier. The job of a SASO is to run a staff and a staff properly responsive to command direction requires its own leadership and management. On the other hand, all senior air force commanders need to find time to continue flying. If they don't and technology continues to dominate the development of both air power doctrine and tactics, there is a risk of a gap of understanding developing between the leader and the led which will lower the credibility of the former and the confidence of the latter.

Before the AT and AAR squadrons left the group towards the end of my tour I flew all the 'heavies' and thoroughly enjoyed the expansion of my education. My first visit to RAF Lyneham, home of the Hercules Force and with the largest number of aircrew in the service, was memorable. I entered a briefing room crowded to overflowing with commissioned and non-commissioned aircrew sporting a wide variety of brevets and squadron badges. Well aware of their quizzical appraisal I spotted in the front row a face from the past. To break the ice I immediately approached the squadron leader who was a navigator. I stuck out my hand, and asked when we last met. "At Cranwell Sir, when you chopped me from pilot training," came the reply. That broke the ice. After this unpromising start some serious work in the flight simulator and a dual handling sortie gave me a rather dodgy captaincy qualification on the K-model Hercules which allowed me to fly to and from RAF Goose Bay with a load of Tornado spares under the closest scrutiny of a training captain in the right-hand seat. Thereafter I flew day and night sorties with the Special Forces Flight to learn about their capabilities before flying with the detachment based at Ancona in Italy on airlift operations into the besieged city of Sarajevo.

The weather was poor. Low cloud and drizzle shrouded the surrounding mountains as we approached the airfield for a Khe Sanh descent, a legacy of the Vietnam War which involved the aircraft making the steepest practical approach to touchdown. Full flap, undercarriage down and throttled right back gave a rate of descent of several thousand feet/minute to round out so to minimise the threat of small-arms fire from Serb forces. A day or two before a Luftwaffe Transall tactical transport had been hit; the captain was exceedingly miffed because the bullet penetrated his schnapps flask. But I was most impressed by the handling skills of our Hercules pilots and fascinated by the activity of an electronic warfare officer (EWO), working alongside the navigator, with a piece of kit that looked distinctly old-fashioned. The operator said it was and while it worked to give the aircraft an adequate measure of electronic protection he very much hoped that the RAF would accelerate the procurement of new kit to counter the evolving electronic warfare threat. Point well made and point taken. The relief operation into Sarajevo, code-named 'Cheshire', lasted from July 1992 until January 1996. RAF Hercules flew 1,997 sorties delivering 20% of the total UN airlift, an average of some 200 tonnes of supplies per week.

The Falklands War and Gulf War I had both highlighted the operational importance of the RAF's in-flight refuelling capabilities as a single force-multiplier. The range of tactical fighter aircraft could be extended in conflict to achieve strategic effect. To protect vulnerable airfields the airborne endurance of defensive fighters could be similarly lengthened. Although I had refuelled from tankers when flying Javelins and Harriers, the opportunity to have an insider's view of flight refuelling was irresistible. In September 1991 I was airborne in a VC10 to RV with a Tristar tanker for mutual training and to have a go myself. However, the Tristar was called off to support an operational air defence task so I enjoyed the pleasure of a general handling sortie with circuit flying following a couple of radar approaches. The weather was perfect with a cloudless sky, unlimited visibility and a breeze straight down the runway. It may sound absurd, but it was rather like flying a large Hunter. In the crew debrief the captain, Flight Lieutenant Evans from my logbook, said it had been all too easy and he hoped I would return to try my hand at refuelling which would really test my mettle. This I did and it was good preparation for an operational sortie with 101 Squadron on Operation Northern Watch – policing the 'no-fly zone' over northern Iraq.

I must now admit to cheating. The AAR staff in the HQ told me that the most challenging aeroplane for in-flight refuelling was the Victor tanker. So I arranged my first sortie in a Victor based at RAF Marham to get the hang of controlling the inertia and momentum of a large aircraft as well as learning the best technique for hooking up. I then returned to Brize and to my delight, and to the crew's reasonably well disguised chagrin, achieved a first time hook-up. But military aviation is a great leveller and I should have been aware of hubris.

Shortly afterwards I flew my first and only sortie in the one remaining Vulcan in service which was a 1 Group aircraft. It was displayed by Flight Lieutenant Paul Millikin and as his AOC it was my responsibility to authorise his sequence. Rather than watch from the air traffic tower at RAF Waddington I flew with him and his three rear crew members who, like their captain, were all doing a full time job on 55 Squadron, Victor tankers. I was allowed to fly the Vulcan for 45 minutes to investigate its unique handling techniques; at low speed and to turn the aircraft you led with rudder rather than the elevons that replaced conventional elevators and ailerons. All went well and after my final landing I handed control back to Paul to observe his display. While the aircraft never exceeded an indicated airspeed of 170 knots, the steep climbs powered upwards by 80,000lbs of thrust with huge wingovers (low speed, stick hard back and bags of rudder) was breath-taking and, with my mind conventionally attuned, rather a good way of getting into a spin. But Paul had that air of disciplined confidence that is always recognisable in pilots on top of their game which allowed me to authorise the display with no misgivings. Back on the ground the five of us sat down for a debrief which Paul opened with some complimentary words about the way I had got to grips with the Vulcan. As a sucker for flattery I was beginning to glow when the nav plotter, a grizzly veteran of the V Force, interrupted. "Don't get carried away sir," he said "Paul says that to all the air marshals." That put me back in my box.

Following the withdrawal of the Royal Marines and other coalition land forces from northern Iraq in July 1991, coalition air power imposed a no-fly zone over Iraq above the 36th Parallel. The RAF's contribution to enforcement was taken on by the Jaguar and Harrier forces in rotation with VC10 tanker support all operating from Incirlik. A year after Northern Watch started the Southern Watch no-fly zone was set up to monitor and control Iraqi air space south of the 32nd Parallel; in 1996 this was extended to the 33rd Parallel. The RAF and principally 1 Group sustained these commitments without a break until the start of Gulf War II in 2003.

As I had only previously flown single familiarisation sorties in the Jaguar and Tornado I arranged further flights to get a better feel for the aircraft and an understanding of their weapons systems. At RAF Lossiemouth Squadron Leader Paddy Roche overcame my Harrier prejudice to improve my opinion of the Jaguar but time available and bad weather prevented me from flying solo. I had better luck with the Tornado at RAF Honington. After a day's ground school, a day in the simulator, and two dual sorties with Squadron Leader Bob Joy I went off as captain with the TWCU senior navigator joining me as crew. The comfortable and roomy cockpit was a real joy after the Harrier, and indeed Jaguar, albeit I retained my single-seat mentality. I asked Squadron Leader Benny Bentham for a map of our low level route. He looked rather surprised and reminded me that I not only had a moving map in the front cockpit that was extremely accurate, but he was indeed a navigator and one of his jobs was to know where we were. Eventually I managed to persuade him that for me a map in hand was as a cuddly to a child and it was far too late to change the habits of a lifetime. Rank alone carried the day.

Thereafter our shakedown sortie together was satisfactorily completed without any tantrums from the front or back cockpits. In subsequent trips with Benny I was introduced to the automatic-weapons delivery system, loft bombing and the terrain-following radar. The Tornado GR1 was a formidable weapons system and the upgrade to GR4 standard assured that the aircraft remains operationally viable at the time of writing. Perhaps it was a sign of advancing years, but I thoroughly enjoyed flying the Tornado while the occasional trip in a Harrier to keep my hand in helped me appreciate the comfort and smooth ride of the former.

As the station's AOC I was a frequent visitor to RAF Aldergrove in Northern Ireland. The point needs making because there was also an Air Officer Scotland and Northern Ireland. His duties in the province were purely representational and Lieutenant General Sir John Wilsey, GOC Northern Ireland at the time, made it plain that he considered me to be his primary point of Air Force contact. Fine by me, not so appreciated by AOSNI. But the operational chain of command was important as the command and control of helicopters in the province at that time was split between the Army Air Corps and RAF. To get a feel for their operations I flew with the Puma and Wessex squadrons (230 and 72) and was introduced for the first time to night-vision goggles. Up until the introduction of NVGs, night support helicopter operations were confined to landings in locations previously recce'd in daylight. The use of NVGs provided an opportunity to eliminate the need for pre-recces so introducing far greater operational flexibility and a larger element of surprise. However, the province was criss-crossed with a web of telephone wires and power cables which required me, as the ultimate authorising officer, to ensure that new procedures would not add an unacceptable element of risk to the dangers that were part and parcel of everyday helicopter operations. After three night sorties I was content that the procedures developed were satisfactory and I signed off the necessary authorisation.

My visits to Northern Ireland also gave me the opportunity to have a good look at the RAF Regiment's contribution to security there. With the RAF Police Squadron responsible for on-base security at Aldergrove, the deployed Regiment squadron looked after a tactical area of responsibility (TAOR) outside the wire to ensure the arrival and departure lanes to and from the runway were secured against the threat of MANPADS or other weapons of less lethal capability. Given that most VVIPS, both civilian and military, flew in and out of Aldergrove in the easily recognisable HS 125 this threat was a constant concern. When required the squadron also supported 39 Brigade in Belfast, under the command of Brigadier Mike Jackson, as well as undertaking VIP protection duties and prisoner guarding in Belfast gaols. Command of the TAOR was exercised by Group Captain David Niven, the station commander and old friend from Gütersloh days. At times of heightened tension the resident Regiment Squadron was reinforced by detachments from other UK-based squadrons with some gunners spending more time in Northern Ireland than elsewhere in the UK on what was theoretically a home tour at their parent station. Although modest in numbers the RAF Regiment never failed in the duty of securing its tactical AOR and the safety of the many who travelled through it in the air and on the ground. For a purely personal observation I went out on patrol with 2 Squadron RAF Regiment, rather poorly disguised as an elderly regiment gunner, armed with a self-loading rifle. I have never felt better protected in my life.

The geographical spread of my command responsibilities, ranging from RAF Lossiemouth in the north to RAF Goose Bay in the west and with operational detachments to the south and east in Italy, Turkey and Kuwait, required a lot of transit flying. Most of this was achieved in the HS125s of 32 Squadron that would pick me up at nearby RAF Boscombe Down. I gained a first pilot qualification on the 125 and I owe a considerable debt to Squadron Leader Mick James and Flight Lieutenant Paton; one or the other captained the aircraft on the majority of my trips. They were both great company on the flight deck, patient instructors and impressively professional in the conduct of their transit flying, often undertaken at short notice, to meet tasking from commanders-in-chief, ministers and other big beasts in the MoD jungle. My shorter range trips were normally flown in Gazelle helicopters (also of 32 Squadron) which could fly in and out of Upavon airfield. Most convenient.

I cannot deny the pleasure I got from flying such a wide range of aircraft but the breadth and variety of the group's operational commitments required me to do so. When I was away, and for the greater part of my tour, the HQ was in the safe hands of David Hurrell who was the longest serving of my SASOs. David was a superb staff officer. He had an innate talent with the pen and was a witty and eloquent speaker. Most importantly his judgement of proposed solutions to complex problems, both operational and administrative, was underwritten with absolute integrity and unadulterated common sense. I could not have been better supported.

Visiting stations and flying with squadrons at home and on detachment gave me an impression that there was something of a gulf between the operational front line and the various organisations established to meet their requirements. Gulf War I rammed home the reality of the comfort zone that I, for one, had lived in during the latter years of the Cold War. Although the Falklands experience had gingered up some of our peacetime training only the flag exercises in North America and, to a lesser extent, the NATO Tactical Leadership Programme (TLP) provided the facilities for realistic training with full and accurate debriefing. However, experienced crews attended flag training every three to four years while new crews could either miss out completely on their first tour or, with luck, attend right at its end. Moreover, there was a vital need for operational training with representative weapons loads no matter the level of individual experience. These observations and much else besides were drawn together in an excellent critical analysis by one of my staff, Wing Commander Ray Horwood, who had served at Bahrain as OC Operations for the duration of the Gulf War.

Ray's paper, a personal initiative, pointed out that the test and evaluation at Boscombe Down was flawed. As an example he quoted that weapons clearances were often planned from academic flying patterns without trialling the delivery of full operational loads. And while CTTO did a good job, their location at Boscombe Down left them isolated from the operational RAF. A similar observation was made about the Electronic Warfare Operational Support Establishment (EWOSE) similarly isolated at RAF Wyton. Ray's analysis concluded with the recommendation that the RAF should set up a central air warfare establishment that would not allow doctrine to become dogma. To ensure its continuing relevance doctrine needed to reflect a process of unremitting review that examined definitions and concepts, the roles and missions of air power, and by no means least, the influence of emerging technologies particularly in the field of electronic warfare.

I forwarded his paper to HQ Strike Command where his proposals were enthusiastically adopted with the establishment of the Air Warfare Centre (AWC) at RAF Waddington in 1995. CTTO, EWOSE, and the Strike Command Scientific and Intelligence Branches were eventually all co-located in the Thomson building at RAF Waddington. This enabled the rapid passage of operational data to squadrons deployed on operations. The aim was to get electronic warfare and intelligence information from one mission directly into the planning of subsequent missions. This involved operational decisions being made on the principle that informed information that might not be 100% accurate was better than delayed or no information at all. The AWC also took on responsibility for tactical leadership training and the expansion of operational evaluation units to include all front-line war fighting and support activities. I am in no doubt that Ray Horwood's initiative made its own most important contribution to the combat effectiveness of the service in the years ahead. Ray received his due reward when he was appointed commandant of the AWC in 1998.

While at Upavon I managed to fulfil a long-held ambition to learn to ride. During a short-leave break I drove over to Larkhill, home of the Royal Regiment of Artillery, where a meeting had been arranged with Staff Sergeant Harnett, riding master of the Royal Horse Artillery. He asked me whether my intention was serious or if I was just looking for some fun. I replied "serious" and in the next two weeks sometimes wished I hadn't. Walking around the stables I noticed a very large horse, a grey, named Foden. I commented on his size and was told I would soon get to know him better. In the tack room all the equipment needed to ride a horse was patiently explained to me before my first lesson – how to prepare my horse (Foden) for inspection. I was then taken to the indoor riding school where I heard that I would not leave it until fit to be seen in public on horseback. Four days later I emerged to start riding out on Salisbury Plain. While I frightened myself a few times, it was exhilarating and I was pleased as punch to have learned the basics of a new and exciting activity. And having Foden pass inspection in the second week of my course gave me an unforgettable sense of achievement.

Not long after my introduction to equitation I was visited in June 1992 by the air secretary, Air-Vice Marshal Bob Honey, who I had worked for in RAF Germany. Bob asked me how I saw my future. I replied that a small extension to my tour expired date would see me past my 54th birthday. With accumulated leave and resettlement courses I would then be well placed for compulsory retirement at 55. I would leave the service a happy and fulfilled man. All this I had worked out before Bob arrived with my thinking influenced by a couple of comments made to me by CAS (Sir Peter Harding) when he visited Upavon; I interpreted them as indicating that I had reached my ceiling. So having given Bob my thoughts I was then told that I was to be short-toured at Upavon. My disappointment was brief as he went on to say that after handing over the group to Peter Squire I was to return to Strike Command with promotion to air marshal to take over from Kip Kemball as the chief of staff/deputy commander-in-chief. This was all good news albeit early departure from Upavon was not so welcome, but I could have no grounds for complaint.

The last few months of the tour passed in a blur. Much travelling, a lot of talking and more listening (I like to think so) continually reminded me of how fortunate I had been to enjoy an association with so many splendid people whose company had given me considerable pleasure both on and off duty. In my outer office and on my travels Squadron Leaders Noel McGonigle and Ian Jenkins and Flight Lieutenant Nick Newman had been boon companions whose ever-ready help and patience with my occasionally intemperate nature could not have been bettered. And for his part Nick learnt that in Westminster there was a cathedral as well as an abbey. Ian and Nick and many others at Upavon and in the group provided me with a perpetual reminder that my ascent of a shaky ladder had depended greatly on the strength and goodwill of those holding it steady beneath me. And hand in glove with that understanding was my deep pride in the group's achievements at home, in Northern Ireland, the Balkans and the Middle East. Within the group there was a rich abundance of proven physical courage which excited my respect and admiration. But as we navigated our way through choppy waters which still stretched beyond the horizon I became more and more aware of the importance of the moral equivalent. The survival of the service would depend very much on the integrity of those entrusted with its care, its wellbeing and its future evolution. And this was not guaranteed as the service was soon to move forward from choppy waters into stormy seas.

CHAPTER 22
STRIKE COMMAND

I had not taken my full leave entitlement at Upavon and spending two weeks learning to ride was rather selfish. But with Victoria and Douglas now settled into universities and Harriet approaching the end of her secondary education it was not easy to harmonise leave with student extracurricular activities, other family interests and my own duties. That was my justification so to atone for this self-interest I planned a two-week skiing holiday in Austria between postings. Elizabeth agreed the arrangements and off we set to Alpbach accompanied by Harriet. But disaster struck. A few days into the holiday I crashed and broke five ribs, punctured a lung and did some collateral damage to my liver.

I ended up in a hospital in Kufstein. The doctors seemed to take an age X-raying me along with other examinations; I thought at the time that they were probably checking the validity of my insurance. Eventually I was wheeled into a small ward on a stretcher. There were four other elderly occupants and one greeted my arrival with the words "Ach, ein Englander". The scene was straight out of the sort of World War II stories I used to read in comics as a boy. I just could not resist saying to my attendant "please take me to Wings Day and the escape committee". I considered that a very witty crack but not surprisingly it fell on stony ground. While previous quips I had sprayed around over the years may have similarly lacked in subtlety this time I learnt a disagreeable lesson. Laughing at one's own rib ticklers is not good form at the best of times; to do so with five broken ribs triggered a painful reminder of one's misfortune.

After four days of utter tedium in hospital I was assessed as fit to travel by a nurse sent out by the insurance company. During the trip home – ambulance to Salzburg airport, flight to Gatwick, ambulance to RAF Hospital Halton – I persuaded the nurse that he should enlist in the Royal Auxiliary Air Force Aeromedical Squadron at RAF Brize Norton. I do hope that he did so but free from my cajoling he might well have breathed a sigh of relief and got on with his life. Once admitted to Halton I was very aware that Kip Kemball would be rather anxious about the possibility of a delayed handover as he had a pre-retirement holiday booked in the West Indies. Apart from some injections in my back soon after admission there seemed little else that doctors could do so I discharged myself in time to take up my new post on 24th February 1993.

My AOC-in-C was Sir John Thomson who had taken over from Sir Michael Graydon in November 1992 on the latter's appointment as CAS. I had known Sir Michael since the day we were enlisted as Cranwell flight cadets in No.76 Entry. I also knew Sir John well. While he was junior to me at Cranwell, we had served together in Aden, he had been an usher at my wedding and he was CAS's PSO for 18 months during my tour as DASB. I recall one briefing session for CAS involving all the great and good of the RAF hierarchy at the time. Halfway through a long discussion John pushed a note to me. It read: "do you realise we are the only two present with natural hair colour?" Swapping notes during briefings was not unusual as we agreed on who would pick up various actions arising. But to share such impertinence in the presence of the Air Force Board Standing Committee was perhaps beyond the level of tolerable cheek.

The story, however, is a pointer to John's character. He enjoyed living on the edge and from time to time burning candles at both ends. Time spent with John was never dull. That said, his prodigious energy, the capacity of his intellect and the forcefulness of his personality earned rapid and deserved promotion. He was recognised to be the heir apparent as CAS in eventual succession to Sir Michael. And thereafter he was in my judgement a strong candidate for appointment as CDS. So I knew that working as John's chief of staff was not going to be an easy ride. We may have been friends but I had no doubt that he would be a demanding task master with a work ethic fashioned by his time as Sir Michael Beetham's PSO. And so it turned out.

Taking over as chief of staff was not too taxing as I was well aware of various matters of moment involving Strike Command. Following the formation of 38 Group within the command, 2 Group (formerly RAF Germany) was now a subordinate HQ responsible for Germany-based Tornado, Harrier and Support Helicopter squadrons. There were some 700 combat and combat support aircraft within a command of 54,000 personnel of whom 5,000 were civilian employees. However, this total was reducing and would continue to reduce as Options for Change decisions were implemented. The command's operating budget at the time was just under £1.8bn.

Strike Command forces were spread far beyond the 17 main operating bases in the UK and Germany. Small units were based in Cyprus, Hong Kong, Labrador (Goose Bay), Belize, Ascension Island, Gibraltar and Decimomannu.

Tornado F3s, Hercules, Chinook and Sea King helicopters along with a Rapier SHORAD squadron from the RAF Regiment were based in the Falklands Islands to provide security and to deter the possibility of future Argentine aggression. Eighty aircraft were assigned to SACEUR at 72 hours notice to move. Meanwhile operations over the north and south of Iraq continued. From November 1992 the command then contributed eight Tornado F3s, two E-3D Sentry aircraft and TriStar tankers to the NATO mission Deny Flight which enforced the no-fly zone over Bosnia. At the same time Nimrod maritime patrol aircraft supported Operation Maritime Guard to monitor the movement of shipping in the Adriatic as part of the enforcement of the UN arms embargo against former Yugoslavia. Finally a Jaguar squadron was deployed and positioned to respond to any UN request for fire support in Bosnia and Her-zegovina. All these detachments were based on Italian air force airfields.

The scale of commitment is best illustrated by the flying effort required to meet UN and NATO tasking. In one year alone (1994) more than 2,000 sorties totalling 6,000 hours were flown over Iraq and Jaguars and Tornados together amassed 10,000 flying hours on Operation Deny Flight; these figures do not include the huge amount of flying undertaken by the command's combat-support aircraft. I have used this inventory of tasks to show that all conventional roles and capabilities within Strike Command's order of battle were being applied on, or in support of, operations. In essence the command was meeting the most disparate operational demands for many years as cuts imposed on the service under Options for Change were beginning to bite.

Notwithstanding these operational pressures, the 1993 Public Expenditure Survey required further savings from all departments to reduce the size of the budget deficit and the MoD would not be immune from this process. Thus in his budget statement made in November 1993 the chancellor gave notice of the launch of a major review which in the MoD took the form of the Defence Costs Study otherwise known as Front Line First. The aim of DCS was to "identify further areas where we can reduce costs….to enable our armed forces to discharge their military tasks and commitments properly, to the full and with formidable capability". A familiar drum beat down through the ages could not assuage my feeling, shared by many others, that some in government saw defence savings as a passport to higher office and more generally offering an opportunity to re-deploy money into vote-winning budgets.

The atmosphere in Whitehall and Westminster at that time was feverish. The Conservatives, re-elected in April 1992 with a majority of only 21, were soon beset by infighting on the issue of Europe. In September that year the government suffered the indignity on Black Wednesday of forced withdrawal of the pound sterling from the European Exchange Rate Mechanism to the huge benefit of currency speculators. The following year Prime Minister John Major launched his 'Back to Basics' campaign intended to be a nostalgic appeal to traditional values encompassing such topics as education, the economy and policing. But public opinion regarded the PM's plea as more of an entreaty to return to family values conventionally associated with the Conservative Party. Unfortunately this initiative was soon torpedoed by a series of debilitating scandals mostly involving Conservative politicians that were joyfully reported in salacious and embarrassing detail by tabloid newspapers. In one year alone (October 1993-October 1994) 13 Conservative MPs resigned their posts after revelations of various financial and social misdemeanours. All of this was, of course, long before the parliamentary expense claims scandal that came to light in 2009. But back in the early 1990s the tabloid press seized upon the undermining of the prime minister's appeal for decency as justification for publishing risqué stories irrespective of how private the matter. As ever, public interest was quoted as vindication which camouflaged some measure of both hypocrisy and treacherous behaviour.

The first military casualty was the chief of defence staff, Marshal of the Royal Air Force Sir Peter Harding, who resigned in March 1994. Max Clifford, the publicist and later a convicted sex offender, revealed in *The News of the World* that Sir Peter had had an affair with the wife of a Conservative politician. Alleged details of the affair filled five pages of the paper and Sir Peter immediately resigned from his appointment on grounds that he had not acted in a manner that befitted the holder of the post. I could not help but observe that amongst his distinguished military predecessors there were others known to have been uncomfortable in their private lives who had survived revelation of such escapades. Shortly after Sir Peter's resignation an early day motion was tabled in the House of Commons "that this House wishes to express its appreciation of the distinguished service to the nation of Marshal of the Royal Air Force Sir Peter Harding; expresses sadness at his untimely resignation and records its relief that neither Admiral Lord Nelson nor the first Duke of Wellington were subject to the attention of the tabloid press". Enough said.

Unlinked to Sir Peter's sudden and unexpected downfall another senior RAF officer was the principal target of a sustained and sanctimonious battering in the pages of *The Mail on Sunday*. Air Chief Marshal Sir Sandy Wilson was castigated for expenditure on the renovation and refurbishment of his official residence, Haymes Garth, after his appointment as AOC-in-C Personnel and Training Command. The hostile publicity provoked a political storm and an inquiry that investigated expenditure on official service residences. The consultant's report, at a cost of £100,000 to the public purse, concluded as reported in Parliament that there was no question of "illegality or culpable impropriety" at Haymes Garth or any other of the official residences examined. The report, discussed at the highest level in the MoD – only six people were said to have read it – was then leaked to *The Daily Telegraph* which reported, under a banner front-page headline, that Sir Sandy was " almost certain to be forced to leave the RAF after a damming report into the bill for refurbishing his official home". So-called 'authoritative defence sources' were then quoted as saying that there had been misjudgement on such a scale that Sir Sandy's position was no longer sustainable. The source of the leak was officially investigated with no proven conclusion albeit with strong suspicion of the perpetrator's identity.

The deliberate leak of the report before Sir Sandy had seen it let alone been invited to comment plus selective quotes from 'authoritative sources' constituted a spiteful attack against Sir Sandy personally and the RAF in general. Mindful of reputational damage to the service and acutely aware of the stress endured by his family Sir Sandy elected to take early retirement. After handing over command of Personnel and Training Command in May 1995 he retired in August that year. Many within the service felt he had been harshly treated and were angered by the manner the matter came into the public domain. Mr Rifkind, secretary of state for defence, said in Parliament that "all members of the services carry responsibility for their actions including their judgement". Twenty years later he stepped down as chairman of Parliament's Intelligence and Security Committee following exposure of his involvement in the 'cash for access' scandal. In *The Guardian* Sir Malcolm (now knighted) was reported as saying: "I don't think I did anything wrong. I may have made errors of judgement but we all make errors of judgement. We are all human beings in that sense." Biter bit.

I was one of those caught up in a maelstrom of bad publicity for the service. As chief of staff at Strike Command I authorised an extension to Queen's Gap – an air officer's residence in the married quarters site at Bradenham Beeches – to accommodate the incumbent of the newly established NATO appointment of commander Allied Forces North-West Europe (AFNW). I did not know at the time that a tragedy, not too far distant, would have me appointed as C-in-C AFNW after only six weeks as AOC-in-C Strike Command. It was in the latter appointment that I received a letter from an MoD official stating that an investigation had cleared me of mismanagement or misuse of public money in expenditure on official service residences at RAF High Wycombe. I was astounded and angered to receive this communication which in effect told me I had been subject of an inquiry by persons unknown against unspecified charges without any notification. I wrote to CAS saying that if this was symptomatic of the MoD's attitude to its commanders-in-chief I would immediately resign my commission should I be subject to any repetition of such disgraceful conduct. I heard no more of the matter.

The whole process of DCS work was undertaken against a background of consistent bad publicity for the armed forces and particularly the RAF. As the study progressed leaks to the press fuelled a strong suspicion that the Treasury were behind a campaign to denigrate the armed forces as profligate in expenditure and inefficient in financial management. In a speech to the Air League Sir Michael Graydon called on those behind the campaign to stop undermining, not just the RAF, but all the armed forces. Sir Michael's words were construed as a thinly-veiled attack on the efforts of Treasury ministers to cut the defence budget. The very next day he was hauled over the coals by the secretary of state for defence for overstepping the mark in making public criticism of cabinet colleagues even in an oblique way. After his interview with Mr Rifkind, Sir Michael wrote a letter of apology to the chancellor of the exchequer (Mr Kenneth Clarke) and the chief secretary (Mr Michael Portillo) regretting that his remarks had been interpreted as an attack on them. Today, with the advantage of hindsight, Sir Michael much regrets making the apologies and believes he should have braved out the storm and risked the possibility or indeed probability of being sacked. But at the time he did not have a successor ready and primed to take over. Moreover the pressures on the service emanating from operational commitments, the close down of stations, the disbandment of squadrons and the implementation of a redundancy programme let alone further stress being generated by DCS persuaded Sir Michael that it would be in the RAF's best interest for him to continue in post for the immediate future. I think he was right.

A further consequence of Sir Michael's speech was a statement from the Treasury saying that "officials had not offered any briefing to the press on the defence programme". Reading these words at the time it seemed to me this was a case of 'if the cap fits wear it'. The use of the word 'offer' did not rule out the suspicion that officials 'gave' rather than offered. Most recently Sir Michael has confirmed that the suspicion was well founded as journalists had privately acknowledged to him that this was the case. Furthermore Sir Michael's words were specifically aimed at the bad mouthing of the services rather than any detail in a defence programme yet to be decided. Within the span of a year the retirement of Sir Peter Harding, the public wigging inflicted on Sir Michael Graydon and unremitting press attacks against Sir Sandy

Wilson culminating in his early retirement may well have pleased those who for a variety of reasons savoured the misfortunes of the RAF. In the febrile atmosphere of the time for those of us remote from the Whitehall bear garden it seemed that the service was becoming the victim of some malignant force.

While this may have been true from the personal perspective of all of us involved much worse was to follow. On 2nd June 1994 a RAF Chinook helicopter crashed in fog on high ground on the Mull of Kintyre in Scotland. Twenty-five senior intelligence experts from the Royal Ulster Constabulary, MI5 and the Army were being flown from Belfast to attend an intelligence conference in Inverness. All died alongside the four RAF crew members. The cause or causes of this appalling tragedy, the subject of almost continuous review for the best part of two decades, officially remain undetermined.

The progress of DCS work, as directed by a steering group chaired by the secretary of state, was not disturbed by either defamation or calamity. The minister of state for defence procurement, Mr Jonathan Aitken, chaired an executive group that supervised the work of 33 separate studies of which 20 were designated as 'major' and 13 as 'minor'. The studies were intended to cover all aspects of defence other than the front-line capabilities of the armed forces; there was to be one notable exception. Most studies were designed to look across service and other organisational boundaries to consider possibilities for rationalisation and to bring best practice from one area to another. The structures and management of each service were examined separately in 'vertical' studies. Study teams were encouraged to investigate sacred cows. Each team, chaired by one or two-star officers with a few led by outsiders, included a Treasury representative. In April 1994 the conclusions of each study were drawn together into a single document for ministerial consideration before onward passage to the cabinet.

The intensity of the work required John Thomson to attend many meetings in the MoD. My role as his chief of staff was to oversee the preparation of briefs which involved the staffs in a considerable volume of complex work to protect the essential components of the command's organisational structure while minimising the pain of inevitable further manpower reductions. In addition we were soon deeply involved in the staffing of work that went beyond the DCS remit to conclude with proposals concerning the RAF's operational capabilities. A separate report exclusively focused on the RAF titled Defence Costs Study 19 was co-authored by Air Marshal Sir John Walker and Mr David Hart.

I knew John Walker, not well, but we had touched swords when he was SASO Strike Command and I was SASO RAF Germany. I recognised John as a forceful personality and a top-notch operational leader fuelled with outstanding energy and drive. His commitment to the operational efficiency of the service was beyond question as was his understanding of air power, both its strengths and limitations. I had also observed that once John had formed an opinion it would be expressed with either aggressive rhetoric or in purple prose that brooked no argument. In sum John Walker was a formidable personality not given to self-doubt.

I did not know Mr Hart but heard that he had played an important part in helping Mrs Thatcher overcome the miner's strike in 1984/85 by organising and funding strike-breaking miners in Nottinghamshire. Although remaining a convinced supporter of Mrs Thatcher, Mr Hart fell out of favour as a 'Downing Street irregular' until his re-emergence in Whitehall as an independent advisor to Mr Rifkind after his appointment as secretary of state for defence. David Hart was known to have "a technicolour approach to life in which boredom and predictability were always the enemy". As a political manipulator with a keen interest in defence his alliance with John Walker, the military authority, presented him with the opportunity to use John's expertise to his own ends. For his part John Walker, filling a central staff appointment and outside the RAF chain of command, recognised that his partnership with David Hart presented a heaven-sent opportunity. John's views on how best to improve the RAF's operational capabilities would have a guaranteed conduit to the highest levels in the MoD and the Treasury and had already been paraded to interested parties. The consequence of the Hart/Walker partnership was DCS 19. This study was to embroil CAS and his board colleagues in a sustained and at times bitter debate with ministers readily persuaded that implementation of DCS 19's recommendations would achieve further substantial savings.

I had many long chats in the evening with John Thomson as he kept me abreast of developments in London. There appeared to be a widely held view in Whitehall that Options for Change had let the RAF off the hook compared to cuts inflicted on the RN and the Army. Although reductions to the RAF's front line were acknowledged particular criticism was levelled at the allegedly slow pace of concomitant manpower reductions. The responsibility to balance the equipment-manpower equation, however, had already been formally acknowledged by the Air Force Board Standing Committee when Air Vice-Marshal Andrew Roberts was appointed to lead the Manpower Structure Study Team in 1993. His wide-ranging and detailed report concluded that by 2000 the RAF could operate with a trained strength of 55,210, some 20,000 less than the 75,000 previously agreed under Options for Change.

In DCS 19 Hart/Walker went further in recommending a trained strength of 50,000 to be achieved by the end of 1997 after an immediate call for voluntary redundancies and the imposition of a parallel compulsory redundancy programme as soon as possible. Achievement of the 50,000 manpower figure would be reached when the Hart/Walker recommendations concerning the service's command structure, its training methods, its basing policy to include the closure of a further eight airfields plus a raft of other measures, were implemented. The carrot dangled in front of ministers was the prospect of £3bn further savings. To sugar the pill for the service Hart/Walker proposed that this saving should be invested in a leasing arrangement with the USAF to procure F-16 C/D aircraft for air superiority operations until the eventual deployment of Eurofighter. But there was a practical snag with the F-16 proposal. For air-to-air refuelling the F-16's system was incompatible with the RAF's tanker aircraft which all used a probe-to-drogue method. Our air operations had become increasingly dependent on AAR to extend the reach of national air power which posed an obvious conundrum about the F-16's acceptability into RAF service. Whatever the solution it would certainly be expensive.

At the time I was well aware that the Tornado F3 (the RAF's front-line air defence aircraft) was not an air superiority fighter; it was a long-range interceptor aeroplane. By 1994 the introduction of a Stage 2 radar which would soon be followed by the joint tactical information distribution system and advanced air-to-air missiles was turning the Tornado F3 into a credible, even formidable, weapons system as was to be proven on Red Flag exercises. To me the procurement of F-16 C/D aircraft was pie in the sky given the service's investment in the Tornado and its commitment to Eurofighter not to mention its incompatibility with our in-service AAR system.

Although DCS 19 was to commit the AFBSC to some bruising encounters with ministers – a final three-hour inquisition as opposed to a 90-minute review for each of the other two services – the report contained a number of recommendations that I fully supported and in time would become reality. Total withdrawal from RAF Germany and the future command and control of the RAF's Support Helicopter Force come immediately to mind. My major misgivings about DCS 19 centred on its treatment of service manpower. Command of a group had already given me a feel for the entirely understandable discontent and rancour provoked by redundancy programmes. I felt that implementation of the Hart/Walker manpower recommendations would bring the service to its knees and destroy forever any trust that had survived Options for Change and memories of the 1970s notorious redundancy programme.

Moreover, the scale of our global commitments stretching into the foreseeable future fully justified a cautious rather than a hasty approach to the complex issue of manpower control.

The Front Line First conclusions required the RN and the Army to reduce military manpower by 4% and 1.9% respectively; the RAF was reduced by 11.6% with an accelerated timetable for implementation. Very shortly after publication of the DCS final report *The Times* journalist Mary Ann Sieghart wrote an article peppered with criticism of the RAF in general and its senior officers in particular. Much of the disparagement reflected arguments supporting some of the DCS 19 recommendations that were not accepted by ministers. No comment was offered on the level of the RAF's commitment to current operations and I was saddened to see my service's leadership so publicly traduced for reasons that I suspected had much to do with thwarted political and military ambitions. Sitting on the periphery of a fierce debate in Whitehall about the future structure of the RAF I was so relieved that rational argument as deployed by CAS, so ably supported by my old friend and colleague John Willis, eventually won the day.

Although the DCS review did preserve the front line within a reduced budget there was still bad news for many as job losses and redundancies were the inevitable consequence of civilianisation of some activities with others transferred to the private sector. The most high profile casualty of the process of civilianisation was The Queen's Flight which was disbanded with the aircraft embedded in 32 Squadron at RAF Northolt; servicing was then contracted out to the private sector. The rationale behind some other decisions escaped me. As an example, the chosen site for the amalgamation of service hospitals was the RN facility at Haslar, near Portsmouth. To my mind the obvious location was the RAF hospital at Wroughton which was close to the airheads at Brize Norton and Lyneham into which casualties from overseas operations would be flown.

The proposed formation of a new JHQ and the establishment of the post of commander Joint Operations were debated within and without the MoD. We at HQ Strike Command in alliance with HQ Land opposed the proposition arguing that the formation of a new HQ at a time of significant reductions in equipment and people was inappropriate, and particularly so after the JHQ at High Wycombe had functioned perfectly well during Gulf War I. The MoD judged that the current ad hoc approach of only setting up a joint headquarters in response to a developing crisis had shortcomings, in particular a high risk that a hastily assembled staff would lack cohesion when confronted by a rapidly developing predicament. The MoD also argued that the establishment of a Permanent Joint Headquarters (PJHQ) would enable an unambiguous connection between the policy and strategic functions of the MoD and the conduct of operations at the operational level. From the outset the plan was supported by the Royal Navy eager to provide a home for the new HQ co-located with HQ Fleet at Northwood in the belief – soon proven mistaken – that close proximity would bring with it influence. The RN got their wish on location and future events were to prove the validity of the MoD's case. But what was right in theory would not necessarily prove achievable in practice.

Preceding the PJHQ issue and separate from the national defence debate, the demise of the Soviet Union and the reunification of Germany had convinced the North Atlantic Council (NAC) – NATO's governing body – of the need for change. Political expectations for reductions in defence expenditure were not confined to the UK. Indeed the clamour was even stronger in the majority of nations that contributed military forces to Allied Command Europe (ACE). It was soon agreed that the SACEUR would retain his HQ in Mons, Belgium, with three subordinate regional commands – North, Centre and South. To satisfy the need for change a four-nation steering group (Denmark, Germany, Norway and UK) was then set up to examine the command structure in Northern Command with a view to achieving significant savings. The steering group recommendation that Channel Command, Northern Command and UK Air Forces should be fused in a new smaller and joint command to be named Allied Forces North-Western Europe (AFNW) was accepted by the NAC. High Wycombe was chosen as the site. The construction of a completely new HQ building on a cricket pitch within the Strike Command estate made me a glorified clerk of works which involved continuing discussion with our allies, particularly the Norwegians, and NATO HQ at Mons in Belgium.

In the spring of 1994 John Thomson was appointed commander-in-chief designate of AFNW to take command on 1st July that year. I, in turn, was to succeed John as AOC-in-C Strike Command two weeks before the new NATO HQ was formally opened by SACEUR, General George Joulwan, US Army. The day, attended by the NATO hierarchy, military and civilian, as well as national ministers and flag officers from all three services went off without a hitch. As our HQs were co-located I agreed to keep John in touch with purely RAF business as he was expected to succeed Sir Michael Graydon after two years at AFNW. The plan, however, disintegrated when John died on 10th July in RAF Halton hospital after a short illness. His death, so sudden and so unexpected, at the early age of 53 was a dreadful blow to the service let alone his family. In direct consequence my tour as AOC-in-C Strike Command lasted for only six weeks before I moved across to HQ AFNW as the new C-in-C. This came as something of a surprise as I was not privy to any discussion beforehand. Sir Michael told me of the move in the RAF High Wycombe officers' mess following the wake which concluded John Thomson's funeral. I had supposed that Air Chief Marshal Sir Michael Stear, then deputy commander-in-chief of NATO's Central Region, was the obvious successor to Sir John. I could only surmise that the Norwegians played an important part in the decision-making process as I had got to know their key senior men while setting up the new NATO HQ and finalising arrangements for the parade.

CHAPTER 23
ALLIED FORCES NORTH-WEST EUROPE

I travelled a lot during my six weeks in command of Strike Command visiting subordinate HQs and stations in an effort to check widespread concerns about the future of the service. The certainty of further and continuing manpower reductions was the most prominent issue. But I was surprised to be quizzed on the service's command structure such as the need for groups. The future equipment programme also came in for some caustic comment which reflected DCS 19 thinking and recommendations that had not been accepted. Taken all together it was not surprising that pressures from without the service and free-ranging argument within were generating disquiet that was undermining morale. As a new C-in-C on a short-term contract I could do no more than to take questions full on and to answer them as honestly as I could. To what effect, if any, only others could judge. During my travels I left the HQ in the safe and highly competent hands of John Allison who had taken over from me as chief of staff. John was also preparing for the arrival of Air Chief Marshal Sir William Wratten who was to succeed me as AOC-in-C.

I was a full member of the Air Force Board during my brief time in Strike Command and attended two meetings in London, both dominated by discussion of progress in the implementation of DCS decisions. At the AFB Standing Committee Meeting (AFBSCM) which preceded the full board meeting I got into a spat with the then second permanent under secretary on the issue of manpower reductions as I tried to argue on grounds of operational commitments for some easing of the pressure. I didn't win. At the AFB meeting soon afterwards I clearly recall a defence minister sitting opposite me gently slumping forward in his chair. I thought for a moment or two that he had died as had happened to a visitor to my office at Upavon. But a gentle rumble of postprandial content communicated no need for resuscitation as Flight Lieutenant Nick Newman had provided at HQ 1 Group, but sadly without success.

Attendance at these two meetings at least gave me an informed impression of what Sir Michael and his uniformed colleagues were facing and would continue to confront as I moved across the road to the brand new HQ AFNW. I was distressed to leave Strike Command at a time of obvious difficulties and sad not to end my career in the Royal Air Force. I was 55 and the retirement age of 58 for four-star officers meant that AFNW would be my last tour of duty. On the plus side I readily acknowledged that the challenge of setting up a new NATO major subordinate command (MSC) HQ from scratch to bring it to full operating capability was both novel and exciting.

When John Thomson had taken command the headquarters was by no means a settled in organisation. The chief of staff, a Norwegian three-star general, had spent the greater part of his time in Oslo rather than at High Wycombe during the critical setting-up period when a firm hand and clear direction was required to manage staffing and infrastructure issues including the installation of office-based IT in the form of a computer network. This innovation was to provide a workstation for every staff officer, a new venture in 1994. The assistant chiefs of staff from Germany, the Netherlands, Denmark, Belgium and the UK arrived at a time of their convenience. In short, when John had assumed command the HQ structure was not just disjointed but marking time with some senior staff obviously out of step; they had yet to recognise that the aftermath of the Cold War was creating a complex web of political and military problems. But thanks mainly to the hard work of Captain Terry Tull US Navy, Group Captain Paul Luker (PSO to C-in-C) and Colonel Ian Campbell (director of staff operations) John at least entered a brand new HQ in which he had his own office supported by a fully manned and ready to go outer office expertly managed by Warrant Officer Joe Bradshaw. After John's death, the reluctance of the chief of staff, an Army logistician by professional background, to give a firm lead to his subordinate ACOSs meant that no progress had been made in establishing a staff-training programme. This was quite obvious when I moved in as was the frustration of the ACOSs, in particular, ACOS Ops, a rear admiral in the German Navy.

As previously explained AFNW was created and intended to represent the new face of the Alliance. The HQ was designed as a small, streamlined, multi-national and tri-service HQ which used high grade technology to get the job done with a comparatively small staff. An effective MSC was to be shaped with one tenth of the staff numbers in the Central and Southern Region HQs of Allied Command Europe. The establishment of 284 personnel was drawn from nine NATO nations (Norway, Denmark, Belgium, Germany, the Netherlands, Italy, Canada, UK, USA). One hundred and fifty officers filled staff appointments. The command AOR covered the Eastern Atlantic, Norway and the UK together with their territorial waters and associated airspace. For the first time the defence of the UK mainland became a NATO responsibility while the AOR was extended into the Baltic Sea for maritime and maritime air operations. Blue uniforms, both light and dark, predominated in the HQ and admirals headed four of the five HQ divisions. In sum, the personnel establishment, the use of high grade contemporary technology and extensive cost sharing with the RAF landlords cost NATO a mere £5m per annum – 80% less than the individual running costs of the Central and Southern Regional Command HQs.

I had no involvement in the discussions that led to the formation of AFNW but I was surprised by some of the consequences. In peacetime HQ AFNW was supported by four principal subordinate commanders (PSCs). Two of the HQs, in Norway and Denmark, were manned and organised for joint operations; two others, both in the UK, were purely functional in nature, one looking after air operations and the other maritime affairs. Also in the UK was C-in-C Land Command who would come under NATO command in TTW. Although AFNW personnel were under my command I should stress that I had no powers of command over subordinate HQs until they were 'chopped' to me by SACEUR on exercises or in response to a real time crisis.

Four of the HQ's subordinate commanders held national command duties which in the normal course of events had priority over their declaration to NATO; in the jargon of the day they were 'dual hatted'. The fifth, Admiral Sir Peter Abbott at Northwood, was not only a national C-in-C but also a NATO MSC in the East Atlantic while at one and the same time being a PSC within the AFNW AOR. Elsewhere, commander Baltic Approaches was primarily a Central Region PSC under C-in-C Central Region who had primacy for overland military operations but with maritime responsibilities vested in HQ AFNW. Within this overall set-up there were, to say the least, structural inelegancies that were far from being an ideal division of responsibility for joint operations. This structure had been fashioned out of an amalgam of political, economic and geographic factors with scant consideration of harsh military realities. Nevertheless, the task of HQ AFNW was to train up within this structural framework in time to play its full part in NATO crisis-management exercises, the first scheduled for January 1995.

SACEUR's mission statement required me to ensure the security and territorial integrity of AFNW's AOR. Second to this primary task was responsibility to enhance peace and stability through cooperation and dialogue with non-NATO nations in Scandinavia and the Baltic while being prepared to plan for and execute peace support operations outside traditional boundaries.

Achievement of the primary mission required a phased training programme with clearly identified objectives at each stage along the road to full operating capability. Although starting with a clean sheet of paper and a lean staff, most with open minds, was advantageous, it was imperative that the potential offered by new and unique equipment was not stifled by simply rewriting old procedures left over from the Cold War. The challenge we faced as a brand new MSC was to establish our operational credibility and authority in national capitals and with our superior and subordinate HQs. Success hinged on our ability to satisfy the difficult task of reconfiguring a slim but efficient peacetime establishment into an equally slim but no less efficient emergency establishment capable of handling all but the largest crises without need of extra manpower. Within a year the HQ had publically demonstrated in three major NATO exercises satisfactory operational planning capability within a wide range of crisis scenarios.

Fundamental to this achievement was a shared understanding in the HQ of massive change in the threat environment as Russia had moved from the centre of a menacing and totalitarian empire to an economically weak country whose armed forces we judged at the time to be generally undermanned, underfunded and poorly disciplined. Although immediate dangers to stability in Europe were posed by violent terrorist groups and by ethnic, religious and other types of disputes that could flare into vicious armed conflict, we did not overlook Russia's inheritance of the dangerous remnants of the Soviet war machine. As a heads up Russia's rapid military deployment into Chechnya in December 1994 was an impressive demonstration of strategic mobility with concentration of force within time and space.

The savagery and brutality of Russian behaviour in Chechnya was also a timely reminder that proportionality and collateral damage did not figure in their military lexicon. So we did not dismiss the possibility of a resurgent and threatening Russia in the longer term, a point of particular concern to the Norwegians who, alone in NATO at that time, shared a common border with Russia. The border was adjacent to the Leningrad military district, Russia's most important and sensitive military region west of the Urals. Moreover, Russia's need for access to the world's oceans via the Baltic Sea meant a continuing requirement for open sea ports in the Gulf of Finland and the Kaliningrad Oblast, a small Russian province sandwiched between Poland and Lithuania. Elsewhere in the Baltic, the Russians and particularly the military were extremely irked by the granting of independence to Estonia, Latvia and Lithuania. But their displeasure was more than matched by the sense of outrage within the Baltic States provoked by the conduct of Russian forces as they withdrew. As I saw with my own eyes they left behind a trail of wanton destruction in the facilities they had occupied. Departing Russian lorries bearing the inscription 'we shall return' underlined the legacy of bitterness on one side and fear on the other which continues to this day.

At the sub-strategic level there were a range of other issues that were potential contributory factors to regional instability. The most prominent of these strands were ethnic tensions in Estonia and Latvia caused by the presence of substantial Russian minorities (over 25% of the population in both countries), access to Kaliningrad through Lithuania, the spread of organised crime from Russia, and nuclear safety particularly in and around the Kola Peninsula. Russia's Northern Fleet could not cope with the task of maintaining the huge number of active reactors within its nuclear-powered vessels let alone provide proper care and maintenance for disused reactors unattended in laid-up submarines and ships awaiting safe disposal. In addition to disputes between the Baltic States concerning natural resources, there was also friction between Kaliningrad and Lithuania over fishing rights and access to oil deposits close to the coast of the Kaliningrad Oblast. None of these tensions or risks in themselves constituted an immediate threat to the security of my AOR, but I judged that northern Scandinavia and the Baltic region would remain for some time to come the focal points for diplomatic pressure and military sabre rattling. Careful monitoring of the risks and tensions within this important area of interest to ACE would remain a primary task of HQ AFNW throughout the relatively short time of its existence.

Within a year I was confident that my staff were trained and adequately equipped to fulfil their responsibilities. Some sceptics had thought that AFNW would soon come to grief during the work-up period as a consequence of insoluble difficulties arising from the delineation of maritime and air responsibilities within my AOR and particularly in the Baltic. Quite apart from political and military sensibilities that would be aroused by boundary configurations, the establishment of seamless command and control procedures would be obviously problematic. An early meeting with General Helge Hansen, the German C-in-C of the Central Region, removed my private concerns. Helge, an exceptionally tall and slim man with impressive bearing and easy charm, was a military professional to his very core. It was immediately apparent that he was a strategic thinker well attuned to the politico-military changes that had reshaped the command structure within ACE. We were both acutely aware of our shared responsibility to make the new model work and in the process to avoid friction. As commanders we accepted that notwithstanding boundaries clearly drawn on maps and charts, we had overlapping interests and concerns that required us to think in terms of broader and more flexible spheres of influence. If and when push came to shove, operations in the Baltic would be conducted by Helge or me as directed by SACEUR on a case by case basis. A practical consequence of this early meeting was the production and publication of the Central/Northwest Regions Operational Planning Process document – the first time in NATO's history that the mechanics of joint planning which translated a strategic objective into operational plans and directives had been documented with the agreement of two MSCs. I was rather proud of this achievement.

Responsibility to SACEUR 'to enhance peace and stability' in my AOR fell out of the Partnership for Peace (PfP) programme initiated at the NATO summit in January 1994. The initiative subsumed the previous military coop-eration programme by aiming to move beyond dialogue and cooperation to forge real partnerships with non-NATO countries. Cooperation rather than confrontation was the order of the day to include the emerging democracies of East Europe while strengthening ties with non-aligned nations. In AFNW we supported the programme by developing military activities with Sweden, Finland, Estonia, Latvia, Lithuania and the Polish navy. Initial effort was focused on specific goals associated with search and rescue, delivery of humanitarian aid and maritime peacekeeping operations. AFNW was thus soon involved in a broad spectrum of PfP activities embracing seminars, workshops and live exercises. As a consequence of my first visit to the Baltic States in the autumn of 1994 a search and rescue workshop was conducted in the Maritime Rescue Coordination Centre at Gothenburg in Sweden in May 1995. The foundations were laid for the first live PfP search and rescue exercise in the Baltic, hosted by Sweden and including the Russians. Most of our early efforts had a distinctive maritime flavour with our first land exercise outside the traditional NATO boundaries hosted by the Czech Repub-lic in September 1996.

Thirteen countries from Scandinavia, East Europe and including the Baltic States participated in an exercise designed to develop and share basic peace-keeping skills. The programme included competitive events utilising ranges in the Boletice military training area close to Cesky Krumlov, 100 miles south of Prague, which in 1992 had been declared a UNESCO World Heritage Site. Renais-sance and baroque buildings crowned by a spectacular castle, and all untouched by war, surrounded an elegant, cobbled, old town square where I gave a speech of welcome to participants. Sadly the British Army was not represented.

I struck one personal blow for the military reputation of NATO. At the end of a competitive shooting exercise against snap-up targets the Czech defence minister, a large and florid man marked with the bullying character of Soviet officialdom, loudly invited me to shoot against half a dozen of his generals with a bottle of vodka as the prize. I was handed an AK47 and told to get on with it. Sensing a reputational joke in which I would be the butt, I accepted the inevitable and blazed away with relaxed abandon. To my astonishment and to the Czech minister's very obvious displeasure, I won. The vodka was handed over with singular bad grace and no offer of congratulations. My MA, Lieutenant Colonel Clive Knightley, a keen shot himself shared my surprise. "I didn't know you could shoot like that," he observed before challenging me to a competition that evening. I was determined to win this and ditched my approach of relaxed abandon. The consequence of trying too hard was inevitable. I lost but happily had not wagered the bottle of vodka on the result.

The following afternoon we left the authentic old world charm of Cesky Krumlov to return to Prague in a Hind helicopter modified for VIP transport. The modification included a leather armchair in the centre of the cabin. It was certainly very comfortable but lacked any safety harness. After lift-off and as the nose tilted down to accelerate the helicopter I also discovered that the seat, mounted on small wheels, was not attached to the floor as it gently rumbled across the cabin. This was not to be my last experience of flight-safety standards in countries of the former Warsaw Pact which fell more than some way short of western norms.

As well as these practical activities we welcomed to the HQ partner staff officers to take part in our own operational planning exercises so to prepare them for possible integration into command and control structures created for NATO peace support operations. The importance of this task was emphasised by the shameful reality of Bosnia and Herzegovina. After the collapse of Tito's federalist system of government in Yugoslavia, wars of independence in Slovenia and Croatia preceded Bosnia's declaration of independence in 1991 following a referendum which had been boycotted by Bosnian Serbs. Another war was the inevitable consequence and a region of ethnic and geographic complexity was soon transformed into a charnel house of violence and ethnic cleansing pursued with medieval brutality.

Early in 1992 the multi-national United Nations Protection Force (UNPRO-FOR) had been established to create peaceful conditions for the settlement of the Yugoslav crisis and ground forces were deployed. By the summer of 1994 some 2,500 British soldiers were committed to UNPROFOR, a contribution second only to the French. But the total UNPROFOR strength was insufficient for peacekeeping let alone peace enforcement. Moreover, the widespread dispersal of small and often isolated detachments of multinational ground forces required the exercise of caution. It had been hoped that the presence of soldiers acting as observers on behalf of the international community would deter violence and encourage peaceful settlement of disputes. This was not to be. Well aware of NATO air power deployed to bases in Italy the Bosnian Serbs took many of the detachments hostage, in effect using them as shields to deter NATO bombing. Thus from 1992 to mid 1995 air power was only applied irregularly and in small doses. Further difficulties ensued from extended and duplicated chains of command within the UN and NATO. In essence the UN had deployed a peacekeeping force on the ground and NATO a peace-enforcement force in the air. But procedures were improved and perceptions which may have been created in 1993 and 1994 of the relative impotence of air power were shattered when land forces under the command of Lieutenant General Rupert Smith were progressively re-deployed for self-protection and NATO air power unleashed on 30th August 1995 in Operation Deliberate Force. Rupert Smith, who had succeeded Lieutenant General Sir Michael Rose, was prepared to accept the need for a coercive bombing campaign to force the Serbs to the negotiating table.

A few weeks earlier SACEUR had required me as his senior airman to go down to CINCSOUTH's HQ in Naples to be briefed on an air campaign plan. SACEUR sought my assurance that the plan applied an appropriate level of coercive force which would make a significant if not decisive contribution to the totality of pressures that would force the Serbs to accept the demands of the international community. I felt uneasy about the task because both Admiral Leighton Smith, C-in- C of NATO's Southern Region, and Lieutenant General Mike Ryan USAF, commander 5th Allied Tactical Air Force, had operational pedigrees born of considerable experience in Vietnam. My own operational flying in South Arabia and Oman was very small beer in comparison. But I need not have worried. I was warmly received by Leighton and Mike and fully briefed on their plan which tasked NATO air packages against target complexes including command and control facilities, SAM sites, microwave radio relay towers and military compounds within which there were 338 individual aiming points. I particularly noted Mike Ryan's sensitivity to the proportionality of usable force and his awareness of the dangers that collateral damage could do to NATO let alone UN solidarity if the plan was executed.

My questions concerning the composition of force packages, rates of effort and command and control of the air space were all answered to my entire satisfaction and this I reported to General Joulwan after I had returned to High Wycombe. I had noticed that only US and UK officers had been present at the briefing and Leighton explained that the targeting details of any op plan shared with other nations within his HQ would quickly find its way into Serb hands, hence the limited attendance. I could only observe that any attempt to apply such a restriction in my HQ would have provoked mayhem.

Two significant and appalling events in Bosnia triggered the launch of Operation Deliberate Force against the Bosnian Serbs. The first was the massacre in July at Srebrenica of some 8,000 Muslims. Shortly afterwards Air Chief Marshal Sir William Wratten, my successor as AOC-in-C Strike Command, was sent by the government to meet with General Ratko Mladic, chief of staff of the Bosnian Serb Army. He was accompanied by the commander USAF Europe and the deputy commander French Forces. In essence Bill, leader of the delegation, was instructed to inform Mladic that unless Serbian armed forces immediately stopped all military activities they would be subject to heavy and unremitting air attack. The full story of the mission is included in Appendix 1, but the threat of coercive force did not prevent a mortar bomb attack on the Sarajevo market place that killed 38 civilians and injured hundreds more. These atrocities caused the UN and NATO command keys to be turned with a single purpose as NATO air power was coordinated with UNPROFOR artillery provided by the newly created British, French and Netherlands Rapid Reaction Force (RRF). The UNPROFOR artillery, positioned high up on Mount Igman, was tasked to neutralise Bosnian Serb heavy weapons around Sarajevo. Further pressure on the Serbs was exerted by the Croat-Muslim Federation ground offensive in the Serb Krajina region.

NATO attack aircraft flew 3,515 sorties against the targets approved by NATO and UNPROFOR. One thousand and twenty-six munitions were launched of which some 700 were precision guided. Air operations lasted for an overall three weeks with a six-day pause after 48 hours of operations as the Serbs hoped to benefit from the timidity of some UN and NATO members. Once resumed and 13 days later the Serbs gave in and not before time as the authorised target list was almost exhausted. The Serb leaders signed an agreement to respect safe areas and attend peace talks. Further negotiations followed leading to the Dayton Agreement that was formally signed in December. UNPROFOR troops were replaced by the NATO Implementation Force (IFOR) of 60,000 troops in theatre which put an effective stop to violence in Bosnia and Herzegovina.

I have never claimed success was achieved by air power alone. Over a long period ground forces had held the ring while international leaders and aid agencies played out their hands. The Croat offensive in the Serb Krajina would certainly have helped weaken Serb resolve as did the deployment and support of UNPROFOR artillery. But General Sir Michael Rose's assessment of the air campaign as "no more than a useful signal to the Serbs that the peacekeeping option had been suspended" underestimated air power's contribution to the aggregate of pressures which forced the Serbs to negotiate. For my part I shared Leighton Smith's judgement that it was the relentless pressure and precision of up to seven NATO air-attack packages a day against authorised targets that finally persuaded the Serbs that the West really meant business. Some may still disagree, but for certain without the commitment of NATO air power the savage war in Bosnia would have ground on much longer.

NATO's support of the UN in the former Yugoslavia brought with it important lessons for future crisis-management operations: to beware of deploying neutral and lightly armed peacekeepers into a civil war if there was no peace to keep; the inherent difficulty of trying to combine a peacekeeping effort on the ground with a peace-enforcement mission in the air; the need for a clear and attainable mandate from the UN and the vital requirement for unity of command. But, above all, NATO operations in Bosnia underlined the crucial importance of understanding the true nature of a conflict before the commitment of armed forces into situations of instability within which ethnic and cultural differences complicated objectives of political or territorial control. For far too long General Joulwan's appeals to the North Atlantic Council (NAC) for clear definition of purpose and unity of command fell foul of political wrangling, excessive caution and from the French ambassador downright obstruction. But when the UN and NATO eventually got their acts together the harmonisation of air and land operations provided a classic demonstration of the use of structured force in the service of diplomacy.

The subsequent deployment of IFOR marked the transition of military success into a permanent achievement that was eventually to involve 134,000 personnel from 32 different countries tasked to implement military aspects of the Dayton Peace Agreement. For the first time non-aligned countries placed their forces under NATO command exercised by Admiral Leighton Smith armed with robust rules of engagement. My role and that of General Helge Hansen in the Central Region was to support Southern Region operations.

There were two aspects that involved my HQ. As we approached Christmas 1995 SACEUR tasked AFNW to certify contributions to IFOR offered by non-aligned countries. Certification of land forces required me to send teams of specialist officers to check what was on offer – not just numbers, but equipment, professional competence in identified roles, English language fluency and by no means least, having the wherewithal to deploy into and survive in the harsh conditions of the Bosnian winter. By the end of the year we had inspected and certified units from Poland, Morocco, Malaysia and Pakistan. In January a team was sent to the Czech Republic to provide essential pre-deployment training for the Czech contribution to IFOR. General Joulwan also required me to provide staff augmentation to IFOR which depleted my staff by10%. Meanwhile we continued to participate in NATO's Article 5 exercises that demonstrated the unique and enduring principle of collective defence that was at the very heart of the Alliance's founding treaty.

The pressures on my HQ were containable but I had soon learnt after taking command that nations had their own individual work ethics. For the Norwegians this meant the working day started at 0800 hrs and ended at 1600 hrs. Work outside this period earned overtime pay. However, the first submission to MoD Norway for payment of overtime was refused as it had not been included in their budget for the new HQ. Hence my concern that tasking Norwegian officers to surrender their Christmas stand down to undertake certification duties and then short notice detachments to IFOR might provoke rebellion in one form or the other. My fears were unfounded. Everyone in the HQ understood the urgency of these tasks and deployed without complaint to contribute to the success of the IFOR mission; we all recognised that the potential consequences of failure were dire. Pleasingly the format of the reports designed by the staff – principally soldiers but with cerebral contributions from the light- and dark-blue elements – and the accuracy of military judgements earned SACEUR's commendation.

In June 1996 a communiqué from NATO announced in Berlin was to have far-reaching impact on AFNW as national leaders reaffirmed their commitment to open the Alliance to new members. I was surprised by the decision. The Balkan experience had highlighted difficulties within the NAC as had debate concerning the first re-structuring of the ACE command boundaries. Expansion of the Alliance from 14 members to potentially more than 20 could only create a larger complexity of decision making. Moreover it didn't seem entirely sensible to cock a snook at the Russians just when the first green shoots were appearing from the seeds sewn by Partnership for Peace. But this was all about politics and in my AOR the ambitions of Poland and the Baltic States to join NATO were well known. The French military mission attached to my HQ under command of an air force brigadier also led me to believe that France was serious about re-joining NATO's military command structure. Had I been more politically astute I would have picked up warning bells from the Berlin communiqué that recorded NATO's objective of moving onwards from Cold War military structures towards more flexible arrangements that would allow coalitions of the willing to use NATO assets for military missions beyond the Alliance's borders. France's interest as a member of the NAC focused on enhancing the effectiveness and visibility of the European Security and Defence Identity, the name given to the intended European 'pillar' within NATO. For the Americans, the primary concerns were the preservation of American leadership of the Alliance and unity of command in NATO.

After two years of wrangling the NAC agreed that the Western European Union could undertake peacekeeping, humanitarian and peace-enforcement missions beyond the Alliance's borders using NATO's military assets under European command. Although Washington retained a veto over European use of NATO assets on missions of which they did not approve, the French had achieved their main goal. Political enthusiasm to return to NATO's formal military structure consequently withered on the vine to the dismay of the French military.

In discussion with CDS, Field Marshal Sir Peter Inge, I sensed that MoD UK would not press hard for the preservation of AFNW should the NAC conclude that the responsibilities of AFNW and AFCENT could be merged into one HQ Regional Command North based at Brunssum in the Netherlands. CDS felt that a French decision to re-join NATO's military structure would save the day for AFNW by giving an extension of its AOR and attendant responsibilities. I suspected at the time that the MoD's primary interest, and certainly the Army's, was not to prejudice the acquisition in 1992 of command of the Allied Rapid Reaction Corps. Maintaining a Corps HQ capability through command of the ARRC was an imperative to the Army following structural changes and manpower reductions in the wake of Options for Change and DCS decisions. I also knew full well that the formation of AFNW was not popular in Norway and Denmark and for understandable reasons. The Norwegians were upset by the departure of an MSC HQ from Kolsas to High Wycombe and the Danes were less than enthusiastic about the delegation of responsibility for maritime operations in the Baltic to a UK-based HQ. The Germans took a similar view.

Throughout my 2¾ years in command I enjoyed cordial relations with senior officers in Norway, Denmark and Germany and I never had cause to suspect that any of my NATO military colleagues were seeking to undermine the authority and credibility of my HQ. However, I have since learned that our reputation within NATO's political officialdom was not particularly favourable. In its early days the HQ was visited by a party of senior NATO officials. I was absent having been called to an audience with HM the Queen of Denmark. I delegated responsibility for giving the command presentation to my chief of staff who in discussion afterwards was, I am told, myopic in failing to demonstrate any informed concern about the future of the Alliance beyond the purely national self-interest of Norway. His mindset was focused exclusively on the Article 5 responsibility of the HQ. I thought, wrongly as it turned out, that this would soon be forgotten and notwithstanding this blot in our copybook I was quietly confident that my HQ would not go to the wall. AFNW also had a powerful ally in General Joulwan who argued for the retention of three commands in ACE on the grounds that a two-command structure, one for north of the Alps and one for south of the Alps, would create an excessive span of control. I agreed. Moreover, having established the authority of the HQ in its primary Article 5 mission, AFNW staff had played their full part in the dramatically successful IFOR mission. Elsewhere and under the banner of PfP the HQ had built bridges to former adversaries and to other countries of long-standing and robust neutrality. These new friendships didn't happen by accident. They were the result of the staff's hard work that dug the practical foundations of PfP within the Command's AOR. Such was the score card of achievement when my tenure at AFNW ended and I returned to national duty on my appointment as CAS. The impressive performance of the HQ was most generously and publically acknowledged by General Joulwan in his address to the parade on 11th March 1997 when I handed over command to Air Chief Marshal Sir John Cheshire.

I regretted having to leave with a question mark hanging over the future of AFNW and with two important questions still unanswered. The first was who would assume the tasks and responsibilities of AFNW if the axe should fall on the HQ; second, at what financial cost and to what military effect? Overlaying both these questions was my concern that operations in the Southern Region were taking NATO's eye off the military and political complexities of life in AFNW's AOR. We certainly had not dismissed the possibility of Russian resurgence as an aggressive and untrustworthy neighbour, a judgement that reflected much time and effort spent on PfP activities, home and away, as well as discussions with political and military leaders in the Scandinavian and Baltic countries. Apart from losing the expertise and bank of knowledge within AFNW, its replication in a new Command HQ would certainly involve extra cost to the NATO budget. It would be ironic if the financial motivational forces that inspired the formation of AFNW would be reversed more by political whim than military judgement.

Uncertainty about the future was resolved in December 1997 when NATO defence ministers reached agreement that AFNW and AFCENT would be amalgamated into the new Regional Command North (RCN). This meant that henceforth NATO would be represented in the UK only by CINCEASTLANT

at Northwood. On the plus side, and in the context of influence, British command of the ARRC was not challenged. This success was supplemented by
securing the appointment of deputy commander-in-chief RCN and a British
general was appointed as the single deputy SACEUR – hitherto there had been
two deputies, one German and one British. In retrospect I have come to believe,
after discussion with others better informed, that in the highest echelons of
the UK MoD AFNW was valued as a bargaining chip in negotiations that
secured these appointments. Achievement and military relevance were less
important than the possession of influence, political as well as military.

When the decision was made to do away with AFNW it needed a man of
real stature, presence and character to keep the show on the road and to sustain
the morale of a multinational tri-service HQ until closure. John Cheshire was
the man for the job. In his last ten years of service he had filled a succession
of international appointments with distinction. Coming to High Wycombe
direct from Brussels where he had been the UK military representative at HQ
NATO, John was well aware of continuing uncertainty about the future of
AFNW. He was not at all discouraged and before the decision to shut down
AFNW was made he had set up a PfP cell within the HQ manned by officers
from Sweden, Finland, Latvia, Lithuania and Slovakia. More the pity that the
effort AFNW expended in carrying forward the imaginative and constructive
PfP concept was not sustained by RCN. But over and beyond the obvious pride
John took in his command and his persistent good humour in the face of many
difficulties, his exceptional leadership throughout three very tough years earned
the unqualified admiration of everyone who had dealings with HQ AFNW.

The story of AFNW's short life merits recording as but one piece of NATO's
restructuring in the wake of the Cold War. For my own part command of
AFNW continued a process of education within which new experiences, some
sought after and some quite unexpected, expanded my knowledge of military
operations. My comprehension of air power was well informed and close
association with soldiers in a variety of appointments had given me some
appreciation of the difficulties born of the inherent friction of land warfare.
But my understanding of maritime warfare was strictly theoretical rather than
practical, a deficiency that I was determined to ameliorate as C-in-C of an
AOR within which two thirds of the surface area was water. In the round the
wide variety of experiences I enjoyed involving participation in events and
activities at the strategic, operational and tactical levels were to prove invaluable in my next appointment as the professional head of the RAF. And
particularly so when faced with the prospect of another Defence Review after
the election of the New Labour government in May 1997.

CHAPTER 24
RECOLLECTIONS AND REFLECTIONS

As already recorded I went to AFNW in the firm belief that I would retire at the end of my tour on reaching the age of 58. Two years earlier we had bought a cottage in Dorset as our retirement home having secured a mortgage on favourable terms from Lloyds Bank, but conditional on full repayment when I retired in July 1997. My gratuity would fund the outstanding debt. So all was set fair for Elizabeth and me to enjoy the last two years of our military life together. Everything was proceeding to plan when in mid-June 1996 CAS's PSO rang me to fix an office call in MoD. No subject for discussion was mentioned and I assumed Sir Michael Graydon wanted to discuss the future of AFNW. Not so. No sooner had I settled in my chair than he asked if I wished to be considered as a potential successor following his retirement in spring 1997. The question was a true bolt from the blue and it is embarrassing to admit that I asked for time to think about it. Sir Michael generously agreed.

My hesitation reflected more than surprise. I had got used to the idea of retirement in a year's time and had been contemplating the future. A job somewhere in the defence industry held no attraction and I was thinking about studying for a degree in military history through enrolment in a distance-learning programme. This was no more than an attractive aspiration but I had not forgotten my distaste for the MoD in particular and Whitehall in general; this had not mellowed since my departure in 1981. In considering whether or not I should accept Sir Michael's invitation, my thinking first recognised practical inexperience of working at the highest level within the MoD and, secondly, absence of direct contact with the RAF now stretching back for two years with more than nine months to run. I was certainly proud to be considered as a potential CAS but as pride comes before fall I had to ask myself whether or not I was up to the job of leading a service still recuperating from the consequences of Options for Change and Defence Costs Studies. And while I had been distinctly unimpressed by the Conservative government's attitude to defence, the probability of New Labour winning the next election introduced a further element of uncertainty into an already unpredictable future.

In drawing up a balance sheet of pluses and minuses I recognised that since leaving the MoD, and with the exception of a year at RCDS, I had been exclusively involved in single service and joint operations for more than two decades. More recently director of operations for Gulf War I, command of 1 Group during a rapid expansion of the RAF's operational commitments followed by appointments in Strike Command and AFNW had given me a well-informed insight to the practical difficulties associated with national power projection at a time of rapidly declining defence expenditure. Politicians banging on about punching above our weight remained an unfortunate turn of phrase and I had little doubt that sooner or later we would catch a cold if not a bloody nose. Meanwhile, two years in AFNW had already presented valuable experience in working at the highest military level in NATO in a joint and multi-national environment. So perhaps at this stage in my story I will be forgiven if I digress from the matter at the forefront of my mind to reminisce about experiences, some of which were unique for a NATO C-in-C and others that were to influence my final decision.

My NATO tour was set on firm domestic foundations. The extension of Queen's Gap that had previously caused me some grief and which we had moved into in July 1994 gave Elizabeth and me room to put up a steady flow of senior visitors from NATO HQ and PfP nations. VVIP visitors to the HQ including King Harald V of Norway and the Prince of Wales provided welcome opportunities to include AFNW staff in receptions at Queen's Gap. Such social occasions were part and parcel of the bonding process that helped create a distinctive AFNW identity. It was good fun too. NATO provided us with an apartment in Oslo and the Norwegian MoD gave me an office suite in the courtyard of Akershus Castle, a medieval fortress that overlooked Oslo and dominated the sea approaches to the national capital. Through the centuries the castle had successfully withstood many sieges by foreign enemies, principally Swedish. I soon discovered that Scandinavian history was riven by violent regional rivalries. So it was not until 1940 that Akershus Castle was first surrendered and to the Germans after the Nazis' unprovoked assault on Denmark and Norway. My office, a haven of peace and quiet, was the perfect place for speech writing and letter drafting. The apartment in Oslo's diplomatic quarter, comfortably furnished and well equipped, was the ideal setting for entertaining my Norwegian hosts, political, military and civilian. The high price of alcohol in Norway guaranteed heroic consumption of my duty-free hooch.

Regular visits to Norway were important to reassure the Norwegians that their national interests were not being overlooked in a UK-based regional HQ.

Oslo also served as a convenient launch pad for many journeys throughout the long length and thin breadth of Norway as I set about familiarising myself with the topography of the country. Travelling by land and sea was pure delight. Whether viewed from a train window or the bridge of a ship, I never lost my sense of wonderment at the spectacular beauty of Norway. Glaciers and fast running rivers flowed down from the rugged terrain of a predominantly mountainous landscape to the sea where 16,000 miles of coastline were gashed by steep-sided fjords that stretched far inland. There was unlimited scope for energetic outdoor activities: hiking, cycling, kayaking and rafting in the summer and all forms of skiing and snowboarding in the winter. Ski jumping and bobsleighing opportunities were available for more adventurous souls.

With a population of 16 per square kilometre there was plenty of room for everyone including a NATO C-in-C who qualified as a bobsleigh brake man after two hair-raising descents of the Olympic course at Lillehammer. I wisely – in my view – ignored ski jumping but attempted to master the skill of cross-country skiing. My instructor was Major General Oernulf Tune, recently retired from the RNoAF, an expert skier and a man in whom patience was indeed a virtue. I could cope on the flat and going downhill in a straight line. But controlled turning at speed using a snowplough technique was beyond my limited ability. To change direction I deliberately fell over, stood up, pointed on the new heading and set off again much to the amusement of Oernulf. But his patience, which gave me some understanding of the requirement, was eventually rewarded when I was introduced to 'NATO planks'. These cross-country skis were at least twice the width and significantly shorter than the skeletal skis I had previously used and consequently were much more manageable when I visited winter exercises in north Norway.

Major NATO exercises were well supported and particularly so by the UK/ Netherlands Amphibious Force, elements of the US Striking Fleet Atlantic and a US Marine Corps Expeditionary Force. As the regional C-in-C, much of my time was spent in briefing and escorting senior visitors from ACE – General Joulwan downwards – military observers from other NATO and PfP nations and accredited ambassadors to Norway from participating countries. The safe transportation of this throng plus hangers-on around exercise locations in dangerously changeable weather conditions made programme time keeping rather tricky. But it drove home the message to our senior visitors that the hard and uncompromising blend of topography and climate created unique difficulties should NATO be required to fight on its northern flank.

In addition to the major exercises I spent separate time with Brigade 6 of the Norwegian Army on exercise in north Norway where the Arctic wastes of Finnmark give way to the plains around Kirkenes immediately adjacent to the Russian border. From the start of the tour at AFNW I considered it an essential responsibility to get a well-informed feel for the tactical environment, a responsibility not only borne of my joint appointment but in acknowledgement of NATO's intellectual investment in the Combined Joint Task Force (CJTF) initiative – a developing concept proposed by the Americans that aimed to draw on NATO's existing military capabilities to head off or respond to crises. The operational requirements for a CJTF HQ were twofold. First, it should be capable of rapid formation when the probability of commitment was high. Secondly, it should have the capacity and capability to exercise command and control of sea, land and air forces, to assess and disseminate intelligence and all while sustaining operations in a hostile environment. NATO's thinking centred on the identification of a core staff nucleus with plug-in staff modules specific to an identified operational task. However, my experience as Gulf War I director of operations led me to question its practicality as I was not convinced that such an arrangement would be capable of rapid formation that would be sufficiently robust to withstand the pressures of an operational deployment.

My doubts led me to choose the Battles of Narvik in 1940 as the subject of a HQ study period in October 1995. I chose Narvik as battles within the overall Norwegian campaign required the combination of the three British services in a totally joint operation together with French, Polish and Norwegian forces – arguably the first CJTF in history. Professor Richard Holmes led an impressive array of military historians, British and German, who covered all aspects of the battles from planning to denouement. The two-day study period was attended by a distinguished company of guests including ambassadors from PfP nations, the NATO military hierarchy and London-based defence attachés all in addition to my own staff and representatives from our PSCs. In the round the campaign was a disastrous episode in the Allied war effort from which many lessons would be learnt. To emphasise their importance I was fortunate to enlist support and contributions from two most distinguished warriors.

First was Air Chief Marshal Sir Kenneth Cross who happily had forgotten our short-lived encounter in 1962. Sir Kenneth immediately gained the attention of the audience by admitting that he now knew far more about what went on than he did in May 1940. He then spoke about his experience of the conflict and the tragic consequences for his squadron, No. 46, and 263 Squadron, not to mention Fleet Air Arm aircraft after embarkation on HMS *Glorious* following receipt of the evacuation order. The loss of all 20 RAF aircraft, nearly all the pilots along with most of the ship's company in the major naval disaster of the campaign reminded us all of the harsh realities of conflict far removed from the interesting but dispassionate historical presentations. Sir Kenneth filled his remit to introduce authentic experience to conclude the first morning session.

Field Marshal Sir Nigel Bagnall was the second distinguished interlocutor. His comments were predictably precise and very much to the point. He noted that Allied operations in Norway were impaired by political indecision and strategic improvisation. When committed to operations Allied forces were handicapped by ignorance of the climate and topographical characteristics with no detailed knowledge of harbours, airfields and storage facilities in Norway. On the other side of the coin, German success was firmly based on a clear aim, thorough planning, sound intelligence, operational security, the achievement of surprise and audacious execution. Sir Nigel concluded with some sharp comments about glaring deficiencies in the British command and control arrangements. His observations underlined the relevance of the Battles of Narvik to contemporary consideration of the CJTF concept and allowed me to conclude with questions, as still recorded in my note book, for others to consider in NATO HQ.

Mindful of the foundations of German success was it any longer possible to achieve operational security in multinational coalitions in the (then) new age of CNN? Was the acceptance of risk, bedfellow of audacity, any longer politically acceptable when the media would be quick to portray any hint of possible failure? Would public opinion in western democracies have the stomach, where national sovereignty was not under threat, to see their armed forces committed to sustained and unpleasant operations with ever increasing casualties? Had public expectation of surgical accuracy in contemporary military operations now overridden the eternal truths of our principles of war which laid stress on such dictums as offensive action, concentration of force, surprise and so on? I concluded by expressing the hope that the study period had helped to illuminate hard-earned lessons that underlined important operational questions that the Alliance had to address if it was to move forward into the next century with confidence in its capabilities.

I did not mention my concern about NATO enlargement. Whilst enlargement would be eventually decided by politicians I was worried about Russia's reaction to an extension of NATO's boundaries that could be interpreted as both unnecessary and aggressive. But visits to the Baltic States had left me in no doubt about their eagerness to join NATO. Without pouring cold water on their ambitions I believed that the process of enlargement needed to be gradual, deliberate and transparent. My efforts to explain to military counterparts the responsibilities of membership, its costs and risks as well as benefits, received a polite hearing, but their ambition was to prove much stronger than cool consideration. The Latvian chief of defence told me that his first priority was the procurement of airborne warning and control (AWACS) aircraft. Some gentle questioning soon revealed he had absolutely no idea of the cost of an airframe let alone the associated training and logistics bills. For decades the armed forces of the Baltic States, equipped by the Soviet Union, had no accountability for procurement, introduction to service and the maintenance of equipment. With independence the Baltic States had to learn to think for themselves and within the military, break with practices instilled by Soviet hegemony.

I have already mentioned that 70% of my AOR was water but the characteristics were far from uniform. While the moderating influence of the Gulf Stream kept coastal waters of the UK and Norway free from ice, unlike parts of the Baltic and Barents seas, much of the northern areas of the AOR were inshore waters or shallow seas which made maritime operations particularly demanding. The coastline was vulnerable at many points to sea-borne attack. Moreover a country in which terrestrial movement could range from problematic to the nigh on impossible was significantly dependent on sea-borne communications. My practical experience of winter maritime operations at sea started with a day passage through the Norwegian Leads, the water between the mainland and a long string of offshore islands. The sea state was predictably rough as I set off in a fast attack craft of the German navy on an excursion that was both instructive and invigorating. The Albatross-class, now decommissioned, were capable of 40 knots and armed with a potent mix of Exocet missiles, guns and torpedoes with electronic warfare and decoy countermeasures. The German navy certainly got a big bang for their bucks and in my judgement was the most operationally efficient of the German armed forces. German naval officers and non-commissioned ranks had self-confidence, pride and an aggressive mindset that I noticed not only at sea but within the walls of the HQ at High Wycombe.

My nautical education on NATO winter exercises was further extended by a day with the Special Boat Service (SBS) operating from a small island not far distant from the entrance to Trondheim Fjord. Admiral Bjorn Kipsgaard, the regional PSC and a good friend and colleague, had asked for my help to resolve a difficulty concerning exercise boundaries that defined the scope of special forces activity. To get both sides of the story I helicoptered to the island and after briefing from the SBS commander it didn't take long to sort out the problem. I was then asked if I would like a ride in an SBS rigid raiding craft.

These small craft, capable of reaching 40 knots and carrying a coxswain plus ten troops, were used for rapid beach and riverbank insertion/extraction. I accepted the invitation and shortly afterwards was at sea accompanied by my MA at that time, Lieutenant Colonel Bob Hendicott. The temperature in February was below freezing, the wave tops well over a metre high and the interval between was short and sharp. A windshield gave some protection to the coxswain and me from continuous sheets of spray as the craft maintained its maximum speed up and down the waves; it was an exhilarating helter-skelter of a ride. After 20 minutes or so I started to wonder how long we would stay out as the Royal Marines corporal gave no indication of returning to base. I did not want to appear a wimp but face-saving salvation was at hand. Bob Hendicott, sitting behind us, had no shelter and was already turning into a block of ice. I pointed out his understandable discomfort, bravely borne dare I say, and suggested we should return to prevent the onset of hypothermia.

Once ashore, and after Bob had thawed out, I was then asked if I would like to return to Trondheim in a long-range insertion craft (LRIC). Again I accepted with pleasure and was introduced to the craft and its three-man crew with a colour sergeant in command. From memory one steered, one navigated and one operated the throttles and trim. The hull carried a roofed cabin, to Bob Hendicott's obvious relief, and saddle seats for eight assault troops. The LRIC could act as a mothership for smaller craft and was also deployable on maritime interception operations. We took two hours to get to Trondheim as we manoeuvred at full tilt in the fjord up to the maximum speed of some 70 knots. The sea state had got rougher which added a larger element of exhilaration to that I had enjoyed in the rigid raider. We seemed to fly between the wave crests with the throttle man setting full power (approximately 2,000 hp) each time we hit water. Now and again with longer gaps we ploughed straight in and the world around us turned green until we emerged into daylight. I now understood the critical importance of trimming. As we disembarked at Trondheim I appreciated I had enjoyed one of the most memorable days of my life. Chatting to the crew I asked if operating a LRIC was dangerous. The colour sergeant gave me a pitying look. "Dangerous," he replied "it's ******* dangerous." I don't think he was winding me up.

At this point some may well ask why a C-in-C was gallivanting around with the German navy and the SBS. First, these outings presented a matchless opportunity to experience conditions far beyond those I had encountered during offshore sailing expeditions. Secondly, at the back of my mind was the vulnerability of shore installations to mining, a thought that also applied to AFNW's maritime responsibilities in the Baltic. So my next port of call was to NATO's

Mine Warfare School run by the Belgian navy in preparation for a couple of days at sea with Royal Navy mine countermeasures vessels (MCMV) in the Firth of Clyde. The first day and night was spent on a Sandown-class MCMV, the latest addition to the Fleet before moving to an older Hunt-class MCMV in a rigid inflatable boat (RIB) that guaranteed an uncomfortable passage between the two vessels. Soaking wet I clambered up a rope ladder and was piped aboard as I sprawled onto the deck. Watching seamen made a fair effort suppressing their mirth at such an undignified arrival by a king crab.

Observing the MCVMs at work from the bridge reminded me of a well-run combat operations centre on an RAF station except that the latter was stationary rather than pitching and rolling. The Sandown MCMV deployed remote-controlled mine-disposal vehicles controlled by fibre-optic cables while the older Hunt-class used a traditional wire-sweeping system combining acoustic and magnetic detection. Mine hunting and sweeping clearly required cool nerves, sustained concentration and well-disciplined team self-confidence. Having admired the professionalism of both crews and having thoroughly enjoyed the warm hospitality of the wardrooms, I returned to High Wycombe with some informed understanding of a potential threat to maritime security within the AFNW AOR. One final visit and a submerged day at sea on a RN nuclear attack submarine, Trafalgar Class I recall, introduced me to a truly formidable weapons system and one that remains an essential component of national defence.

Further afield in January 1995 I travelled to Norfolk, Virginia, to fly out to the USS *Theodore Roosevelt* in the Greyhound carrier onboard delivery (COD) aircraft. I had met Admiral Jay Johnson, commanding Striking Fleet Atlantic, at a NATO conference hosted by Admiral Peter Abbott. Jay, sensing my interest, invited me to spend a few days on the *Theodore Roosevelt,* a nuclear-powered Nimitz-class aircraft carrier. Three hours after landing on I was strapped into the back seat of a F-14 braced for a catapult launch. The aircraft captain warned me that after running up to full power and completing pre-take-off vital actions he would salute the flight deck. He added that then there would be no turning back. After two tours flying Harriers I was well-conditioned to rapid acceleration but the F-14 experience was a quite definitive upgrade – about two seconds to 140 knots. A 50-minute sortie introduced me to the air defence capabilities of the aircraft before it landed back on. Slamming to full power as we hit the deck in case the hook missed the wire was a novel experience but all was well as the aircraft rapidly slowed down. After unhooking we taxied to our parking slot which required the aircraft to turn through 180 degrees. With the nose wheel aft of the cockpit I had an unobstructed view of the sea well below as we turned in prior to shutdown which I found just a little unsettling. The day was 25th January 1995 as recorded on a certificate presented to me by Captain R.L Christenson US Navy that appointed me an 'honorary tailhooker'. Above the certificate is a colour photograph of my first launch, a treasured memento and so typical of American kindness.

The *Theodore Roosevelt* was in the final stages of working up before deploying to the Red Sea in support of Operation Southern Watch over Iraq. The 100,000-tonne carrier had 98 aircraft embarked with a total complement of some 5,000 men split almost equally between those running the ship and those operating an air wing that covered all constituent roles of air power. On deployment the Carrier Strike Group included six surface combatants and one or two attack submarines to provide all-round defence with supply ships of Military Sea Lift Command contributing logistic support. In 1995 the US Navy had commissioned seven Nimitz-class carriers with three more to follow up to give the USA a force of maritime power projection that far exceeded the total combined capabilities of all other navies. While touring the ship escorted by the two Fleet warrant officers I was struck by the youthfulness of the crew and their highly disciplined energy in all aspects of operating this hugely complex engine of war. This was most evident on the flight deck where everyone wore coloured jerseys that denoted their specific job. I learnt that all aspects of aircraft operations on the flight deck to airborne aircraft out to five nautical miles were controlled by the air boss, assisted by a mini boss, perched in a tower high above the deck.

I met the air boss, a US Navy captain and himself an aviator, during a short lull between the launch and recovery of two aircraft packages. Over a cup of coffee I commented that naval aviation was a nice way to earn a living. He agreed but added it was at night that the pay cheque was really earned. Point taken. After dinner that evening the programme gave me an hour to watch night flight deck operations from the admiral's bridge. I stayed there for four hours totally fascinated by the choreography of launching, recovering and turning around individual aircraft types within varying package sizes of up to 20 aircraft. The next day after a morning in the operations centre watching the myriad aspects of command and control of the ship itself and its escorts I said farewell and thank you to Captain Christenson. An hour later and back in the COD I was catapulted off to return to Norfolk in time to catch a return flight home.

Gulf War I had given me an insight into military power in all three dimensions of conventional warfare, but it was the visit to the USS *Theodore*

Roosevelt that left me with an indelible impression of American military reach. The combination of USAF air power and the continuous presence at sea of three Nimitz-class aircraft carriers enabled unmatched power projection and was a forceful reminder of the simple fact that all western democracies relied on the USA for their ultimate security. And although the UK remained America's most potent military and diplomatic ally in Europe I was worried that continuing reductions in our national defence spending and political addiction to the concept of 'punching above our weight' with internal emphasis on influence rather than capability, would reduce our armed forces to paper-tiger status. However, it is only fair to remember that in the search for peace dividends most other European members of NATO were ahead of us in reducing their force levels. But while the Pentagon was not immune from post-Cold War cuts, the USA continued to foot three quarters of NATO's bill. In the round the Americans owed no thanks to their European allies for their contributions to collective defence.

I also had my doubts about our 'special relationship' with the USA. British politicians were ever ready to emphasise its enduring importance, but American acknowledgement of its contemporary relevance seemed to me to be little more than courteous recognition of our shared history and common language. Since the end of World War II the Americans had not always been sympathetic to the UK's strategic concerns nor for that matter generous in economic assistance following victory in 1945. Since then fluctuations in the relationship left me in no doubt that American diplomacy would continue to be defined by their purely national self-interest. We might seek to influence American thinking but when decisions have to be made power rather brains holds the whip hand. In all my dealings with General George Joulwan I was thus respectful of his appointment and his person and offered advice and opinion only when invited rather than gratis. George, with the build of an American football player – he told me he only joined the Army to play football – was blessed with quite incredible stamina that ignored time zone differences between Washington DC and Europe. When staying overnight at Queen's Gap he would be on the phone in the early hours to the Pentagon and then up fresh as a daisy for breakfast at 0630 hrs before departing to the USAF base at Mildenhall to catch an aeroplane to Washington to attend a Congressional hearing that afternoon. His tireless energy, unwavering during my 2¾ years under his command, earned my admiration. But his unceasing search for clarity in an ever more complicated and multi-polar world could not defeat the impact of confused and incompatible national interests. George Joulwan never gave up trying and that merited respect.

It was easy to warm to my colleague, Admiral Leighton Smith US Navy, C-in-C of the Southern Region. His achievements as a naval aviator which I have already referred to included three tours in Vietnam and more than 1,000 deck landings, outstanding achievements by any comparative yardstick. But I never heard him utter a boastful word. There wasn't a shred of arrogance in his makeup which I soon discovered was hallmarked by absolute integrity illuminated by an engaging sense of humour. During the Balkan imbroglio Snuffy (as well known to his friends) was under constant pressure from George Joulwan pre-Srebrenica to make greater use of NATO's air power but UNPRO-FOR regarded the use of force "as the absolute last option". Most times when Snuffy offered to use NATO air he was rebuffed by UN commanders. George Joulwan had some difficulty accepting the truth of Snuffy's predicament. Moreover the problem was amplified by the interventions of Ambassador Richard Holbrooke who directly tried to pressurise Snuffy into taking a more aggressive stance; he didn't like it when Snuffy with proper respect for the chain of command told him he took orders from George and no-one else. But relations between George and Snuffy inevitably became strained which was evident in command group meetings and exercises at SHAPE.

The ACE Command Group for most of my tour consisted of George Joulwan, General Sir Jeremy McKenzie (DSACEUR), General Peter Carstens (German chief of staff) and the three regional C-in-Cs – Snuffy in the south, Helge Hansen in the centre and me in the north. The group was thus nicely balanced; two Americans, two Germans and two Brits and individually we all got on well together while recognising that the relationship between our American colleagues was not exactly cordial. But it was worth remembering that US four-star officers were truly big beasts in the jungle; they commanded forces in terms of mass and power far beyond the grasp of their European counterparts. Furthermore, in reaching the top ranks of their services they had triumphed in an intensely competitive environment that was totally unforgiving of failure. In comparison we Brits were soft.

The command group worked efficiently under George Joulwan's leadership first, because no-one doubted either his professionalism as a soldier or his commitment to NATO, and secondly because we collectively recognised that the survival of the Alliance was essential to continuing peace in Europe. Such shared determination laid the foundations for success in Bosnia when NATO's IFOR was deployed in December 1995 tasked to action military aspects of the Dayton Peace Agreement. IFOR had a strength and sense of purpose lacking in its UNPROFOR predecessor. The differences were clear. IFOR had a mission with an appropriately sized force, authority to use that force and resolve to use it without hesitation. Snuffy encapsulated this in his three Rs: Robust force, Right ROE and Resolve to use them.

When I visited Sarajevo Snuffy was fulsome in his praise for Lieutenant General Sir Michael Walker, commander of the ARCC. He later generously described him in a public lecture as "the true hero of IFOR's success". It was Mike Walker who devised a number of ways of immediately demonstrating IFOR's determination to carry out its mandate. One such event was the destruction of the six checkpoints around Sarajevo airport. Within minutes of Snuffy relieving UNPROFOR's General Janvier, Mike Walker's men were bulldozing the checkpoints. The task was quickly completed as two Serb, two Croat and two Bosnian checkpoints were demolished. All factions were similarly outraged at this encroachment on their sovereignty but they could not complain about IFOR's even handedness. And they all learnt a valuable lesson; IFOR was different from UNPROFOR. The IFOR mission lasted for one year before it was succeeded by the NATO-led Stabilisation Force which lasted until 2004 when the European Union took on NATO's stabilisation role.

At command group meetings we were all sensitive to our individual national interests but our responsibility was to work together in the best interests of the NATO military structure within ACE leaving the politics to the NAC. I think we established a sound team ethic because there was no prima donna seeking to impose a dominance of the group in pursuit of their own personal ambitions. And I recognised how lucky I was to enjoy the professional and social company of two men in particular who, despite their difficulties at the time, were great Americans and dedicated servants of the Alliance.

To return now to Sir Michael Graydon's initial question. I recognised that my tour in AFNW had added further valuable experiences to those I had already acquired in the RAF since the end of the Cold War. As a professional airman I had not ignored my aviation responsibilities within the joint command. My logbook records flights with the RAF, USAF, the US Navy, the Polish naval air arm and the air forces of Sweden, Finland and Norway. Two land-based sorties were truly memorable. The flight in a USAF F-15E Strike Eagle provided a remarkable demonstration of true multi-role capabilities as well as convincing me that two heads in the cockpit rather than one were required to make the full use of such potential. The second occasion was a flight over the Baltic in a Saab Viggen. Flying over a flat calm sea with a hazy horizon at 500 knots and a height of 50 feet left me gritting my teeth. The aircraft captain's reassurance that he had a radar altimeter in the front cockpit did little to ease my nerves. Perhaps I was getting just a little too old for this sort of caper. While I shall have more to say later about 'jointery', my nautical experiences had given me the flavour of the difficulties that were part and parcel of maritime warfare to add to theoretical knowledge garnered from much reading, such memorable films as 'The Cruel Sea' and the superb TV documentary 'The War at Sea'. Within my HQ national differences of opinion and character had at times caused me frustration but the search for broad-based consensus before decisions were made and orders issued had curbed my inclination towards impatience which could be wounding when in debate with others speaking a foreign language. And although I was proud to be a senior officer in the British Armed Forces, my dealings with smaller European nations on the one hand and the Americans on the other taught me to avoid any suggestion of arrogance and to beware the pitfall of hubris. Both admirable principles but I cannot in all truth swear I was absolutely unswerving in their observance.

In terms of my military professionalism I felt confident in my ability to represent with conviction the RAF's contribution to national defence while engaging in wider debate on the future size and capabilities of our armed forces. As for leading my service and continuing the process of recuperation from wounds inflicted after the Cold War I was well aware that if appointed CAS I would be far older than all my post-World War II predecessors on taking up office. Later I was to discover their average age on retirement was 57.7 years – a month or so younger than I would be if appointed. But I was in excellent health, well endowed with energy and stamina and various activities in AFNW had kept me physically in good shape. Finally and crucially was the issue of duty which was a much more important consideration as I pondered Sir Michael's question. The answer had to be an unqualified "yes". I confirmed my decision to Sir Michael who told me I would know the outcome of further deliberations in the MoD by mid-September. It was then that I received his letter of congratulations telling me that I was to succeed him as CAS.

CHAPTER 25
ATTITUDES AND PREJUDICES

I had served in the RAF for 40 years when appointed CAS and had accumulated in my baggage certain attitudes and indeed some prejudices. But in admitting my own partiality I also had to recognise the existence of a small but vociferous minority whose own prejudiced opinions about the RAF flew in the face of history. So perhaps it is worthwhile to reflect on why the RAF was born of a merger of the Royal Naval Air Service and the Royal Flying Corps each with its own brief but glittering history. And reflection may provide some food for thought to those who emerge from time to time to propose the dismemberment of the RAF.

For the first few years of their existence the RNAS and the RFC were understandably regarded by the Admiralty and the War Office as integral parts of the Royal Navy and the Army. But the Germans were the first to twig that aircraft had a military utility beyond the control of the air space over and near battlefields; they could be used to strike directly at the heartland of an enemy. Sporadic attacks on mainland targets in England came to a head on 13th June 1917 when Gotha bombers attacked London killing 162 people and injuring a further 432. A second successful raid on 7th July caused panic in London and much criticism of the failure of the RFC and RNAS to provide effective defence of the capital. As a consequence of these attacks and the ensuing panic, General Smuts, the South African member of the Imperial War Cabinet, was appointed to examine " the air organisation generally and the direction of aerial operations".

With no air marshals yet available to assist his deliberations General Smuts took advice from a variety of sources before submitting his second and final report on 17th August 1917. He identified failure within the existing set-up to coordinate air operations while drawing attention to competition between the RNAS and RFC for available air resources that provoked disputes over the supply of aircraft and engines to the competing air arms. Having established all the problems associated with the current structure and after explaining in detail why an independent third service was essential he wrote "having secured it (air predominance) in this war , we should make every effort and sacrifice to maintain it in the future. Air supremacy may in the long run become as an important a factor in the defence of the Empire as sea supremacy." Within a week the War Cabinet had accepted its principal recommendation that a new service should be created through the merger of the two existing air arms. Soon afterwards Orders in Council were issued that defined the composition and duties of the Air Council with an announcement that the new service would be formed on 1st April 1918.

The RAF had existed for a mere seven months when World War I ended in November 1918 much earlier than many expected. Thereafter the new service had to survive more than a decade of deep-rooted hostility under cross fire from the Navy and the Army as they argued for the return of the RNAS and the RFC elements to their respective parents. Senior former Royal Navy and Army officers dedicated to the survival of the RAF were regarded as renegades while those more junior were dismissed as upstarts who for the most part were socially unacceptable. In conversation the official military historian of World War I described the early RAF officers as largely "bad hats – fellows with debts from Ascot and so on". But there was more to it than social disdain. Both the Royal Navy and the Army were concerned, perhaps even fearful, of General Smuts' assertion that: "The day may not be far off when aerial operations.....may become the principal operations of war to which the older forms of military and naval operation may become secondary and subordinate."

Such justification for the formation of a third service to master the ocean of the air posed a clear threat to independent sea power and land power, hence the sustained opposition of the other two services to the fledgling RAF. The RAF was indeed fortunate to have within its higher ranks founding fathers of distinction from the Army and the Royal Navy. From the former the names of Henderson, Trenchard, Salmond and Sykes stand apart. From the Royal Navy, Longmore, Bowhill and Courtney elected to transfer to the RAF; all three were to achieve the rank of air marshal. These seven men of aviation distinction were united in their determination to face up to the growing complexity of war and one of them, Hugh Trenchard, was to emerge as a true giant of a man. It was Trenchard who laid the foundations of an enduring service with the creation of the Cadet College at Cranwell, the Staff College at Andover and the Apprentice School at Halton that was to be the bedrock of engineering excellence in the years ahead.

At the sharp end of the miniscule RAF in the 1920s the service was kept busy maintaining order on the North-West Frontier of India and assuming single service responsibility for peace and quiet in Iraq and Arabia. And all with significant savings to the benefit of the Treasury and to the frustration of the Army as the service pioneered a new form of military action known as air control. Forts and other military objects were bombed to subdue rebellious tribes as necessary. But mass killings of the innocent as asserted by critics played no part in the application of air control. The concept embodied the peculiar, and being unorthodox, much derided notion that little wars could be won by making people's lives intolerably uncomfortable and frustrating by such means as inhibiting the harvesting of crops after warnings had been ignored. Apart from operations the RAF blazed trails for what later on became air routes to South Africa and Singapore via the Middle East. And the service went in for air racing winning the Schneider Trophy that so influenced the design of the fighter aircraft that won the Battle of Britain.

Today powered flight is part and parcel of everyday life and taken for granted, but if we look back to 1930 when aircraft had been flying for a mere 27 years, the variety of the RAF's achievements excites my respect and admiration. The men leading the service at that time were true visionaries looking to the future unencumbered by centuries of tradition. But they didn't get everything right as a consequence of financial stringency, political indifference and primacy within the service given to Trenchard's strategic doctrines.

Trenchard's commitment to the concept of strategic bombing was borne of his doctrinal conviction that maximum air effort should be concentrated on offensive operations and the minimum devoted to defence. Although implementation of his expectations was to be undermined as reality outstripped theory, early understanding that air power was the product of technology was eventually to shape a service quick to learn from its mistakes and to accept the need for drastic change when weaknesses were identified. But progress between the wars was slow. The exercise of air control by aeroplanes not so different from their First World War predecessors was partly the consequence of the struggle to spread limited resources to best advantage. Structural foundations were laid at the expense of the strength and capabilities of the front line, and up until the 1930s there was no competitive spur to advance the performance of either aircraft or weaponry. Operating in India and the Middle East with no airborne opposition and in favourable weather conditions obscured fundamental operational weaknesses within the RAF.

At home Trenchard's emphasis on offensive operations led to neglect of the RAF's air defences. So it is indeed ironic that eventually it was fear of the dominance of bomber aircraft that accelerated the re-equipment of Fighter Command in the late 1930s. Both Bomber Command and Coastal Command were to suffer as a consequence of the priority then given to our air defences to counter the threatening and rapidly expanding re-emergence of German air power. In 1939 Coastal Command could muster a front-line strength of 258 mainly obsolete aircraft armed with ineffective weapons. With 480 aircraft Bomber Command was significantly stronger but contained a wide variety of types varying from the obsolescent to more modern aeroplanes that were soon to be proven inadequate for a number of reasons including poor performance in terms of range, speed and bomb-carrying capacity. All aircraft types were deficient in defensive armament to ward off fighter attacks and their bombs "had a serious record of malfunction and were filled with indifferent explosives".

On the credit side the Hurricane first flew in 1935 and the Spitfire a year later. In 1938 at the time of the Munich agreement Fighter Command could muster only 93 of the new eight-gun fighters – the remaining 550 aircraft were outdated biplanes set to oppose a long-range striking force of some 1,200 modern German bombers. A year later on the declaration of war more than 500 of the new monoplane fighters were available for operations. The rapid growth of defensive strength in the air was matched by technical excellence on the ground. The construction of 20 radar stations (the magic eyes), the fitting of an identification friend or foe (IFF) device to our fighters and the establishment of a defence telecommunications control organisation that linked radar sites, operations rooms and airfields were all important developments in the construction of a reporting and control organisation so vital to efficient operations in the air. The creation of Fighter Command in 1936 was to place all air defences, including static defences, under the overall operational command of the AOC-in-C with tactical command and control delegated to each of four group commanders with each group divided up into sectors for close control of a battle. The harmonisation of technology in the air and on the ground into an air defence system within which the structure clearly delineated lines of responsibility was the solution to one of the problems that in 1917 led to the formation of the RAF.

The impact of technology on military operations was not universally welcomed in the Army. According to Field Marshal Lord Carver, who in 1936 was commissioned into the Royal Tank Regiment, "The Army's substitution of motor vehicles for the horse proceeded hesitantly and indecisively". A handful of senior and progressive forward-thinking officers such as Major General J F C Fuller and Major General Sir Percy Hobart drew on their World War I experience to argue for accelerated mechanisation. Fuller was required to retire in 1933 and Hobart exiled in 1938 to command a division in Egypt.

Sir Basil Liddell Hart, another prophet of armoured warfare and a most distinguished military thinker of the time, wrote a number of papers on the strategic and tactical use of armour that provoked resistance and hostility within the British general staff. Elsewhere, and particularly in Germany, Liddell Hart's papers were diligently studied by the German general staff who put into practice his ideas of tank tactics and mechanisation much to the future disadvantage of the British Army – an army that invented the tank went to war in 1939 without a single armoured division and united in its dismissal of the RAF's potential contribution to a land battle.

Between the wars doctrine and technological development within the Royal Navy were similarly torpid. By 1930 the strength of the service had been much reduced by treaties that toppled the Navy from its pre-war position of maritime predominance. Moreover, the transfer of air-minded senior RN officers to the RAF robbed the Navy of talent that had an understanding of the potential of air power. Doctrinal thought was thus dominated by advocates for the battleship that was still judged to be vital for command of the sea. In 1918 the Royal Navy had led the way in the development of air power at sea, a lead that by 1939 had been surrendered to the Americans and Japanese who developed aircraft carriers as long-distance strike forces.

Within the RN carriers were considered to be adjuncts to battle fleets with their aircraft utilised primarily for reconnaissance and air defence. While the growing threat of war in 1936 added much needed urgency to a national programme of rearmament, the Royal Navy's response to operational and technical problems arising from the refurbishment of British sea power suggested in the words of the military historian Correlli Barnett "a narrow professionalism of outlook too much influenced by loyalty to tradition and too little blessed with innovative imagination". Some have argued that to protect its independence the RAF distanced itself as far as possible from the Royal Navy and Army. There may be some truth in this assertion and the blame for this state of affairs may be attributable to all three services. I leave it to others to debate proportionality of responsibility. But for certain in 1939 the Army remained dismissive of the RAF's potential contribution to land warfare whereas the Royal Navy believed their warships could survive in a hostile air environment and the U-boat threat could be accommodated without major air assistance.

It is thus with the best will in the world, and assuming the return of the RAF to its parent services in the 1920s, I have difficulty in believing that the RFC and RNAS, either individually or together, would have created the air defence structure on the ground and in the air that defeated the onslaught of the Luftwaffe in 1940. Many others both within and without the RAF made their contributions to our victory in the Battle of Britain. But it was the pilots of Fighter Command, many from the dominions and including vengeful young men from the occupied countries of Europe, who were our sword and shield in 1940. Had Fighter Command been defeated I am sure the Royal Navy would have done all in its power to keep the enemy at bay. But, with a rampant Luftwaffe operating from forward airfields in France, at what cost? Subsequent evidence from the Mediterranean and the Far East convincingly demonstrated the vulnerability of our warships without air cover to airborne attack. This situation did not arise. The RAF defeated the Luftwaffe and that was that.

Two years later demands for tactical air support from the Royal Navy and the Army almost exceeded the front-line strength of the RAF which posed difficult questions of priorities, and particularly so between the growing strength of the bomber offensive and the vital need to defeat the U-boat threat that reached its zenith in 1942. Within a year the Royal Navy and Coastal Command, operating in true concert, had started to gain the upper hand. By the end of the war Coastal Command had destroyed 189 U-boats and 311 enemy surface vessels. Four VCs were won by their aircrew with some 5,000 aircrew killed on operations.

While writing about the RAF's contribution to the war at sea, it would be churlish to ignore the successes of the Fleet Air Arm. Two come immediately to mind: the damage to the *Bismarck* that enabled the ship's destruction, and the epic of Taranto. Both involved torpedo attacks by antiquated Fairey Sword-fish biplanes with a maximum speed of about 150 mph. At Taranto 20 of these aircraft crippled the Italian battle fleet. Admiral Sir Andrew Cunningham, C-in-C Mediterranean Fleet, accurately described the action as an unparalleled example of economy of force. Taranto marked the opening of a new era of maritime warfare as the Fleet Air Arm demonstrated offensive power that was to end battleship dominance in the Royal Navy.

Elsewhere the tactical employment and effectiveness of RAF fighters and fighter bombers in support of land forces became a model for land/air co-operation in the future; their presence over every notable battlefield from El Alamein to the end of the war heartened our soldiers and inflicted heavy losses on enemy armies with deadly precision. And while Transport Command's airborne operations associated with D-Day and the supply of food and ammunition to maintain an army of 300,000 men fighting in Burma have been largely overlooked, Bomber Command operations that endured without break from the first to the last day of the war have been examined in detail. In some quarters this sustained and highly dangerous effort is dismissed as not only non-effective but ultimately pointless. Such judgements made in hindsight reflect an emotional and political aversion to Bomber Command that have led some to conclude that the RAF's bombing in World War II was not only a war crime but an inexcusable one. I challenge both verdict and judgement which insult the memory of the 55,000 men who died on operations and the 21 Victoria Crosses awarded to Bomber Command aircrew.

In the aftermath of World War I, slaughter in the trenches argued for an alternative method of waging war, hence the attraction to politicians of Trenchard's ideas that were dominated by his commitment to offensive operations and the creation of a strategic bombing force. Prime Minister Baldwin's words spoken in 1932 "that the bomber would always get through" reflected Trenchard's thinking with the obvious conclusion that victory would go to the side with more bombers and the commitment to use them. But in the first three years of the war Bomber Command aircraft, lacking in performance and operated by aircrew inadequately trained in the skills of navigation, were to suffer heavy losses. Aircrew difficulties were compounded by inadequate bomb-aiming and navigation equipment. During the Battle of Britain some 800 Bomber Command aircrew were killed and others taken prisoner as they attacked invasion barges and Luftwaffe airfields. Bomber Command casualties were almost double those inflicted on Fighter Command. Little damage was done to Germany as daylight raids continued to suffer heavy casualties that forced a transition to night attacks and then to area attacks on cities associated with communications hubs and war fighting industries that created and supplied German combat power. This was at a time when the Army had been defeated in Norway, France, Greece and Crete and when the Royal Navy was engaged in a remorseless struggle in the Atlantic and desperate battles in the Mediterranean.

The sum of these disasters and uncertainties was to turn the focus of public attention on to the activities of Bomber Command that alone could attack Germany. Ineffective as they may have been, the operations gave more than hope to the British people. Morale was sustained in the wake of the Blitz on London and other major cities, and there were strategic repercussions. Bomber Command operations demonstrated that Germany was not immune from the consequences of aggression; moreover the Americans and the Russians understood that the UK would continue to prosecute war against Germany with all available means.

In August 1942 after our armed forces had suffered further catastrophes in the Far East 18 bomber aircraft of the United States Army Air Force flew their first mission over occupied Europe. Within a year the foundations had been laid for a combined bomber offensive with the RAF bombing by night and the USAAF by day to weaken Germany to a point when the Allies could invade Europe. At first the Americans suffered heavy losses but the arrival in 1944 of long-range Mustang fighters – newly equipped with Rolls-Royce Merlin engines – provided protection for the bombers and a dramatic increase in the number of German fighters shot down. Also in 1942 Bomber Command squadrons started to re-equip with Lancaster bombers that overcame many of the defects associated with first and second generation bomber aircraft while the accuracy and effectiveness of night attacks was much improved by the use of new navigation aids.

By March 1944 more than 7,000 German fighters had been withdrawn to central Germany to cover Berlin. Some 9,000 88mm anti-aircraft guns, equally effective against tanks with armour-piercing ammunition, were deployed for air defence along with 25,000 guns of smaller calibre. Nine hundred thousand men operated the weapons and a further million Germans were constantly employed clearing up and repairing bomb damage. The deployment of even half of the 88mm guns and manpower to either the eastern or western fronts would have made a significant impact to Germany's advantage. In 1944 Germany lost 35% of its tank production, 31% of aircraft production and 40% of truck production.

I recently heard a military historian dismiss the RAF's operations in 1945 as being no more than continuing to smash German cities. For the record, between D-Day and the end of the war 32% of Bomber Command's effort was tasked against industrial targets, that is cities. A further 32% was devoted to oil and transportation targets and 28% to military targets, installations as well as in direct support of land forces. The combined bomber offensive forced the Luftwaffe on to the defensive such that on D-Day not a single German bomber threatened the landings. In the months that followed enemy defensive strongpoints were eliminated and the effectiveness of German vengeance weapons – V-1s, V-2s and long-range guns – was much reduced. In the context of the war at sea it is worth recording that Bomber Command sank or rendered useless six of Germany's ten major warships, laid 47,000 mines that accounted for 759 German vessels while selective attacks severely disrupted U-boat construction. Sufficient I think to contradict those who in retrospect judge Bomber Command operations to have been ineffective and ultimately pointless.

Air Chief Marshal Sir Arthur Harris, AOC-in-C Bomber Command from February 1942 until the end of the war, has been the target for venomous criticism as the inventor of area bombing. In fact the decision to attack industrial areas was taken long before his appointment because it was, as already explained, the only way that the UK could hit back at Germany. Today Harris is most often associated with attacks on Dresden, which Bomber Command led on the night of 13/14 February 1945, and for which he is held accountable.

Dresden has been described as a "city too far" as Germany was down and out. It didn't seem so at the time. Failure at Arnhem in the autumn and the German surprise winter offensive in the Ardennes that took a month to defeat had quashed earlier optimism that the war would soon be over. The Allies had yet to cross the Rhine, fighting on the eastern front continued with ferocious intensity and British sailors, soldiers and airmen were dying every day. The Germans were deploying new revolutionary weapons, notably the Me 262 jet fighter and Schnorchel-equipped U-boats. German technological ingenuity could yet challenge Allied air and sea supremacy. The bombardment of southern England with V-1 'Doodlebugs' – as I well recall – and V-2 rockets continued. Between 12th June 1944 and 24th March 1945 no less than 10,000 V-1s were launched at London of which some 4,000 were destroyed en route. V-2 rockets were far more dangerous. The first hit London (Chiswick) on 8th September 1944 and the last of 1,115 V-2s landed on Orpington on 22nd March 1945. V-1 and V-2 attacks killed some 9,000 civilians and seriously injured 24,000 more.

In January 1945 the Joint Intelligence Committee assessed that the Soviet offensive on the eastern front could be effectively supported by bombing important transport nodes in east Germany. Chemnitz, Leipzig and Dresden were identified as strategically valid targets to interdict the movement of German reinforcements from the west simultaneously sowing confusion in evacuation from the east. The intention to bomb, noted and approved by Churchill, was accepted at the Allied Air Commanders conference on 1st February 1945. Soon afterwards Churchill was told that the cities would be attacked as soon as weather and moon conditions allowed. Churchill did not demur and Dresden's fate was finally sealed at the Yalta Conference (4-11th February 1945) when he met with President Roosevelt and Premier Stalin to discuss the post-war settlement of Europe. At the conference the Soviets asked for the bombing of rail centres in eastern Germany and according to the official British interpreter Dresden was specifically mentioned by General Antonov, deputy chief of the Soviet general staff, and Stalin himself. While this is not confirmed in the official record, there is no doubting Allied determination to support the Soviets by bombing eastern German cities and Bomber Command and the US 8th Air Force were tasked accordingly.

Aside from its importance as a transportation node in the German railway system Dresden was a major industrial contributor to the enemy's war effort and so far had escaped Harris's attention because of the distance of penetration required to reach the city. The loss of 95 bombers and 545 aircrew attacking Nuremberg in March 1944 clearly demonstrated that deep penetration raids were very high risk operations. For this reason Harris sought confirmation from the Air Ministry that the Dresden attack was to proceed; this was confirmed. The subsequent destruction of Dresden, its architectural treasures and the horrendous casualties cannot, however, be judged in isolation. Account has to be taken of the political and military circumstances at that time and it was the amalgam of complex factors that forged the military purpose of the attack which quite simply was to shorten the war. For the British, who had been fighting for five years, any effort including Bomber Command operations that helped to achieve this enjoyed the almost unanimous support of the country. But when the scale of devastation of Dresden became evident Harris was cast as the villain of the piece as many others, his military and political superiors including Churchill, sought to distance themselves from responsibility.

There can be no doubt that German morale did not prove the soft target assumed by pre-war theorists and Harris himself concluded after the war that: "The idea that the main object of bombing German industrial cities was to break the enemy's morale proved to be totally unsound." So best perhaps to leave the last words to a German who as a young man suffered first-hand experience of Allied bombing. As the chief historian in the military research office in Freiberg, Dr Horst Boog wrote: "If the morale of the civilian population is defined as their will to continue work for the war effort, then German morale was not broken. But it was certainly weakened, as recent studies have revealed, especially in cities suffering heavy attack. People continued to do their duty in a fatalistic and apathetic mood, and this did not increase their devotion to the political cause and productivity. It was not morale in this sense that kept them on the ball. Rather it was the desire to survive – which, under the circumstances of the political surveillance system, also meant doing what one was told and not shirking in the presence of others – and the hope that one day their dreadful existence and experience would be over."

In reflecting on RAF history I am constantly reminded that in the formative years of my career I worked directly for men who fought and won the Battle of Britain and then survived another four years of fighting. I worked for others who against all the odds survived more than one tour in Bomber Command and some who had enjoyed similar good fortune in Coastal Command and the Tactical Air Forces. I revere their bravery that set the gold standard for later generations of aircrew to emulate. At the higher command levels, RAF C-in-Cs had little past experience to shape their operational and tactical thinking on how best to employ the full range of air power capabilities that were developed and deployed for the first time in a global war. But they learned quickly.

In terms of strategic effect the Battle of Britain bought time, the Bomber Command offensive opened a second front long before D-Day and maritime supremacy in the Atlantic, a truly joint endeavour, enabled the transfer of vast resources from the USA that empowered the invasion of Europe and ultimate victory. Although there were some failures of leadership and judgement these were few, and in my estimation the names of Dowding, Portal, Tedder, Harris, Freeman and Slessor all merit honoured memory in the history of our nation.

World War II demonstrated that although air power was an entity in itself, it was almost invariably interlocked with sea and land power; the ultimate achievement of victory demonstrated that all three were essentially interdependent. The most efficient and economical use of our armed forces was achieved when the operational focus was on cooperation rather than competition. But both before and after the war Treasury parsimony and political indifference motivated each service to fight its corner for resources which stimulated competition at the expense of cooperation. Three years were thus to pass in World War II before the Allies started to win victories that brought together Fleets, Army Groups and Tactical Air Forces in massive joint operations. In the years that followed the war our national concern with withdrawal from empire and eventual concentration of military effort within NATO diminished interest in joint operations as our services were again forced to fight for their individual interests during years of fluctuating financial circumstances.

Although land/air operations were regularly – and in my opinion rather ineffectually – exercised in Europe, the Falkands War came as a sharp reminder of the realities of conflict and the importance of joint planning at both the operational and tactical levels. Post-Cold War we moved into a new world order within which the security environment was more complex, more varied and more volatile. This meant that our armed forces had to be prepared to meet a new range of operational commitments and security challenges that could arise at short notice anywhere in the world. Thus the priority given to joint operations had gradually subsided from the Army Group/Tactical Air Force level to much smaller force mixes tailored to the needs of a specific operation.

Gulf War I experience and later my tour as C-in-C of a NATO joint command had convinced me of the need for force contributors from all arms to have a clear understanding of the roles that each constituent part would play when committed to operations. The cement to hold structures together was born of practical experience of joint training and dedication to a common cause. Beyond this statement of the blindingly obvious, I recognised that as an airman, who almost inevitably would be involved at some stage of an operation with soldiers and sailors, it was my duty to gain an understanding of what concerned them, why it concerned them and what air power could do to alleviate their operational difficulties. All fine and dandy in concept but not so easy to achieve as I was reminded from time to time after lecturing at staff colleges. Too often questions reflected an inability, perhaps unwillingness, to think of warfare as being at least a three-dimensional activity; more annoying were questions born of ill-informed prejudices and preconceptions.

In my experience each service had within its senior ranks 'military obsessives' who signed up to 'jointery' as long as you did it their way. That said, identifying an 'obsessive' required a distinction between determination, admirable, and stubbornness, tiresome; this was not always a simple judgement. As an advocate of 'jointery' I defined the word as a collective noun embracing all aspects of tri-service joint training, the development of joint doctrine and joint concepts of operations, the process of joint planning and the execution of joint operations. I also recognised that while 'obsessives' had their usefulness as experts within their specialisation, blinkered obsession that denied sensible debate stifled strategic thought and could spawn spectacular inefficiency and distortion of the defence equipment budget.

As I prepared to assume the responsibilities of CAS I concluded that in any kind of warfare control of the airspace in the theatre of operations could determine the outcome. I also recognised that sea power, the consequence of geography, history and national temperament, remained a vital component of national defence. The protection of global sea lanes, an essential element of our economic wellbeing, argued for power projection while nearer to home the security of the nuclear deterrent required the constant protection of surface and subsurface vessels as well as maritime patrol aircraft. The Royal Navy shared with the RAF a responsibility to deploy combat power at far distances and a need for expensive and technologically advanced equipment.

The end of the Cold War and the effort devoted to the achievement of a peace settlement in Northern Ireland removed the first and within a decade the second of two operational props that had supported the Army's case for manpower in numbers twice the size of the RN and RAF. While the Army had a lesser requirement for expensive, high technology equipment, the enduring uncertainties of conflict that moved with variable speed and changeable direction had argued for a sustainment of Army manpower numbers that was in direct budgetary conflict with the future equipment costs of the RN and the RAF.

However, the Army's problem was compounded by public sensitivity to the impact of casualties and a growing intolerance of war. But evidence from the Middle East, the Balkans and sub-Saharan Africa demonstrated that intolerance of war was not universal. Future conflicts would not be merely asymmetrical in terms of weaponry but asymmetrical as far as the societies that fought them were concerned. Thus casualties suffered in the pursuit of obscure political purposes, and especially if the purposes lay beyond the realms of the relatively quick fix, would appear to many western societies as being nothing short of criminal. Signs of political aversion to risk and a yearning for casualty-free solutions, already evident in the mid-1990s, were becoming a strategic determinant. Professor Sir Michael Howard summed up the predicament. He wrote: "People who are not prepared to put their forces in harm's way fight at some disadvantage against those who are. Tomahawk Cruise missiles may command the air, but it is Kalashnikov sub-machine guns that still rule the ground. It is an imbalance that makes the enforcement of world order a rather problematic affair."

I concluded that unless national security was under direct threat, the commitment of ground forces to combat would be unacceptable unless the certainty of casualties had been reduced to a level of political acceptability. And this meant that the RAF had to be ready, most probably in a coalition of the willing, to shape the ring for friendly ground forces and then to provide direct support for their activities within it. Moreover, if the UK was to remain in the business of power projection there was a clear case for the retention of aircraft carriers in the Royal Navy. I recognised that my opinion would not be shared by some RAF colleagues, past and present, but in the circumstances of the world in the mid-1990s we shared with the Fleet Air Arm a responsibility for the generation of air power with global reach.

While the significance of air power had once suffered from over-expectation, its utility and effectiveness had been transformed by advances in technology. First and foremost, the introduction of precision guidance in air weapons systems, and secondly the availability of stand-off air-launched weapons that extended terminally accurate and threatening reach deep into an opponent's heartland. With precision the cudgel had been transformed into a scalpel. I also thought it timely to question the assumption that tactical air operations would continue to be associated with the traditional battlefield.

During Gulf War I B-52 bombers had carpet-bombed Iraqi ground forces and tactical F-117s had struck strategic targets in Baghdad. Later on in the Balkans elements of NATO air power were targeted against supply routes and war stocks. These traditional tactical targets were of huge strategic significance because of Serbian dependence on their availability to achieve political objectives. If airmen were to continue to refer to strategic air attack it needed to be precisely defined, not by the nature of the aircraft or weapon, nor by the distance covered, nor even by the nature of the target, but by the direct relationship of a specific target to the overall political objective. With an eye to the future I had a clear understanding that the future of air power would stand or fall not by promises and abstract theory but like any other kind of military power by its relevance to political objectives and its ability to secure them at a cost affordable to the government of the day. When the future was so difficult to divine our defence capabilities should not remain shackled to the past.

In the wider context of defence I judged it essential that the RAF was seen to be a willing contributor to the most efficient application of military effort through the harmonisation of air and surface operations. This could only be achieved when the effectiveness of our armed forces was based on an appropriate balance of mobility, firepower and manoeuvre capabilities. I decided that my contribution as CAS to future defence debate would be based on four main propositions:

• First, the primary role of the RAF would be to win and sustain control of the air in an operational theatre, and be prepared to do so in conjunction with allies.

• Second, such control would remain essential to the success of military operations in the contemporary and future joint environment.

• Third, air power's inherent characteristics of height, speed and reach enhanced by technological advances in target acquisition and weapons precision had made it the first political choice in the containment of crises or, in the event of conflict, as the primary tool for shaping the battle space to permit the effective and winning employment of surface forces.

• Fourth, and by no means last, the vital need to recruit, train and retain highly motivated personnel able to operate in a joint environment but imbued with the ethos and history of the Royal Air Force and pride in its achievements.

In giving a full airing to my prejudicial thoughts I have not disguised my conviction that, when allowed to, the British armed forces work far better in cooperation rather than in competition. And I would never ignore one overriding imperative. The Royal Navy, the Army and the Royal Air Force are ultimately all in the business of winning battles and to do this the nation needed people prepared to do difficult and dangerous things; things that tested not only the quality of their inner steel but also their loyalty and commitment to their fighting unit whether it be ship, regiment or squadron. The motivational and other reasons that persuade people to put their lives on the line are complex, but ethos and tribal identity are certainly vital factors. Because of our history and the structural organisation of our armed forces, ethos and identity within the British military remain based on the individuality of each service. The challenge of leadership was unqualified commitment to joint operations where it made operational sense in terms of military effectiveness, while maintaining a clear sense of belonging and loyalty to the parent service.

CHAPTER 26
CHIEF OF THE AIR STAFF

Arrival

On 9th April 1997 I was driven from our new home, a government-owned flat in Knightsbridge, to the MoD. I entered at the Richmond Terrace end of the building and ascended by lift to the sixth floor where I walked into CAS's office. Nothing had changed in either layout or decoration since my tour as DASB 16 years earlier. Some uncomfortable episodes at that time, logged in the archives of my memory, were instantly revived but not for long. The boot, as it were, was now on the other foot as my day was gladdened by the outer office staff who made me feel most welcome.

It had been the custom since Trenchard's day that CAS would have a civil servant as his private secretary, familiar with Whitehall working practices and with a keen intellect untarnished by military training and experience. Jonathan Ironmonger was the man for the job. I also inherited from Michael Graydon a personal staff officer, Wing Commander David Haward. David, a 4 (AC) Squadron pilot during my tour as Harrier Force commander, was one of the cluster of highly talented junior officers most of whom were to fulfil their early potential and reach air rank. It was a pleasure to meet up with David again whose sunny disposition, sense of humour and natural courtesy were the characteristics of a man whose devotion to the service was not tainted by selfish or inordinate ambition. Tragically, David was killed in a Harrier flying accident not long after leaving MoD on promotion to take command of RAF Wittering. Many others joined me in mourning the death of a charismatic and popular leader who had been destined to reach the top.

The third man in the outer office was Flight Lieutenant Peter Brown. Peter, an education officer in the administrative branch, was at first sight a rather unlikely incumbent of an ADC post. Well above 6ft tall, powerfully built and exuding fitness and energy he appeared better suited to the rugby scrum than the flummeries of an ADC's life. But I was soon to discover that a first in mathematics, his relentless energy, his eye for detail and a most amiable personality all came together to forge a formidable identity – one that was equally effective on the rugby field and in my outer office. I was thus supremely confident that I would be well looked after by the triumvirate of Ironmonger, Haward and Brown who in turn enjoyed the support of a registry staff and typing pool superbly led and managed by Flight Sergeant Jerry Barnes. I was not to be disappointed.

The round of arrival calls started immediately. The first was to General Sir Charles Guthrie, recently appointed chief of the defence staff. Charles and I first met in Aden and thereafter we had regularly bumped into one another. During my previous time in MoD we had been tasked to brief a visiting American delegation on desert operations following their aborted attempt in April 1980 to rescue 52 American diplomats held hostage by the Iranians in Tehran. The US Armed Forces were, as ever, prepared to recognise and learn from their mistakes. Charles was no stranger to the MoD having served there in four appointments before his promotion to CDS. His impressive blend of operational soldiering and understanding of the Whitehall/Westminster labyrinth would be tested by the challenge of a Defence Review that would inevitably follow the outcome of the general election that was to take place three weeks later. I looked forward to working with him.

My old friend and colleague John Willis was VCDS, an appointment ideally suited to his calm temperament, his intellectual capacity and his staff skills. Although John was filling a 'purple' appointment, I knew he would help me find my feet within a structural and working set-up much changed since 1981. The First Sea Lord was Admiral Sir Jock Slater. We had only met once before when he visited the JHQ during Gulf War I. But as a former VCDS and having served two previous tours in the MoD I recognised he also was well versed in the working practices of Whitehall. General Sir Roger Wheeler, successor to Charles Guthrie as chief of the general staff, I had first met when he was serving as GOC Northern Ireland and he was another experienced Whitehall warrior having served in Army Plans and as assistant chief of the general staff.

Defence politicians were occasional visitors to the MoD as most of their time was spent electioneering. I only met one before the election, Mr Nicholas Soames MP, minister for the Armed Forces. He recalled flying with me in a Jet Provost Mk 5 when he was equerry to the Prince of Wales. He bubbled over with genial bonhomie which led me to conclude that he was confident of keeping his seat unlike many others in his party. Richard Mottram, the permanent under secretary, was next on my list followed finally by Roger Jacklin, the second permanent under secretary. My reception by both civil servants was polite but seemed rather guarded. I was an unknown quantity and I knew that I was going to have to earn my spurs. So perhaps no surprise that some in my own service doubted the wisdom of my appointment as CAS given three previous years' absence in NATO and total lack of contemporary experience in the MoD. The probability of a change of government and the inevitability of a Defence Review added to their misgivings. On the other hand I received letters of congratulations and encouragement from retired RAF friends who I held in high regard and perhaps, rather surprisingly, from senior sailors and soldiers whom I had worked with in Germany, Gulf War I and during my NATO tour. I needed no encouragement to get on with the job but this support was both heartening and stimulating.

During my comfortable and enjoyable NATO tour the RAF had endured three more tough and rather dispiriting years. The cumulative consequences of the search for the peace dividend by now had involved the disbandment of 14 front-line squadrons and the closure of a similar number of front-line stations and support units including hospitals. The uniformed strength of the service has been reduced from 92,000 in 1989 to 55,000 with a further planned reduction of 3,000 to meet a government-imposed cciling. Seventeen thousand civilians now supported the uniformed RAF most of whom worked for contractors who were quick off the mark to employ redundant servicemen and women; this was attractive to civilian employers who did not have to pay a training bill, at least in the short term, and similarly appealing to politicians and their accountancy apparatchiks.

At my first meeting with Air Force Board Standing Committee (AFBSC) colleagues the three commanders-in-chief agreed that morale was on the cusp between marginal and satisfactory. With this in mind I felt it imperative to identify my personal objectives and to state them clearly and concisely to the service. I thus sent a signal to all in command appointments that set out my ambitions. It read:

> "First, to lead a service in which we all share an appreciation of the value of the individual.

> "Second, to lead a service in which we all share confidence in our ability to do the air power job.

> "Third, to lead a service in which we can all share justifiable pride."

While I meant every word of it I recognised that it would most probably appear rather banal to the cynics and the permanently dissatisfied in the service but at least they could hold me to account if they suspected I was straying from these three tenets. And they did during many question and answer sessions as I visited a variety of stations to catch up on the service's activities. These visits were to shape and condition my whole approach to the Strategic Defence Review (SDR) that was soon under way following the election of a Labour government on 1st May 1997.

I met the new secretary of state for defence, Mr George Robertson MP, on his first day in the MoD. I was ushered into his office by the PS where I found him standing behind his desk. Grinning broadly he pointed to his ministerial red box and told me that until that day the highest security classification he had encountered was 'Restricted'. In there, he went on, were papers with security classifications he had never previously heard mentioned. I warmed to him immediately and in our subsequent conversation I noticed the directness of his questions concerning the RAF's current activities and how carefully he listened to my answers. Mr Robertson said his appointment had come as something of a surprise and that he had a lot to learn. I didn't doubt for one moment his determination to do so. Accompanying him to the MoD was a fellow Scot, Dr John Reid, appointed as minister of state for the Armed Forces. The two Scots, both political activists in their younger days, ascended to ministerial office at a time of reform and modernisation within the Labour Party. While George Robertson was a newcomer to defence, John Reid had served in opposition as a defence spokesman and was clearly well-informed on contemporary military matters. Together they shared intellectual agility, political guile and to my mind appealing but quite different personalities. George Robertson represented the acceptable face of socialism in New Labour with John Reid personifying all the characteristics of a Glaswegian political bruiser. I could not imagine George Robertson subscribing to John Reid's reported motto of "better a broken nose than a bended knee". Together they were a formidable duo and ably supported by John Spellar as parliamentary under secretary of state and Lord Gilbert as minister of state for procurement. I recognised that if I was to stay true to my three tenets it was vital to establish a sound working relationship with my political masters and to earn their trust in my integrity and judgement.

Strategic Defence Review
The SDR started three weeks after the election. The Labour government came to power with a manifesto commitment "to reassess our essential security interests and defence needs and to consider how the roles, missions and capabilities of our armed forces should be adjusted to meet strategic realities". The SDR would be foreign-policy led such that the future shape of our armed forces would be decided by defence and security needs rather than a Treasury-led quest for further financial savings. This was an encouraging start as the Conservative's search for a peace dividend had already reduced defence spending by 23% since 1989/90 when it was set at 2.7% of GDP.

The SDR was divided into three main stages which delineated a policy baseline, identified appropriate force structures and then finally synthesised the work for cabinet consideration. Phase one, setting out the foreign policy baseline upon which subsequent phases would be built, required the MoD to work closely with the Foreign and Commonwealth Office. Together they looked forward to 2015 trying to judge our place in the world and in Europe while preserving the strength of our transatlantic links. Account also had to be taken of significant changes in social and technological trends, likely areas of risk and the possibility of a re-emerging and direct threat to our national security.

The overriding conclusion was that European security would remain fundamental to our own national security and economic wellbeing and that membership of NATO would continue to provide the UK with its best insurance against new risks or instability. And while we could not afford to ignore the Western European Union, strong links with the United States would remain an essential element of national strategy. There was nothing surprising in this but the examination did underline how much the end of the Cold War had transformed the security environment. The likely main areas of conflict in which we could be involved were judged to be the Middle East and North Africa. If operationally committed to any of these three areas we would expect to operate alongside allies with similar important interests and friendships. The outcome of this phase was accepted by the prime minister and cabinet colleagues in August 1997.

Building on these findings, phase two examined the force structures and capabilities required. First, the military missions were defined, next military targets were set, scales of effort decided and finally concurrency assumptions and readiness states were agreed. Simple as all this may sound, phase two involved some 46 different study groups working to a three-star implementation steering group thence to the financial planning and management group (FPMG). The FPMG involved the MoD's military and civilian hierarchy in debate before recommendations were submitted for ministerial endorsement in March 1998. The consequent discussion across Whitehall – phase three – against the backdrop of the government's Comprehensive Spending Review, involved further departmental time and effort before agreement was finally reached. The White Paper went to print in July 1998 marking the completion of 14 months consultation and presentation within a review initially planned for completion within six months.

Looking back at the process of the SDR, ministers made a genuine attempt to consult as widely as possible both within and outside the MoD to achieve consensus. For my part, most ably supported, briefed and encouraged by Air Vice-Marshal Tim Jenner (assistant chief of air staff) and Air Commodore Steve Nicholl (director air plans) I was content with the opportunities given to argue our case.

For the RAF our analysis of future scales of effort was based on three key assumptions. These were, first, to have the capability to respond to a major international crisis that required a military effort of a similar scale and duration to Gulf War I. Secondly, to be capable of undertaking a more extended deployment on a lesser scale while retaining the ability to mount a further substantial deployment if made necessary by a second crisis; most importantly both deployments were not expected to involve war fighting or to be sustained simultaneously for longer than six months. And thirdly, given much longer notice, to be able to increase our order of battle (ORBAT) as part of NATO's collective defence should a major threat re-emerge in Europe.

Based on these SDR planning assumptions the methodology used led us to conclude that:

• Our offensive forces could be reduced by 23 aircraft to include 12 Tornado GR1s (which would have been taken from the ORBAT in any event for reasons of fleet management), nine Harrier GR7s (mostly by removing planned enhancements under the previous government's Front Line First exercise) and two Jaguars which would have minimal effect.

• The air defence force would be reduced by 13 aircraft; six through detailed analysis of readiness states and the retention of some Tornado F3 OCU instructors as combat-ready aircrews for deployment on larger-scale operations. The remaining seven would be at risk against the forthcoming introduction of the Eurofighter Typhoon.

Acceptance of our recommendations only came after a long and gruelling debate with potentially far worse consequences for the service. Happily, the excellent equipment programme which I inherited from Michael Graydon was preserved in its entirety. The government's commitment to the Eurofighter programme was particularly welcome. The aircraft was due to come into service in 2003 and ministers recognised that withdrawal from the programme would incur severe penalties from partner nations. Moreover, the UK's considerable investment in the programme would be lost. The Eurofighter project had been the target of fierce and ill-informed criticism from those who ignored the simple military fact that the RAF was in desperate need of an air superiority fighter to replace Tornado F3 and eventually Jaguar aircraft. A well-known military historian told me there was no need for an aircraft that was little more than an expensive bauble. "Did I think we would be squaring up to the Russians?" he asked. He certainly got that wrong and although progress has been slow, the development of the Eurofighter/Typhoon into a true multi-role aircraft capable of carrying the full arsenal of contemporary weapons is close to achievement.

Typhoon apart, ministers also accepted the cases for the Hercules C130J, Merlin helicopters, Chinook Mk 3 and a whole raft of new weapons including Storm Shadow cruise missiles, the Brimstone anti-armour weapon and beyond visual range air-to-air missiles (BVRAAM). The only difficulty I had with the programme was Nimrod MRA4. I had not forgotten the Nimrod AEW fiasco, the doomed attempt to cram into a Nimrod airframe the technical capacity – radar, electronics, power generation, cooling systems etc – plus six operator consoles all necessary to provide acceptable AEW performance. Simply put the airframe was too small for the job. The programme was cancelled in 1985 and Boeing E-3D aircraft bought, an in-service system with most impressive performance. By then Nimrod AEW had cost £1 billion against the original project costing of £200-300 million. Every intuitive bone in my body told me that there was a very high risk that the Nimrod Mk 4 airframe was again not big enough to accommodate and integrate the full suite of proposed sensor detection systems along with additional weapons to include Storm Shadow.

My preference was an off-the-shelf buy of the proven American P-3 Orion to be fitted out with our own sensor systems and weapons. The US Navy had a considerable number of airframes surplus to their requirements. But my intuition carried no weight with ministers who were easily persuaded by BAe Systems that my fears were groundless. I take no pleasure from recording that when Nimrod MRA4 was cancelled in the 2010 SDSR it was nine years late, some £800 million over budget and still plagued with unsolved functional flaws. The cancellation of Nimrod MRA4 and the absence of an MPA aircraft remains a most significant operational gap in the RAF's ORBAT at the time of writing – one that is thankfully soon to be filled by P-8 Poseidon multi-mission maritime aircraft bought from the United States.

To return to 1998 we also secured the development of a future offensive air system to replace the Tornado GR4 around 2020 with the commencement of a study into the replacement of the Harrier GR7 and Sea Harrier with the joint strike fighter. It was also finally agreed that we should lease four Boeing C-17 heavy-lift aircraft to augment the transport fleet with long-range strategic and tactical capability. I would have preferred outright purchase but leasing, in the long run a far more expensive option, was the only way to guarantee the procurement of the aircraft. It took the best part of two years to persuade the MoD that the C-17 was the only aircraft that met the operational requirement.

Throughout the process of the SDR as it affected the RAF there was one issue that caused me continuing worry. George Robertson's special advisor (Mr Bernard Gray) argued strongly for the disbandment of the Jaguar Force and the subsequent closure of their base at RAF Coltishall which would achieve considerable savings. Notwithstanding recent and considerable expenditure on upgrading the performance and capabilities of the Jaguar fleet, acceptance of Mr Gray's proposal would have had serious consequences. Our offensive forces remained committed to continuing operations over the Balkans and north and south Iraq and there was no suggestion of reducing the level of involvement. The removal of three squadrons from the ORBAT would inevitably increase the pressure on the Tornado and Harrier Forces to an unsustainable level. During a long-drawn-out debate I enjoyed the private support of CDS which may well have tipped the balance in favour of my arguments. But I did not know that I had won until formally informed by George Robertson of final cabinet approval of the SDR decisions that affected the RAF.

Before the meeting, and after very careful consideration, I had privately drafted a letter of resignation to the secretary of state if the decision went against me. Only Elizabeth knew of its existence as I believed that any public hint of my going would have conceded the possibility of losing the argument. But assuming the worst I judged that resignation would have represented no more than a one day wonder in the media and I recognised that I would most probably depart helped along by a good kick in the pants from the Downing Street spin doctors. The dispute about the future of the Jaguar Force was common knowledge in the service. I thus felt very strongly that defeat at the hands of a special advisor, who knew next to nothing about the generation and application of air power let alone the pressures on our front line, would have fatally wounded my professional reputation. Moreover, I didn't pretend to myself that resignation would somehow save the Jaguar Force from disbandment. But the service would most certainly have lost confidence in my leadership and ability to protect its operational concerns. I had no wish to continue as a lame duck CAS and thought it best to hand over to a successor untarnished by reputational damage. But thankfully it didn't come to that and tearing up my draft resignation letter came as a relief.

'Jointery'

Throughout the SDR process ministers placed considerable emphasis on the importance of 'jointery' within which the debate on the future of support helicopter (SH) ownership had been a constant wrangle between the RAF and the Army since 1986. I was first involved when serving as SASO in HQ RAF Germany where I judged the Army case to be rather puerile as it reflected the worst of cap badge mentality which had little to do with operational capabilities in the best interests of national defence. Before the start of the SDR an operational audit of support helicopter forces was carried out by the directorate of operational capability led by a brigadier. The audit in the clearest possible terms concluded that the RAF was the most efficient operator of support helicopters. I thus proposed, with the agreement of Roger Wheeler, that there should be an SDR study of the possible creation of a Joint Helicopter Command (JHC). In so doing we beat the Civil Service to the punch.

To lead the study I had up my sleeve the ideal candidate, Air Vice-Marshal David Niven, who had served on exchange tours with both the Royal Navy and the Army. As I expected David did a first-class job acceptable to both the other services which led to the formation of a new JHC within which AOC-in-C Strike Command retained full command of all RAF personnel but with operational command delegated to C-in-C Land. The force included the Army's new Apache attack helicopters as well as RN support helicopters but not their anti-submarine warfare Lynx helos that were an integral part of a ship's tactical war-fighting capability.

Enthusiasm in the RAF for the formation of the JHC was at best lukewarm. Many feared that service in the JHC would cut them apart from mainstream career progression and that operational command as exercised by C-in-C Land would effectively remove the SH squadrons and their personnel from the RAF chain of command. I had to spend some time explaining to the doubting Thomas's the meaning of 'full command' while making the point, forcefully, that it was now our duty to make it work. And if it all turned to a can of worms they knew who to blame – me.

Some 12 years or so later the three most senior appointments in the RAF, including CAS, were all filled by men with a SH background. So much for career progression and I certainly owe a debt of gratitude to Air Vice-Marshals David Niven and Paul Luker, the first two commanders of the JHC, for all they achieved in forging its joint identity as they brought together the separate elements into a force that could operate with equal effectiveness in support of either land or amphibious operations. The JHC most certainly earned its spurs in Iraq and Afghanistan.

The second joint initiative was known as Joint Force 2000, the brainchild of Tim Jenner and Jonathan Band, assistant chief of the naval staff. They proposed that RN Sea Harriers and RAF Harriers should come together in a joint force equally capable of operating from shore or ships. Jock Slater and I accepted their recommendation and submitted a paper signed by both of us to the secretary of state. The fact that the RN and the RAF had come to such an agreement came as something of a surprise to those in the MoD centre who predicted that the Navy and the Air Force would soon be at each other's throats to the eventual benefit of the Treasury. A very senior official accused me of trying to stitch up the MoD. I could only laugh and reply that we were consistently being asked to come up with sensible proposals in the best interests of 'jointery' and financial prudence. That was what we had done and I was surprised that our initiative had caused disquiet, presumably because it had fallen into 'the not invented here' trap. The joint submission was greeted by ministers as a most positive and welcome proposal.

It is worth recording that soon after the start of the SDR, Jock and I met for a long chat in which we both agreed that on past evidence if not traditional form we would be expected to fall out on the question of aircraft carriers. I believed that no decision could sensibly be reached until phase one of the SDR was completed that would decide whether or not the UK was to remain in the power projection business with intervention capabilities. If this was the outcome I would support the replacement of the three Invincible-class aircraft carriers and that is what happened.

At the time two new carriers were envisaged as being in the order of 30,000 to 40,000 tonnes and I thought they would be similar to the US Navy's Wasp-class amphibious assault ships that could operate a mix of fixed-wing aircraft (Harrier) and SH as required by operational circumstances. Wasp-class carriers could also embark 1,500 marines and their landing craft. Given the SDR's emphasis on sustaining an intervention capability they seemed just the ticket. But I kept my thoughts to myself as it was not my job to teach the Navy to suck eggs. However, I had absolutely no idea at the time that the new carriers would within the next seven years morph into the 65,000- to 70,000-tonne monsters that are the largest and most expensive warships to come into RN service. The original budget for the two ships has been exceeded by some £2bn, and the first carrier commissioned, HMS *Queen Elizabeth,* still has no aeroplanes to fly. The Strategic Defence and Security Review conducted in 2010 decided that all the Harriers and their logistic support would be sold. The US Marine Corps was the happy beneficiary of this largesse.

The growth in size and cost of the new carriers has led not only to a substantial decrease in the surface and subsurface fleet numbers required to protect them but also to a distortion of the future equipment programme to the disadvantage of both the Army and the RAF. Had I known that in 1998 I most certainly would not have agreed and, like me, Jock Slater may not have foreseen the consequences of our agreement. I also know that today many in the Royal Navy recognise the damage that has been done to their service. It lacks the spread of capabilities in sufficient numbers necessary to meet the many challenges in an unpredictable world that our national sea power has to confront.

Another main theme of the SDR was sustainability which aimed to repair damage to defence medical services, inflicted by defence costs studies, as well as improving other logistic capabilities. Improvements to RAF medical services were part of a defence-wide upgrading that included the provision of an additional RAF Aeromed Evacuation Flight that would increase medical support to deployed operating bases and support helicopters. The RAF also gained increased investment in logistics, particularly Harrier and Tornado deployment packs, engines and avionics spares packages and support helicopter tactical fuel vehicles. All this and further small enhancements significantly improved the deployability and sustainability of the services' readiness to respond to future crises.

The SDR of 1997/98 was probably the first time that a searching examination of our national defence capabilities did not question the existence of the RAF Regiment. I did not have to deploy well-rehearsed and militarily legitimate arguments for the Corps' retention in the RAF as I had to do during Front Line First when briefing John Thomson. The Regiment's sustained excellence of operational performance in Northern Ireland, Gulf War I and the Balkans had not gone unremarked. RAF Regiment expertise in NBC warfare was acknowledged to be the best. Moreover, the Army conceded that they could not provide force protection from within their resources for our expensive people and equipment deployed on overseas operations. Subsequently 27 Squadron RAF Regiment was removed from the ORBAT and combined with 1 Royal Tank Regiment to form a new joint NBC regiment under RAF control. At the same time its Rapier SHORAD squadrons joined with Royal Artillery air defence units to form a new joint air defence command. The loss some years later of the regiment's SHORAD role came as a timely reminder that Whitehall people could still reach decisions that flew in the face of all available evidence. That said, the Corps' responsibility for aggressive ground defence today at least provides a single point of operational focus for the RAF Regiment.

Within the whole process of the SDR I lost one significant argument. From the outset there was growing interest in the formation of a Defence Logistics Organisation (DLO) drawing together under one commander the three separate services' engineering/logistic support elements. Much of this interest seemed to me to come from the Treasury who were represented at all significant SDR meetings within the MoD. I got the impression that the formation of the DLO was a done deal agreed by ministers and officials within both departments and that the debate was essentially no more than going through the motions. I felt that the formation of the DLO at a time when the services were all involved in implementing many other decisions, both operational and financial, was a step too far.

While acknowledging that some may have considered that the exercise of logistic functions within each of the services was both functionally and financially inefficient, I argued that we should be given a yellow card and two years to prove an acceptable level of performance. At the final decision-making meeting I put my case which was politely listened to but John Reid countered with the argument that it was necessary to act now rather than endure continuing expensive inefficiency – his assessment and not mine as it applied to the RAF. Richard Mottram gave a masterly summation of the more detailed considerations before a decision was reached. I lost and went to HQ Logs Command to give them the bad news but it was interesting to note that many of the middle-ranking officers were not at all put out. They quickly recognised that within a much larger DLO their career prospects had taken a turn for the better. Air rank officers accepted the news with stoical resignation. Royal Air Force Logistics Command was disbanded and its headquarters closed on 31st October 1999.

Doctrine

SDR debates brought home to me the simple fact that not only senior officials but colleagues in the Royal Navy and Army had no informed understanding of the complexity of contemporary air operations and attendant risks. But, first, we needed to put our own house in order. Air Publication 3000, Air Power Doctrine, was first published in 1990 to set out the characteristics of air power, both strengths and limitations, and fundamental tenets for its employment. The end of the Cold War and Gulf War I prompted an update of AP 3000 in 1993 but in my judgement it did not go far enough in attempting to define the core capabilities of our national air power as we looked forward to the 21st century. Nor did it consider changes in the strategic environment and how we should address change in concert with our sister services. I thus commissioned a complete rewrite of AP 3000 that took full account of 'jointery' and multinational operations. I had just the man for the job, Group Captain Stu Peach, the then director of defence studies (RAF). The drafting of the document to my satisfaction took longer than I anticipated as Stu Peach gamely confronted some of my prejudices and attitudes. As far as I can remember he won his fair share of our debates so it's no surprise that as I write he is chief of the defence staff.

The eventual publication of AP 3000 in 1999 provided an authoritative and contemporary doctrinal statement to guide commanders at all levels, no matter the colour of their uniform, by shaping their thinking on the successful employment of air power in crisis or war. This came with a health warning that doctrine should not become dogma in a strategic environment that remained fraught with uncertainty. Doctrine needed to reflect a continuing process of review that examined definitions and concepts as well as the roles and missions of air power.

I also instructed the Air Warfare Centre to produce a booklet for wide distribution that catalogued all of the RAF's aircraft and weapons with their performance capabilities and characteristics. I found it a most helpful aide memoire but I am confident that it was not a 'bestseller' amongst the MoD's accountants more concerned with balancing budgets than understanding the cost of competitive capabilities that gave best value for money – capabilities that relied on innovative technology to stay ahead of potential adversaries.

People

The SDR recognised that the armed forces had suffered from overstretch as a consequence of under-manning and in some cases having too few units to meet certain commitments – hence my determined opposition to the disbandment of the Jaguar Force. Under-manning fuelled overstretch that caused dissatisfaction which led to problems in retaining high quality people.

Recruiting and holding on to these personnel was a major and continuing concern throughout my tenure of office.

During the SDR process I fully supported initiatives which addressed overstretch, under-manning, education and welfare. I was relieved that there would be no redundancies in the RAF. The manpower savings in the fast-jet forces following the reduction in aircraft numbers were not lost to the service. Establishment vacancies elsewhere were filled to bring an end to gapping that had become almost institutionalised. Moreover, the strength of the Royal Auxiliary Air Force was increased by 270 which represented a minor success given the large reduction in numbers inflicted on the Territorial Army.

I welcomed the 'Policy for People' package that emphasised the importance of education and training, both vocational and academic, that would underpin the RAF's commitment to investment in people. Other initiatives, such as improvements to operational allowances and leave entitlement, were intended to ensure that our personnel and their families would remain attracted to service life. Equally important, they would not be disadvantaged when they returned to civilian employment. At the time I was well aware of a certain cynicism within the service about messages delivered from on high and that failure to deliver the goods could only exacerbate the retention problem.

Two early visits to stations underlined my concern. At RAF Lossiemouth I met four Tornado pilots who had fought in Gulf War I and since then completed 12 more detachments on Southern Watch duties. They told me, apologetically, that they were taking premature voluntary retirement. I learned they were all graduate entrants, they were all married with young families and their wives were pursuing their own careers. Family life stability had become increasingly important and they could not foresee any easing of the operational pressures that had dominated their lives since 1990. I told them that while I regretted their decisions they would leave the service having done their duty and with my thanks.

At another station I met a group of junior technicians in the avionics trade group. I heard that the rapid reduction in service manpower had reduced promotion opportunities such that in their trade group promotion had ground to a complete standstill with no immediate prospect of a return to normal promotion quotas. Their situation was by no means unique in the service. I then discovered that trade group managers had stopped promotion to retain a recognisable pyramid structure within individual groupings. I felt that life without hope of promotion was asking too much of young men and women who had committed to a career in the service. So personnel staff were instructed to reintroduce promotion to get things moving; shape and structure would be addressed in happier times. I also wrote a personal note to Dr John Reid pointing out that the service was still bound by the previous administration's instruction to reduce our personnel strength by a further 3,000 which gave no room for manoeuvre in addressing a serious retention problem. I asked to be given freedom to manage our personnel numbers within budget but without the pressure of having to implement the Conservative government's directive. Approval was given.

During my station visits I noticed that a number of junior officer appointments in the engineering and administrative branches were filled by warrant officers as recruiting targets for commissioned officers had not been met. Apparently warrant officers were not applying for commissioning which seemed to me hardly surprising if the consequence of selection meant subjecting themselves to the full initial officer training syllabus at the RAF College Cranwell. The Army, on the other hand, as I had discovered at RAF Gütersloh, had no problem with the immediate commissioning of warrant officers suitably qualified by personal character, experience, education and age.

I was thus determined to introduce a similar system into the RAF and did so despite the misgivings of some members of the AFBSC. Almost inevitably there were efforts to prolong a process that I asked to be contained within a long weekend. But I did stamp my foot when I heard that an extra day was being added on so that the warrant officers could be instructed in sword drill. It stayed a long weekend. All's well that ends well and I presented scrolls to the first group of warrant officers commissioned under the new system. For me, the real reward was talking to their wives all of whom were professional women mainly involved in nursing and teaching careers. Without exception they expressed their pleasure at recognition of their husbands' value to the service and the new opportunities now offered them as commissioned officers.

Higher up the scale I was concerned that the appointments and promotion of air rank officers was too much of a closed book with no formal record of discussion on how decisions had been reached. I decided that we would set up an air rank Appointments and Promotion Board again modelled on the Army system. I chaired the board with the three commanders-in-chief as members plus the air secretary who was responsible for the preparation of briefs and the minutes of meetings that formally recorded our discussion and decisions. Apart from reassuring candidates for promotion that their prospects and competitiveness had been judged without fear or favour, the proceedings proved helpful in the joint arena when the Senior Appointments Committee met under CDS's chairmanship to choose the best candidate from any of the services to fill a 'purple' appointment. Our purely RAF deliberations were also helpful when I had to tell air rank officers that there was no prospect of further promotion that inevitably came as a disappointment to most.

Two other initiatives merit mention. If the RAF was to achieve a better return of service, particularly from pilots, it was essential to lower the average age of entry. By far the majority of prospective pilots entered the service in their early twenties with a degree. Driving down the age of entry thus inevitably required candidates to forego a university education. While a degree course during RAF training had proved an unachievable aspiration, I thought it could be achieved after commissioning at a time of an individual's choosing if the necessary arrangements could be made for distance learning. Such courses would focus on the subjects relevant to a military career within a syllabus that acknowledged the value of some aspects of service training. Happily, and after detailed negotiations led by Air Marshal Sir Anthony Bagnall, agreement was reached with Exeter University and the Open University for serving officers to take a degree course so they would not be disadvantaged in searching for civilian employment after leaving the RAF.

The second initiative, and at the time more controversial, was the production of a booklet titled 'Core Values and Standards in the Royal Air Force'. In recognising that the RAF was built on a foundation of shared values, expectations and commitment it seemed to me that in 1999 the need to maintain common values and standards presented a greater challenge than had been the case in the past. We could not afford to ignore attitudinal changes in contemporary society from which we recruited men and women from all ethnic, religious and cultural backgrounds. The booklet thus set out the values and standards that should govern daily life within the service. Seven key qualities were identified as core values. These were integrity, courage, commitment, professionalism, pride, loyalty and teamwork. The RAF was the first to publish such a document but I gained the impression that it was not warmly welcomed by the rank and file in the service. There was a general feeling that other more pressing matters required the attention of the service's senior leadership. That said, I did not regret a successful attempt to set out with crystal clarity the values and standards that characterised service life and that were more demanding than those found in the civilian world.

While I could take some satisfaction from a few successful initiatives, I was in no doubt that far-reaching changes in the armed forces since the end of the Cold War had left many feeling that the RAF no longer offered a rewarding career. Defence cuts, increased emphasis on business culture, changes to conditions of service, frictions arising from integration with contractors' personnel and by no means least a deterioration in quality of life, had bred cynical and negative attitudes. I had also underestimated the influence of 'jointery' that served to emphasise rank disparity between the services and particularly between the Army and the RAF. The Army retained a younger service rank for rank that reflected both its military roles and structure particularly within the non-commissioned ranks. This caused frustration in the RAF especially in the less technical joint service areas.

In sum, poor promotion prospects, overstretch, civilianisation and failure to recognise and reward endeavour were all powerful incentives to leave at a time of uncertainty about the future. Although a number of in-service initiatives had achieved some improvements to conditions of service the requirement to achieve a much closer match of resources to task was an imperative that needed to build on the SDR baseline. Confidence in the future meant that the RAF's senior leadership had to show sympathetic recognition of widespread concerns that could not be allayed by the rhetoric of formal briefings. Thus was born the idea of formulating a strategic view of the service's future that could be distributed throughout the rank structure. Implementation of the idea was however delayed as in March 1999 the RAF once more went to war.

In recording concerns and achievements as they affected RAF people I may have given the impression that I was working as a one-man band. Not so. My requirements placed huge demands on Personnel and Training Command staff as they grappled with a raft of issues that influenced morale and commitment to the service. I owe a particular debt of gratitude to three people. First, Warrant Officer Jim Andrews who filled the appointment created by Michael Graydon as CAS's warrant officer. I had previously served two tours with Jim Andrews and knew that this quietly spoken Scot was a man of unquestionable integrity whose judgement was invariably well balanced and precisely presented. In routine meetings with him after his regular visits to stations at home and abroad I always got the unvarnished truth as it concerned morale and the wellbeing of our people where it affected their commitment to the service, their careers and family life within the RAF.

I was also indeed fortunate to enjoy the wholehearted and energetic support of Air Marshal Sir Anthony Bagnall, the AOC-in-C Personnel and Training Command, and Air Vice-Marshal Ian Stewart, the air secretary. Individually and together they never failed to satisfy my expectations while sustaining patient good humour as demands were piled upon them from many quarters. Keeping the RAF on an even keel during a time of uncertainty owed much to their judgement, their example of sympathetic understanding and firm handling of the many challenges posed by circumstances beyond the immediate control of the service.

CHAPTER 27
OPERATIONS

In the early 1990s the Federal Republic of Yugoslavia (FRY) was devastated by destructive forces generated principally by multiple ethnicities and religious differences. The cruel brutality of the conflict in Bosnia and Herzegovina had been terminated by military force with a political settlement agreed in Dayton that secured peace in the immediate region. But the status of Kosovo, an autonomous province within the Republic of Serbia, was not addressed. Within Kosovo tensions between the Albanian and Serbian communities had simmered for decades with occasional violent eruptions that came to a head in 1997 when the Yugoslav Army entered Kosovo to destroy the Kosovo Liberation Army (KLA). Although the Yugoslavs denied any armed conflict in Kosovo there were many reports of Serbian brutality that culminated in a massacre of villagers in the Drenica area in March 1998. At the end of the month the UN Security Council imposed an arms embargo on the FRY and warned of additional measures if there was no progress towards a peaceful solution.

In the year that followed more than half a million Kosovans were displaced or had fled across the borders as diplomatic initiatives continued. These concluded with an invitation to Serbian and Kosovan representatives to attend peace negotiations at Rambouillet near Paris under the auspices of the Contact Group (US, UK, Russia, France, Germany and Italy). The Contact Group required, inter alia, an immediate ceasefire, the withdrawal of nearly all Yugoslav forces from Kosovo, the demilitarisation of the KLA and the insertion of a peace-implementation force, KFOR, into the province. On 19th March 1999 the Serbian delegation rejected the terms for a peaceful settlement and another 80,000 ethnic Albanians fled their homes as heavy fighting resumed.

President Milosevic rebuffed a formal and final request from the American, Ambassador Holbrooke, to halt attacks on Kosovo Albanians or face air attack. NATO planners had ruled out the option of a land campaign on the grounds that it would probably be protracted in duration and expensive in casualties. The coercive use of air power was judged to be best suited to stopping Serbian aggression. Thus on 24th March 1999 air strikes were launched on the authority of the North Atlantic Council. Operation Allied Force lasted for 78 days before Milosevic agreed to the withdrawal of Serbian forces from Kosovo.

From the start of the campaign there was disagreement in NATO about strategy. According to USAF doctrine the focus from the first night should have been on a massive strike at the strategic centres of gravity that supported Milosevic and his oppressive regime. However, gaining agreement to this concept among NATO's 19 nations proved impossible. Some argued that air attacks should only be made on troops and vehicles carrying out ethnic cleansing in Kosovo. Others took the view that potential targets near Belgrade should not be attacked. Much to the frustration of my friend, General Mike Ryan now the USAF chief of staff, the need for consensus within the Alliance led to acceptance of a phased option that went through a series of escalatory steps each within exceptionally stringent rules of engagement. Phase one prioritised the destruction of the FRY's integrated air defence system (IADS), Phase two moved on to attack military targets south of 44 degrees north (to include command and control centres, hostile forces, lines of communications and operations and logistic sites) and phase three extended the campaign throughout the FRY. Unlike Deliberate Force I had no say in or influence on initial Allied Force planning but I judged that unchallenged claims emanating from Washington that Milosevic would be brought to heel in a relatively short time were far wide of the mark. I was not asked to express an opinion by either my political or military superiors in the MoD.

Optimistic expectations were based, first, on an assumption that the USAF would launch a 'shock and awe' air campaign and, secondly, on misunderstanding of air power's contribution to ending the war in Bosnia and Herzegovina. Fine weather prevailed throughout Deliberate Force, air defences were ineffective and aircrews could make repeated passes to confirm their targets and best attack profiles. Moreover, I judged that on past form Milosevic would exploit divisions within NATO and use every trick in the book to delay or minimise the effects of an air campaign.

NATO's stated intention of relying on air power and excluding the option of a ground invasion immediately ceded an operational advantage to the Serbs. Their formidable array of surface-to-air missiles, including SA-3, SA-6 and SA-7 Strela missiles, were put on an immediate war footing with radar crews dispersed in hardened bunkers some distance from radar heads. Decoys representing artillery, tanks and other armoured fighting vehicles were widely deployed, and troops and their equipment not actively fighting the KLA were dispersed and hidden among the Albanian population. The possibility of NATO changing its mind to include the option of a ground offensive was ruled out – not that there were forces in a position to do so or indeed any certainty that sufficient numbers and capabilities could be generated by European nations. President Clinton had made quite clear his opposition to the deployment of American troops as part of an invasion force. Moreover, the decision that the air campaign would be shaped by a policy of gradualism inevitably signalled an extended rather than a short and sharp period of offensive action. This was the unavoidable consequence of the need to keep cohesion within NATO while Prime Minister Blair was developing his concept of humanitarian intervention.

Differences of opinion as how best to target air power were also soon evident within NATO's military chain of command. Phase one operations were hampered by bad weather while explicit ROE required positive identification of targets validated from two sources. When there was a risk of civilian casualties only PGMs could be used. Priority given to force protection imposed an absolute lower operational flying altitude of 15,000 ft. Cloudy weather below this height limited the use of laser-guided bombs that required uninterrupted line of sight from the aircraft to the target; 33% of Harrier LGB attacks were aborted because of failure to achieve or sustain laser-target designation in bad weather. Numerous other Allied aircraft returned to base without bombing because of fears that civilians could be in the target area. Such concerns were amplified by the altitude limit that made it difficult to identify smaller targets with the equipment then available.

NATO's initial air assault, constrained by bad weather, tight ROE and emphasis on force protection, quite predictably failed to impress Milosevic who immediately intensified ethnic cleansing in Kosovo. In response NATO directed that Kosovo Albanians should be protected by direct targeting of fielded Yugoslav Army and ministry interior police units in Kosovo rather than their supporting infrastructure. This was to be undertaken whilst sustaining the phased air campaign. But there were not enough attack aircraft to do both in tandem. The intensity of effort planned for phase one was thus diluted by increased tasking into the Kosovo Engagement Zone (KEZ). The shift of focus was supported by SACEUR, General Wesley Clark. His natural inclination as a soldier was to target enemy ground forces rather than strategic target sets. The shift of air campaign priorities away from the previously endorsed three-phased operation provoked a fundamental difference of opinion between SACEUR and Lieutenant General Michael Short USAF, the Combined Forces Air Component commander.

While he recognised that SACEUR shouldered political pressures over which he had little or no influence, General Short argued that the marginal tactical benefit achieved by KEZ missions did not warrant the level of effort expended. Although by the beginning of May the air campaign had achieved some impressive results – the establishment of air superiority, the disruption of civil and military communications, significant damage to military infra-structure supporting the Yugoslav Army and the disruption of rail and road links into Kosovo – these successes failed to match political expectations and not least those of Prime Minister Blair.

Short's argument that tactical successes were not exerting sufficient coercive effect on the FRY leadership eventually won the day. By 25th May SACEUR had accepted the need for reorientation of effort to include attacks on targets that were "leadership sustaining" as well as parts of Serbia's industrial base. Two weeks later, and after the air campaign had been intensified to an average of 280 offensive sorties per day, Milosevic finally conceded to NATO's demands. Lieutenant General Mike Jackson, commander Kosovo Force (KFOR), met with a Yugoslav delegation to present them with a military technical agreement (MTA) for signature. The document set out details of the withdrawal of all FRY security forces from three designated zones in Kosovo to be completed within 11 days. KFOR troops would enter the zones in phases as FRY forces withdrew. After 100 hours of negotiation the MTA was signed on 9th June 1999 and Operation Allied Force was suspended the next day.

Predictably the debate on "who won the war?" started immediately hostilities ended. Critics of the air campaign, a hotchpotch of politicians, commentators, armchair warriors and historians, joined together to argue that it was the threat of a NATO ground offensive that finally persuaded Milosevic to accept a negotiated settlement. One notable exception to this view was Sir John Keegan, arguably the foremost military historian and commentator of the time, who initially was a critic of the campaign but at its conclusion accepted that air power rather than land power was the deciding military factor. However, the majority view reflected frustration at the failure of the initial air assault to achieve a quick solution to the crisis hence their judgement that the ground threat solved the impasse. But in June 1999 how realistic was this threat?

Only the UK was prepared to accept the need for a forced entry into Kosovo. No other NATO nation had started to prepare for offensive ground operations and the concept was not supported by Germany and France. President Clinton, without European consensus, restricted US involvement to no more than planning. When Milosevic agreed the terms that ended the conflict some 15,000 KFOR troops were deployed for peacekeeping and humanitarian duties, a little more than half of the 28,500 originally envisaged by NATO. UK military planners calculated that an opposed ground invasion required 140,000 troops. There was thus no practical possibility of launching an opposed ground campaign before the onset of winter assuming the Americans, French and Germans could be persuaded to participate. In sum, the reality of the situation on the ground and political and military disagreements within NATO can hardly have come together to exert any coercive effect on Milosevic. Claims that the threat of a ground offensive was the decisive factor in ending the conflict on NATO's terms appear unfounded.

Only Milosevic knew for certain why he capitulated so suddenly. His decision was probably influenced by three factors. First, his indictment along with four other senior figures in his regime by the International Criminal Tribunal for the Former Yugoslavia may have exercised an unsettling effect on his personal morale. Secondly, apart from the damage to his military capabilities and the devastation of their supporting infrastructure, NATO's attacks seriously damaged the wealth of the industrialists and fat cats who underpinned his hold on power. Thirdly, and most importantly, international isolation of the FRY achieved by diplomatic processes culminated in the withdrawal of Russian support for Milosevic. With due allowance for the influence of these factors, what is undeniable other than by distorting facts beyond recognition, is that had NATO not sustained its air campaign, a negotiated settlement, the end of ethnic cleansing and the return of refugees would have been long delayed.

In stating my conviction I have not forgotten that Allied Force was a joint operation within which NATO sailors and soldiers made their own contributions. The navies provided launch platforms for aircraft and cruise missiles while land forces made an invaluable contribution to humanitarian relief and by their very presence on the ground helped prevent further regional destabilisation and conflict spill over. Thus, and in the words of General Wesley Clark: "The conflict ended on NATO's terms. The Serbs are out. The refugees are going home. Peace is in place."

Throughout the 78 days of the air campaign CDS kept a very tight grip on military staffs in the MoD. As the principal air advisor to the government I did not speak directly to the prime minister or the secretary of state about either the overall conduct of the air campaign or our national contribution to NATO air power. All communication to our political masters went through Charles Guthrie who was determinedly protective of his position as CDS. It should be understood that I was not in the chain of command. Thus my role at the chiefs of staff early morning briefings was to give an overview of operations and my interpretation of air matters before CDS went off to a ministerial meeting. At our first COS briefing I had to explain why Harriers returned from their mission without bombing. Many commentators have since recorded they missed their targets. Untrue, they did not bomb for reasons previously explained. I also emphasised that ministers should be reassured that the self-discipline of our aircrews would minimise the risk of the RAF inflicting collateral damage that could cause political embarrassment.

The failure to bring Milosevic immediately to heel generated ever-increasing impatience within Whitehall. In mid-April and just before the prime minister flew to Washington to meet President Clinton, CDS asked me to present a paper setting out my own professional judgement on the prospect of the air campaign achieving FRY acceptance of NATO's demands. At that time there was increasing and hostile criticism of air operations perhaps best reflected in an article in *The Times* by Simon Jenkins who wrote: "No amount of NATO bombing will make Milosevic see sense in Kosovo," and, "It is inconceivable (that) the Serb leader will suddenly withdraw."

I was given six hours to produce my piece. Sadly I don't have a copy of it and no trace can be found in my archived files. But I did know that SACEUR had directed that the primary weight of air effort was to be targeted against the Yugoslav Army and ministry interior police units in Kosovo. I knew this was an inefficient use of most aircraft types available and a diversion of scarce resources from where they were really needed. I had also observed that the enemy's strategic and operational centres of gravity had not been defined and that there were no timelines or target priorities. Correction of these omissions, the arrival of reinforcement aircraft and better weather would, however, intensify the air campaign that under phase three would include Yugoslav military industrial infrastructure, media outlets and other strategic targets.

I judged that *if* NATO moved to full implementation of phase three the FRY, with no means of retaliation, could not withstand the piecemeal dismemberment of national infrastructure that included power generation, the transport system, communications and water supply. If these conditions were met I assessed that Milosevic would be coerced into negotiation of Yugoslav withdrawal by September at the latest. My prediction proved pessimistic. I don't know what happened to my note although some senior officials complemented me on a sober and realistic appraisal. I appreciated their kind words.

It may be, with emphasis on the 'may', that my note never reached the prime minister because it was not fully in tune with MoD military thinking. From the start of the campaign it was generally accepted that if air power failed in its coercive purpose, we had to be prepared for the slower and more dangerous option of using ground forces to forcibly evict the Serbs. NATO thus needed to develop a coherent air/land campaign plan and the construction of a Plan B seemed to be no more than sensible contingency planning. I thus had no difficulty in giving it my support but without changing my formal assessment that I don't believe was accepted by everyone of influence. Soon after I had presented my assessment CDS met with his American counterpart General Henry Shelton, US Army. They shared misgivings about the conduct of the air campaign and SACEUR's misplaced and uneconomic focus on KEZ targets. They agreed that their concern should be raised directly with General Wesley Clark and I was allocated the rather unenviable task of doing this.

I set off for HQ SHAPE accompanied by two brigadiers from Army Plans. My brief was to raise the issue of the strategic direction of the air campaign and its associated planning as the UK needed to achieve a broader understanding of SACEUR's strategy. In other words, what were the FRY's centres of gravity and how could they be most effectively targeted? I was also instructed to confirm the UK's support for General Short's concept of operations that would take full advantage of extra aircraft being committed to the campaign – and in doing so to emphasise the need for concentration of force and economy of effort. The unspoken and not so subtle purpose was to convince SACEUR that he should cease micromanagement of the air campaign and to delegate authority to the appropriate subordinate commanders; and then let them get on with the job. SACEUR listened intently and while I believed he accepted General Short's mission plan I was not entirely convinced. My suspicion was confirmed when soon after SACEUR issued strategic guidance to NATO's C-in-C South stating: "My highest priority is the attack of ground forces in Kosovo."

I had two other messages to deliver. Although the UK accepted US primacy in operational control of the air campaign, we were concerned by the preparation of two separate air tasking orders one of which was only releasable to US personnel. Operational planning was thus complicated and the principle of unity of command, so important to the preservation of Alliance cohesion, was undermined. A near collision at night involving a RAF Tornado and an unknown USAF stealth aircraft operating outside the NATO air tasking order prompted our practical concern. Secondly, and finally, I was instructed to inform SACEUR that the UK government was prepared to field 50,000 troops to a NATO invasion land force should the air campaign fail in its purpose. General Clark's surprise was reflected in his immediate question asking if I had been authorised to say this. I replied my authorised statement demonstrated the government's determination to bring Milosevic to book and NATO had to win if the Alliance was to survive.

NATO aircraft flew 38,004 sorties during Allied Force of which 10,484 were offensive missions that released 23,614 air munitions. The RAF flew 979 attack sorties. Of these, Harriers, operating out of Gioia del Colle in Italy, flew 850 against tactical and fixed military targets in Kosovo. RAF Brüggen Tornados contributed a further 129 missions delivering LGBs against individual aiming points in the FRY. These missions, the first flown from a home base since the end of World War II, gave the aircrews and their families concern absent from deployed operations. "Counting them out and counting them back" had added poignancy.

Until the end of April the Tornados had to fly a circular route over France, Corsica and Italy before entering FRY airspace. These missions, some seven and a half hours long were critically dependent on air-to-air refuelling often accomplished at night in the most difficult of weather conditions. In late April a more direct route was authorised through the Czech Republic, Slovakia, Hungary and Croatia that reduced sortie time to around five hours with only two as opposed to four air-to-air refuelling brackets. Tornados, spending significantly more time in hostile air space than the Harriers, were engaged by surface-to-air missiles and heavy anti-aircraft artillery on 70 of these missions. At the end of May Brüggen deployed 12 additional Tornados to the French air force base at Solenzara in Corsica. This detachment flew three missions each involving six aircraft before operations ended on 10th June.

The UK's contribution included 100 combat air patrols flown by RN Sea Harriers from HMS *Invincible* and Tomahawk cruise missiles launched from HMS *Splendid.* VC10 and TriStar tankers and AWACS aircraft flew a further 500 combat support missions with hundreds more sorties contributed by RAF air transport aircraft in support of our deployed forces. The RAF's offensive operations, some 10% of the total NATO effort, played an effective role in the achievement of NATO's strategic objective. Tornados and Harriers contributed to the degradation of FRY's integrated air defence system and the disruption of transportation and communication links between Kosovo and Serbia. The Harrier KEZ missions forced FRY forces to conceal or disperse troops and their weapons which constrained the effectiveness of their operations against the KLA. But while no collateral damage was attributed to the RAF, several errors of others such as the bombing of the Chinese embassy in Belgrade caused considerable embarrassment that played into the hands of those ever eager to criticise NATO's air campaign.

Throughout the course of the campaign air operations were subject to continual and critical analysis from a number of media and military 'experts' who presented a predictable litany of prejudices and fixed ideas. Their reports gave an impression that NATO aircraft were raining down bombs on a largely defenceless Serbia. Furthermore, they suggested that many of the bombs missed their targets and no damage was done apart from the destruction of dummy tanks because NATO aircrew would not come down to low level to close with the enemy. It is true that the NATO chain of command placed a high premium on the safety of its aircrew and aircraft. As we were not fighting a war of national survival, rather a war of choice, it seemed eminently sensible not to fly consistently in range of Serb MANPADS and light AAA. And as already mentioned 15,000ft was not a safe haven. While the FRY air force quickly threw in the towel, their GBAD fired more than 700 SAMs at coalition aircraft and engaged with heavy AAA on numerous occasions. The battle for control of the air space was quickly won, and thereafter the effectiveness of counter measures, the skills of our aircrews and a measure of luck brought home all but two of the 829 aircraft from 14 nations that operated under NATO control.

Flying at low level would have obviously increased the probability of the Serbs knocking down more NATO aircraft which would have given a substantial boost to their morale. I have to wonder whether the cohesion of NATO would have been sufficiently strong to accommodate a steady flow of aircraft losses. It seemed to me that a lot of otherwise well-informed and intelligent people could not get to grips with the fact that war is not an exercise in chivalry that demands an even-handed and fair contest. War is and will remain a nasty and brutal business in which the aim is to achieve political objectives with the least possible loss to one's own side. Your strengths and advantages are thus concentrated on the enemy's weaknesses with no prizes awarded for manufacturing an evenly balanced fight let alone for sustaining unnecessary casualties.

At the end of hostilities Harriers were held at a high state of readiness at Gioia del Colle to respond rapidly to any call for air support from KFOR units. Elsewhere RAF personnel provided essential service and security to sustain peace support operations. The vital air head at Pristina was protected by the RAF Regiment with crash and fire cover provided by RAF firefighters. The RAF Medical Service deployed a 25-bed field medical facility to the airport which was soon home to a detachment of Puma helicopters. RAF Police assisted Special Investigation Branch officers in collecting evidence for the International War Crimes Tribunal with 5131 Bomb Disposal Squadron fully engaged in the removal of unexploded bombs, mines and booby traps. To the north three Chinook helicopters operating from Split transported troops and supplies around Bosnia in support of the NATO Stabilisation Force.

Tactical Supply Wing maintained refuelling points at various locations throughout the country to provide an essential service for the aircraft of all contributing nations.

During 1999 events in the Middle East necessarily took a back place as international attention focused on the Kosovo crisis. Soon forgotten by many was the RAF's contribution to Operation Desert Fox, a four-day bombing campaign on Iraqi military targets in December 1998. The operation, led by the USAF, was provoked by Saddam Hussein who blocked access by UN weapons inspectors to various sites in Iraq associated with weapons of mass destruction. RAF Tornados flew 28 attack missions, 15% of the total, dropping 52 LGBs on a variety of targets of which some 60% were destroyed or severely damaged. In the year that followed and in response to Iraqi SAM attacks, our Tornados dropped LGBs on Iraqi air defence installations hitting 49 separate targets. The Tornado GR1s' bombing and recce missions were escorted by Tornado F3 air defence aircraft. Jaguars continued to patrol the northern Iraq no-fly zone with all detachments supported by VC10 tankers and the air transport force.

The scale and geographic dispersion of RAF operations in 1998 and 1999 came as a surprise to many when I lectured even to knowledgeable audiences in the Houses of Parliament and at various academic institutions. I was worried that many, including those well-informed on aviation matters, had no practical understanding of the complexity of contemporary air operations and attendant risks. The possibility of planning miscalculations, operating errors in the accomplishment of the mission and unforeseen developments in enemy air defences inflicting unexpected losses of aircraft and their crews, remained a constant concern. To help spread some gospel of understanding I asked Peter Squire, now AOC-in-C Strike Command, to prepare a briefing on Kosovo operations to be presented to retired air marshals at the annual gathering of the 'Old and Bold' at Cranwell.

The briefing, given by squadron commanders from all RAF elements involved in the air campaign, was an impressive presentation. There was no exaggeration of difficulties that were precisely and unemotionally set out and cockpit video evidence of Serbian SAMs narrowly missing our aircraft left no-one in any doubt about the associated dangers. With apologies for taking them away from their primary duties, I asked for a rerun of the presentation at the MoD. I did so in the hope that apart from military education those holding the purse strings would understand that air operations were not a risk-free option and there remained a continuing and pressing need to use technology to stay ahead of possible enemies.

Listening to the presentations I was aware that some operational deficiencies identified in Gulf War I had not yet been resolved. Although aircrew were better trained in medium level operations there remained a desperate need for precision-guided weapons, procured in quantity, that could be dropped through cloud. The Harrier needed a better anti-armour weapon for medium level attacks against ground forces. No less essential was the procurement of secure air-to-air communications equipment and an effective missile approach warning system. Above all I had been embarrassed to learn that at the start of the Kosovo war not one of the Harrier pilots had dropped and guided an LGB during peacetime training because of the scarcity of TIALD pods and the cost of the weapons. So it was not just a question of needing better weapons, there was an essential need to improve the frequency and quality of training. Shortcomings in weapons performance had been recognised in the SDR and were in the process of correction at a pace conditioned by available funding but not in time for Allied Force.

Overall I was proud of the scale and breadth of the RAF's contribution to operations that came to a head during my last year as CAS. The performance of our Harrier and Tornado aircrews merited particular respect. Although poor weather had caused much frustration their discipline never faltered and they demonstrated admirable courage and determination from start to finish. Outstanding airborne leadership by Wing Commander Andy Golledge (OC 1[F] Squadron) and Wing Commander Tim Anderson (OC 14 Squadron) was recognised with the award of the DSO to these two exceptional airmen. And for his part in Operation Desert Fox, Wing Commander Steve Hillier earned a most well-deserved DFC.

RAF personnel ensured that the cutting edge of the service remained as well-honed as possible given some equipment shortcomings. I felt it a true privilege to be its professional head at a time when all elements of the service (air and ground) had convincingly demonstrated their professionalism and commitment to duty. Their example underlined my own responsibility to do my utmost to stabilise the service after the buffeting it had endured for the greater part of the decade. As I approached the last six months of my time as CAS I judged that the SDR had established the foundations on which the AFBSC could construct a strategic plan that would give all ranks of the RAF confidence in the future.

CHAPTER 28
RAF STRATEGIC PLAN

By the end of 1999 there had been some important changes in senior appointments within both the MoD and the service. Much to my regret George Robertson and John Reid had departed, the former to take over as secretary general of NATO and the latter on appointment as secretary of state for Scotland. I had enjoyed their company and developed a healthy respect for their genuine interest in defence and the wellbeing of the armed forces. Their replacements had big boots to fill and in my judgement fell some way short. Mr Geoffrey Hoon, the new secretary of state, was a lawyer and a rather aloof man with some intellectual arrogance that he made no effort to disguise – not uncommon amongst politicians. I have forgotten the name of John Reid's successor and only remember him as an anti-smoking obsessive with no apparent interest in defence and no obvious concern for the welfare of servicemen and women.

Michael Boyce had succeeded Jock Slater as First Sea Lord and Peter Abbott had taken over from John Willis as VCDS. Richard Mottram had been replaced by Kevin Tebbit as permanent under secretary. I was fortunate to enjoy continuing good relationships with my new colleagues from the Royal Navy while sustaining friendship with Charles Guthrie and Roger Wheeler. For my part I knew I would be handing over to my successor in April 2000. Shortly before George Robertson's departure in October 1999, Charles Guthrie asked me if I would wish to be considered as a possible successor in the appointment of CDS. I immediately declined. During my tour the government had introduced annual appraisal reports on all individuals, including the chiefs, who filled senior appointments in the MoD. In my 1999 report Charles Guthrie wrote that I "might lack the dexterity to manoeuvre through and round the byzantine labyrinth of the Whitehall and Government machine". Spot on and there was no might about it as I had already reached that conclusion. At about this time I was also asked if I would extend my tour as CAS to four years. I refused the invitation on the grounds that acceptance would mean retiring aged 62 – four years beyond the nominal retirement age for my rank which seemed excessive. More importantly staying on would necessitate the premature retirement of a subordinate air marshal who had deserving and justified promotion expectations. It was thus the appropriate time to think about the future of the Royal Air Force and to develop the strategic plan that had been at the back of my mind since the conclusion of the SDR.

In considering how a strategic plan would be best constructed I was determined that the shape would reflect top-down direction to the staffs rather than issuing a broad remit and waiting for the output as had happened during my time in the directorate of Forward Policy with no satisfactory conclusion. With the kind permission of the commandant, the AFBSC met in Seaford House during the Royal College of Defence Studies summer leave period for a brainstorming session. I hoped we would define clear direction that could then be given to the responsible staff for wordsmithing the final document which could then be circulated throughout the RAF. The aim was to shape a strategy for the future based on an honest and critical analysis of the service's strengths and weaknesses and the identification of opportunities and threats – what is commonly known as SWOT analysis.

By the time of the meeting only two members of the AFBSC had served with me from the start of my tour – Air Marshal Sir Peter Norriss (controller aircraft) and Roger Jacklin (second PUS). Air Chief Marshal Sir John Allison had retired from his final appointment as AOC-in-C Strike Command and I knew I would miss his intellectual vigour, personal integrity and manifest commitment to the operational efficiency of the RAF. His replacement, Peter Squire, well-known to me from 3 Squadron days, had commanded and led with distinction 1 (F) Harrier Squadron during the Falklands War and subsequently completed two tours in the MoD, the first as ACAS and the second as deputy chief of defence staff (programmes and personnel). He was eminently well suited and qualified to succeed me as CAS. Air Marshal Sir David Cousins had been replaced at Personnel and Training Command by Tony Bagnall whose energy and determination I have already mentioned. Air Marshal Sir Colin Terry retired following the disbandment of Logistics Command. His replacement as the RAF's senior engineer, Air Vice-Marshal Peter Henderson, filled a new appointment within the Defence Logistics Organisation under the rather grand name of director general of Equipment Support (Air). Finally Tim Jenner, my most trusted ancillary throughout the long process of the SDR had departed for Strike Command with well-earned promotion. His replacement, Air Vice-Marshal Jock Stirrup, ensured that one big brain would be replaced by another of similar intellect and acumen. I enjoyed and indeed needed the support of clever subordinates, and as long as they left me to make the judgement calls and thereafter did what they were told, we worked in perfect harmony.

To keep debate focused on the purpose of our gathering we needed a facilitator, a recently retired senior officer with the status and intellectual liveliness to command authority. I knew of no-one better than John Willis to do the job and was delighted when he accepted my invitation to return from his retirement home in the distant north.

My approach to the day was shaped primarily by the outcome of the SDR. Power projection and intervention capabilities reflected the prime minister's conviction that the armed forces should operate on the global stage as a 'force for good'. His ambition was in harmony with the statement in the SDR White Paper that the UK should not "stand idly by and watch humanitarian disasters or the aggression of dictators go unchecked". Post-Cold War the armed forces had at last been given a new sense of purpose but I remained well aware that the Defence Council had accepted a financial settlement at the conclusion of the SDR that required cuts in defence spending. The Treasury had pressed for long term cuts of £2bn, or 10% of the current budget but this had been reduced to £915m before a further reduction to £685m was achieved by increasing the scope of the property disposal programme. The reduction from the original Treasury target allegedly owed much to Charles Guthrie's personal intervention with the prime minister with whom he had established a mutually agreeable working relationship. As a member of the Defence Council I had supported the judgement that the budgetary shortfall should be accepted. We were not going to get a better deal and we lived to fight another day.

Acceptance of the deal removed what little flexibility there was in the SDR planning assumptions that had shaped our future force structures, capabilities and manning levels. In effect, the strategic plan had to be developed within a financial straight jacket and in the hope that our commitments would be contained within the bounds of the planning assumptions – albeit in an uncertain world we had to be prepared to go beyond them if the situation warranted. But I had not forgotten my chat with Tornado aircrew at RAF Lossiemouth in the early days of my appointment. If our resources, material and people were unavoidably stretched, our ministers had to understand the need for a commensurate period of recuperation.

The meeting at Seaford House remains a happy memory. A gathering of lively minds under John Willis's watchful eye ensured that no punches were pulled in a full, free and frank discussion. Whilst the planned equipment programme was identified as a key strength, as it needed to be in any air force that aimed to retain operational effectiveness, there was general agreement that the quality of our people was our biggest strength. The strategic plan thus needed to set out a vision for the future within which RAF men and women would be at the centre of our thinking. The vision, an aspiration for the future of the RAF, had to be a declaration of the kind of organisation we intended to be. Discussion identified four key strands. The RAF had to be trained and equipped to generate air power as an essential contribution to the security of the UK and as a 'force for good' in the world. The service should be proud of its heritage and foster professionalism and team spirit founded on commitment and self-discipline. Most importantly, the RAF should offer opportunity to all while providing a rewarding career and skills for life.

The identification of what the nation, the government and our people expected of the service defined key strategic objectives. These boiled down to recruiting, training and maintaining the commitment of all our servicemen and women while contributing effectively to military operations in both joint and multi-national environments and organisations. The discussion about environment was particularly stimulating. We all recognised that government policy would be the overriding factor in determining demands made of the service. The demands would be driven and shaped by the economic climate, the impact of legislation (particularly European), demography and technological advances. Moreover, structural change would become a recurring theme in our future which persuaded us that the inevitability of change in an uncertain world should be recognised as more of an opportunity than a threat; an opportunity that we would do our best to use as a positive influence while setting a manageable pace for change.

In terms of equipment there was much to look forward to but reductions in investment had led to a noticeable and continuing deterioration in the standard of our estate that affected people's morale and commitment. If not rectified this would feed through into worsening retention. Underfunding property management and capital works was in the long run bad value for defence. So it was not at all surprising that every avenue explored led back to the quality of our people and the vital need to give them confidence in their future. The framework of our strategy was broad in width as we discussed recruitment, training, equipment support, the management of resources and external linkages. John Willis ensured that identification of strengths and weaknesses was honest and specific. By the end of a long and busy day I judged we had done sufficient to give the staff clear direction to help them paint in the fine detail that could be translated into action with appropriate performance indicators. This they were to do to my entire satisfaction composing as I had hoped a clear vision and direction for the RAF over the next ten years and beyond. But my optimism, although honest, was soon proven to be misplaced and naïve.

The first meeting of the AFBSC in January 2000 was attended by Peter Abbott (VCDS) and Vice-Admiral Sir Jeremy Blackman (deputy chief of defence staff, equipment capability). They introduced a Central Staffs paper setting out concern about the MoD's financial position. Although there was some uncertainty about the costing figures as they had been derived from a new financial planning system – resource accounting and budgeting – the paper established a framework for taking options for savings (cuts) on operational costs and the equipment programme. For the RAF proposed cuts in operational capabilities included a further reduction in the Tornado F3 force to be taken on top of the SDR cut which was in itself not justified by planning assumptions. Other proposed measures included dispensing with two BAe 146 communications aircraft, a reduction in the VC10 tanker force and reducing Strike Command's annual flying task by 20%. Such a reduction in the flying task would save no more than £20m a year but then only half of the Tornado force would remain combat ready.

It was obvious to all of us that implementation of such measures would undermine the credibility of the SDR. There would be inevitable negative consequences concerning such key issues as retention, the pressure of existing operational commitments, infrastructure and the quality of life. My optimism for the future of the service took a backwards step. Notwithstanding the apparent success of the SDR, there remained a fundamental distinction between the government's desire to play a military role on the global stage and the ability of the country to pay for it. In no time at all the MoD would be falling back on traditional budgetary expedients. The introduction to service of new equipment would be delayed and future projects postponed or cancelled. The knife would be taken to support services with the possibility of general salami slicing to cut budgets across the board. Each of these measures ran counter to the thrust of the SDR which in terms of combat power aimed to promote increased levels of readiness and much improved logistic sustainability.

In preparing for negotiations with the Treasury the scale of the problem had to be presented to ministers as the level of cuts contemplated could undermine the recent good achieved in improving retention. The case for an uplift in funding was undeniable but I was not confident of the outcome and I was only too well aware that my successor would inherit a plateful of problems that threatened implementation of the strategic plan. I thus handed over to Peter Squire on 19th April confident that he was the best man for the job and best placed to defend the service against continuing Treasury raids on the defence budget in general and the RAF's share of it in particular. This was not a happy note on which to conclude my active service career.

Reflections

SDR work dominated the first half of my tour with the second half focused on the implementation of SDR decisions while operations in Iraq and the Balkans reminded me that the generation of air power was the RAF's over-riding responsibility. Relating the story of the SDR and its consequences may present an impression of an unremitting grind overcast with gloom only occasionally penetrated by a ray of sunshine. This was not the case.

After my NATO tour and notwithstanding pride in my appointment as CAS I was delighted to be back in the RAF enjoying the company of my light-blue kith and kin. I grasped every opportunity to get out of the MoD to visit RAF stations and units at home and overseas. The availability of 32 Squadron BAe125s and helicopters sped me on my way and allowed me to keep my piloting hands in reasonable trim. I tried to meet cross-sections of our people from all ranks, branches and trades and in doing so had to answer some tough questions. By and large such exchanges were polite and at times enlivened by the black humour that is characteristic of service banter. On occasion when confronted by an officer of the permanently dissatisfied persuasion I felt obliged to use sharp words to remind him of his duty of leadership. Working for permanently miserable individuals could not have been rewarding for those blessed with proper ambition and commitment to the service. Although they were relatively few in number, palpable differences in morale at various locations quite obviously reflected the quality of leadership. It was not difficult to spot station commanders enjoying their job and comfortably carrying the weight of their responsibilities. Some others, however, while equal to the task found it difficult to inspire confidence in their subordinates.

I looked forward to my first warrant officers' conference held at RAF Uxbridge early in my tour. I had benefited from the support of some outstanding SNCOs who had well-earned their royal warrant. But the meeting got off to a bad start when I was told that some master aircrew had already returned to RAF Lyneham because they were dissatisfied with their accommodation. Although I couldn't care tuppence if this reflected personal dislike of me, I felt that such disrespect insulted the office of the CAS. My immediate reaction was to condemn them as unworthy of their warrants and to ban them from future conferences. When I had cooled down I realised that such a response would be similarly childish and best to keep a cool head before deciding on a formal reaction.

A good thing that I did because the conference revealed a depth of discontent far deeper than I had imagined possible. Expression of dissatisfaction with conditions of service, work pressures and quality of life came from a vociferous minority but there were no obvious signs of disagreement from the ranks of the majority. When I spoke about my intention to introduce fast-track commissioning for warrant officers the reaction was cynical disbelief. I needed no spurring on and departed the conference both angry and disappointed. But I had been left in no doubt of the cumulative effect on morale inflicted by compulsory redundancy, under-manning and the contractorisation and civilianisation of service posts. I hoped that fast-track commissioning of warrant officers when announced and the SDR 'Policy for People' package would help heal the wounds inflicted on our servicemen and women by the Treasury and their political acolytes.

So my return to the RAF was not an experience always illuminated by sweetness and light. On the other hand, with the support of Wing Commander Andy Pulford, when firmly established as my PSO, and encouraging goodwill from the many who shared my affection for the service, my resolve was steeled and for the most part I was kept in reasonably good humour. I had not forgotten my much-publicised precept that no-one enjoyed working for a miserable bugger.

I was surprised that I found the MoD a rather congenial working environment. Tim Jenner, who seemed to know everyone, service and civilian, was adept at sniffing out potential difficulties during the SDR as well as offering imaginative proposals that kept us on the front foot. Jock Stirrup had no difficulty in sustaining high quality and adroit advice when he took over. Steve Nicholl, serving in the Central Staff throughout my tour, provided a most helpful conduit of information as did Air Marshal Sir John Day as deputy chief of defence staff (commitments) on the RAF's contributions to operations, most importantly Kosovo.

Outside the light blue circle I was fortunate to enjoy and sustain agreeable and amicable relations with my COS colleagues. Unlike some of our predecessors, and perhaps successors, we all got on well together and occasional disagreements were never allowed to sour our collective and individual relationships. Much of the credit for this was due to Charles Guthrie. As previously recorded Charles kept a firm grip on the COS committee and within Whitehall and Westminster he was a military wheeler/dealer in a class of his own. While he could and would deal ruthlessly with professional failings, he only rarely bared his sharp teeth relying more on an easy charm that cloaked a steely determination to achieve his objectives. My only serious disagreement with Charles concerned the formation of the Defence Logistics Organisation. He did not look best pleased when I argued in public forum against the proposal but then I was to lose the dispute so harmony was quickly restored.

As SDR work approached final decision time Charles instituted breakfast meetings in our flats where he and Peter Abbott (VCDS) would meet with the single service chiefs to hammer out an agreed line. Apart from disagreement over the DLO, these meetings meant there was no dissent on military matters when the findings of the SDR were announced. This came as something of a surprise to many, not least of all to the House of Commons Select Committee on Defence.

I was summoned to give evidence to the committee on 15th July 1998. Mr Bruce George, chairman, welcomed me warmly to my "interrogation" – his word not mine – and we immediately got down to business that was to involve a three-hour grilling. To help out I was accompanied by Steve Nicholl and Trevor Woolley, a civil servant who was assistant under secretary (systems) during the SDR. At the outset I was surprised to learn that the message I had sent to all in RAF command appointments at the end of the SDR had received a much wider circulation that included members of the committee, presumably at ministerial direction. The committee immediately fastened onto my references to hard decisions and regrets. After I had explained that these referred to the disbandment of one Tornado F3 and one Tornado GR1 Squadron and the need to remove 36 aircraft from the front line, the examination focused on the planning assumptions that underwrote these decisions.

This presented the perfect opportunity to stress the importance of the planning assumptions particularly in the context of operational commitments. Thereafter questions ranged far and wide as recorded in the 8th Report of the Select Committee that is available online. The very last question, put to me by Mr James Cann, asked me to identify the unique functions of the RAF that made it important to preserve it as a separate service. I welcomed the question because it allowed me to fire a full broadside at those who suggested splitting up the RAF between the Army and the RN would save money. Some proponents enjoyed teasing the RAF, others were quite serious. But when one answered that if reducing three air arms to two would save money, would not reducing three to one save even more, money was then no longer an issue as discussion moved on to operational matters. Arguing the case for an independent air force never caused me any concern so perhaps no surprise that at the end of my peroration Mr Cann said, "in the interests of my health I am very satisfied with that answer, chairman" .

Overall I was impressed by the questions that revealed a well-informed knowledge of contemporary defence matters along with a willingness to challenge SDR conclusions in the hope of identifying a weak spot in the SDR assessment of our strategic interests. The armed services commitment to joint initiatives was regarded with some suspicion, but the committee could not drive even the smallest wedge between the evidence I provided and the views expressed by the First Sea Lord and CGS. Three hours passed very quickly and at the end of a good-humoured session I was confident that the RAF's position had been satisfactorily protected without giving ministers any cause for concern or embarrassment. Mr Bruce George kindly thanked me for attending and concluded with his hope that "other people (would be) as honest with us in the future". I returned to my office with a rather immodest glow of self-satisfaction and most grateful to Steve Nicholl and Trevor Woolley for filling in the finer financial detail that lent weight to my answers to questions that concerned so-called efficiency savings.

My self-satisfaction could not disguise the simple fact that the outcome of the SDR maintained all of the armed forces existing commitments that would have to be met with fewer resources and less money. A year later raising the efficiency savings target set for 2% in 1998/99 to 3% was in MoD-speak "challenging". Many judged that the achievement of the new target "would represent heroic efforts". It would appear that having finally decided how much money was available the armed forces were to be squeezed to fit within an arbitrary budget rather than be given the funds to sustain operational credibility.

CHAPTER 29
FLYING VISITS

I had joined the RAF with a limited but praiseworthy ambition of becoming a fighter pilot and life in the higher ranks of the service never dulled my interest in the practical skills of flying aeroplanes. Rather to my surprise and pleasure three years as CAS was to provide some exciting opportunities to bring a satisfactory conclusion to a career in military aviation as I travelled the world at government direction.

At home flights with the Red Arrows flown with Simon Mead (leader) and Gary Waterfall (No.9) – both well known to me from Harrier Force days – presented the opportunity to show my appreciation of the hard work, flying skills and discipline all vital to sustaining a consistently exceptional standard of display flying. At Warton Airfield, I met up with Paul Hopkins, who I had last flown with in August 1975 when I did his arrival check to 3 (F) Squadron. Paul, who sadly died recently, was now the chief test pilot at BAe Systems where he gave me my first and only flight in a pre-production Eurofighter/ Typhoon. Paul, one of the nicest men it's been my pleasure to know and a genuinely exceptional pilot, let me fly the aeroplane from start to finish.

It was the first time I had piloted an aircraft in which I felt no need for more thrust as we eased along at Mach 1.3, the limiting speed for the aircraft at that time, in cold power. At the end of the sortie the BAe public relations people pressed me for my first impression. I could only say how much I envied those who in the future would fly the aeroplane as a matter of course as opposed to enjoying a one-off familiarisation sortie. Elsewhere I reacquainted with the Tornado, Jaguar, Harrier, Chinook and Puma while enjoying regularly flying about the country in the BAe125 and Twin Squirrel helicopters. My final sortie in the service was flown with son Douglas. Together we flew a Hercules out to Cyprus and back delivering Tornado spares and recovering unserviceable items. As nice a way as any of ending my career in military aviation.

On overseas trips I flew in various aircraft types with the air forces of the USA, Canada, France, Argentina, Chile, Oman, Jordan, Japan, South Africa, Saudi Arabia, Romania and New Zealand when visiting on official defence business. There were three other particular visits that I vividly recall: one with pride, one with lingering consternation and one which had emotional overtones and a surprising conclusion.

In July 1997 I visited the Irish Air Corps as a guest of the commander, Brigadier General Patrick Cranfield. The IRA had just announced a ceasefire and ministers approved acceptance of his invitation and my intention to travel in uniform. I flew to Baldonnel Airfield, just south of Dublin, accompanied by Elizabeth where Patrick met me at the start of a truly memorable visit. At lunch, hosted by the chief of the Irish Defence Forces, conversation avoided political matters as we chatted over the recent successful tour of South Africa by the British and Irish Lions.

After lunch we drove to the airfield and a tent especially erected for VIP visitors. It was already crammed to overflowing with chaps enjoying their first Guinness of the afternoon so with our wives Patrick and I sat outside on the grass to watch the flying that included some adventurous piston-engined aerobatic displays. As 3pm approached there was a lull until the display commentator announced a surprise item and asked spectators to look to their left. About ten seconds later the Red Arrows appeared flying fast and very low to break into the circuit.

The roar that went up from the crowd was both breath-taking and thrilling. The Arrows had flown direct from a display venue in Belgium and after refuelling the team took off to fly their full display before landing and taxiing in to the accompaniment of rapturous applause. I believe I was the first CAS to visit the Irish Republic and there could have been no better way of doing so than with the Red Arrows also achieving a first that marked a further forward step in our relations with the republic. After the show I basked in reflected glory and was overwhelmed by the number of people who gave me their thanks, many of whom saying they had served in the RAF.

At the end of the programme, accompanied by Patrick Cranfield, Elizabeth and I set off in a car to the aircraft dispersal to board the 125 for the return to London. We didn't get very far before the mass of people leaving the airfield slowed the car to a halt. So we got out and walked enjoying a most memorable atmosphere of goodwill. Wearing the uniform of a senior officer in the British armed forces was no more than incidental. And there could be no denying the goodwill inspired by the Red Arrows and their value to the reputation of British aviation in general and the RAF in particular. I returned home full of pride in the service.

In November 1998 I visited Romania as a guest of General Gheorghe Bucsce. He had paid an earlier visit to the RAF when I learned he was a big fan of Tottenham Hotspur Football Club. So I took with me as presents a

Spurs shirt and a football autographed by the team that guaranteed a happy start to three days in Romania. My brief visit presented a dire picture of the Romanian air force. Fighter pilots were flying no more than four hours a month, aircraft availability was worse than poor and the price of spares bought from Russia for their Mig 21 aircraft had increased by 300% since the end of the Cold War.

The first day of the visit involved arrival calls on defence officials, service and civilian, and air force briefings that supplemented without contradiction our national assessment of the Romanian air force. On the second day I was asked to wear flying kit and was taken to an airfield not far from Bucharest. My host warmly welcomed me and explained that his pilots would demonstrate an airfield attack. To my surprise 24 Mig 21s were lined up outside a squadron HQ and soon afterwards 24 pilots emerged and marched to the aircraft – rather different to our way of doing things. After start-up 21 taxied out, took off and disappeared before returning ten minutes later to overfly the airfield in an attack formation; or so I was told. The aircraft were high, a thousand feet or so, and the three aircraft formations were bunched up. Suppressing the thought that they would be easy meat for a RAF Regiment Rapier SHORAD squadron before they reached the airfield, I murmured some appropriate words of appreciation.

We then moved to the squadron crew room for a briefing given by the base commander, Air Commodore Luqa, that was translated by an interpreter whose grasp of aviation matters was somewhat lacking. So it only gradually dawned on me that I was to fly with the air commodore in a two-seat Mig 21 who would demonstrate his low level aerobatic sequence. My two accompanying staff officers could scarce disguise their dismay while I found it difficult to muster appropriate enthusiasm at the prospect. Never mind, it was time to close my eyes and think of England.

Thirty minutes later I was strapped into the rear seat of the Mig 21 having noticed as I climbed the ladder that the tyres on the aircraft were threadbare. No briefing had been given on the ejector seat or any other flight safety subject for that matter. As we taxied out I stared at the instrument panel seeking without much success guidance from words all written in Cyrillic script. By the time of take-off I had identified the air speed indicator and the altimeter both set in metric measurements. This was at least a helpful start as we blazed off down the runway in full reheat before getting airborne and immediately cranking into a hard starboard turn as the undercarriage was retracted. Rolling out, we accelerated for a short while before pulling up into what I guessed would be a loop. I noted the altitude over the top and the airspeed for future reference assuming we didn't hit the ground on the pull out – it looked distressingly close. We bottomed out at about 100 feet or so and this was the introduction to a sequence that involved lots of G, full reheat for most of the time and a quite unforgettable inverted pass down the length of the runway, again at a height of 100 feet.

Although I have forgotten details of the sequence after the loop, the inverted pass that was the penultimate display item remains unforgettable because without a negative G strap and with the seat and shoulder harness straps insufficiently tightened, I ended up in an untidy heap someway distant from the seat pack with my head banging around the canopy. My consternation remains a clear memory but happily we landed soon afterwards and I got out of the aircraft to be greeted with polite applause from the squadron pilots and the presentation of Romanian air force 'wings' first class. Not to be sneezed at when the only controls I had touched were the rudder bars for want of somewhere to put my feet. After returning home I pointed out in my trip report to the secretary of state that I was certainly earning the flying pay that I no longer received.

A year later, accompanied by Andy Pulford and Peter Brown I set off for Argentina. Earlier in the year CDS and the UK chiefs of staff had met with our Argentine equivalents at a service of reconciliation in the crypt of St Paul's Cathedral with lunch following in the Savoy Hotel. Conversation was courteous and respectful and I enjoyed meeting up again with my Argentine opposite number, Brigadier General Ruben Montenegro. We had first met at the USAF 50th anniversary birthday celebration at Nellis Air Force Base, Nevada. Ministers decided that to build on the success of the London meeting chiefs of staff should visit Argentina. After Charles Guthrie had paved the way he decided I should be the first chief to go as the Argentine air force was predictably the most difficult to get on with. Charles's judgement was equally predictable.

The visit did not get off to a good start. We were met at the airport by Brigadier Catala and while driving to the British embassy in Buenos Aires I apologised for my lack of Spanish but complimented the brigadier on his excellent English. "It should be," he replied "I was one of your prisoners of war." A smile removed any sting and Alberto Catala was the kindest and most attentive escort throughout the visit. At the ambassador's residence we were greeted by Mr William Marsden and his wife Kaia. That evening our hosts held a reception to celebrate the 50th anniversary of the Buenos Aires branch of the RAF Association. The first I had heard of its existence was when met on arrival by the defence attaché, Group Captain David McDonnell.

Thirty-five members of the association attended the party led by Group Captain Prince Charles Radziwill who had joined the RAF via the Polish air force early in World War II. Also present was Odette Strugo Gavey who had been a SOE agent. I was told that the group captain – decorated with a DSO and DFC – had dropped Madame Gavey into occupied France on her first SOE mission in 1944. Both were fortunate to have survived the war but I did not discover how they came to live in Argentina. Some 550 Anglo-Argentine pilots served in the RAF during the war of whom 122 died on operations. It was a privilege to present the association with a new pennant in their memory and in return I received a gaucho knife as a memento of my visit.

The formal side of the visit started with a wreath-laying ceremony at the Argentine War Memorial in the centre of Buenos Aires. Afterwards I was invited to pay an office call on President Menem who kindly presented me with a book on the Tango with an accompanying CD. Programmed to lecture at the Armed Forces Staff College – subject NATO air operations in the Balkans – my brief advised me to avoid any mention of the Falkland Islands/ Las Malvinas. Come the hour, in uniform, and face-to-face with a large military audience I sensed some tension in the air and decided the conflict could not be ignored. Going off-script I started by saying that we could not overlook the fact that only 17 years earlier we had been at war which had cost the lives of many brave Argentine and British servicemen. It was thus a privilege and a most welcome duty to speak to them as part of the process of reconciliation between our countries. The tension immediately eased and thereafter the talk went ahead as planned. Subsequent questions and discussions did not digress into purely bilateral political matters.

On the third day I went to the Argentine air force base at Villa Reynolds to fly in a two-seat A-4 Skyhawk as number two on a simulated low level attack mission. The tactics and formation manoeuvres were similar to our own but I was glad that I kept my hand in. The aircraft captain, Major Deluffe, allowed me to fly the aeroplane throughout the sortie. I thoroughly enjoyed getting down in the weeds again to match the leader's height above the ground. Safely back at the airfield the base commander presented me with an Argentine air force medal so I must have earned my keep.

Apart from this flight and a soaking under the Iguazu Falls – Andy Pulford and Peter Brown were totally drenched as I refused to share my umbrella – the visit to the Argentine air force cadet academy at Cordoba gave me an insight to inter-service relations that had been soured by the Falklands conflict. The final item on the visit programme was the canteen, not to be mistaken for a British interpretation of its function. The canteen, an impressively large and ornate room, was the hub of the college where graduation ceremonies and 'wings' presentations were made. As this was being explained to me I was conscious of a muffled conversation behind my back. Briefing over, the college commandant told me that he had decided to do something special that was not included in the programme. I was then led through a doorway into an antechamber.

To my immediate front on the opposite wall was a tattered Union Jack, one of many and the most significant of mementos of the war that had been smuggled out of the Falklands by prisoners of war as they returned home. To my right and within a semi-circular alcove were life-sized portraits of all the Argentine pilots killed during the conflict. The absence of portraits of other deceased aircrew was noticeable. I contemplated the room without comment and as I walked out the commandant said he had shown me the memorial museum to give me a better and informed understanding of the Argentine armed forces. As he explained "the Army surrendered, the Navy ran away and the Air Force was undefeated". In my post-visit report to the secretary of state I recounted his judgement with the comment that prospects for 'jointery' in the Argentine armed forces were not good.

The visit concluded with a formal lunch hosted by Mr Marsden in his residence for our Argentine hosts and their wives. Lunch was a lively and good-natured occasion with no hint of what was to come. As coffee was served, the folding doors between the dining room and drawing room parted. There, posed for action and music, was a pair of Tango dancers who immediately glided into passionate action. It was spellbinding stuff but my enjoyment was truncated at the end of their performance when Her Majesty's ambassador invited me to explore the convolutions of the Tango under the expert tutelage of the lady partner. The prospect of public Tango entanglement with a lithesome beauty at least half my age was just too much. So I politely declined the invitation to audible murmurs of regret amongst which the voices of Pulford and Brown were clearly distinguishable. Later on they claimed disappointment that I had not outsourced the invitation to those more junior in both rank and age. Some hope.

So ended a visit that was the most enjoyable and potentially fruitful of my time as CAS. Encouraged by President Menem's wish to re-establish relations with the UK and with the issue of Falkland Islands sovereignty relegated to a low priority, Ruben Montenegro and I agreed to seek political endorsement of three first-step initiatives. These were a joint air-sea rescue exercise in the South Atlantic and an exchange of Hercules aircrew and flying instructors. These proposals were welcomed in the MoD and when Ruben Montenegro paid a return visit to the RAF in September I understood that progress was being made in Buenos Aires. But I fear that President Menem's departure from office in December put an end to the process of normalisation. The Falkland Islands dispute was soon reinstated as a top political priority. Economic problems and endemic corruption propelled this shift of emphasis to divert attention away from internal political problems.

Where possible my overseas trips to foreign air forces were coordinated with visits to our deployed operational detachments in the Balkans and the Middle East. I was well satisfied with the operational professionalism in our offensive and support helicopter forces but concerned by the shortage of essential kit such as tentage, cooking utensils and so on. Apparently such equipment holdings that supported the Harrier and SH squadrons during the Cold War had been much reduced as a contribution to peace dividend economies. Training of support personnel had also suffered and the SH force had to reacquaint themselves with Cold War hard-earned lessons. On the other hand, Harrier Force people were no longer operating in periodic mud baths in Germany. They were now flying from fixed bases and the comparative domestic comfort of aircraft carriers, albeit some old hands, well known to me from the past, told me they still preferred the mud. Some people are never satisfied.

My travels brought me into contact with many high officials within the diplomatic service. Without exception HM ambassadors and high commissioners were always welcoming and attentive hosts. And I could not fail but to be impressed by the calibre and intellect of men and women whose value to our country was, in my judgement, considerably underrated in Whitehall. One of the few pleasures of office work in the MoD was to read diplomatic reports and in particular valedictory despatches composed by ambassadors as they departed their last overseas posting to retire from the service. It was a sad day when valedictory despatches were effectively ended in 2006 during Margaret Beckett's time as foreign secretary because of their potential embarrassment to ministers and civil servants. My successors would no longer enjoy the elegance of the prose, the clarity and vigour of expression and the candour of their judgements. Reading diplomatic memoirs now remain one of the private pleasures of my life in retirement, an appetite fed and encouraged by candid revelations of life behind the public formality of an ambassador's life.

CHAPTER 30
DEPARTURE

The last six months of duty passed very quickly. Apart from visits to our operational deployments my logbook reports flights to all our front-line stations and major support units. At Cranwell I popped in to the Officer and Air Crew Selection Centre where Group Captain Sid Morris – another old friend from Hunter/Harrier days – asked me if I would like to take the pilot aptitude tests. Up for the challenge and confident of success I accepted. After finishing the test Sid told me with ill-concealed glee that I was assessed as a high training risk. With some 5,000 flying hours in my logbook I thought this was a bit offside, but I suppose Anno Domini were catching up with me; at least that was my rationale.

At the end of February 2000 I flew to and from New Zealand with no intermediary stops apart from refuelling at Bangkok outbound and Los Angeles inbound. Ken Hayr welcomed me to Auckland where I caught up with several old Kiwi chums all of whom were surprised that I was not stopping off in either direction of travel. I was told no-one came to New Zealand without visiting somewhere else. But time pressed and the visit had a purpose. Mrs Helen Clark, newly elected prime minister, was resolutely set on cancelling an order for 28 F-16 A/B aircraft to replace the RNZAF's ageing Skyhawk fleet. The generosity of the deal offered by General Dynamics made my eyes water with envy but Air Marshal Carey Adamson (chief of the defence force) and Air Vice-Marshal Don Hamilton (my opposite number) told me that Mrs Clark would not budge. The RNZAF would be reduced to a small fleet of air transport and maritime patrol aircraft. I did not meet Mrs Clark but visited the RNZAF airfield at Ohakea from where I flew an aerial tour of North Island in a Skyhawk. Talking to squadron pilots and with Don Hamilton's agreement I said they would be most welcome in the RAF should they wish to continue in military aviation with the prospect of flying the Eurofighter/ Typhoon. Many took up the offer and the RAF benefited greatly from the arrival of fully-trained fast-jet pilots who needed no more than type conversion before joining the RAF's front line. When Mrs Clark was told of the exodus her only comment was "good luck to them".

I had one day's relaxation in Nelson, South Island, where in the civic museum I found many references to my mother's family who built the town's first brewery. I am rather proud of that ancestral achievement. Back home one further surprise came out of the blue. Three days before my departure I received a letter from the secretary of state, Mr Geoff Hoon, congratulating me on behalf of the Air Force Board on my appointment, approved by Her Majesty, as the first honorary air commodore of the RAF Regiment. As a member of the Air Force Board this appointment came as something of a surprise as this was the first I had heard of it. Andy Pulford could not explain its provenance so I contacted Air Commodore Richard Moore, commandant general of the RAF Regiment. Without hesitation he offered me congratulations and then explained that rather than involve the Air Force Board he had written to The Queen, as air commodore-in-chief of the RAF Regiment, seeking Her Majesty's approval of the appointment. This had been graciously given. So it was something of a fait accompli and typical of the RAF Regiment's preference for the direct as opposed to manoeuvrist approach to such matters. Whatever, I was flattered, honoured and delighted to take up the appointment.

As the day of departure approached my future has already been decided. In November 1999 my private secretary, Ian Manson, buzzed me to say that he had a 'lord' on the telephone who wished to speak to me – Ian was uncertain of the name. I asked if he was a dissident as at that time I was still shipping occasional bursts of venomous criticism of the RAF's operations against so-called defenceless Serbs. Ian said that he didn't sound like one so the 'lord' was put through to me. "Good morning, my name is Tom Camoys. I am the Lord Chamberlain and I am phoning because The Queen wants to make you an offer," were the first words that came down the line. I nearly slammed down the phone thinking there was a dissident at the other end but held on. "What offer?" I asked rather briskly. "Well I don't want to tell you over the phone but please come and see me," replied Lord Camoys. "Where?" I asked. "Buckingham Palace" was spoken with a touch of asperity. A couple of days later I met with the Lord Chamberlain who asked me if I knew that the constable and governor of Windsor Castle, General Sir Patrick Palmer, was terminally ill with lung cancer and sadly did not have long to live. Would I accept appointment as his successor? My immediate reaction was that I couldn't as I had a done deal with the secretary of state to hand over as CAS in April the following year. "That's all right, we can wait," said Lord Camoys. After 43 years service to The Queen in Her Majesty's Armed Forces I considered it a great honour to continue my duty in direct service to the Crown. Thus was my future decided.

I have no idea as to how this final bolt from the blue was fired but recognised that once more I was the beneficiary of someone else's misfortune. But I do recall an office call on CDS soon after meeting the Lord Chamberlain when Charles Guthrie asked me if I had yet heard anything about my future. I suspect he had some part to play in my appointment and if this is so I remain in his debt.

On 14th April 2000 I was dined out of the service at a Ladies Guest Night at Cranwell. Elizabeth came with me as did our daughters now both married to soldiers who added a splash of regimental colour to the occasion. Douglas, now a flight lieutenant and Hercules captain, was also invited to the dinner that was organised by Tony Bagnall. Sitting at the top table and looking at where I sat at my first guest night in College Hall in 1957 brought back a host of memories. The occasion thus represented the true closing of a circle and I could not think of a more pleasurable and satisfying way to mark the end of active service.

The RAF and the Cranwell that I was leaving was very different from that I joined in 1957 – an Air Force of more than 200,000 men and women with 11 commands and some 3,000 aircraft on 188 squadrons. In 2000, two commands and 45 squadrons told its own story of reduction and compression. But three years at Cranwell for better or worse had left its stamp on me and I owed a debt to the place for four things.

• First, I could still bull a pair of boots or shoes as well as anyone in the service and that could be a valuable attribute as I took up my new post in Windsor Castle.

• Secondly, flying training and particularly the advanced stage on Meteors secured my addiction to military flying that was to remain a constant throughout my career.

• Thirdly, it was at Cranwell that I started to learn the value and some of the mystery of true friendship born of mutual trust and respect. Such friendship was a plant of slow growth and one that needed to be kept in a state of constant repair. A sage once noted that we all need friends to help us grow old and new friends to help us stay young. The friendships I formed all those years ago have been one of the most pleasurable and enduring rewards of my life.

• Fourthly, I think it was at Cranwell that I began to understand something about integrity which to me is all about having the moral courage and determination to tell the truth, and the honesty to be truthful in judgement of oneself. I make no claim to the moral high ground. It was simply that I discovered that lying to keep out of trouble was more bother than it was worth. Somehow you always got found out and long before I discovered golf was not my sporting cup of tea I read somewhere: "Always tell the truth. You may make a hole in one when you are all alone on the golf course." So I came to understand that telling the truth not only saved an awful lot of hassle, it also earned one grudging respect no matter the seriousness of one's misdemeanours. In the year 2000 and perhaps more so today, wherein traditional values of well-proven and lasting merit are at best challenged and at worst belittled, honesty and integrity have their own dignity. And in my judgement they are both to be admired and valued as being beyond compare.

Seven days after the dining out I walked out of the MoD for the last time and with no glow of satisfaction. There could be no disguising the fact that by the end of my tour the RAF's readiness for war fighting and its operational capabilities had declined. Kosovo had demonstrated practically well-known deficiencies in some of our weapons and communications systems as the demands of contemporary air operations were rising faster than the RAF's ability to meet new requirements. Solutions were self-evident, but getting the necessary money to fund them was another matter.

More worrying in my judgement, our engineers were working far longer hours than reasonable to generate sufficient aircraft to satisfy total training needs while sustaining high aircraft availability on operational deployments. Declining experience levels added to my concern. Operational capability was critically dependant on the experience and availability of senior aircrew and too many were leaving the service.

Providing our aircrews with better equipment to meet the increasing demands placed upon them could only be answered by rapid and responsive upgrades. Logistics support required significant investment to achieve the necessary quality of training without flogging our airmen and women to death. Finally, and critically, we needed to retain our experienced and more senior people, both commissioned and non-commissioned for longer. Achieving this would be dependant on satisfying the preceding requirements and giving them confidence in their future.

Such was my legacy to Peter Squire when I handed over to him. My optimism for the future of the Royal Air Force following SDR decisions had been exaggerated and Peter would have to navigate the service through some difficult times before the events of 9/11 upset the strategic apple cart. But, no-one could take away from me my immense pride in the RAF and gratitude for what I had been given in over 43 years of service.

Three weeks later Elizabeth and I started a new life in Windsor Castle where we were to live for the next eight years. Continuing duty to the sovereign in the magnificent fortress and palace of Windsor Castle was to be a privilege that brought with it interests and pleasures hitherto unexplored or unknown. My talent for good luck had not deserted me.

EPILOGUE

Several of Trenchard's principal foundation stones that gave the RAF a permanent structure were removed during my career. The unremitting search for 'efficiency savings' led to the closure in 1992 of the Apprentice School at RAF Halton with all RAF recruit training subsequently undertaken there. The Staff College at Andover had long gone and was to be followed by its successor at Bracknell in 1997. The flight cadet entrance to a permanent commission was abandoned in 1971 in favour of a graduate entry scheme. So the Air Force I led from 1997 to 2000 was very different from the service that fought World War II and which I joined in 1957.

At the end of that war the country was broke. Waging total war for five years had destroyed the basis of the UK's economy. Any hopes that the Americans would be generous in helping the UK to recover from straightened circumstances were dashed when the US refused a request for an interest-free loan of $6bn. Our former enemies were to enjoy far more generous American largesse than their ally who had fought the Germans earlier and longer. Eventually the Americans agreed a 50-year loan of $3.75bn at 2% interest with the pound sterling freely exchangeable for dollars. The loan was finally paid off in 2006 after the country had endured a succession of financial crises under Prime Ministers Attlee, Eden, Macmillan, Wilson and Callaghan.

Many years of financial austerity were imposed with varying degrees of vigour by Treasury officials as guardians of the UK's solvency that brought them into an unavoidable collision with the guardians of the nation's security – the chiefs of staff. The confrontation was complicated by political aspirations. Successive prime ministers wished to adorn the world stage as leaders of a major military power that was a permanent member of the United Nations Security Council. On the other hand, the protection and enhancement of key elements of the welfare state remained a top political priority. At the end of the Cold War in a strategic environment that posed no evident and immediate threat to national security, it was inevitable that the Treasury's grip on defence spending would be tightened.

Economic difficulties and the quest for the peace dividend were not the only factors that conditioned a gradual decline in our national combat power. As an airman I have always understood that air power was based on a foundation of scientific and technological superiority. This fundamental truth was illustrated during my own career by leaps in technology that have seen, for example, the RAF move forward from the Hunter to the Tornado to the Typhoon with the F-35 soon to enter service. For some time now satellite-derived technology and target-acquisition sensors have provided the capability to attack individual targets with terminal precision at night and in all weather. But the cost of technology in the development of airframes and weapons has continued to grow to accommodate the demands of a complex electronic and cyber environment that affects communications, navigation, target acquisition, weapons delivery and precision guidance. One Tornado armed with a single PGM that has the destructive power of 25 dumb bombs can deliver a devastating impact equivalent to that achievable by a squadron of Lancasters. This figure work may be no more than a back of the hand estimate, but it illustrates the point that the loss of one Tornado is equivalent to the loss of a squadron of Lancasters. And that introduces the issue of numbers.

With a unit cost of approximately £90m for a Typhoon comparatively few aircraft can be afforded within a fixed or declining defence budget, nor can the aircraft be quickly replaced. While many more much cheaper aircraft of lesser capability could be bought, there would be a concomitant increase in infrastructure and manpower costs. But as aerospace technology will not stand still it is imperative that the smaller the RAF is numerically, the more important it is that the combat performance of its aircraft should be second to none with the technological superiority to overcome an enemy of greater numerical strength. Mastery of the air will remain the perennial requirement in all operations. Acceptance of this precept assumes that the RAF will be equipped with sufficient aircraft to meet its defence missions as mandated by the government.

It has thus been a combination of national economic circumstances and consistent growth in the cost of equipment and associated rapid advances in technology that has generated irresistible pressures for a steady decline in the size and mass of the service. The RAF is not alone. At the end of the Strategic Defence Review (1997/8) the RN was left with 33 destroyer/frigate warships. That number has now subsided to 19. The Army's manpower, more than 110,000 as agreed in the SDR, has now sunk below the 82,000 target set in the 2015 Strategic Defence and Security Review. All this was in the future when I retired in 2000, but there were factors already evident that were to exercise a malign influence on the size and capabilities of our armed forces.

When I took over as CAS I was surprised by the limitations of my authority. The job specification as set out in the annual appraisal report read that I was responsible for "the operational effectiveness, efficiency and morale of the

RAF. Advice to ministers on all aspects of RAF business and the RAF's contribution to jointery. To contribute to the formulation of defence policy and increased efficiency and to implement such policy within the RAF."

This rather convoluted description of key responsibilities was presumably mirrored in those set out for my RN and Army colleagues. Looking back with the benefit of hindsight I can claim to have made a contribution to jointery. But as already explained the service I left behind was less operationally effective than the one I inherited. Professional efficiency may have remained a constant and morale had, arguably, been stabilised not least by avoiding a further cut in the uniformed strength of the RAF. I had won the argument over the future of the Jaguar Force while the leasing of four C-17s represented my only procurement success. I would have liked 11 but the service was already committed to the procurement of the A400M. Scant attention paid to my concerns about the viability of Nimrod MRA4 illustrates the limitations of my influence on procurement decisions.

I supported the policy of maintaining continuity of an at-sea nuclear deterrent and the sustainment of the necessary forces to project military power with intervention capabilities, but I was not involved in any strategic discussion. Throughout the Cold War and its aftermath successive governments had launched reviews to cut defence expenditure under a cloak of readjusting strategic objectives. But strategic thinking had withered on the vine during the Cold War as the UK accepted US military hegemony. Although the major European contributor to NATO, the UK invariably followed the American lead as her most useful ally to protect in part political addiction to the 'special relationship'. But the strategic certainties of the Cold War, based on the prevention of conflict through nuclear deterrence, ended with the dissolution of the Soviet Union. As NATO grappled with the consequences of this unexpected collapse, strategy became confused with policy; both lacked clarity of definition and strategy within the Alliance became largely synonymous with policy.

In the UK post-Cold War repercussions including the search for the peace dividend complicated the definition of a national defence strategy that reflected the essential differences between strategy and policy. Military strategy, the servant of politically defined policy derived from national strategic objectives, concerns the application of military resources to implement government policy. If the principal policy objective is the security of the nation, potential threats must be identified and how best to deal with them decided after all options and associated difficulties have been thoroughly analysed. In theory this process requires senior military commanders to respond to political ambitions with practical realism that reflects their understanding of the nature of war. This process appears to have been supplanted by another that decides how much money is available and then squeezing the armed forces to fit within the allocated budget. Without a clearly defined national defence and security strategy, policy is made on the hoof and subject to the whims and prejudices of those in government and particularly those holding the purse strings. And if policy is ad hoc, military strategy has to be infinitely flexible and that tends to undermine consistency of thought and process. Perhaps this in part explains the deployment in 2006 of our armed forces on concurrent operations in two theatres of war without adequate resources and against all planning assumptions set out in the SDR.

In recent years politicians have been ever keen to stress that the UK's defence budget is the fourth largest in the world. Expenditure is invariably equated with capabilities but seldom with any convincing explanation of their strategic relevance. There is an obvious difficulty in doing so when the political horizon stretches no further than the next election and particularly so when the cynical cliché 'there are no votes in defence' is as true today as it was in the early 1930s. Competition between government departments to spend the taxpayer's money favours those with short-term relevance to personal well-being. That said it should be acknowledged that when the country's finances are in a mess, national stability is an essential element of national security. And for better or worse, that is the priority the Treasury will always give.

Fear alone as experienced in the late 1930s and sustained at a lower level of public awareness throughout the Cold War provided a rationale for defence spending taking a larger share of GDP than at present – some 5% rather than the current 2% that owes more to creative accounting than strategic realities. If politicians gloss over the dangers associated with global instability and ignore perilous uncertainties of the future, it is difficult for defence professionals to present a case for more spending on defence with persuasiveness that resonates with the voting public. Moreover, it would appear that the MoD's budget-setting process has time and time again failed to match costs to available budgets. The consequence is recurrent huge affordability gaps – black holes – that end up with equipment projects being scrapped or delayed.

During my years of service the story of equipment procurement has included a number of expensive failures that grabbed the headlines. That said, and in all fairness, the introduction to service of many lesser but operationally important systems has been achieved on time and within budget notwithstanding rapid technological advances in all dimensions of warfare. But as intelligence staff assessments sway in their judgement of the most potentially damaging threat to national security, there is an inevitable temptation to readjust procurement decisions. Within a given defence budget the reality is to rob Peter to pay Paul. Threat assessments are subject to one eternal military truth best expressed by one of the cleverest and wise men it has been my privilege to know. Sir Michael Quinlan, one time permanent under secretary at the MoD, wrote:

> "In matters of military contingency, the expected, precisely because it is expected, is not to be expected. Rationale: What we expect, we plan and provide for; what we plan and provide for we thereby deter; what we deter does not happen. What does happen is what we did not deter, because we did not plan and provide for it, because we did not expect it."

There is perhaps no better argument for maintaining a balance of defence capabilities and to resist the temptation to counter an emerging threat by budgetary adjustments that block one potential capability gap while uncovering another threat of continuing relevance.

The authority and standing of the individual service chiefs have been gradually eroded over the years. Power is now concentrated in the MoD centre with the chiefs rusticated to their operational headquarters albeit with access to an MoD office when called to attend meetings. Remote from the centre the chiefs remain responsible to the secretary of state for defence for the operational efficiency and morale of their service albeit now also having to carry the burden of responsibility for their budgets. Taken together morale and operational efficiency depend on the provision of the necessary equipment, manned and supported by adequate numbers of well-trained and motivated personnel. But sustaining morale in circumstances of constant financial stringency is problematic when, for example, demanding exercises necessary to maintain operational effectiveness are cancelled at short notice for budgetary reasons. Doing so in response to a political requirement inverts both responsibility and accountability but it is the chiefs who suffer reputational damage.

As threats to our national security continue to increase and indeed change in nature, the armed forces cry out for strong political leadership. Notwithstanding earlier comment about Treasury priorities, it is reasonable to expect that the services are kept in a high state of efficiency with the social and economic consequences accepted as the cost of our safety and freedom. But the appointment of eight secretaries of state for defence within a decade is symptomatic of political indifference in the high echelons of government. The cost of training sailors, soldiers and airmen to combat readiness varies in degree according to specialisation but is universally expensive. But service personnel are the only defence asset whose value appreciates with time. Once trained their value to their parent service continues to increase as experience is gained and wider responsibilities accumulated. Retention of such people makes both military and economic sense, but successive reviews to cut defence spending leave serving personnel and possibly potential recruits doubting the sincerity of political commitment to the well-being of the armed forces and the security of the nation. 'Efficiency savings' almost invariably involve an erosion of benefits and quality of life. Retention difficulties are consequently inescapable.

Within the RN, the Army and the RAF self-respect, an important constituent of morale, is influenced by public approbation. The popular public attitude to our armed forces is one of pride as clearly evidenced in welcome-home parades for units returning from Afghanistan and the spectacular success of supportive fundraising activities such as 'Help for Heroes'. Such high esteem is, however, sadly lacking in some minority elements of contemporary society and indeed in Whitehall and Westminster. Ritual and unctuous references to our brave men and women cannot disguise the unpalatable fact that complimentary platitudes go hand in glove with the imposition of economies that reduce both combat effectiveness and personal benefits.

Defence of the Realm is the first duty of government. The threats we face and the pace of technological change may be transforming some aspects of warfare but traditional armed force is still relevant to our national interests in deterring armed conflict and assisting friendly allies in unstable regions of the world. Our armed forces can, if adequately equipped, trained and manned make an effective contribution to global security in the interests of sustaining a strong economy so essential for national prosperity. But in focusing on material aspects of combat power – a common political trait – it should always be remembered that it is ultimately the man or woman behind the gadgets that finally count in war. Without adequate equipment the bravest can accomplish little. Without brave people equipment has no value. This simple but eternal military truth should be writ large in the consciousness of all concerned with our national security and international clout.

Acceptance of The Queen's shilling and enlistment in the armed forces is a commitment to a life that is one of "unlimited liability" as most tellingly defined by General Sir John Hackett. It is this liability, setting servicemen and women apart from the civilian world, that merits respect for all who wear The Queen's uniforms. And nor should it be forgotten that the men and women of our armed forces are ever ready to assist civil authorities struggling to cope with natural disasters let alone to respond to acts of terrorism.

As a former CAS I still on occasion wear my uniform. And I do so with pride as I share with many others memories of the RAF's accomplishments in peacetime and at war. Today conflict, that defies simple categorisation, remains common place. Since the end of the Cold War not a day has gone by when the RAF has not been committed to operations somewhere in the world that have ranged from high intensity conflict at one end of the scale to humanitarian relief at the other. The men and women of the service, of every branch and trade, have done their duty with commendable discipline and no small measure of courage. One hundred years after its formation as the world's first independent air force, the RAF now faces a future clouded by strategic uncertainty. But it can do so confident in the knowledge that size for size it still remains second to none. Long may it remain so.

APPENDIX 1
EYEBALLING RATKO

by Air Chief Marshal Sir William Wratten GBE CB AFC RAF
(written for his family in 2009)

In July 1995 over 8,000 Bosniak men and boys were massacred in Srebrenica. This was described by the outside world as genocide. Held responsible for this atrocity, amongst other war crimes, was General Ratko Mladic, the chief of staff of the Bosnian Serb Army. At the time our prime minister was John Major and he held a meeting of other heads of state to determine what should be done about this activity which all agreed was unacceptable. It was decided that General Mladic was to be given an ultimatum; desist immediately from all military activity or NATO forces, primarily the British and Americans, would embark on a bombing campaign that would severely damage his forces and with it his reputation.

Against this background I found myself driving to the RAF base at Northolt to take an aircraft to the annual International Air Tattoo at Fairford. It was a fine Sunday morning, I was in my second year as AOC-in-C Strike Command and I was looking forward to a good day out, a nice lunch and some entertaining flying displays not to mention a chat with many old pals and acquaintances. So it was with growing concern that I took the car phone from my driver who told me that the vice-chief of defence staff in the MoD wanted a word. VCDS at the time was Air Chief Marshal Sir John Willis, another Cranwellian whom I knew well. John gave me the background to the impending ultimatum to be delivered to Mladic, paused to let it all sink in, and then quietly informed me that from a cast of thousands I had been selected to deliver it personally to this perpetrator of such an atrocity. I was to report to the ministry immediately for briefing and would fly to Belgrade the following day to meet Mladic and give him the hard word. I was to be accompanied by a number of officials (civil servants), and collect the C-in-C United States Air Forces in Europe and the deputy commander French Forces en route, as they would be representing the USA and France alongside me. But there was to be no doubt that I was in charge as the leader of the delegation.

In the MoD I was briefed comprehensively on the line to take with Mladic. There would be a C-130 Hercules on standby and I was to take off early on the Sunday for Frankfurt for the USAF general and then Paris for the French-man en route to Belgrade where we would be met by Mladic's representative. From then on no-one was quite sure how it would all evolve. That was to be my problem.

So the first thing I did after being briefed was to contact my staff at High Wycombe and instruct them to change the C-130 to a BAe 146, the four-en-gine jet the royal family used and that had a large Union Jack on the tail fin. It was also a modern aircraft. I wanted the right impression to be given on landing in Yugoslavia from the outset.

All went according to plan until we landed in Belgrade by which time it was dark. Our reception committee, all smiles, told us that General Mladic was waiting to entertain us to dinner and we could discuss whatever it was we wanted to talk to him about in comfort. So, I immediately informed our hosts that we did not come to break bread with this man. Mine was a mission of great importance and seriousness and I insisted we be taken to the general without delay. Dinner with him was out of the question. So a now morose party of Mladic's men ushered us in to waiting big, black cars and off we sped into the dark. About an hour later we arrived seemingly in the middle of nowhere and disembarked to be shown into an unpretentious, small shack-like building where, waiting in civilian clothes, was General Ratko Mladic. Those of my party in the military were all in uniform and I sensed immediately that Mladic regretted his mode of dress. We looked smart and he looked scruffy, and he knew it.

He invited us to sit at a table with me opposite him, my military colleagues on either side of me and our officials in the background. Beside him sat his interpreter (I had brought my own just to ensure their interpretation of what I had to say was accurate) and behind him a few 'heavies' who looked as though they would not need much of an excuse to give us a good going over. So we began by introducing ourselves and our appointments ensuring that he realised the three of us were commanders of major military organisations. I then set out the ultimatum I had been charged to deliver.

Mladic is a charismatic man and I found I had to occasionally remind myself that I was talking to a mass murderer. He has penetrating blue eyes and from the outset it became clear he was not about to give any indication of regret regarding Srebrenica. On the contrary he glared at me throughout and we each soon realised we were competing to see who was going to blink first, literally. I made it quite clear to him, in as calm and controlled a manner as I was able to muster, that if he did not order the cessation of hostilities without delay he and his forces would have the very daylights bombed out of them. This was my message from my prime minister, corroborated and fully supported by my representatives from the USA and France.

I was threatening a war criminal, in his own territory and in words that were not open to misinterpretation, that we would seek to kill him and all under his command if he did not do as he was told. Whilst mouthing these words I wondered to myself if we were going to be allowed to return home in one piece.

Once I had finished and had handed him a written summary of what I had said, Mladic embarked upon a long soliloquy about the history of his country, how the outside world had no understanding of his position, how impertinent it was of others to threaten him in this manner, and so on and so on. After about half an hour of him droning on it began to become rather boring, until he mentioned an area of operations in which a few French soldiers had been killed. At this our French general became extremely agitated and interrupted Mladic when he was in full flow, thumping the table with his fist and calling Mladic a liar. At this Mladic's neck muscles bulged, his already ruddy complexion darkened into a shade of purple as the red mist of his fury descended upon him and then us. I realised instantly that we were in trouble. How do I get out of this?

So I immediately stood up and, smiling at the interpreter, thanked Mladic for his hospitality and said we must now return to our respective countries and report back to our political leaders. Well, not knowing what I was saying, and only seeing I was smiling, everyone waited for the interpreter to tell Mladic what I had said. As she started to do this, I began strolling as casually as I could for the exit hoping all the others in my party, the Frenchman especially, would follow. Thankfully, they did and we began the journey back to Belgrade, our aircraft and home, again via Paris and Frankfurt. Eventually I got to bed in Springfields around 3 a.m., rising a few hours later to report to the MoD to brief the secretary of state for defence on what had happened (Michael Portillo at the time).

The outcome was that Mladic did not cease operations so the bombing campaign against him began.

Author's note: Ratko Mladic, who became known as the 'Butcher of Bosnia', was jailed for life on 22nd November 2011 at the International Court in The Hague for directing his troops to commit the worst atrocities in Europe since World War II.

ABBREVIATIONS

AAA	Anti-Aircraft Artillery
AAFCE	Allied Air Forces Central Europe
AAC	Army Air Corps
AAR	Air-to-Air Refuelling
(AC)	(Army Cooperation)
ACE	Allied Command Europe
ADC	Aide de Camp
ADGE	Air Defence Ground Environment
ADM	Admiral
AEW	Airborne Early Warning
AFB	Air Force Board
AFBSC	Air Force Board Standing Committee
AFD	Air Force Department
AFNW	Allied Forces North-West Europe
AFV	Armoured Fighting Vehicle
agl	Above Ground Level (height)
AHB	Air Historical Branch (RAF)
ANZUS	Australia, New Zealand and United States
AOC	Air Officer Commanding
AOR	Area of Responsibility
AP	Air Publication Anti-Personnel (mines)
ARRC	Allied Rapid Reaction Corps
asl	Above Sea Level (height)
ASOC	Air Support Operations Centre
AT	Air Transport
ATAF	Allied Tactical Air Force
AWACS	Airborne Warning and Control System
AWC	Air Warfare Centre
(B)	(Bomber)
BAI	Battlefield Air Interdiction
BCZ	Berlin Control Zone
BEM	British Empire Medal (Order of the British Empire)
BFNE	British Forces Near East
BMG	Battle Management Group
BRIXMIS	British Military Mission
BTAC	Berlin Tactical Analysis Cell
CAS	Chief of the Air Staff Close Air Support
CBE	Order of the British Empire (Commander)
CBF	Commander British Forces
CCF	Combined Cadet Force
CDS	Chief of the Defence Staff
CENTO	Central Treaty Organisation
CFS	Central Flying School

CGS	Chief of the General Staff
C-in-C	Commander-in-Chief
CIS	Communications Information Systems
CLSP	Composite Launch Sequence Plan
CJTF	Combined Joint Task Force
COS	Chief of Staff
CPX	Command Post Exercise
CTTO	Central Trials and Tactics Organization
DASB	Director of Air Staff Briefing
DCS	Defence Costs Study
DS	Directing Staff
DUKW	Wheeled amphibious assault vehicle/landing craft. A military acronym based on 'D' = model year, 1942; 'U' = body style, utility (amphibious); 'K' = all-wheel drive; and 'W' = dual rear axles. Commonly referred to as a 'Duck'.
EOKA	Greek Cypriot paramilitary organisation
EOD	Explosive Ordnance Disposal
EWOSE	Electronic Warfare Operational Support Establishment
(F)	Fighter
FGA	Fighter Ground Attack
(FR)	Fighter Reconnaissance
FLOSY	Front for the Liberation of Occupied South Yemen
FWOC	Forward Wing Operations Centre

GBAD	Ground-Based Air Defence
GLO	Ground Liaison Officer
HAS	Hardened Aircraft Shelter
HCSC	Higher Command and Staff Course
HCT	Harrier Conversion Team
HF / C	Harrier Force / Commander
HMS	His / Her Majesty's Ship
HQ	Headquarters
HUD	Head-Up Display
IADS	Integrated Air Defence System
IFOR	Implementation Force
IGB	Inner German Border
INAS	Inertial Navigation and Attack System
INF	Intermediate Range Nuclear Forces
IO	Intelligence Officer
IP	Initial Point
IUKADGE	Improved UK Air Defence Ground Environment
JHQ	Joint Headquarters
JIC	Joint Intelligence Committee
JIS	Joint Intelligence Section
Kts	Knots (nautical miles per hour)
LGB	Laser-Guided Bomb
Logs	Logistics
LRIC	Long-Range Insertion Craft
MA	Military Assistant
MAD	Mutually Assured Destruction

MANPADs	Man-Portable Air Defence (missiles)		**PGS**	Portsmouth Grammar School
MCMV	Mine Counter-Measures Vessel		**PJHQ**	Permanent Joint Headquarters
MOB	Main Operating Base		**PSC**	Principal Subordinate Command(er)
MoD	Ministry of Defence		**PSO**	Personal Staff Officer
MPBW	Ministry of Public Buildings and Works		**PWHQ**	Primary War Headquarters
MRT	Medium Range Transport		**QFI**	Qualified Flying Instructor
MSC	Major Subordinate Command(er)		**QRA / N**	Quick Reaction Alert / Nuclear
9/11	Accepted title marking the coordinated Terrorist attack on New York and Washington DC on 11 September 2001		**QWI**	Qualified Weapons Instructor
			(R)	Reconnaissance
			RA	Royal Artillery
NAAFI	Navy, Army and Air Forces' Institute		**RAF**	Royal Air Force
NATO	North Atlantic Treaty Organisation		**RAFC**	Royal Air Force College
			RAFG	Royal Air Force Germany
Nav/Rad	Navigator/Radar Operator		**RCDS**	Royal College of Defence Studies
NBC	Nuclear, Biological and Chemical (capability)		**Recce**	Reconnaissance
NEAF	Near East Air Force		**RFA**	Royal Fleet Auxiliary
nms	Nautical Miles		**RFC**	Royal Flying Corps
NORTHAG	Northern Army Group		**RIB**	Rigid Inflatable Boat
NLF	National Liberation Front		**RM**	Royal Marines
OBE	Order of the British Empire (Officer)		**RMAS**	Royal Military Academy – Sandhurst
OCA	Offensive Counter-Air		**RN**	Royal Navy
OMB	Office of Management and Budget		**RNAS**	Royal Naval Air Station
			ROE	Rules of Engagement
OPCOM	Operational Command		**RRF**	Rapid Reaction Force
OPCON	Operational Control		**R/T**	Radio Telephone/Telegraph
PfP	Partnership for Peace		**RUC**	Royal Ulster Constabulary

RV	Rendezvous
RVL	Rolling Vertical Landing
SACEUR	Supreme Allied Commander Europe
SAM	Surface-to-Air Missile
SAS	Special Air Service
SASO	Senior Air Staff Officer
Sapper	Royal Engineer (known as)
SBS	Special Boat Service
SBA	Sovereign Base Area
SDSR	Strategic Defence and Security Review
SEngO	Senior Engineering Officer
SF	Special Forces
SHAPE	Supreme Headquarters Allied Powers Europe
SHORAD	Short-Range Air Defence
SIGINT	Signals Intelligence
SNEB	Société Nouvelle des Établissements Edgar Brandt (French armament company). Pod housing unguided 68mm air-to-ground projectile.
SOXMIS	Soviet Military Mission
SRT	Short Range Transport
STEM	SHAPE Tactical Evaluation Manual
TACEVAL	Tactical Evaluation
TACON	Tactical Control
TAOR	Tactical Area of Responsibility
TI / TIALD	Thermal Imaging / Airborne Laser Designation
TLP	Tactical Leadership Programme
TOW	Tube-launched, Optically-tracked, Wire-guided. Air-launched Anti-Tank missile
TWCU	Tornado Weapons Conversion Unit
UKADR	UK Air Defence Region
UNFICYP	United Nations Force in Cyprus
UNPROFOR	United Nations Protection Force
VAdm	Vice Admiral
VCAS	Vice Chief of the Air Staff
V/STOL	Vertical/Short Take-Off and Landing
WAAF	Women's Auxiliary Air Force
WOC	Wing Operations Centre
WP	Warsaw Pact

INDEX